FI RCE

ATSUSHI
OHKUBO

27

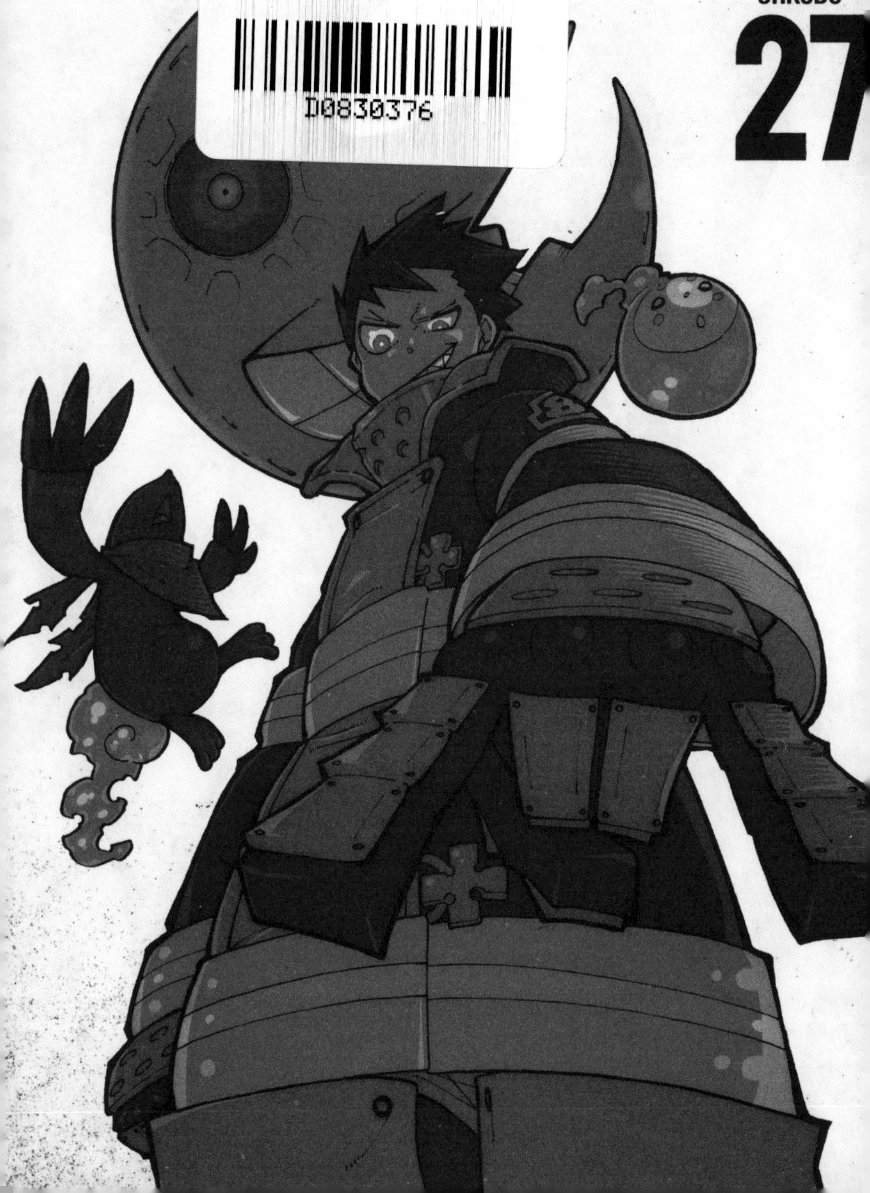

Are the O!!!!

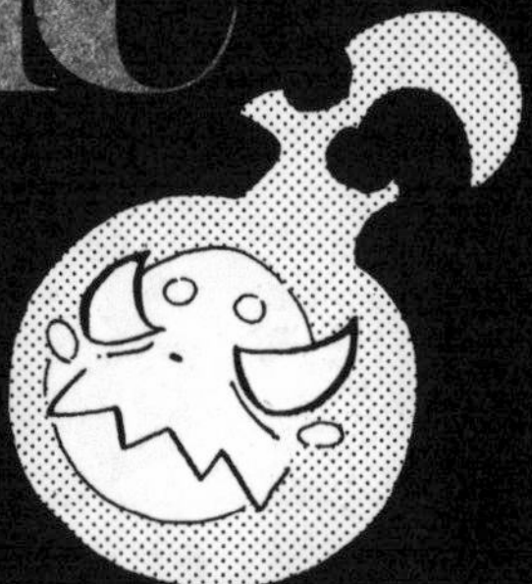

VOL. 27

ATSUSHI OHKUBO

Boy,
You
HER

FIRE FORCE

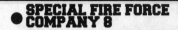

SPECIAL FIRE FORCE COMPANY 8

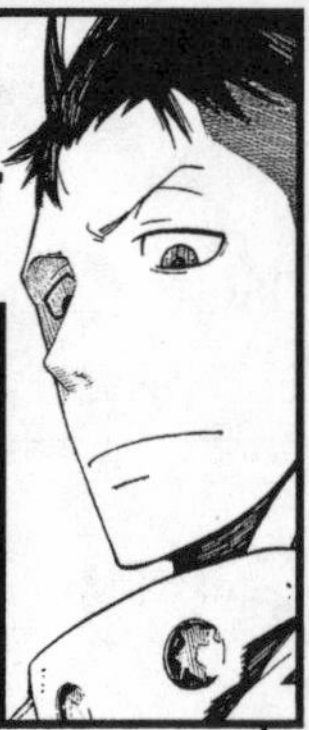

CAPTAIN (NON-POWERED)

AKITARU ŌBI

The caring leader of the newly established Company 8. He has no powers, but uses his finely honed muscles as a weapon in a battle style that makes him worthy of the Captain title. Even when Shinra's personality changed, he refused to abandon him and waited for Shinra's return.

WATCHES OUT FOR

TRUSTS

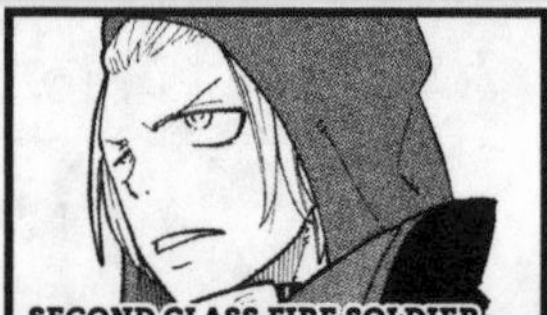

SECOND CLASS FIRE SOLDIER (THIRD GENERATION PYROKINETIC)

ARTHUR BOYLE

Trained at the academy with Shinra. He follows his own personal code of chivalry as the self-proclaimed Knight King. He's a blockhead who is bad at mental exercise. He's a weirdo who grows stronger the more delusional he gets. He noticed something was different about Shinra and explained that Shinra was acting exactly like the devil in the training academy rumors.

IDIOT!!

WATCHES OUT FOR

TRUSTS

STRONG BOND

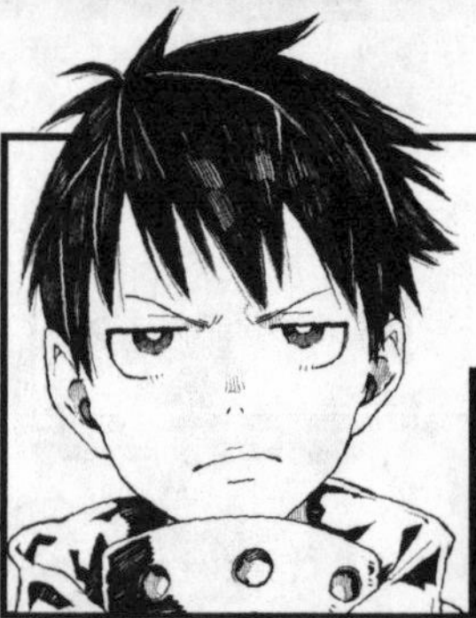

SECOND CLASS FIRE SOLDIER (THIRD GENERATION PYROKINETIC)

SHINRA KUSAKABE

Dreams of becoming a hero who saves people from spontaneous combustion! His weapon is a fiery kick. He wields a special flame called the Adolla Burst. He has no memory of a three-month period in which his personality had apparently been taken over by his doppelganger.

A NICE GIRL

LOOKS AWESOME ON THE JOB

A TOUGH BUT WEIRD LADY

HANG IN THERE, ROOKIE!

TERRIFIED

STRICT DISCIPLINARIAN

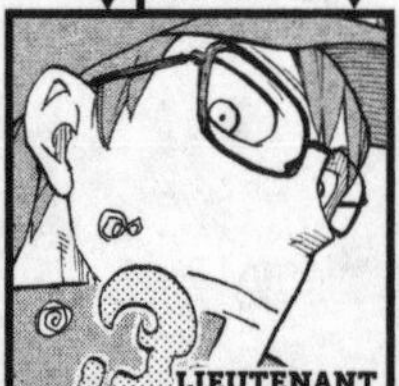

LIEUTENANT (SECOND GENERATION PYROKINETIC)

TAKEHISA HINAWA

A dry, unemotional ex-military man, whose stern discipline is feared among the new recruits. The gun he uses is a cherished memento from his friend who became an Infernal.

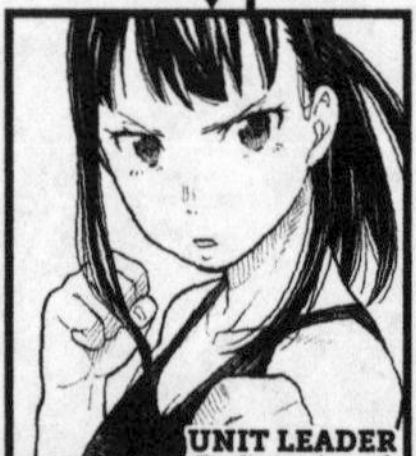

UNIT LEADER (SECOND GENERATION PYROKINETIC)

MAKI OZE

A former member of the military, she is an excellent fighter who controls fire. She's a cool lady, but is mad about love stories, and her beauty is overshadowed by her "head full of flowers and wedding bells."

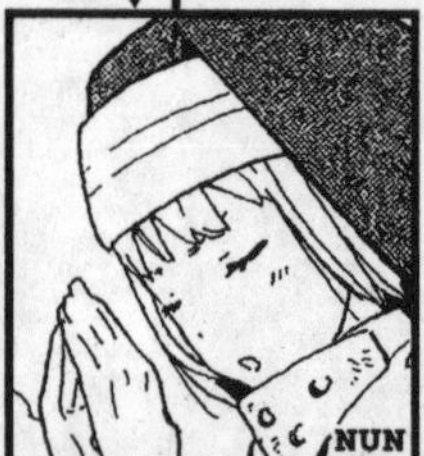

NUN (THIRD GENERATION PYROKINETIC)

IRIS

A sister of the Holy Sol Temple, her prayers are an indispensable part of extinguishing Infernals. Her ignition powers have recently manifested.

THE GIRLS' CLUB

RESPECTS

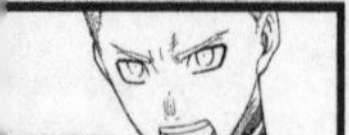

NGINEER

VULCAN JOSEPH

he greatest engineer of the y, renowned as the God of re and the Forge. He inked me tattoos on the ankles of hinra's alter-ego.

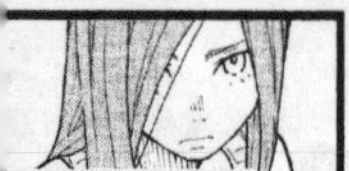

THIRD GENERATION YROKINETIC)

LISA SARIBE

ormerly a spy sent by Dr. iovanni, she is now a member Company 8. She controls ntacles of flame.

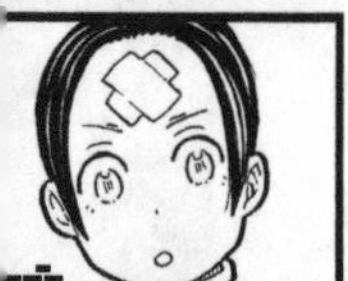

YŪ

self-proclaimed apprentice Vulcan's. Has now recovered om the injuries inflicted by r. Giovanni.

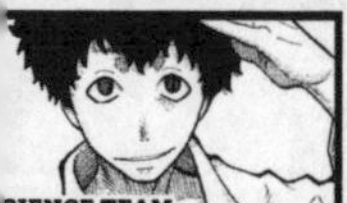

CIENCE TEAM

VIKTOR LICHT

genius deployed to Company from Haijima Industries. as confessed to being a aijima spy.

HAS HIM ON HER MIND

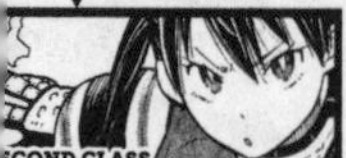

ECOND CLASS RE SOLDIER (THIRD ENERATION PYROKINETIC)

TAMAKI KOTATSU

rookie from Company 1 urrently in Company 8's care. he controls nekomata-like ames.

HOLY SOL TEMPLE + "EVANGELIST"

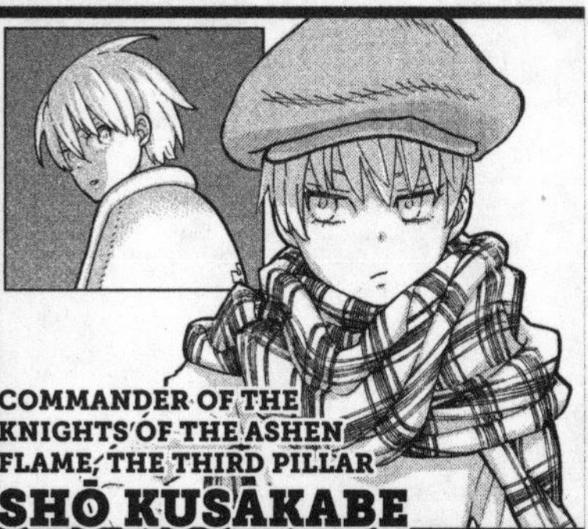

COMMANDER OF THE KNIGHTS OF THE ASHEN FLAME, THE THIRD PILLAR

SHŌ KUSAKABE

Shinra's long-lost brother, the commander of an order of knights that works for the Evangelist. He was made into a doll for Haumea, but is impelled to leave the Church when he feels his brother's warmth through an Adolla Link. Dressed as an ordinary civilian, he is investigating the secret origins of the Kusakabe family.

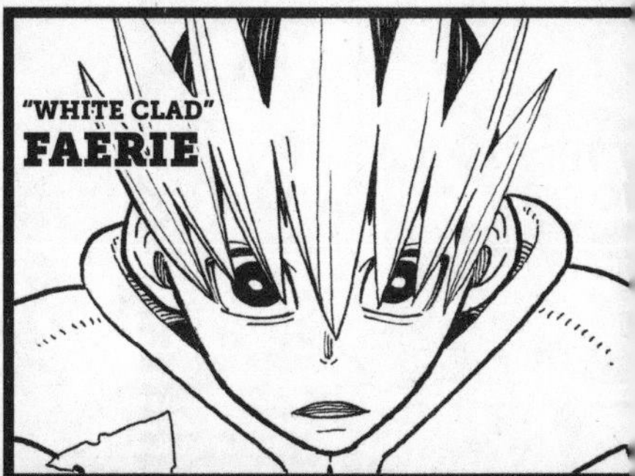

"WHITE CLAD"

FAERIE

A member of the Cataclysm Squad. Can use an Adolla Burst. Apparently was supposed to be Shō's Guardian, and now works in the Cataclysm Squad to remove all of humankind's budding hope before it can bloom.

"GUARDIAN"

ARROW

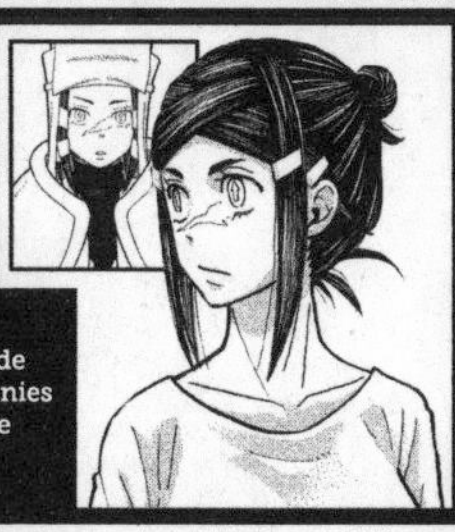

A member of the "White Clad" cult, and Shō's Guardian. Has the power to attack with arrows made of flame. She accompanies Shō when he leaves the Church.

HAIJIMA INDUSTRIES

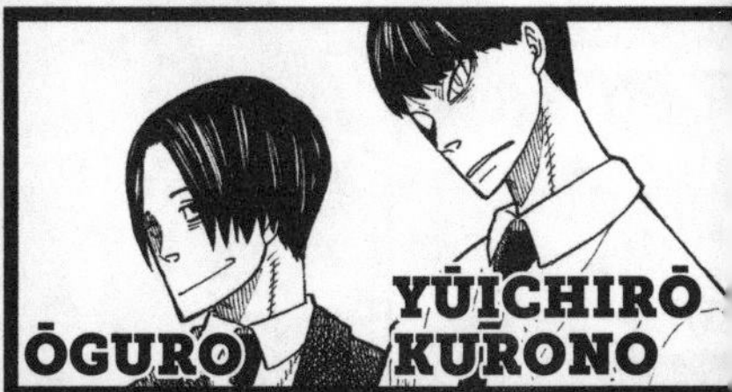

ŌGURO

An elite Haijima executive, who climbed the corporate ladder faster than anyone in history. A horrible human being who nevertheless silences all complaints by continually achieving better-than-perfect results. Non-powered.

YŪICHIRŌ KURONO

The man known as Death, he adores weaklings. Will only take orders from Ōguro and Haijima's CEO, thus forcing Ōguro to accompany him to the field. Third generation pyrokinetic.

SPECIAL FIRE FORCE COMPANY 4

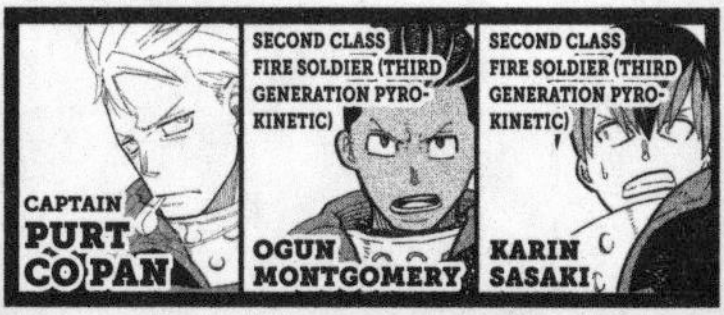

CAPTAIN
PURT COPAN

SECOND CLASS FIRE SOLDIER (THIRD GENERATION PYRO-KINETIC)
OGUN MONTGOMERY

SECOND CLASS FIRE SOLDIER (THIRD GENERATION PYRO-KINETIC)
KARIN SASAKI

SPECIAL FIRE FORCE COMPANY 2

CAPTAIN
GUSTAV HONDA

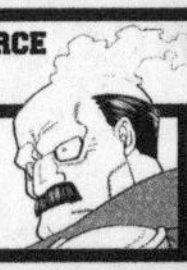

SUMMARY

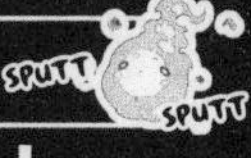
SPUTT
SPUTT

A demon Infernal floats in the air near the pillar that appeared in Sumida Bay—the doppelganger of Shinmon Benimaru's deceased mentor, Shinmon Hibachi. The revived Hibachi lambastes Benimaru for still being unsure of himself as a leader, calling him a "dad-blamed idjit." To prove that he will not disgrace the Shinmon name, Benimaru uses all of his strength to fire a Nichirin at Hibachi, sending his mentor back to the afterlife in a spectacular show of gratitude, ensuring he will never lose his way again. Meanwhile, Shō has has fled the White Clad cult's hideout and is attempting to learn the secrets of the Kusakabe family. He is interviewing a man who knew them back in the day, when suddenly he has an Adolla Link and comes face to face with his mother's doppelganger...!

FIRE FORCE 27

CONTENTS

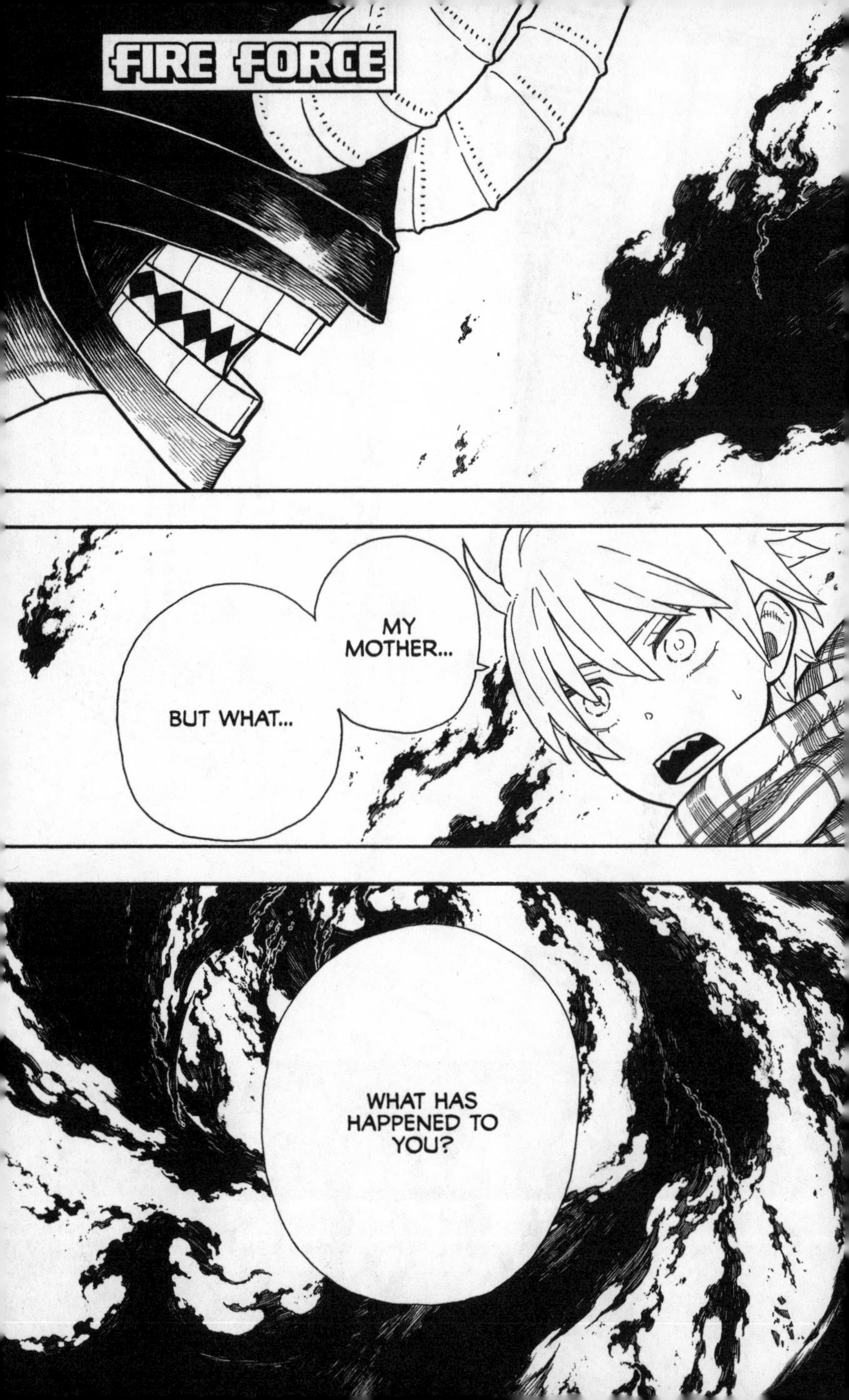
FIRE FORCE
MY MOTHER... BUT WHAT...
WHAT HAS HAPPENED TO YOU?

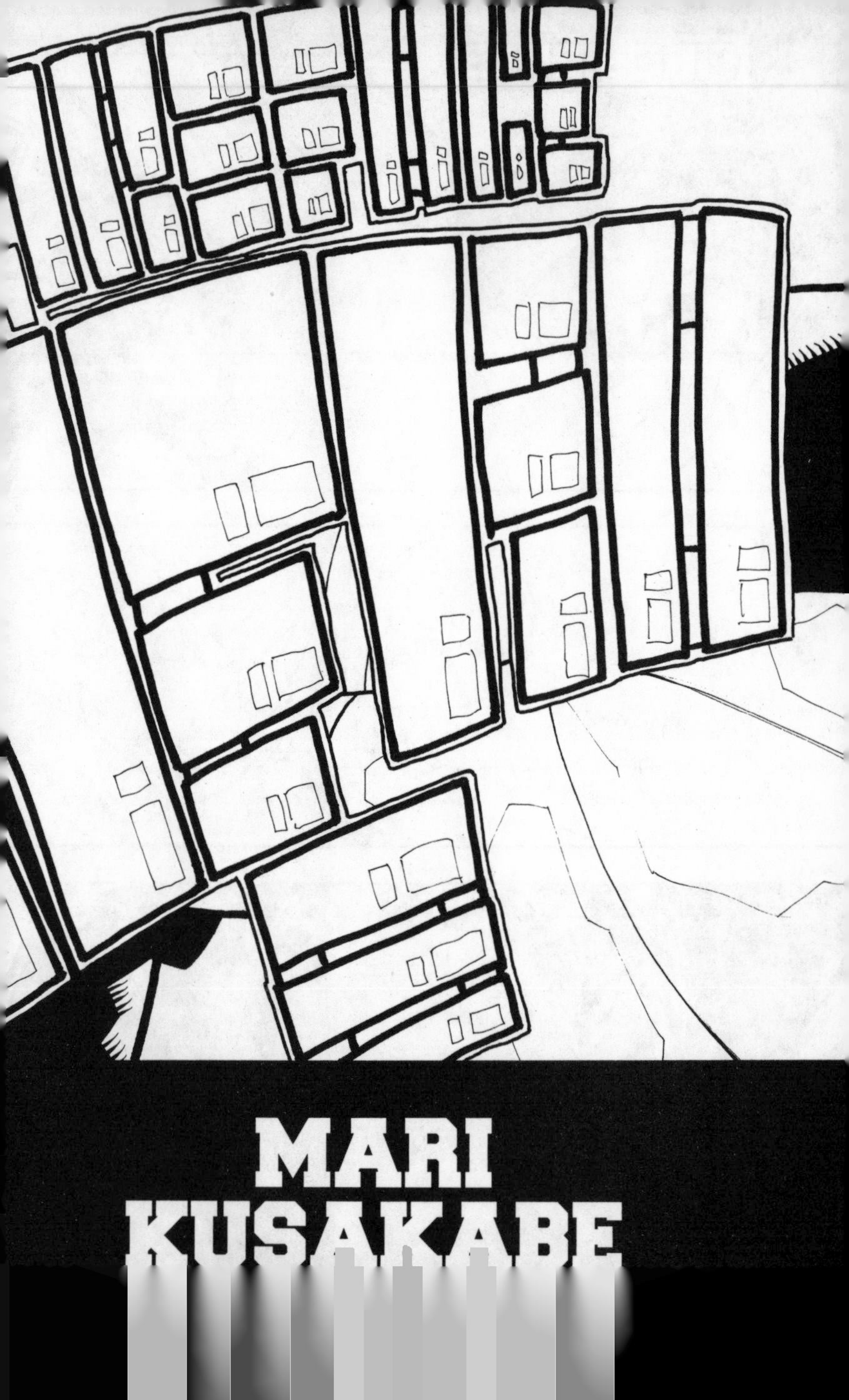

MARI KUSAKABE

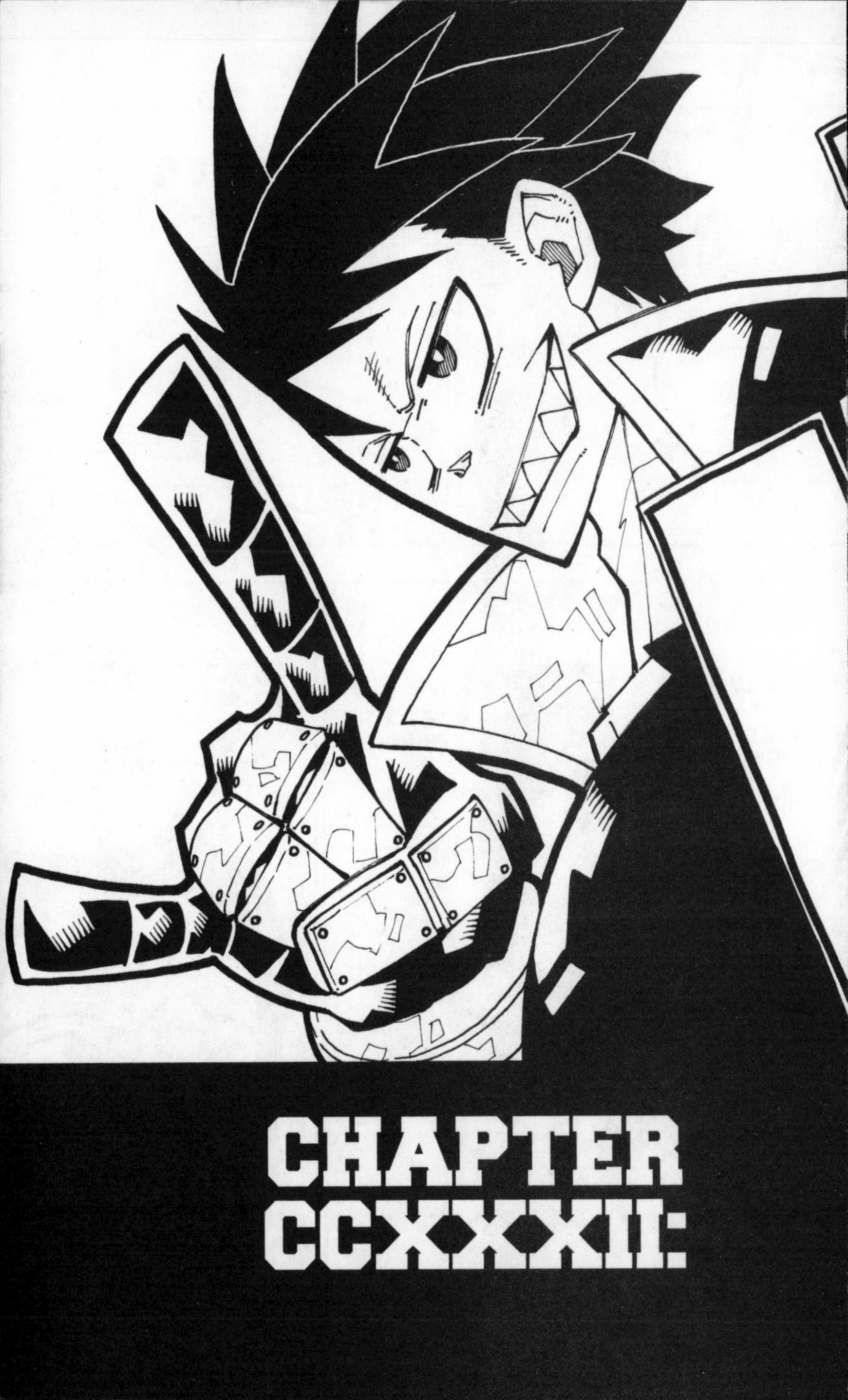

CHAPTER CCXXXII:

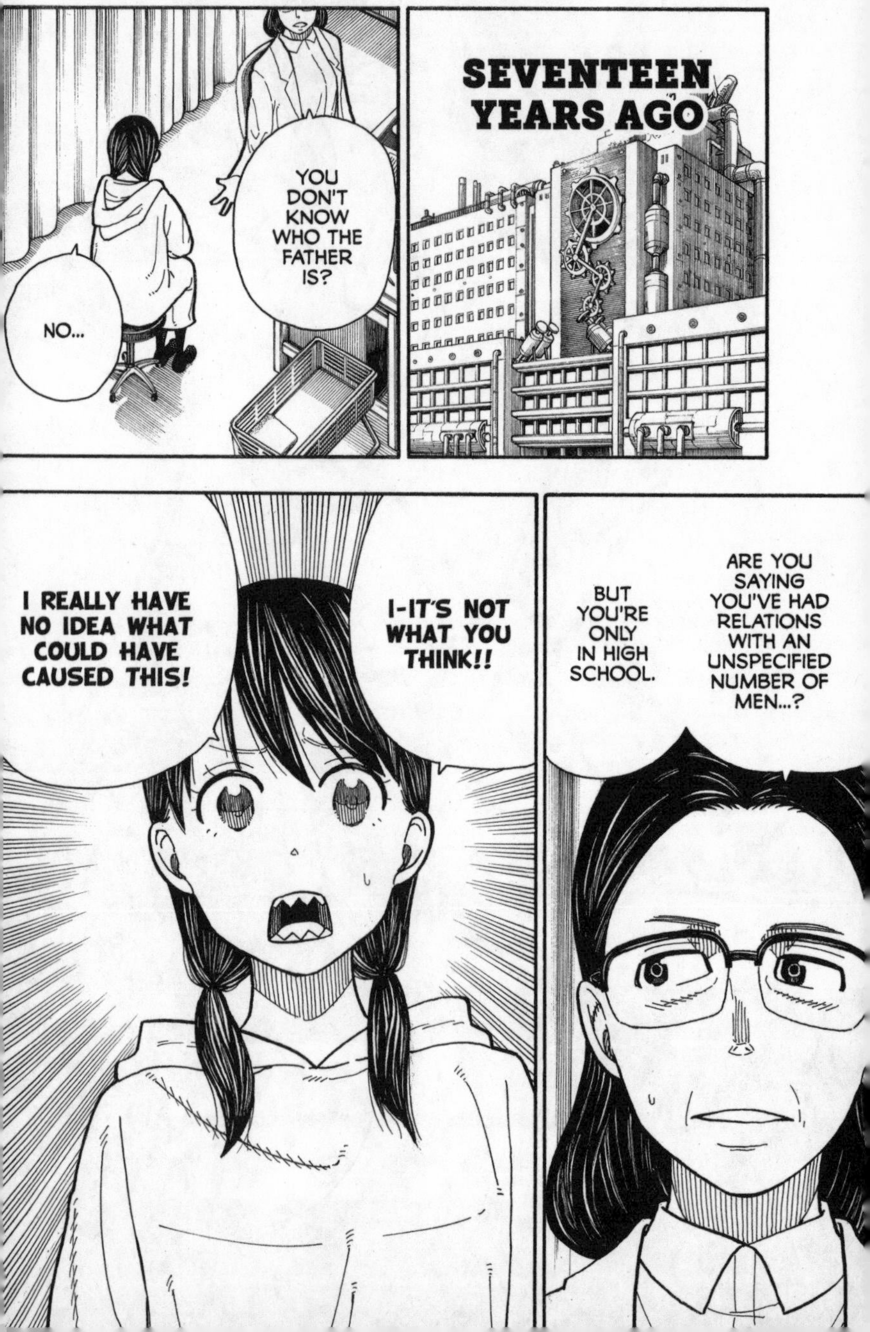
SEVENTEEN YEARS AGO
YOU DON'T KNOW WHO THE FATHER IS?
NO...
ARE YOU SAYING YOU'VE HAD RELATIONS WITH AN UNSPECIFIED NUMBER OF MEN...?
BUT YOU'RE ONLY IN HIGH SCHOOL.
I-IT'S NOT WHAT YOU THINK!!
I REALLY HAVE NO IDEA WHAT COULD HAVE CAUSED THIS!

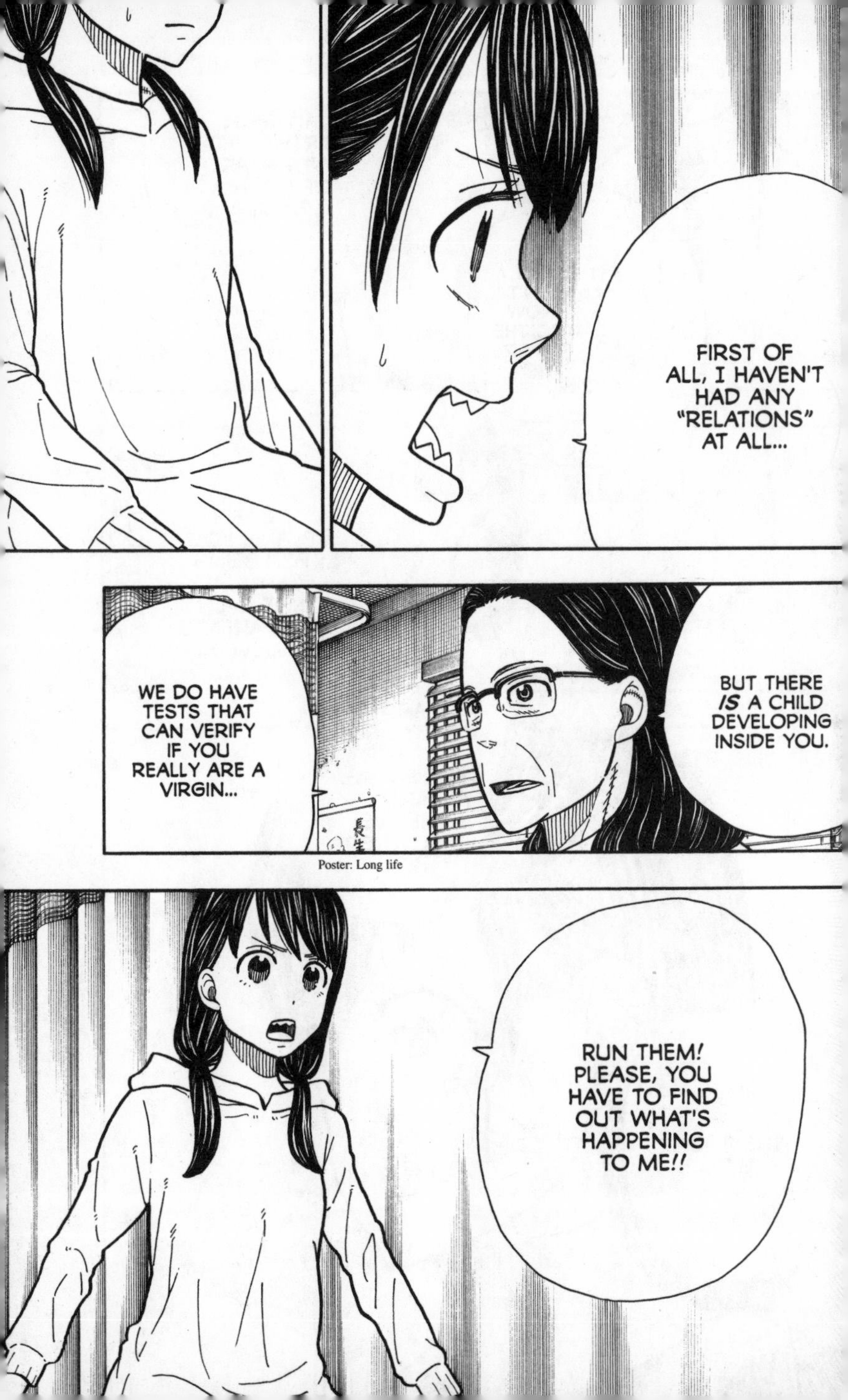
FIRST OF ALL, I HAVEN'T HAD ANY "RELATIONS" AT ALL...
BUT THERE *IS* A CHILD DEVELOPING INSIDE YOU.
WE DO HAVE TESTS THAT CAN VERIFY IF YOU REALLY ARE A VIRGIN...
Poster: Long life
RUN THEM! PLEASE, YOU HAVE TO FIND OUT WHAT'S HAPPENING TO ME!!

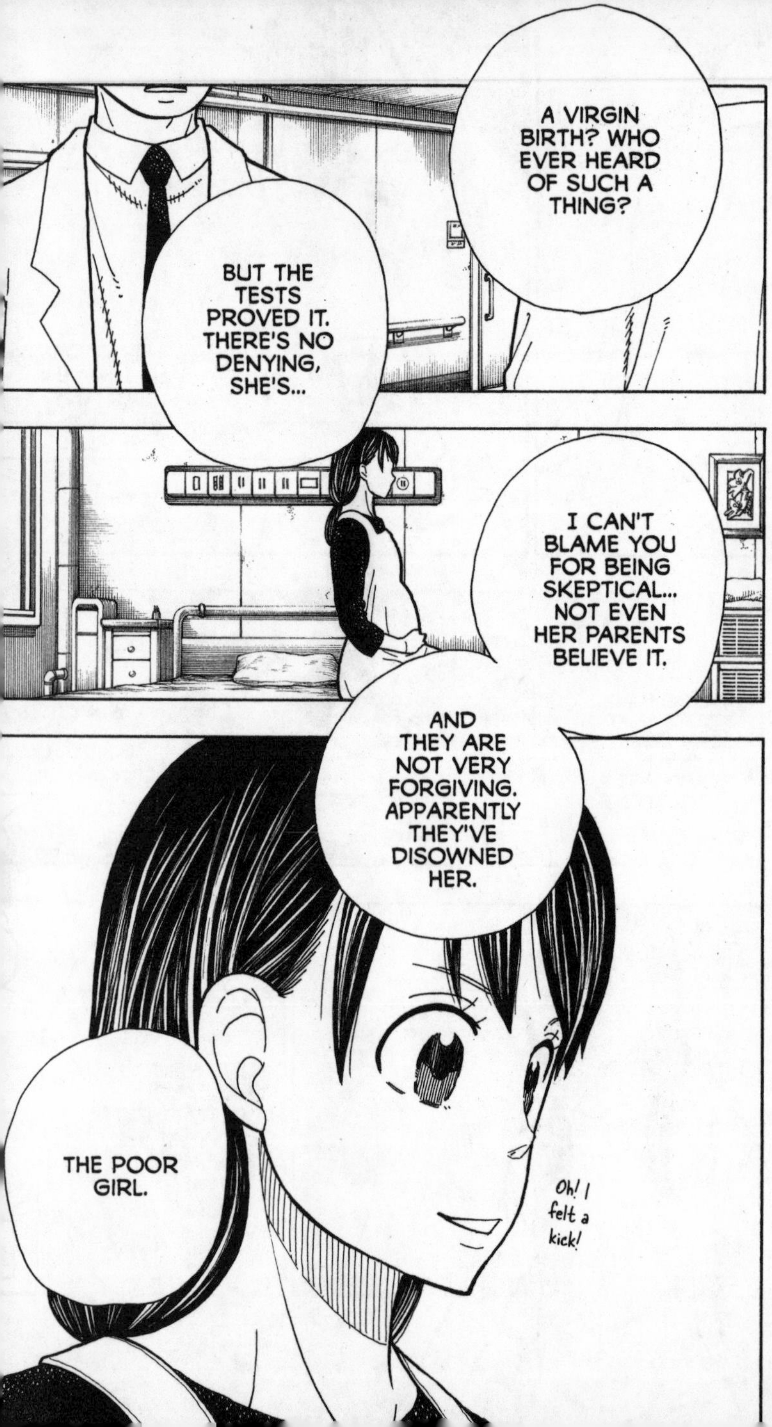
A VIRGIN BIRTH? WHO EVER HEARD OF SUCH A THING?
BUT THE TESTS PROVED IT. THERE'S NO DENYING, SHE'S...
I CAN'T BLAME YOU FOR BEING SKEPTICAL... NOT EVEN HER PARENTS BELIEVE IT.
AND THEY ARE NOT VERY FORGIVING. APPARENTLY THEY'VE DISOWNED HER.
THE POOR GIRL.
Oh! I felt a kick!

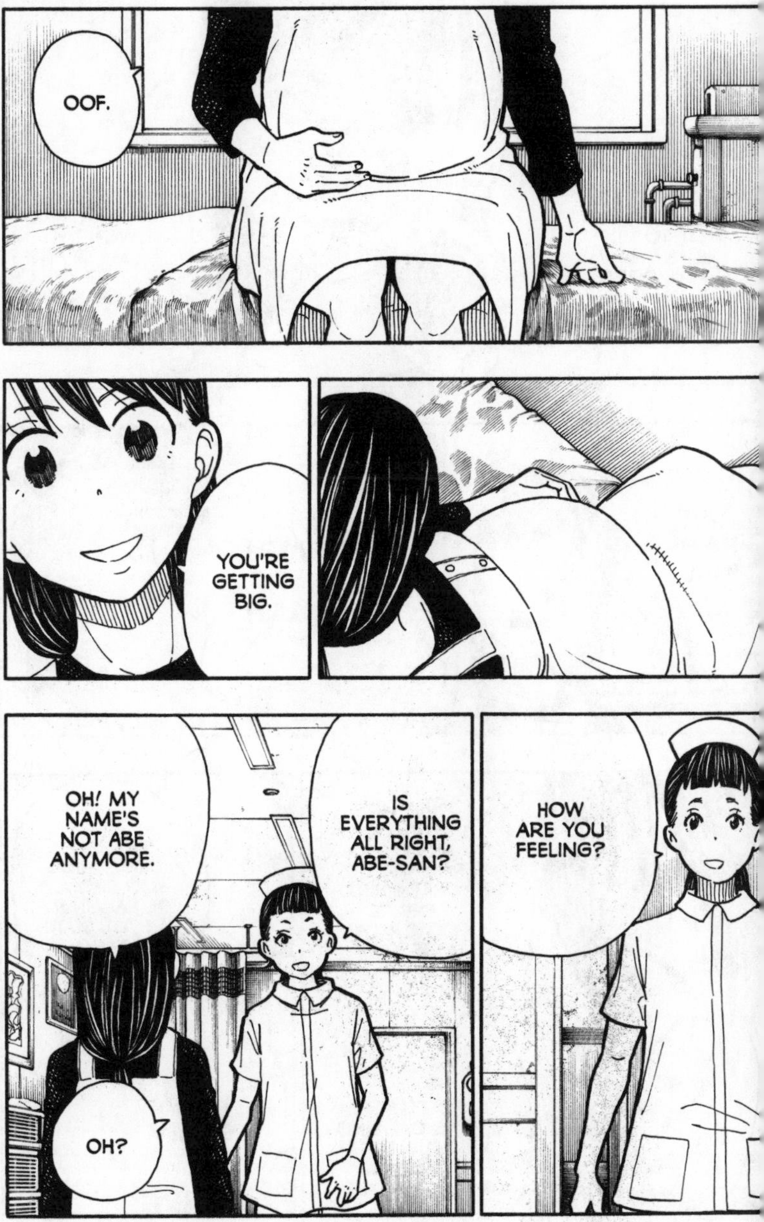
OOF.
YOU'RE GETTING BIG.
HOW ARE YOU FEELING?
IS EVERYTHING ALL RIGHT, ABE-SAN?
OH! MY NAME'S NOT ABE ANYMORE.
OH?

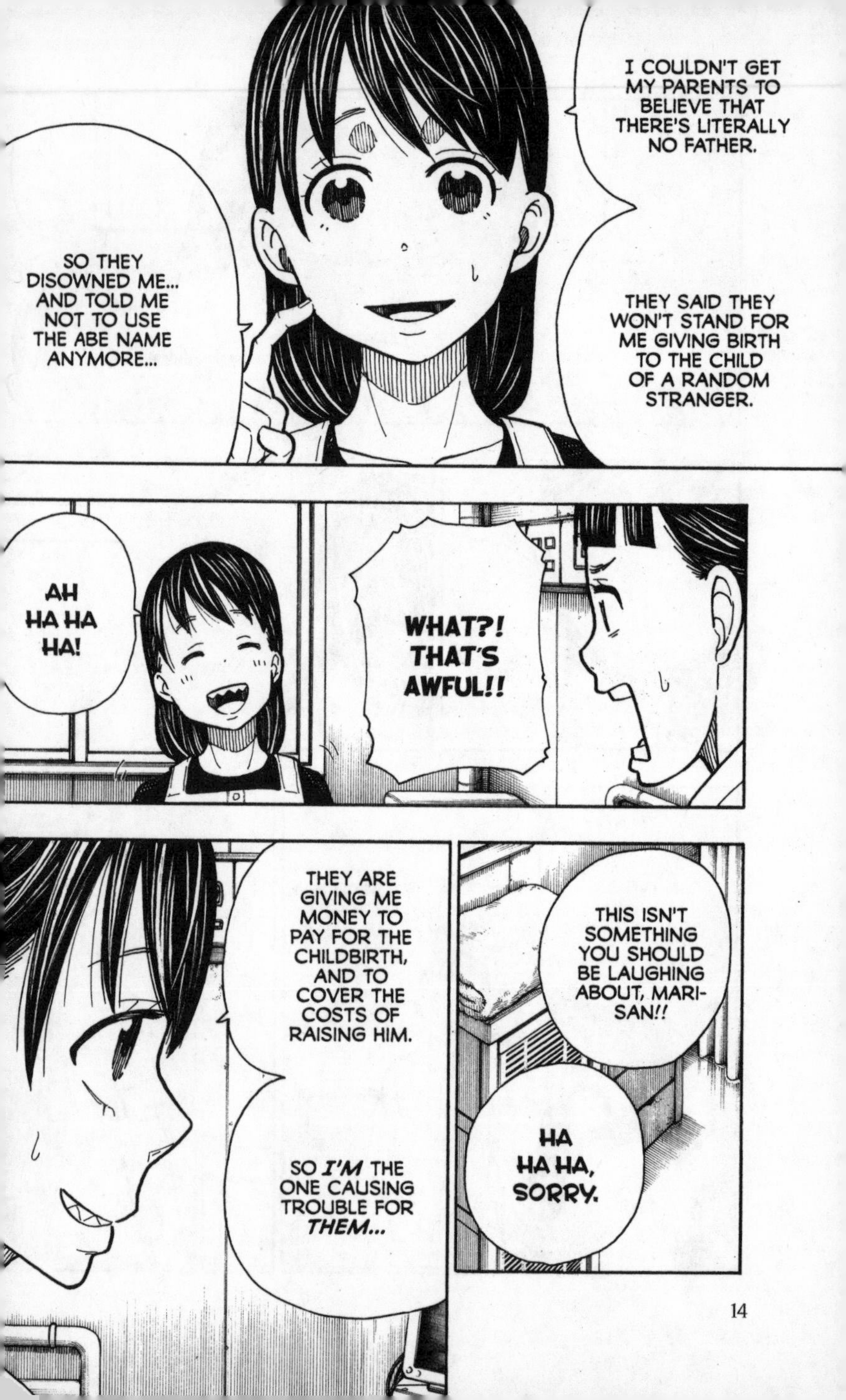
I COULDN'T GET MY PARENTS TO BELIEVE THAT THERE'S LITERALLY NO FATHER.
THEY SAID THEY WON'T STAND FOR ME GIVING BIRTH TO THE CHILD OF A RANDOM STRANGER.
SO THEY DISOWNED ME... AND TOLD ME NOT TO USE THE ABE NAME ANYMORE...
WHAT?! THAT'S AWFUL!!
AH HA HA HA!
THIS ISN'T SOMETHING YOU SHOULD BE LAUGHING ABOUT, MARI-SAN!!
HA HA HA, SORRY.
THEY ARE GIVING ME MONEY TO PAY FOR THE CHILDBIRTH, AND TO COVER THE COSTS OF RAISING HIM.
SO *I'M* THE ONE CAUSING TROUBLE FOR *THEM*...

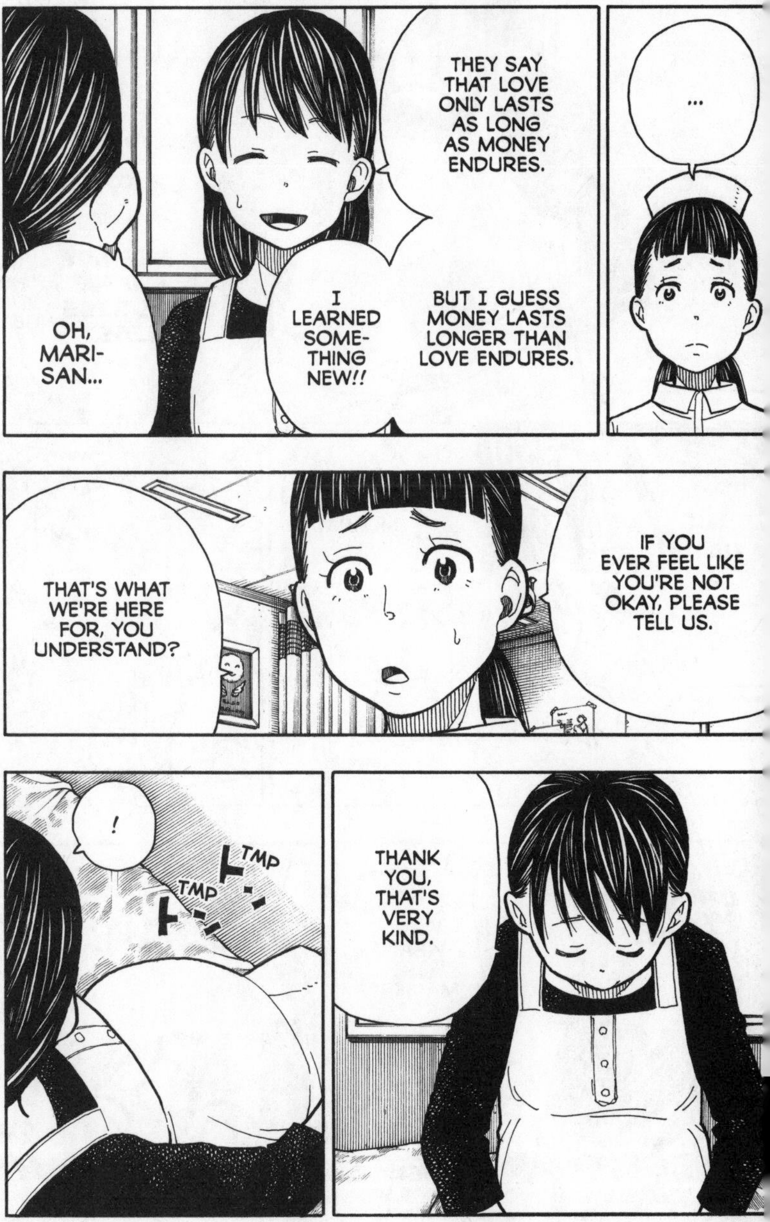
...
THEY SAY THAT LOVE ONLY LASTS AS LONG AS MONEY ENDURES.
BUT I GUESS MONEY LASTS LONGER THAN LOVE ENDURES.
I LEARNED SOME-THING NEW!!
OH, MARI-SAN...
IF YOU EVER FEEL LIKE YOU'RE NOT OKAY, PLEASE TELL US.
THAT'S WHAT WE'RE HERE FOR, YOU UNDERSTAND?
THANK YOU, THAT'S VERY KIND.
!
TMP
TMP

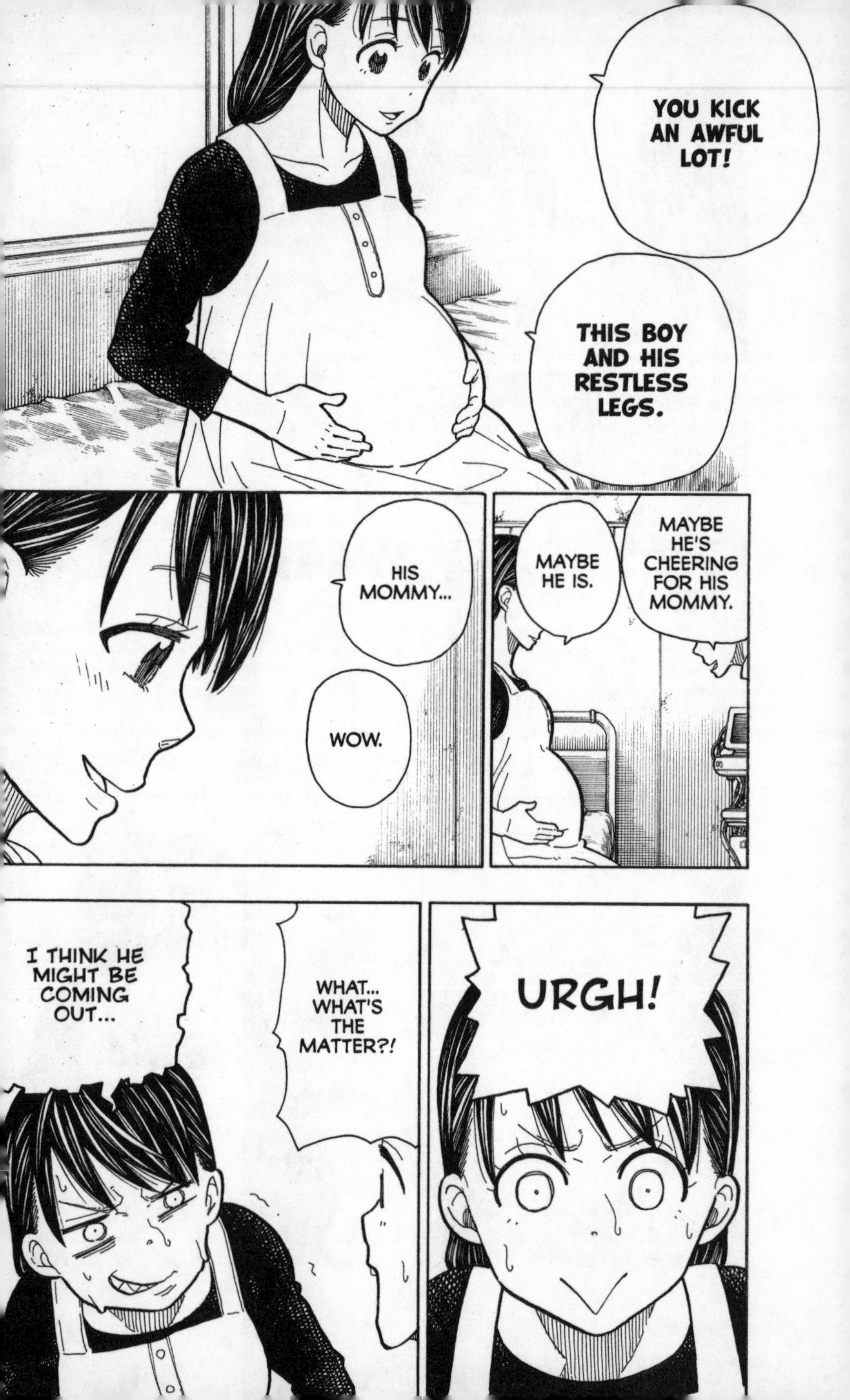
YOU KICK AN AWFUL LOT!
THIS BOY AND HIS RESTLESS LEGS.
MAYBE HE'S CHEERING FOR HIS MOMMY.
MAYBE HE IS.
HIS MOMMY...
WOW.
URGH!
WHAT... WHAT'S THE MATTER?!
I THINK HE MIGHT BE COMING OUT...

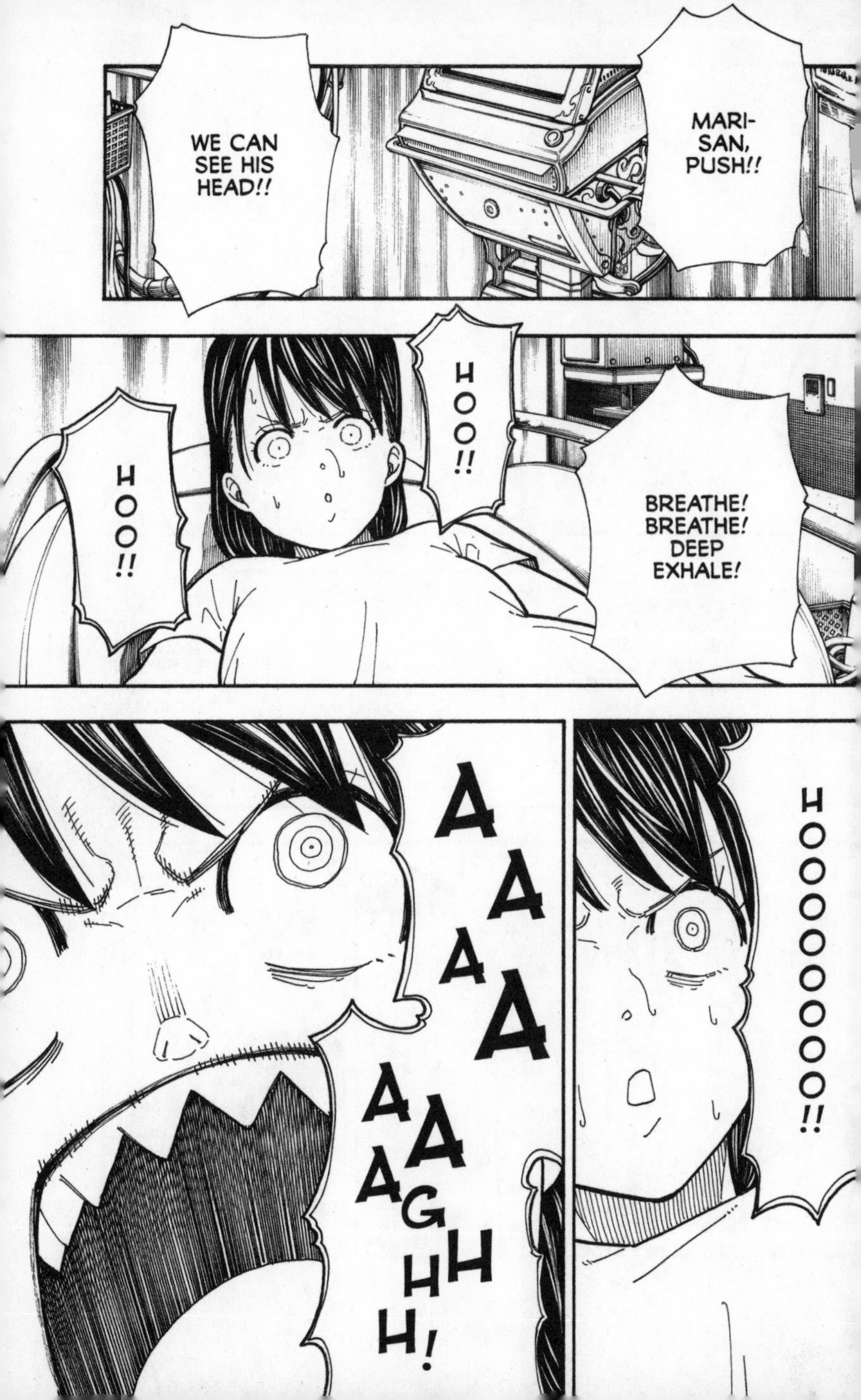
MARI-SAN, PUSH!!
WE CAN SEE HIS HEAD!!
BREATHE! BREATHE! DEEP EXHALE!
HOO!!
HOO!!
HOOOOOOOO!!
AAAAAAAGHHH!

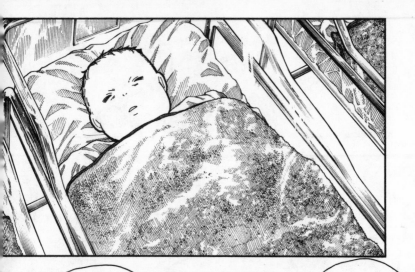

HIS HEART RATE AND BREATHING ARE BOTH NORMAL.
I CAN'T BELIEVE HE'S REALLY HERE...
I'D HEARD STORIES ABOUT BABIES BEING BORN IN A BALL OF FLAMES, SO I WAS A LITTLE WORRIED ABOUT WHAT THIS ONE WOULD BE LIKE WHEN HE CAME OUT...
HOW ARE YOU DOING, MARI-SAN?
HOW'S MY BABY?
THE PICTURE OF GOOD HEALTH.
OH, GOOD.

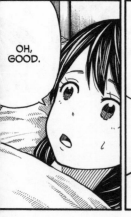

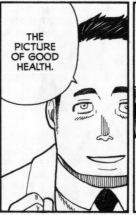

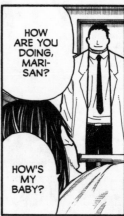

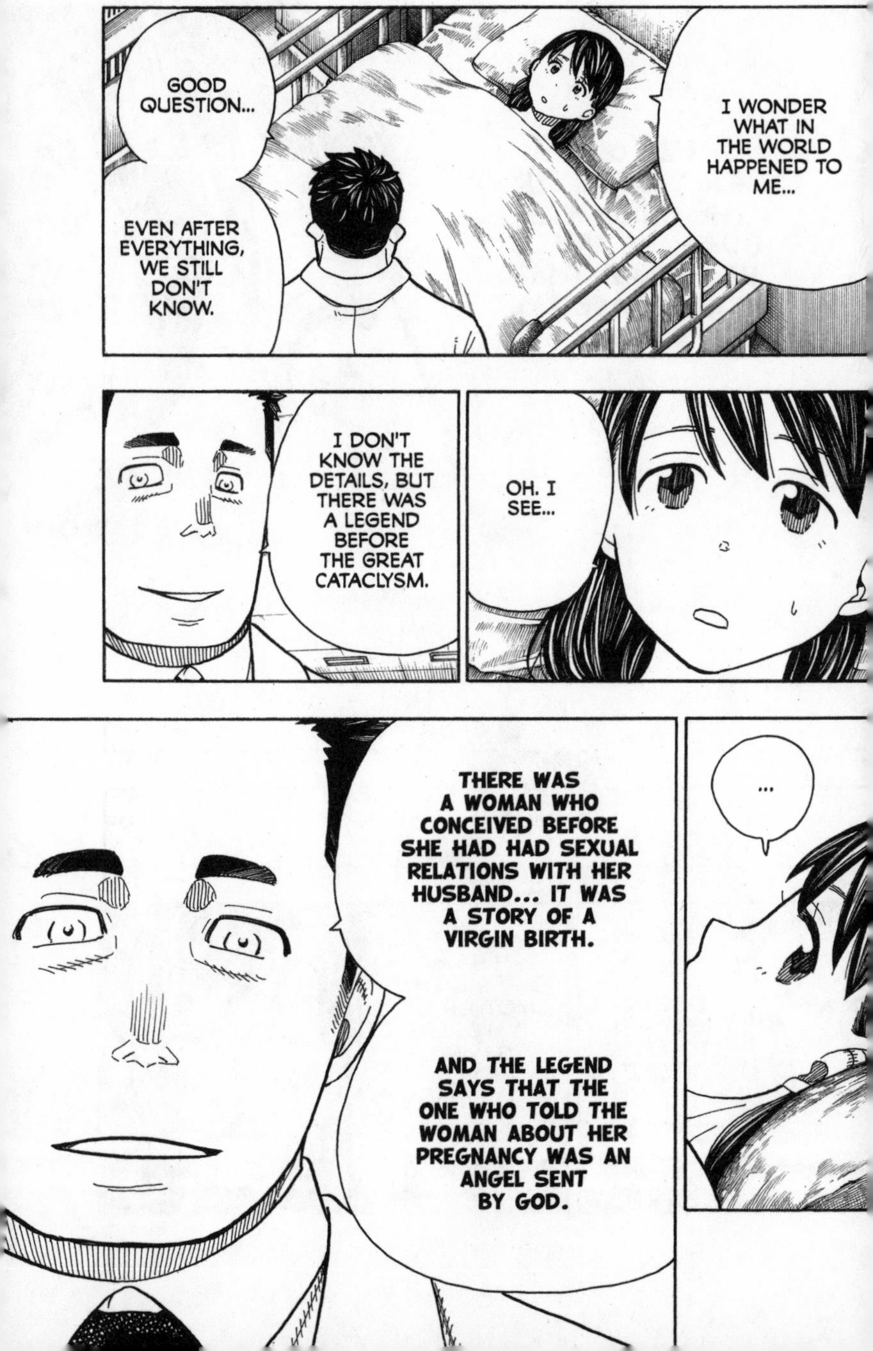
I WONDER WHAT IN THE WORLD HAPPENED TO ME...
GOOD QUESTION...
EVEN AFTER EVERYTHING, WE STILL DON'T KNOW.
OH. I SEE...
I DON'T KNOW THE DETAILS, BUT THERE WAS A LEGEND BEFORE THE GREAT CATACLYSM.
...
THERE WAS A WOMAN WHO CONCEIVED BEFORE SHE HAD HAD SEXUAL RELATIONS WITH HER HUSBAND... IT WAS A STORY OF A VIRGIN BIRTH.
AND THE LEGEND SAYS THAT THE ONE WHO TOLD THE WOMAN ABOUT HER PREGNANCY WAS AN ANGEL SENT BY GOD.

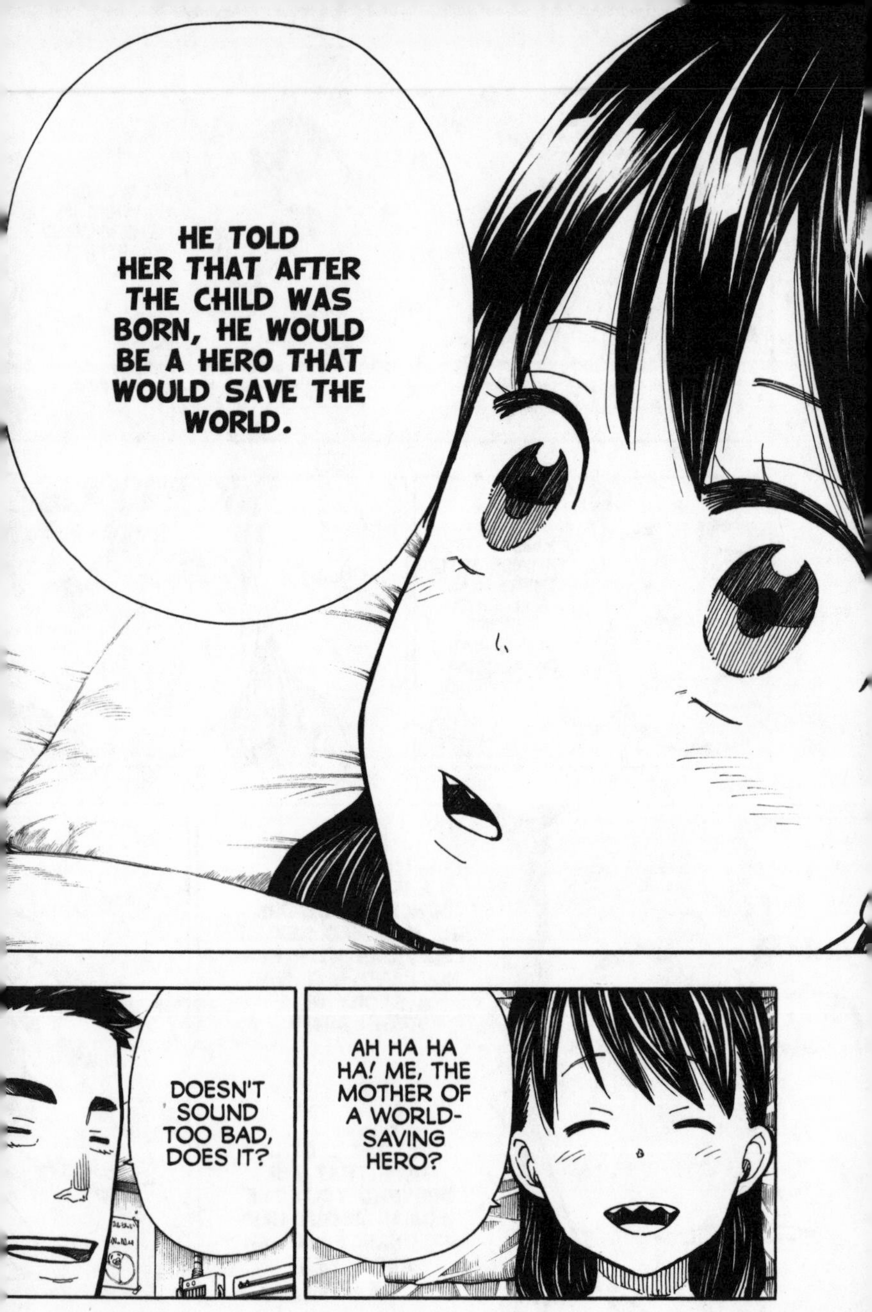
HE TOLD HER THAT AFTER THE CHILD WAS BORN, HE WOULD BE A HERO THAT WOULD SAVE THE WORLD.
AH HA HA HA! ME, THE MOTHER OF A WORLD-SAVING HERO?
DOESN'T SOUND TOO BAD, DOES IT?

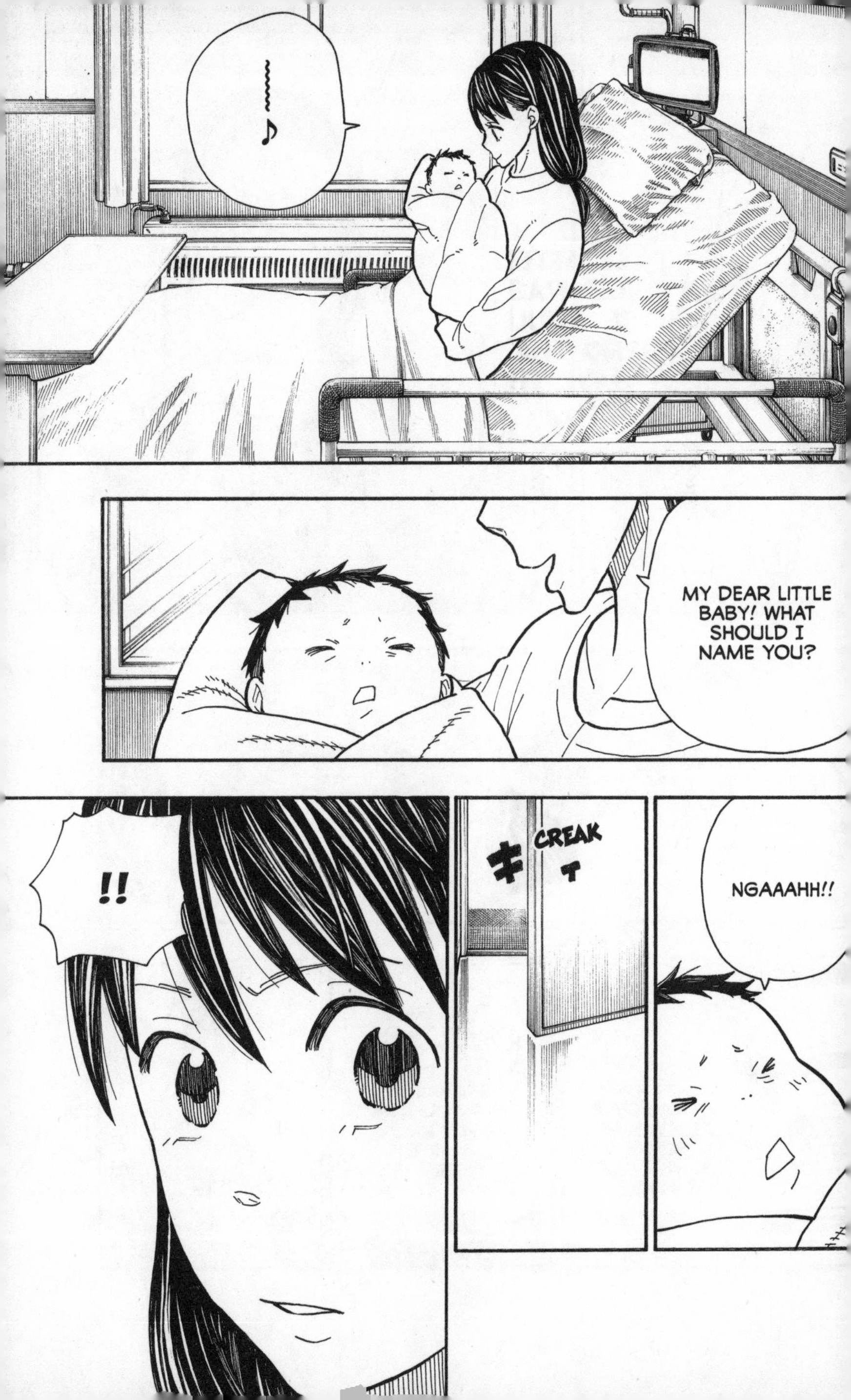
~♪
MY DEAR LITTLE BABY! WHAT SHOULD I NAME YOU?
NGAAAHH!!
CREAK
!!

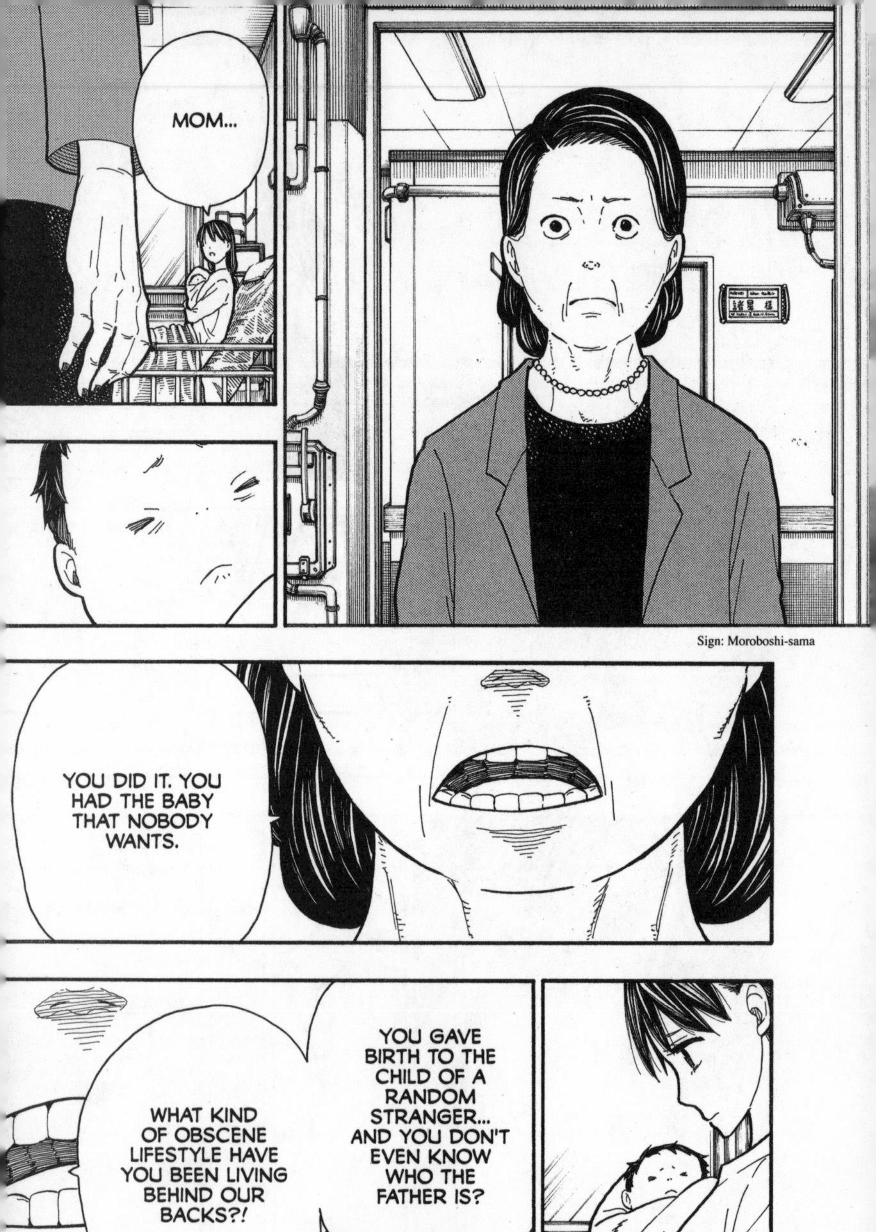
MOM...
YOU DID IT. YOU HAD THE BABY THAT NOBODY WANTS.
YOU GAVE BIRTH TO THE CHILD OF A RANDOM STRANGER... AND YOU DON'T EVEN KNOW WHO THE FATHER IS?
WHAT KIND OF OBSCENE LIFESTYLE HAVE YOU BEEN LIVING BEHIND OUR BACKS?!

Sign: Moroboshi-sama

YOU'RE A TRAMP! THE WORST DAUGHTER A WOMAN COULD ASK FOR!! TO BETRAY YOUR FATHER AND ME LIKE THIS, AFTER ALL WE DID TO RAISE YOU!!

YOU REFUSED TO LISTEN TO US, AND GAVE BIRTH TO A CHILD THAT NOBODY WANTED!!

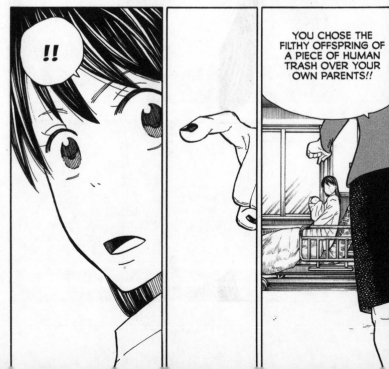

!!

YOU CHOSE THE FILTHY OFFSPRING OF A PIECE OF HUMAN TRASH OVER YOUR OWN PARENTS!!

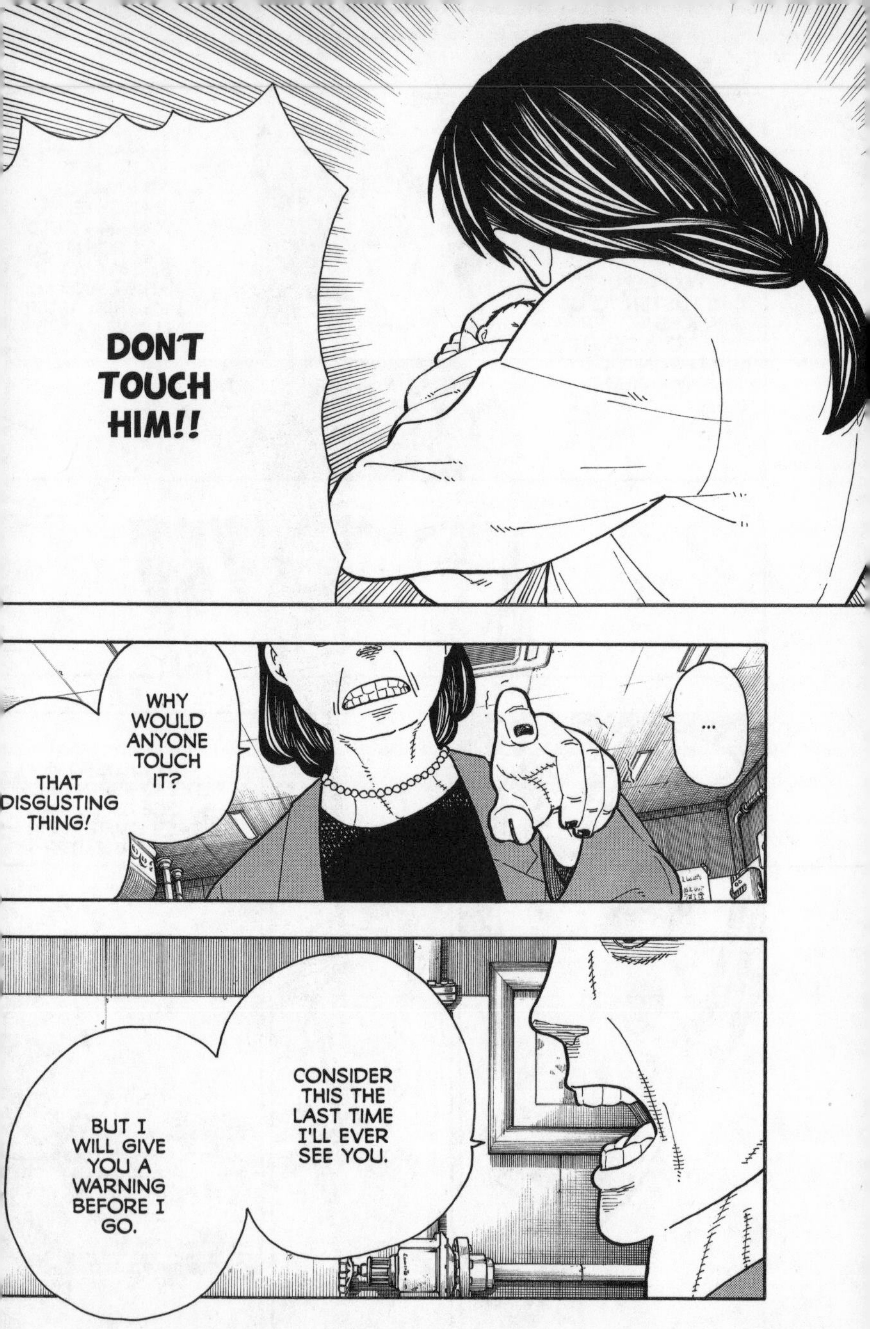
DON'T TOUCH HIM!!
...
WHY WOULD ANYONE TOUCH IT?
THAT DISGUSTING THING!
CONSIDER THIS THE LAST TIME I'LL EVER SEE YOU.
BUT I WILL GIVE YOU A WARNING BEFORE I GO.

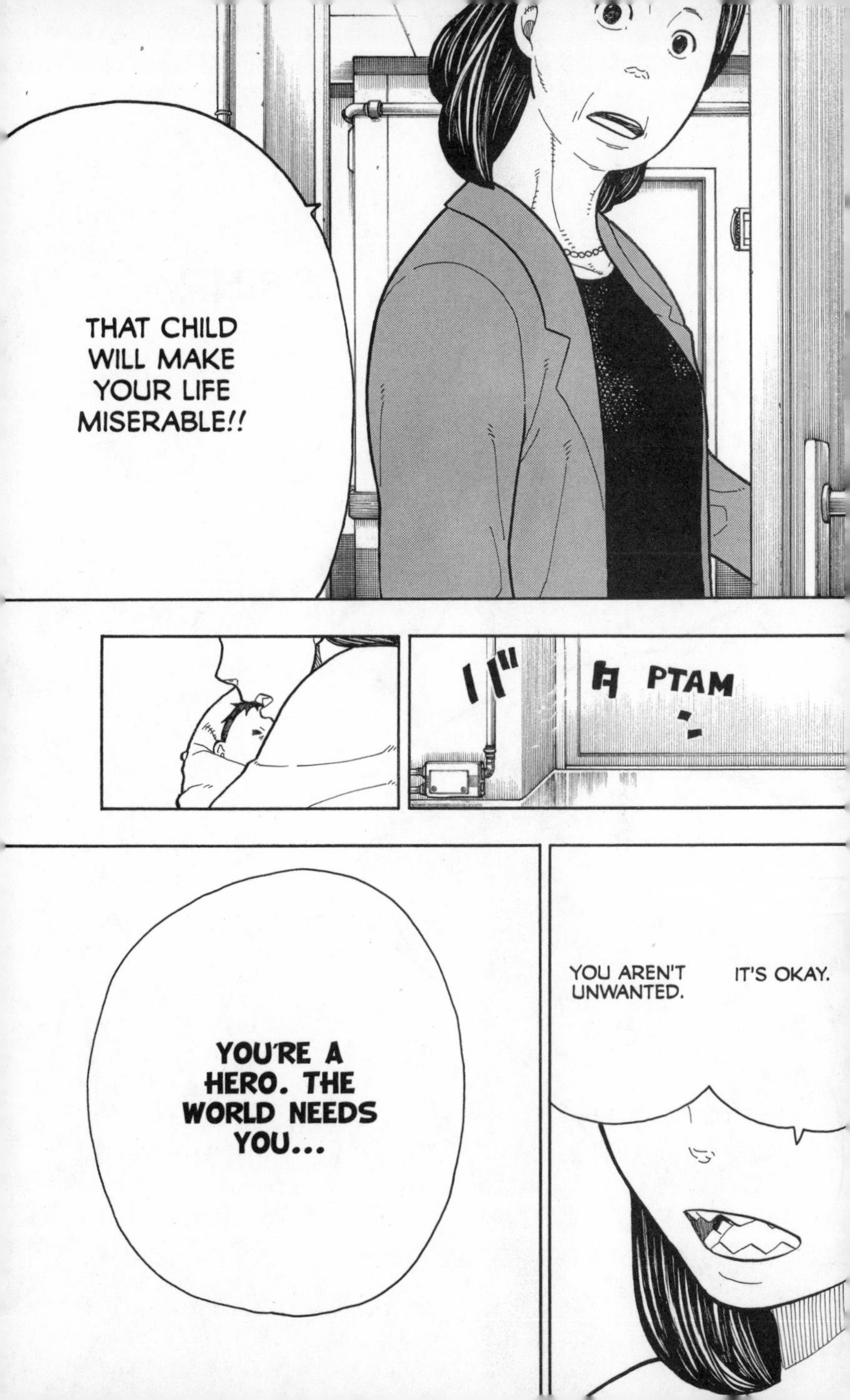
THAT CHILD WILL MAKE YOUR LIFE MISERABLE!!
PTAM
IT'S OKAY.
YOU AREN'T UNWANTED.
YOU'RE A HERO. THE WORLD NEEDS YOU...

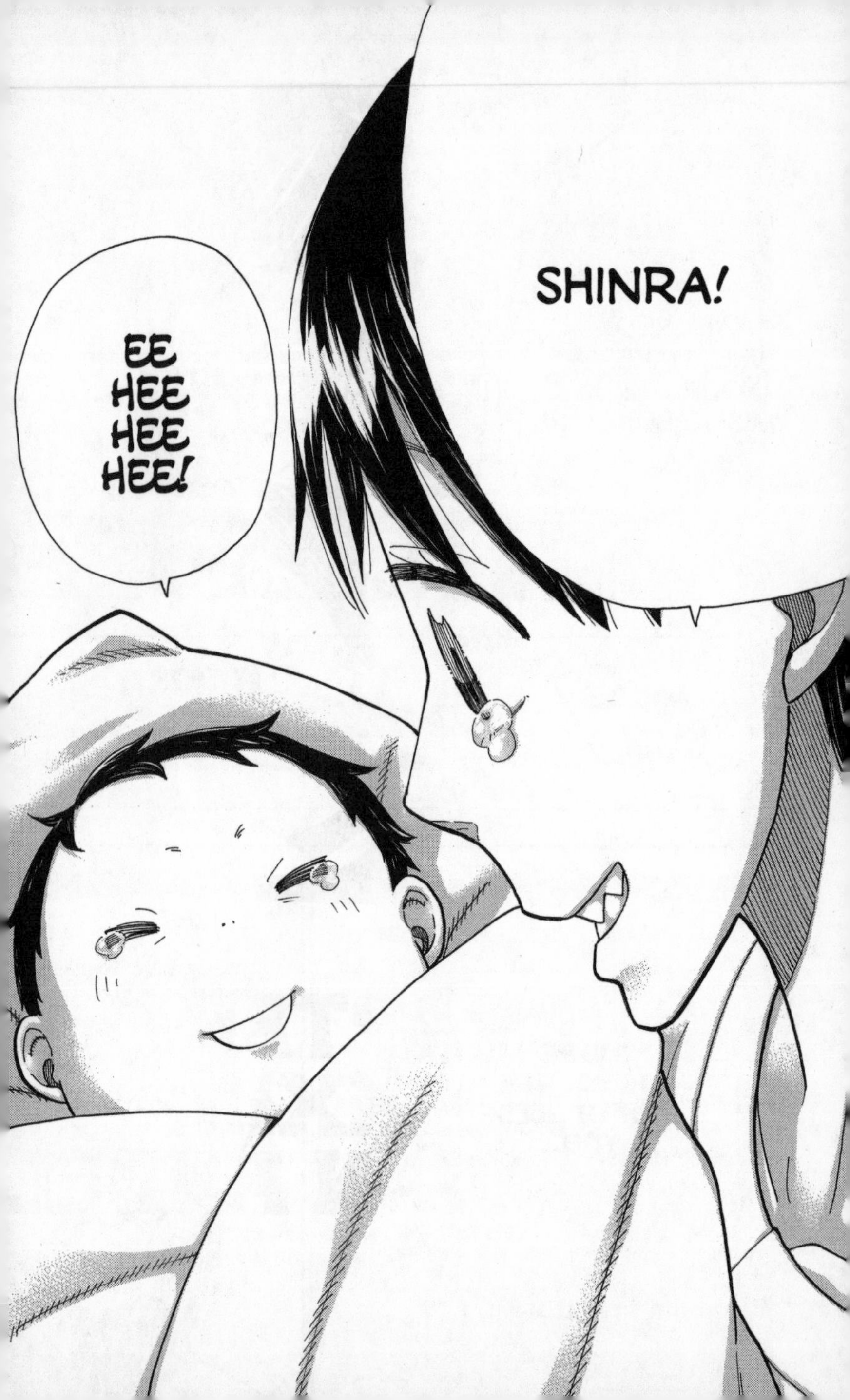
SHINRA!
EE HEE HEE HEE!

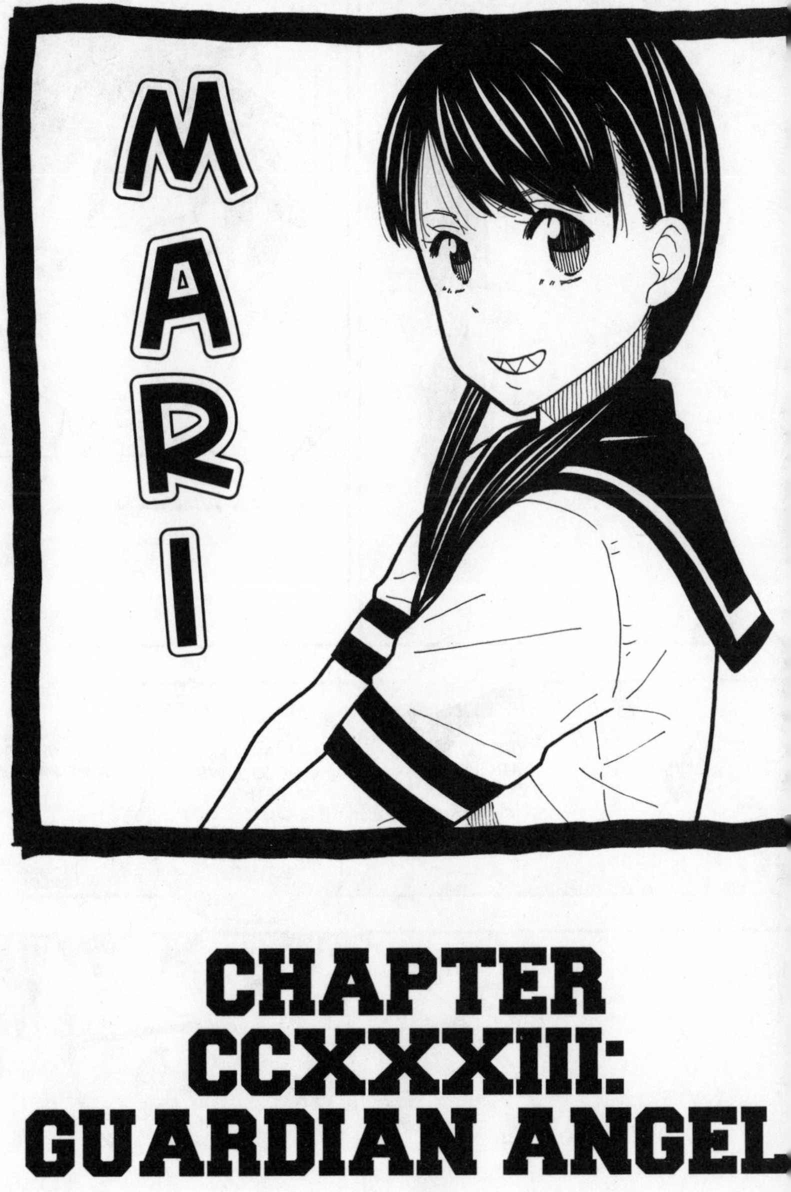
MARI

CHAPTER CCXXXIII: GUARDIAN ANGEL

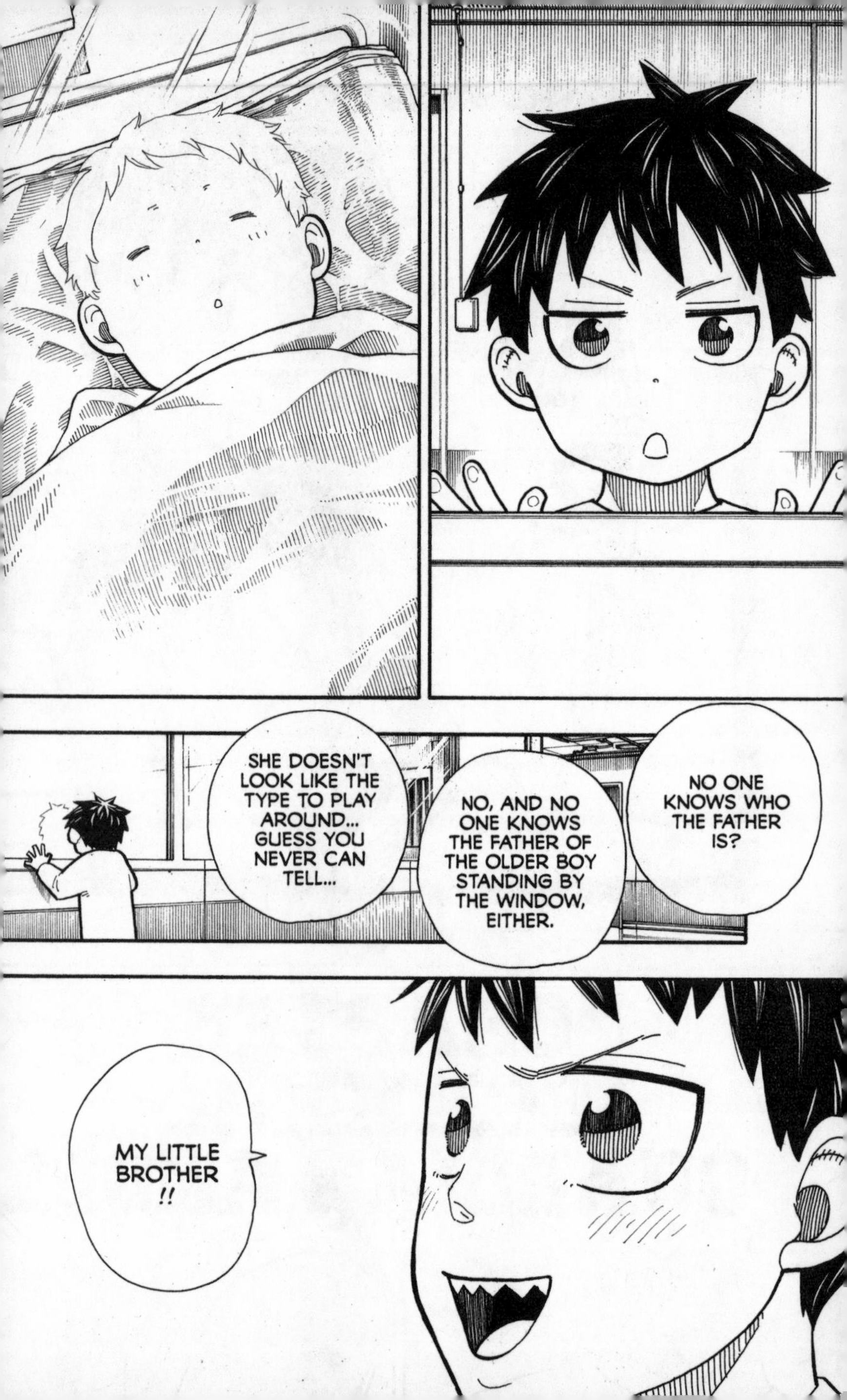
NO ONE KNOWS WHO THE FATHER IS?
NO, AND NO ONE KNOWS THE FATHER OF THE OLDER BOY STANDING BY THE WINDOW, EITHER.
SHE DOESN'T LOOK LIKE THE TYPE TO PLAY AROUND... GUESS YOU NEVER CAN TELL...
MY LITTLE BROTHER!!

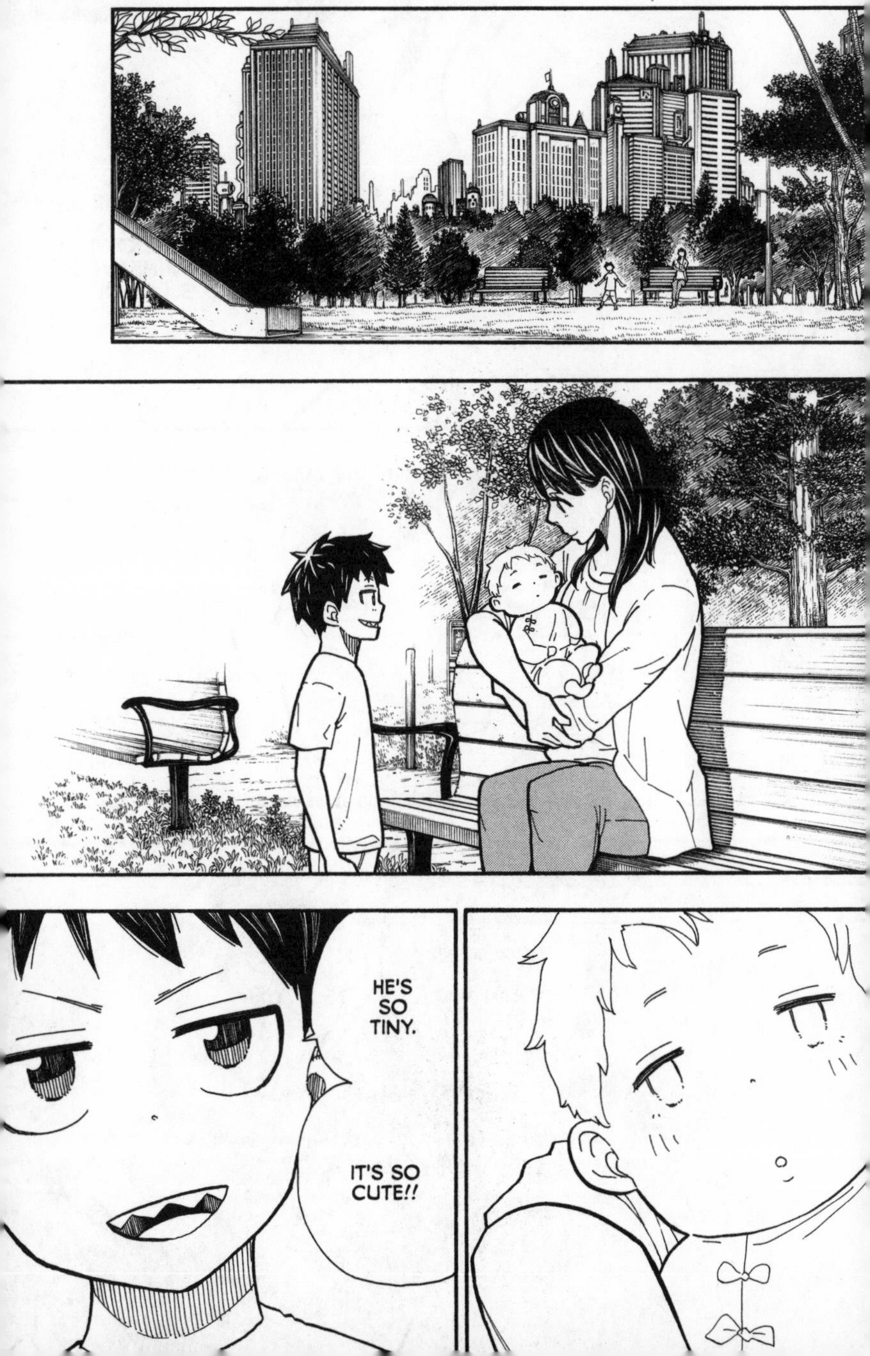
HE'S SO TINY.
IT'S SO CUTE!!

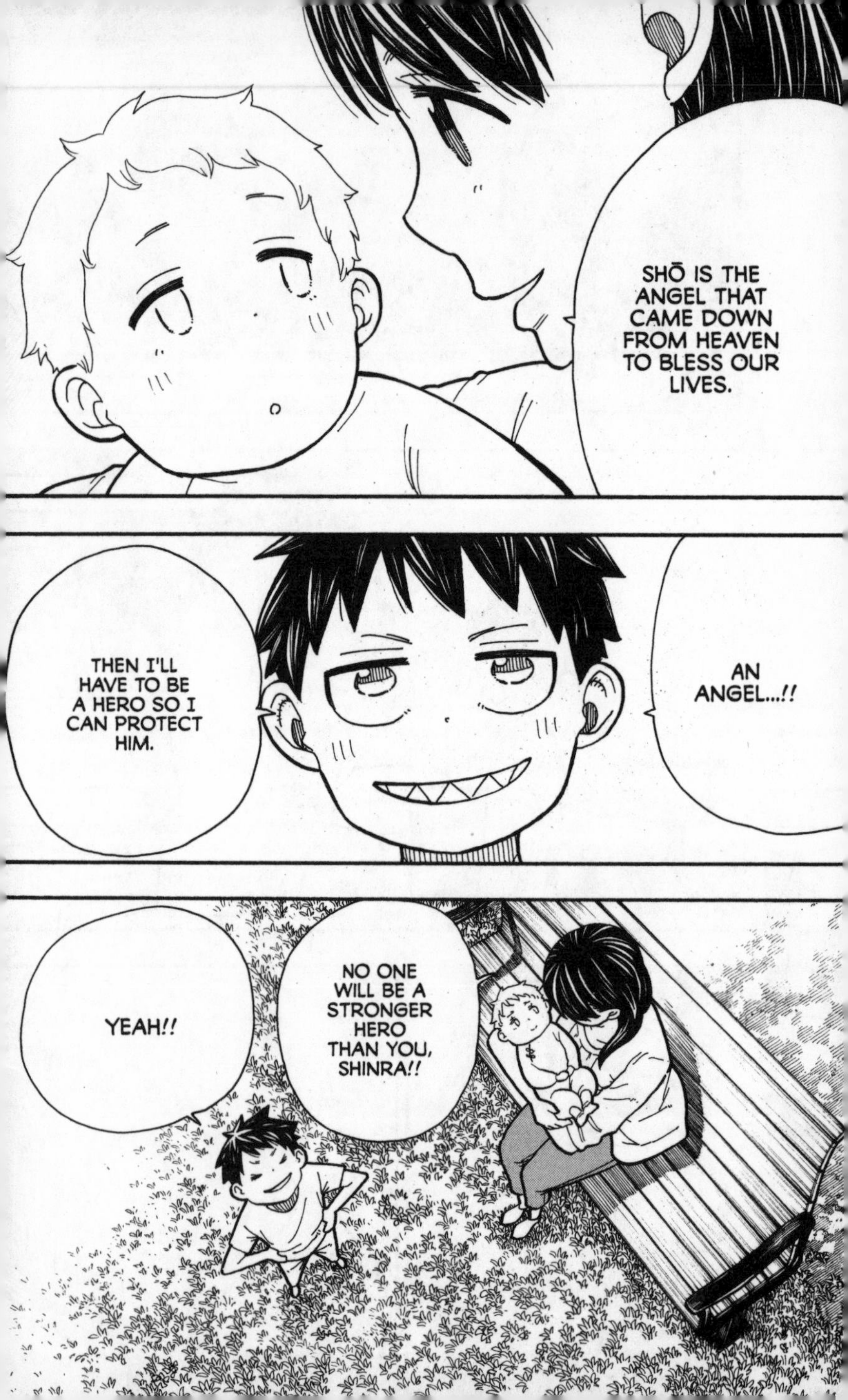
SHŌ IS THE ANGEL THAT CAME DOWN FROM HEAVEN TO BLESS OUR LIVES.
AN ANGEL...!!
THEN I'LL HAVE TO BE A HERO SO I CAN PROTECT HIM.
NO ONE WILL BE A STRONGER HERO THAN YOU, SHINRA!!
YEAH!!

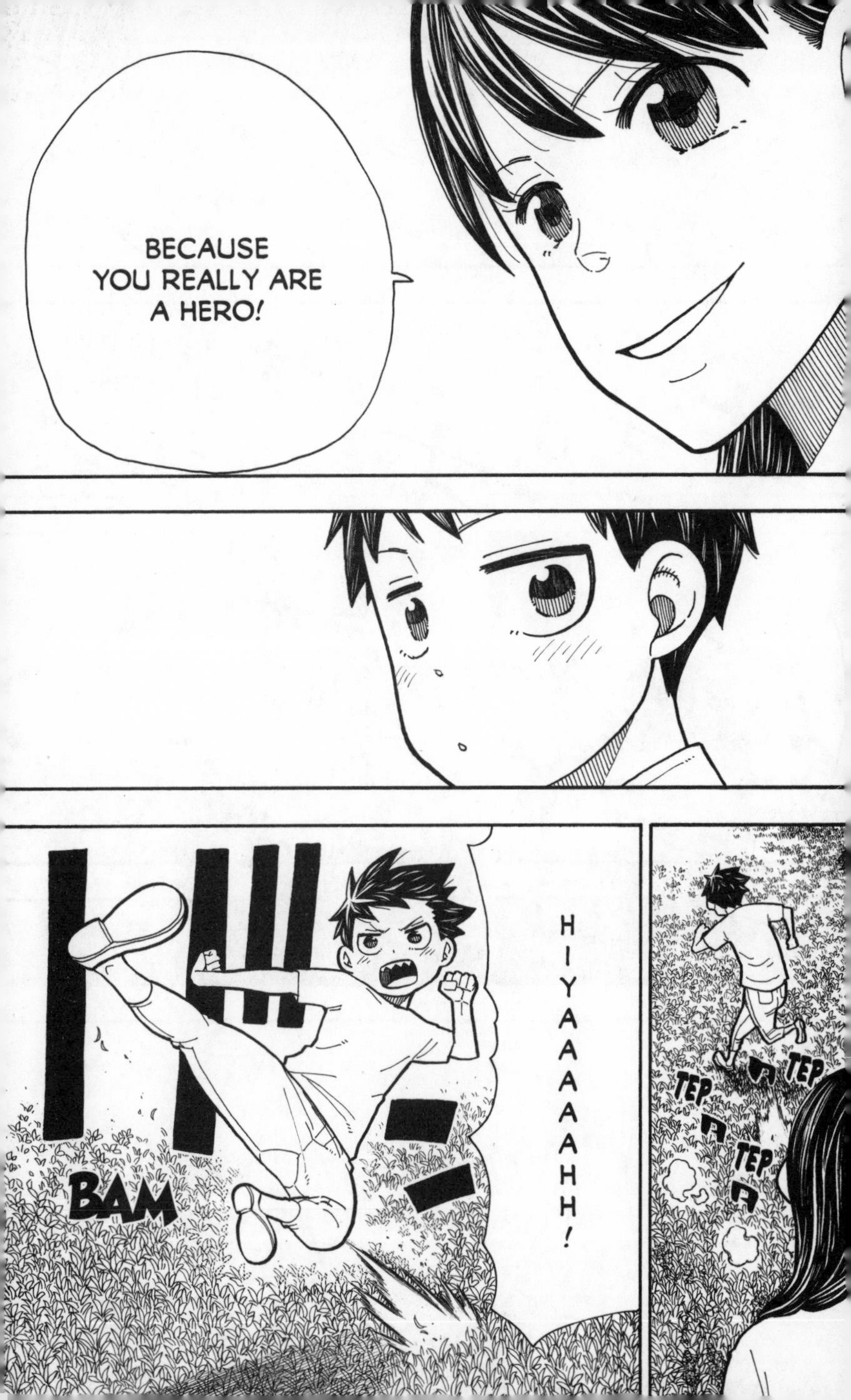
BECAUSE YOU REALLY ARE A HERO!
TEP
TEP
TEP
HIYAAAAAAHH!
BAM

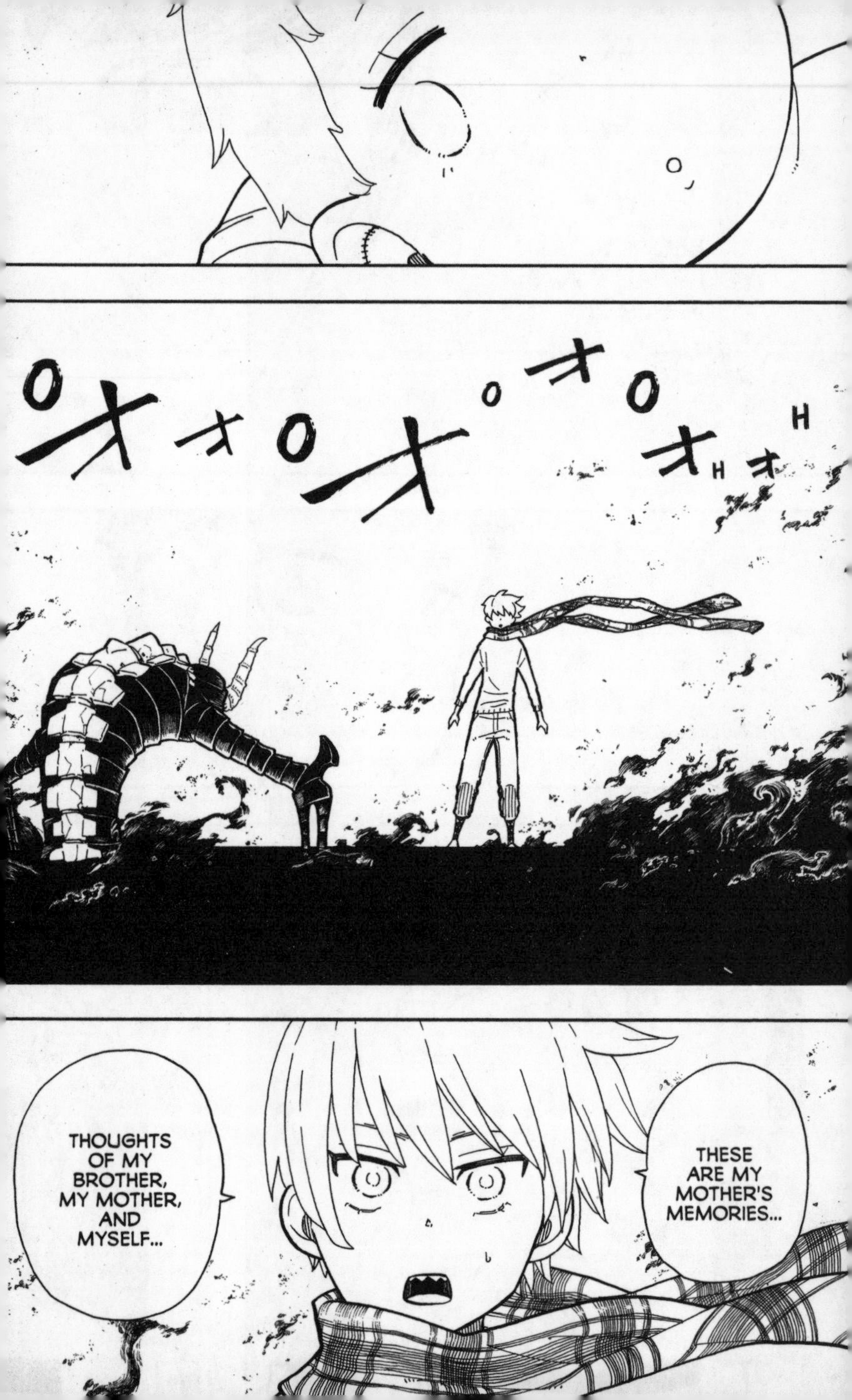
OオォOオoオOオHオH
THESE ARE MY MOTHER'S MEMORIES...
THOUGHTS OF MY BROTHER, MY MOTHER, AND MYSELF...

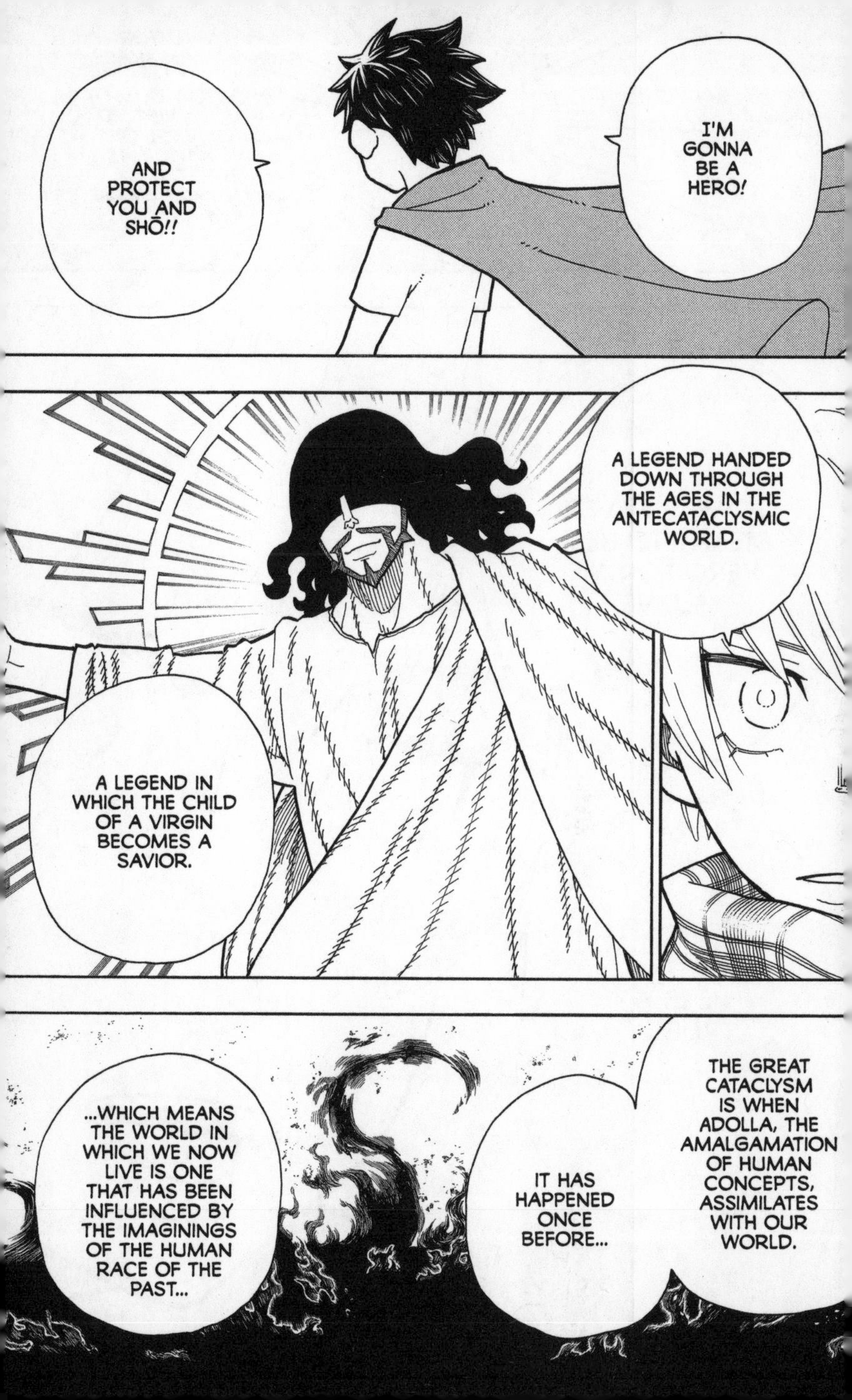
I'M GONNA BE A HERO!
AND PROTECT YOU AND SHŌ!!
A LEGEND HANDED DOWN THROUGH THE AGES IN THE ANTECATACLYSMIC WORLD.
A LEGEND IN WHICH THE CHILD OF A VIRGIN BECOMES A SAVIOR.
THE GREAT CATACLYSM IS WHEN ADOLLA, THE AMALGAMATION OF HUMAN CONCEPTS, ASSIMILATES WITH OUR WORLD.
IT HAS HAPPENED ONCE BEFORE...
...WHICH MEANS THE WORLD IN WHICH WE NOW LIVE IS ONE THAT HAS BEEN INFLUENCED BY THE IMAGININGS OF THE HUMAN RACE OF THE PAST...

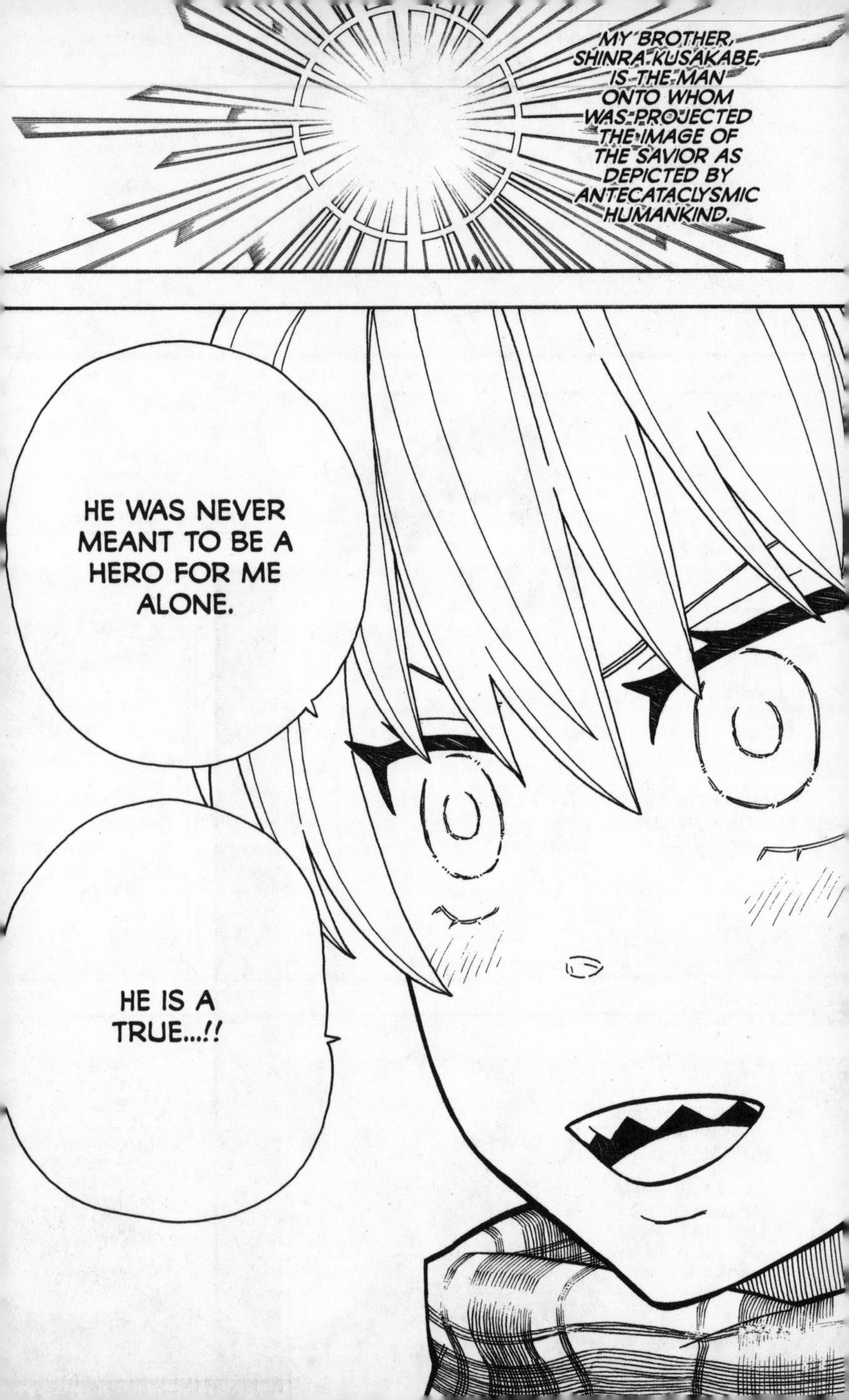
MY BROTHER, SHINRA KUSAKABE, IS THE MAN ONTO WHOM WAS PROJECTED THE IMAGE OF THE SAVIOR AS DEPICTED BY ANTECATACLYSMIC HUMANKIND.
HE WAS NEVER MEANT TO BE A HERO FOR ME ALONE.
HE IS A TRUE...!!

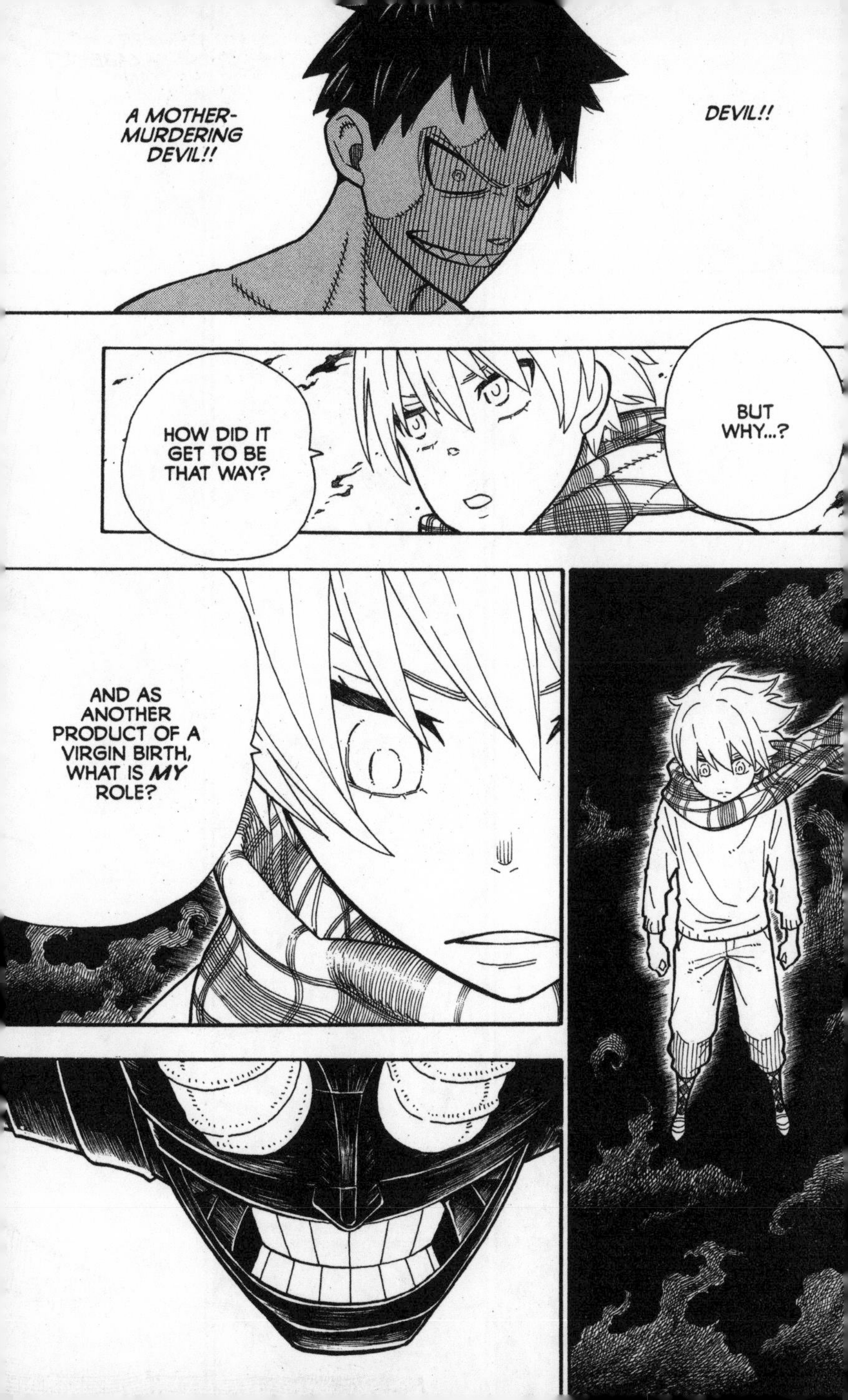
DEVIL!!
A MOTHER-MURDERING DEVIL!!
BUT WHY...?
HOW DID IT GET TO BE THAT WAY?
AND AS ANOTHER PRODUCT OF A VIRGIN BIRTH, WHAT IS *MY* ROLE?

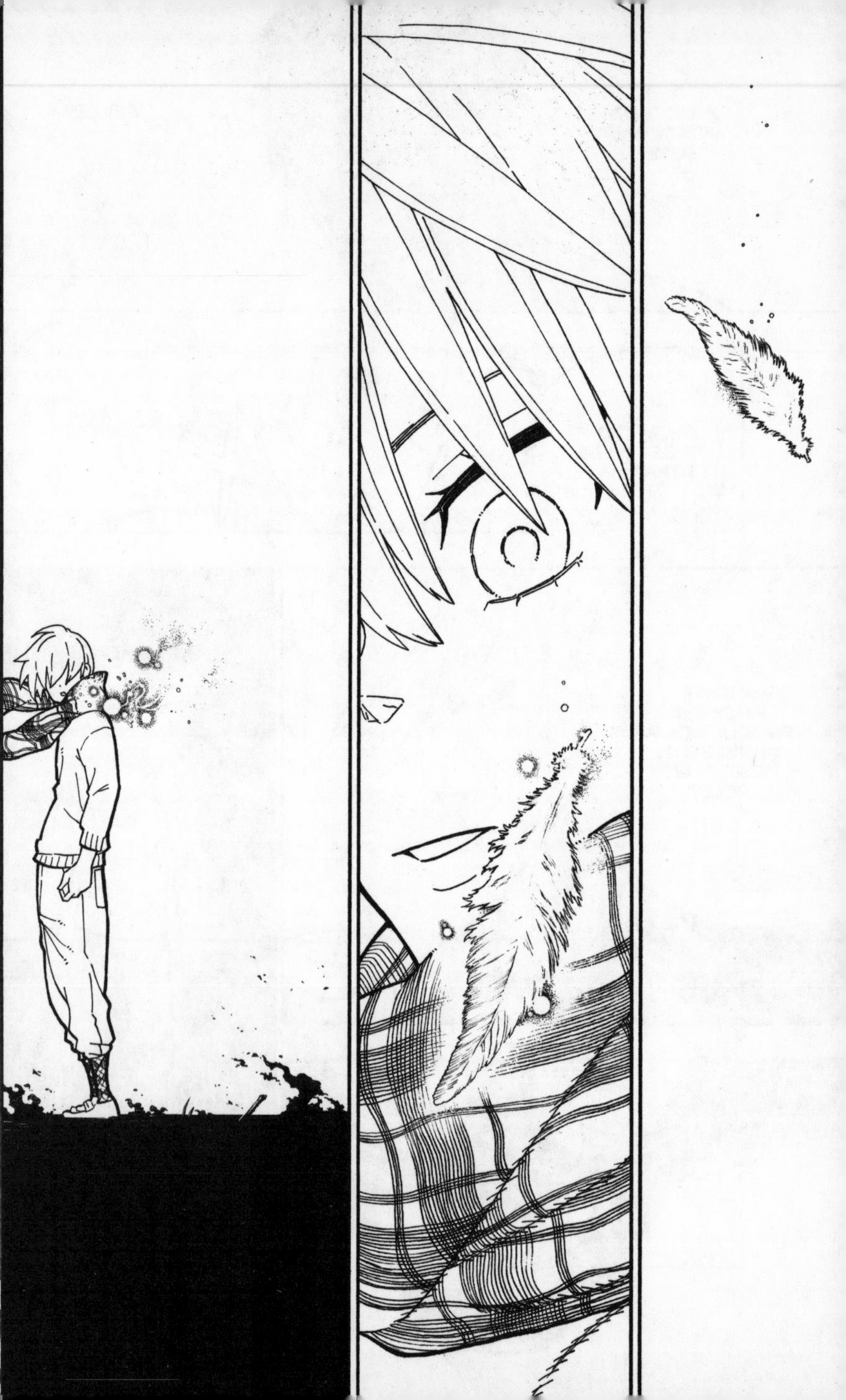

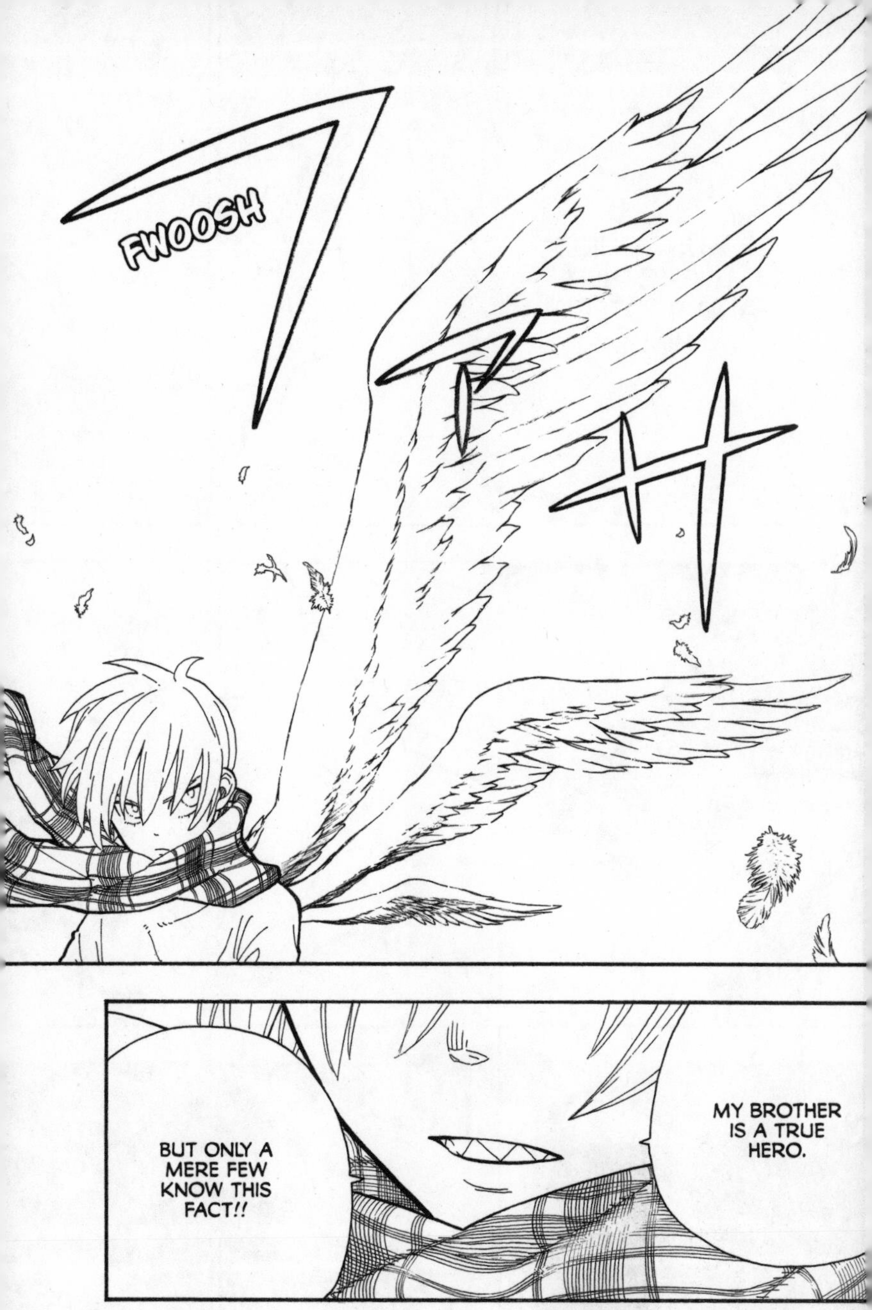
FWOOSH
MY BROTHER IS A TRUE HERO.
BUT ONLY A MERE FEW KNOW THIS FACT!!

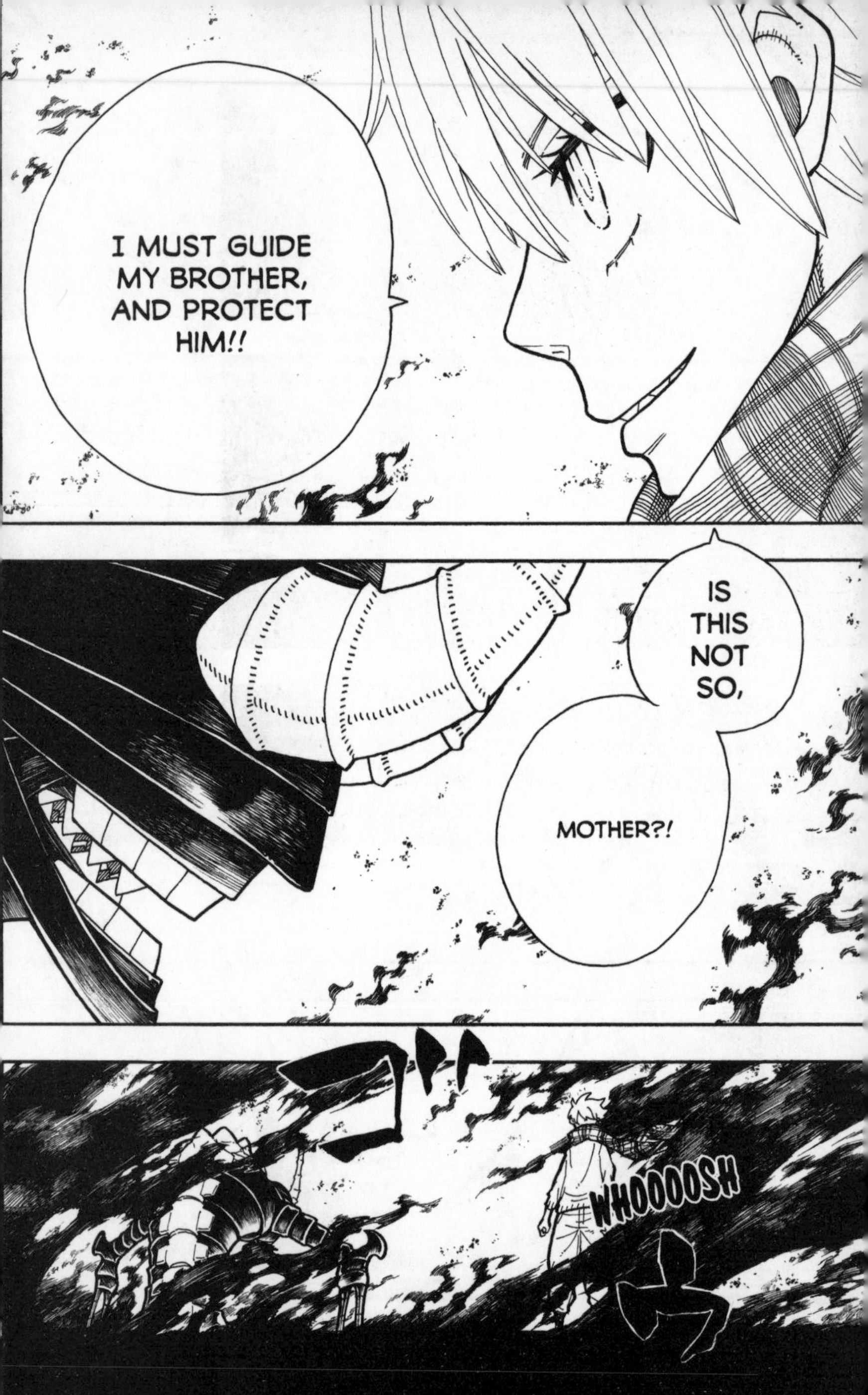
I MUST GUIDE MY BROTHER, AND PROTECT HIM!!
IS THIS NOT SO,
MOTHER?!
WHOOOOOSH

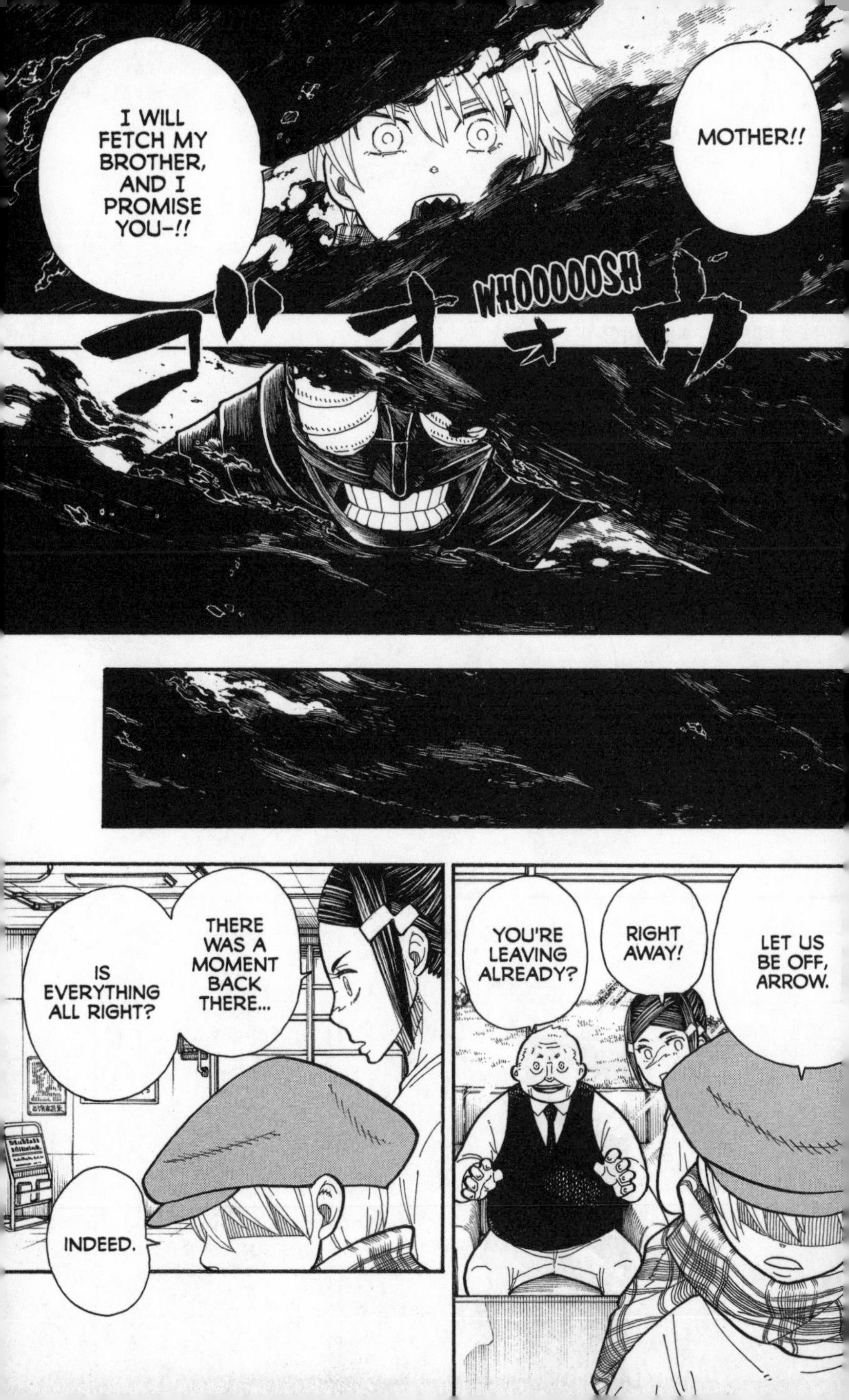
MOTHER!!
I WILL FETCH MY BROTHER, AND I PROMISE YOU-!!
WHOOOOOSH
ゴオォウ
LET US BE OFF, ARROW.
RIGHT AWAY!
YOU'RE LEAVING ALREADY?
THERE WAS A MOMENT BACK THERE...
IS EVERYTHING ALL RIGHT?
INDEED.

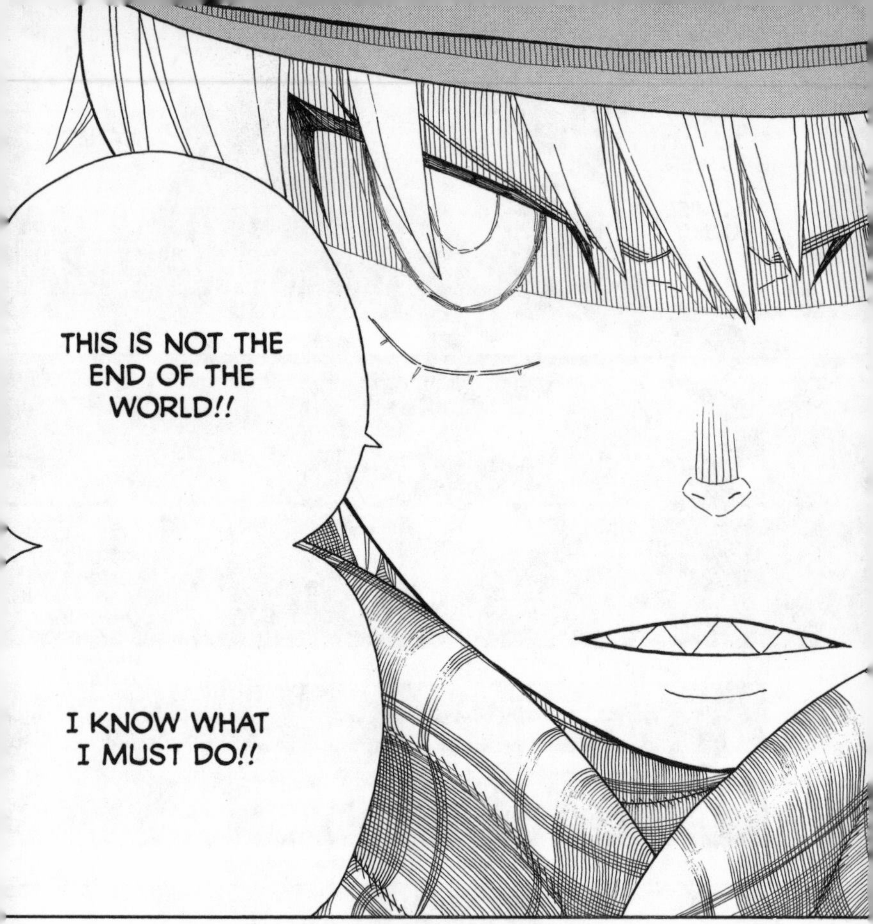
THIS IS NOT THE END OF THE WORLD!!
I KNOW WHAT I MUST DO!!

Sign: Civic Center

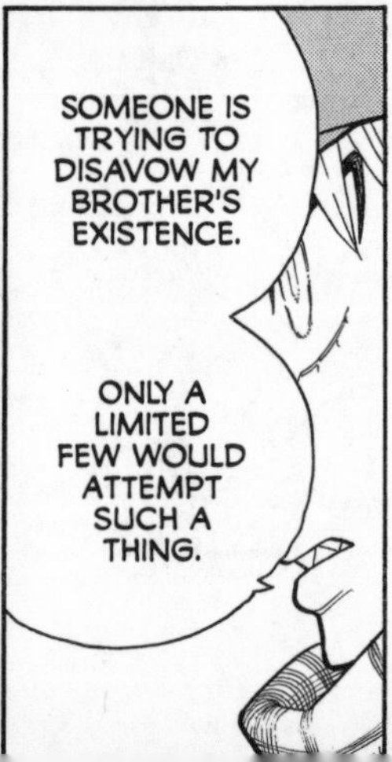
SOMEONE IS TRYING TO DISAVOW MY BROTHER'S EXISTENCE.
ONLY A LIMITED FEW WOULD ATTEMPT SUCH A THING.

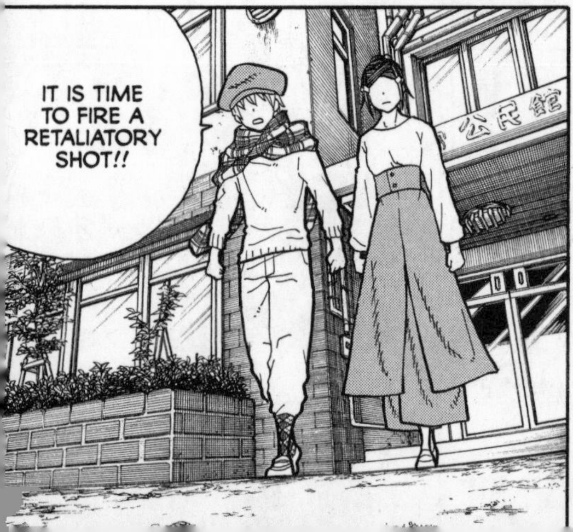
IT IS TIME TO FIRE A RETALIATORY SHOT!!

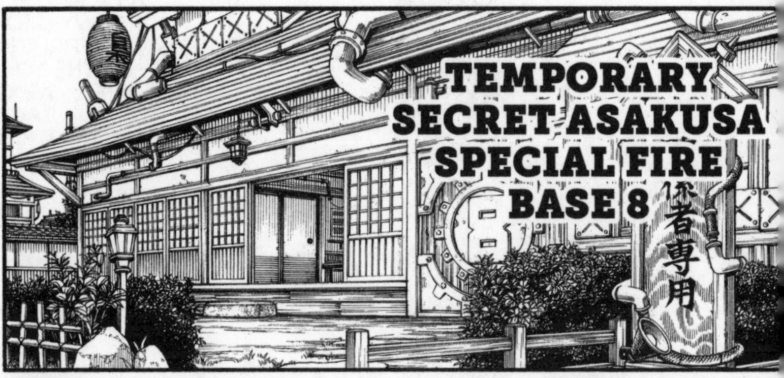
TEMPORARY SECRET ASAKUSA SPECIAL FIRE BASE 8

Lamp: Owl

Sign: Authorized Personnel Only

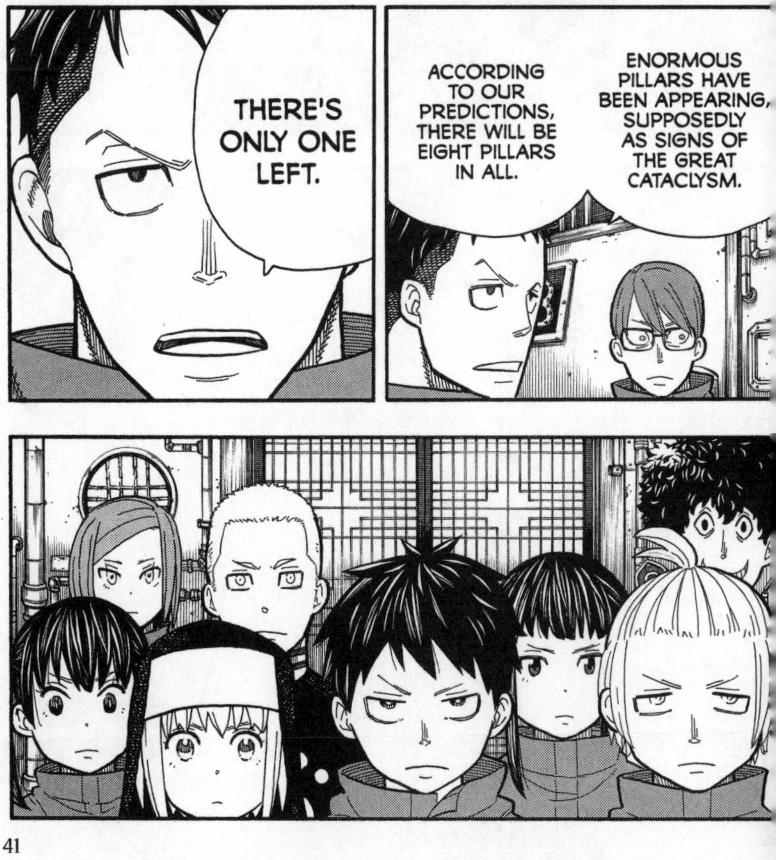
ENORMOUS PILLARS HAVE BEEN APPEARING, SUPPOSEDLY AS SIGNS OF THE GREAT CATACLYSM.
ACCORDING TO OUR PREDICTIONS, THERE WILL BE EIGHT PILLARS IN ALL.
THERE'S ONLY ONE LEFT.

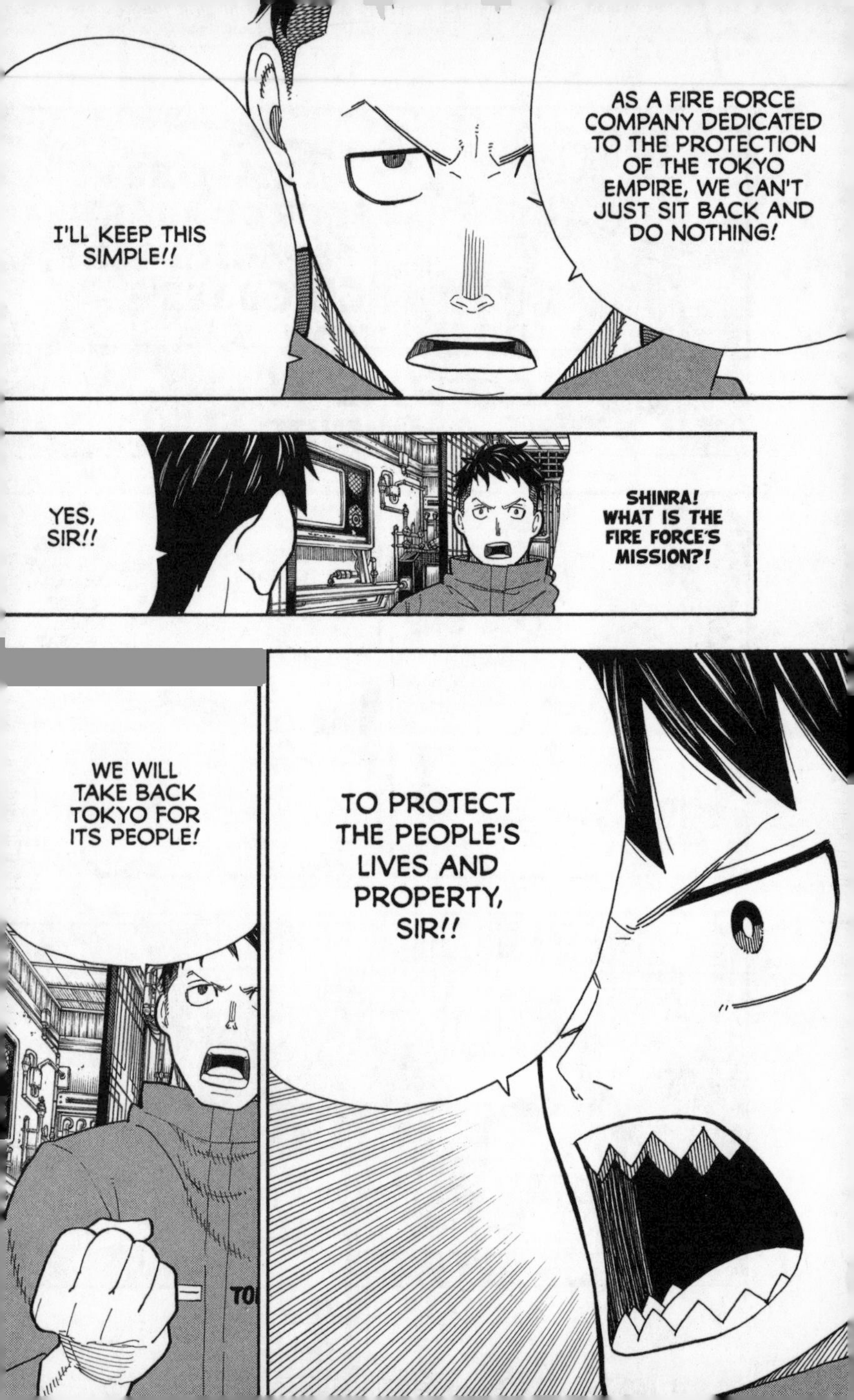
AS A FIRE FORCE COMPANY DEDICATED TO THE PROTECTION OF THE TOKYO EMPIRE, WE CAN'T JUST SIT BACK AND DO NOTHING!
I'LL KEEP THIS SIMPLE!!
SHINRA! WHAT IS THE FIRE FORCE'S MISSION?!
YES, SIR!!
TO PROTECT THE PEOPLE'S LIVES AND PROPERTY, SIR!!
WE WILL TAKE BACK TOKYO FOR ITS PEOPLE!

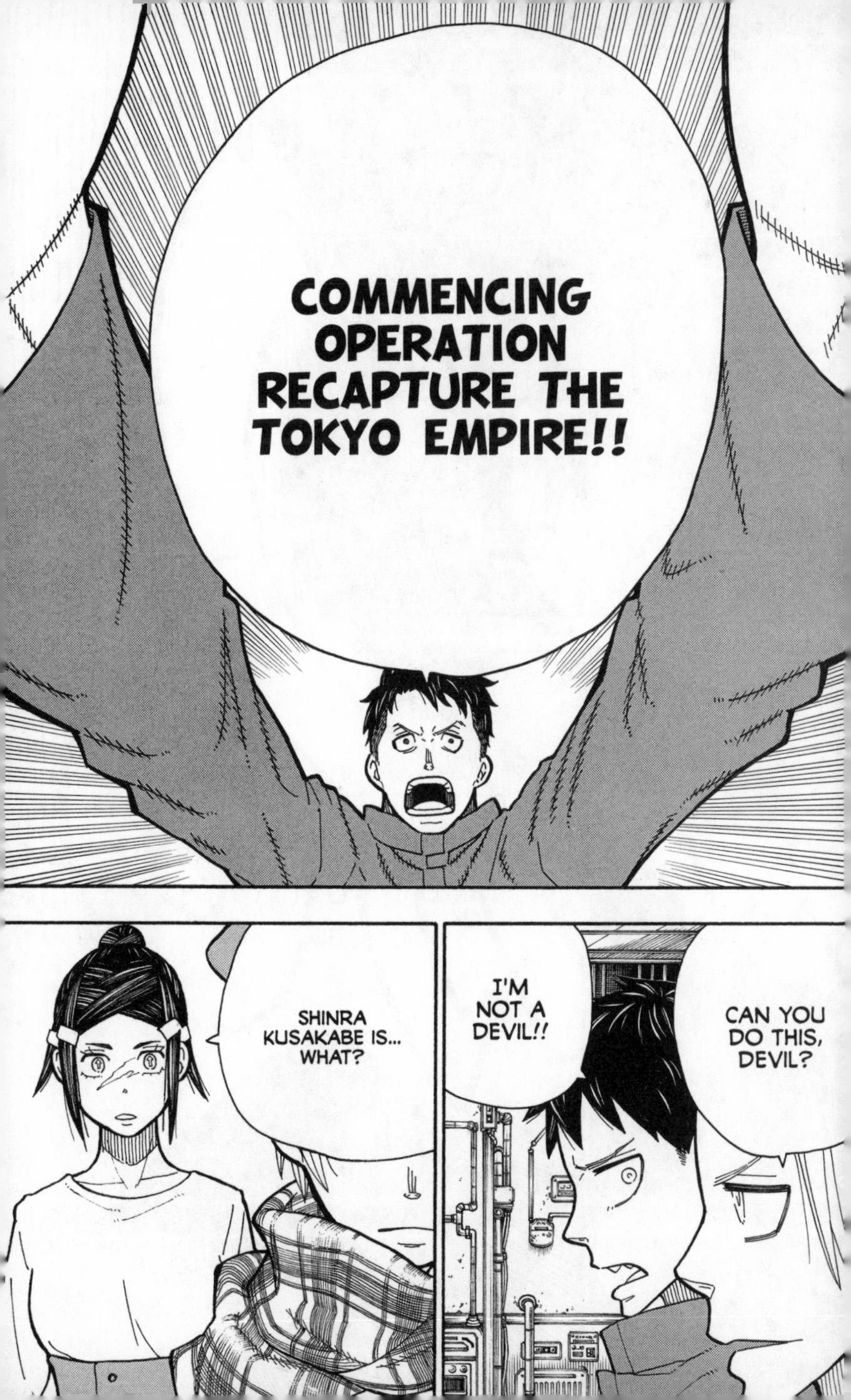
COMMENCING OPERATION RECAPTURE THE TOKYO EMPIRE!!
CAN YOU DO THIS, DEVIL?
I'M NOT A DEVIL!!
SHINRA KUSAKABE IS... WHAT?

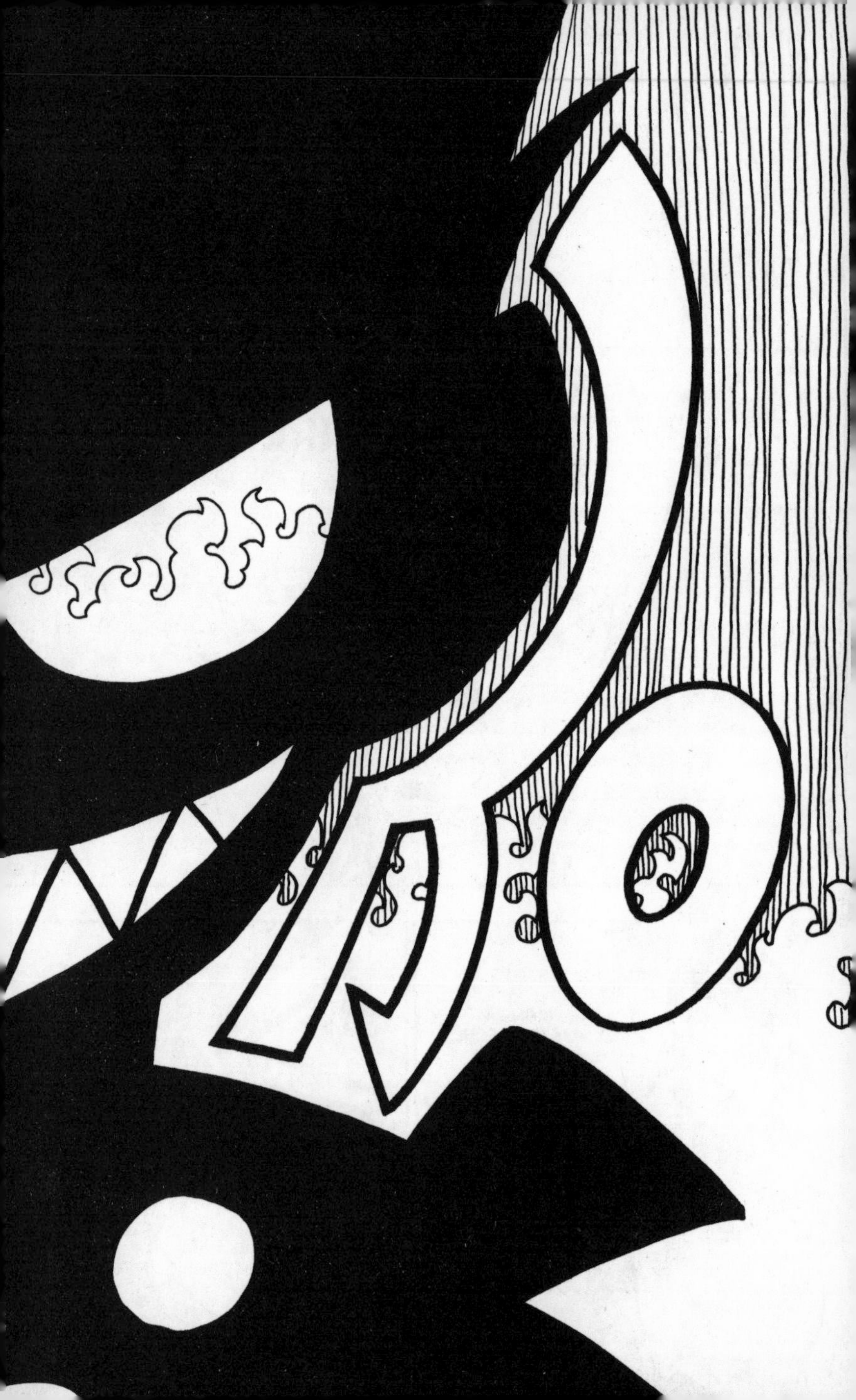

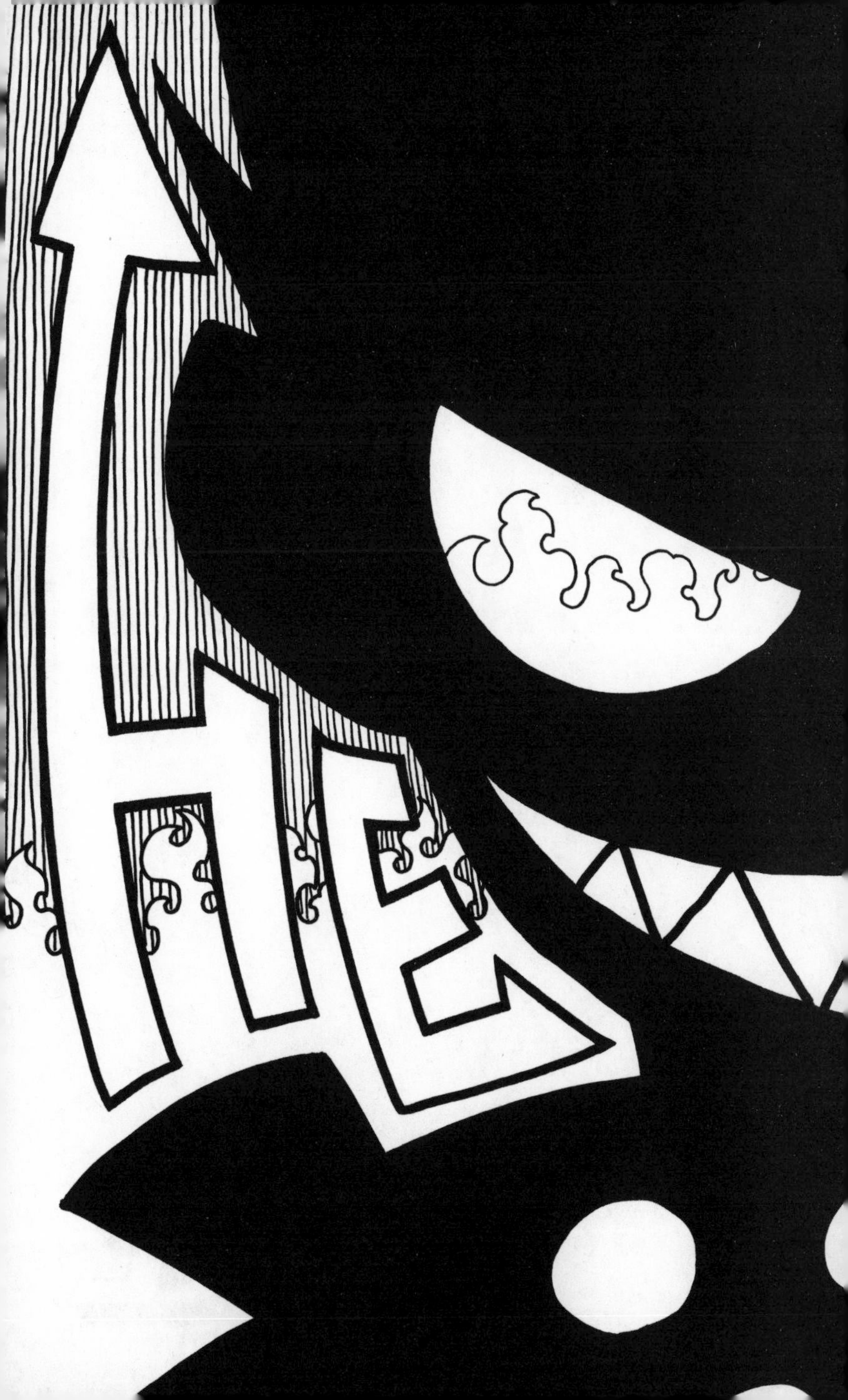
HE

FIRE FORCE

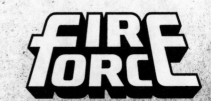

IMAGE GREAT CATACLYSM EXPLOSION

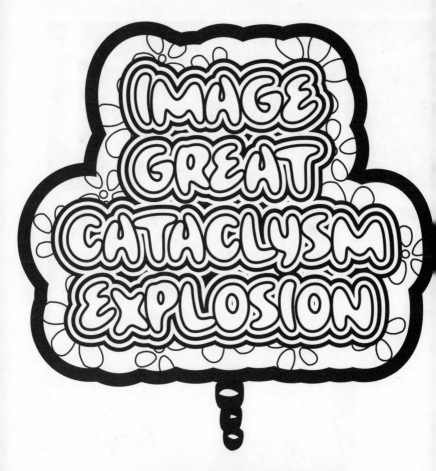

CHAPTER CCXXXIV: THE EIGHTH PILLAR

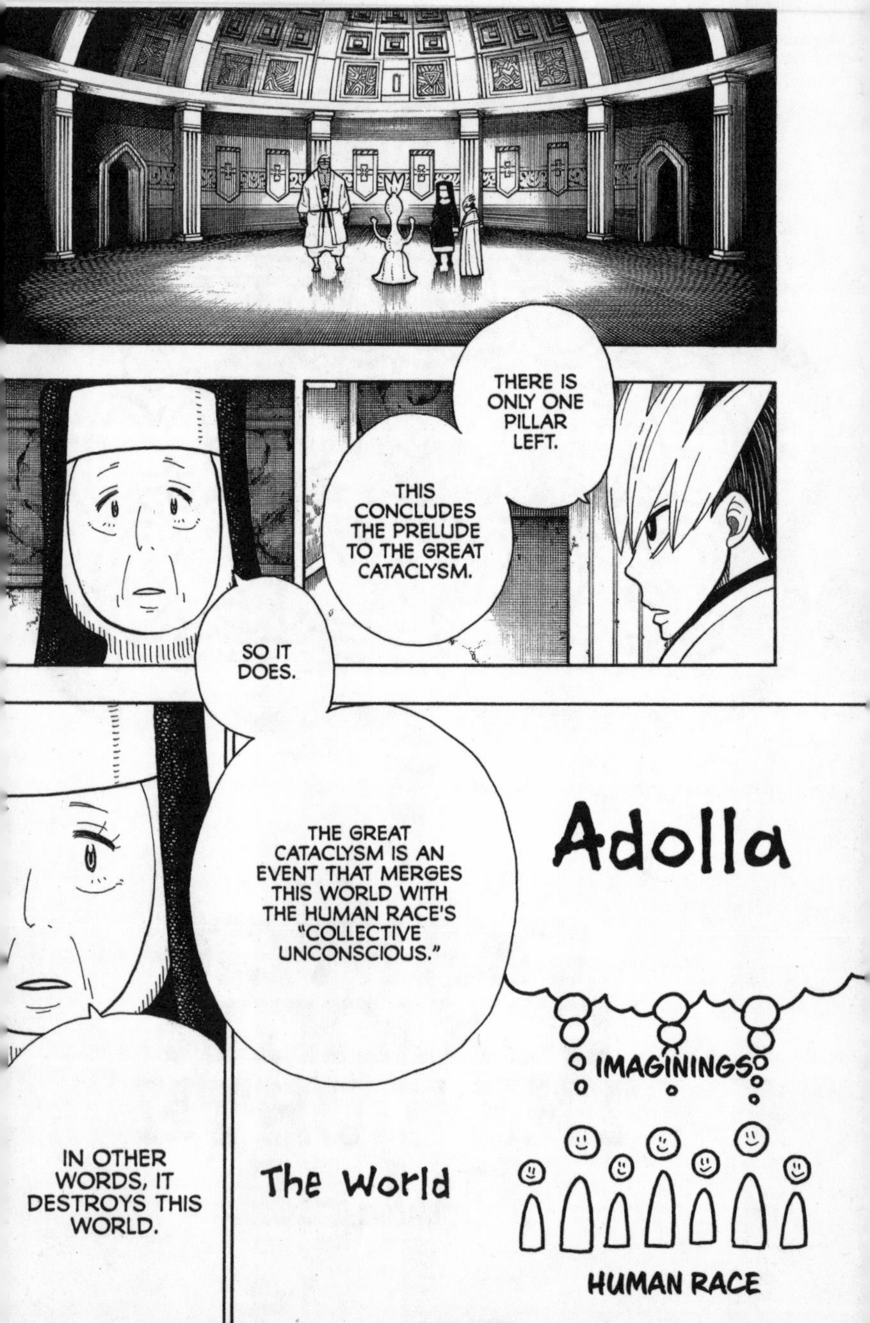

THERE IS ONLY ONE PILLAR LEFT.
THIS CONCLUDES THE PRELUDE TO THE GREAT CATACLYSM.
SO IT DOES.
THE GREAT CATACLYSM IS AN EVENT THAT MERGES THIS WORLD WITH THE HUMAN RACE'S "COLLECTIVE UNCONSCIOUS."
Adolla
IMAGININGS
HUMAN RACE
The World
IN OTHER WORDS, IT DESTROYS THIS WORLD.

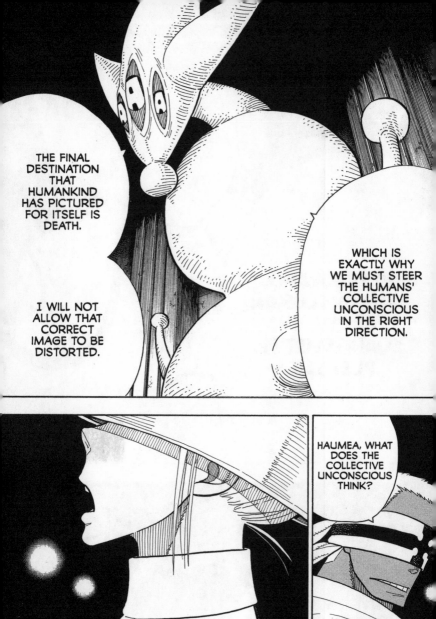

THE FINAL DESTINATION THAT HUMANKIND HAS PICTURED FOR ITSELF IS DEATH.

I WILL NOT ALLOW THAT CORRECT IMAGE TO BE DISTORTED.

WHICH IS EXACTLY WHY WE MUST STEER THE HUMANS' COLLECTIVE UNCONSCIOUS IN THE RIGHT DIRECTION.

HAUMEA, WHAT DOES THE COLLECTIVE UNCONSCIOUS THINK?

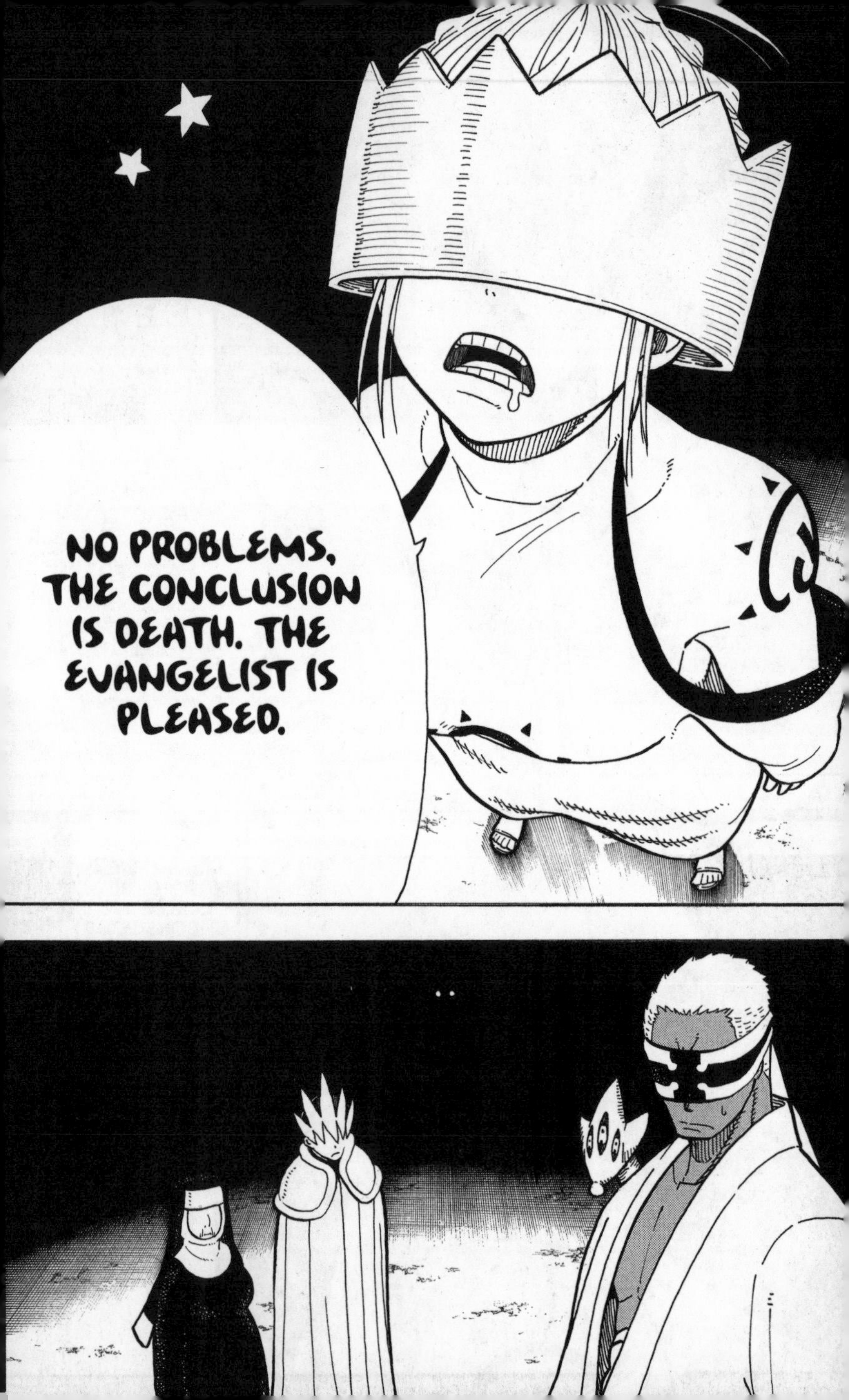
NO PROBLEMS. THE CONCLUSION IS DEATH. THE EVANGELIST IS PLEASED.

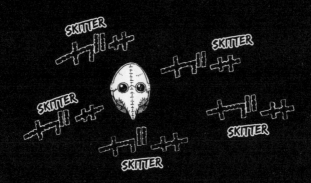

SKITTER
SKITTER
SKITTER
SKITTER
SKITTER
INSECTS FLYING TOWARD A FLAME.
HUMANS HEADING FOR DEATH, FOR DESTRUCTION.
THE SEQUENCES ARE OF DIFFERENT MAGNITUDE, BUT THEY ARE THE SAME.
IT IS TRUE OF THIS PLANET,
AND OF THIS WHOLE UNIVERSE.

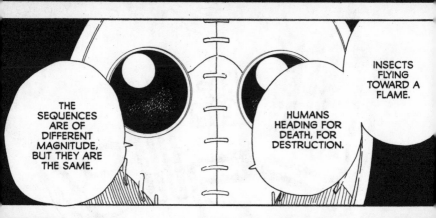

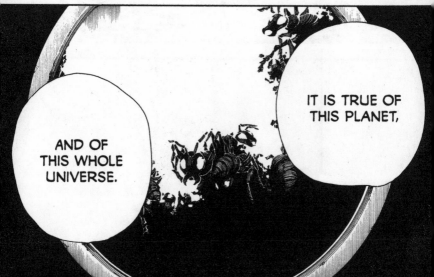

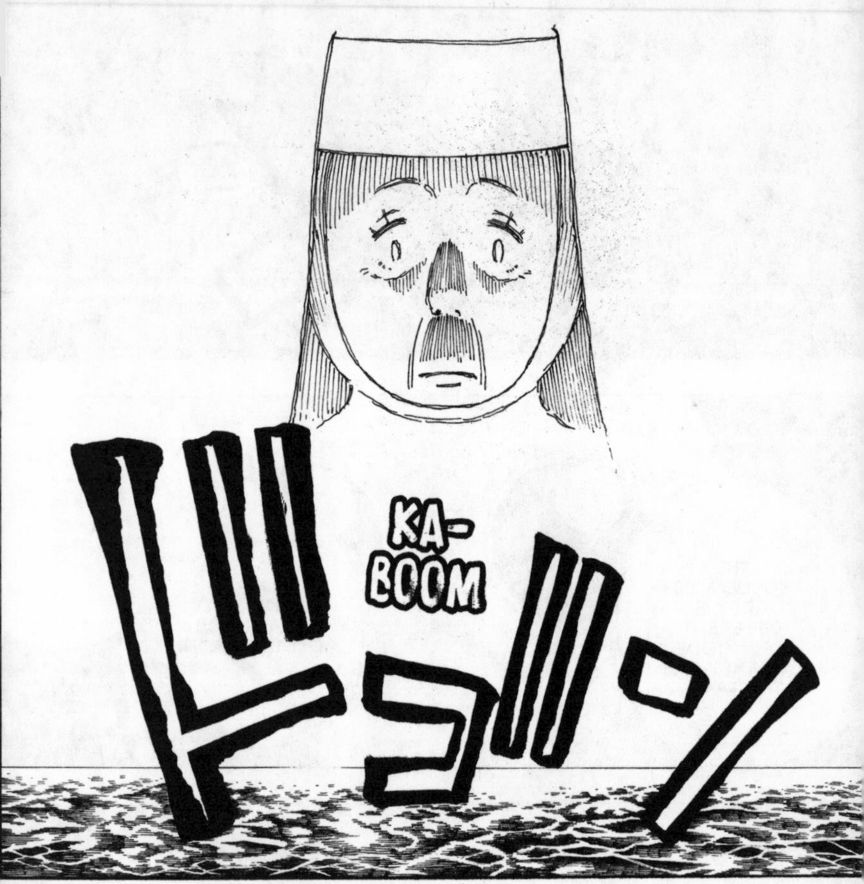
ドゴーン
KA-
BOOM
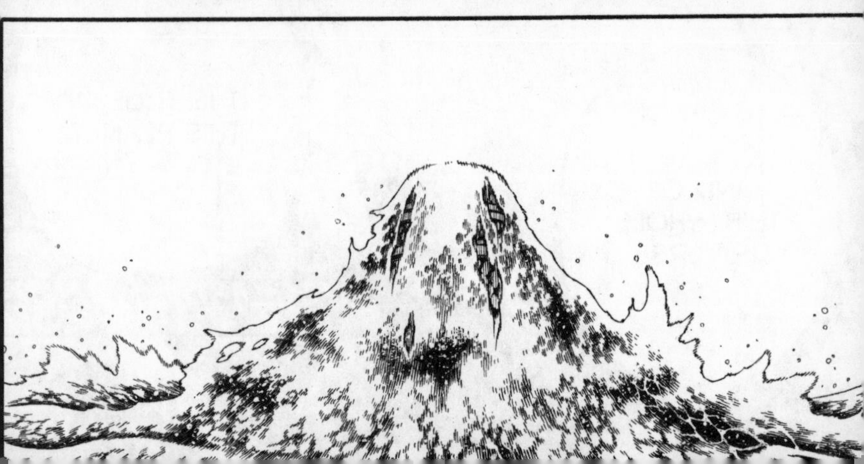

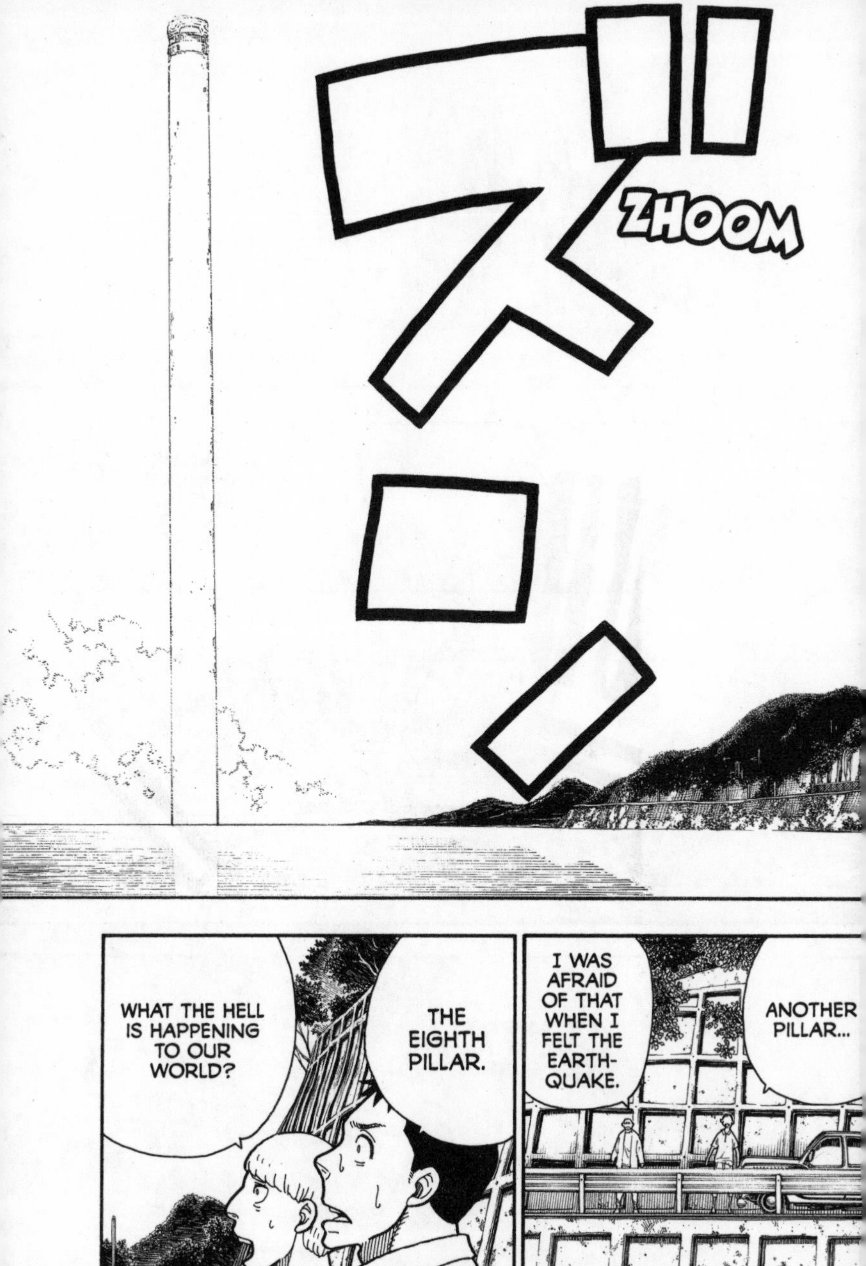
ZHOOM
ANOTHER PILLAR...
I WAS AFRAID OF THAT WHEN I FELT THE EARTH-QUAKE.
THE EIGHTH PILLAR.
WHAT THE HELL IS HAPPENING TO OUR WORLD?

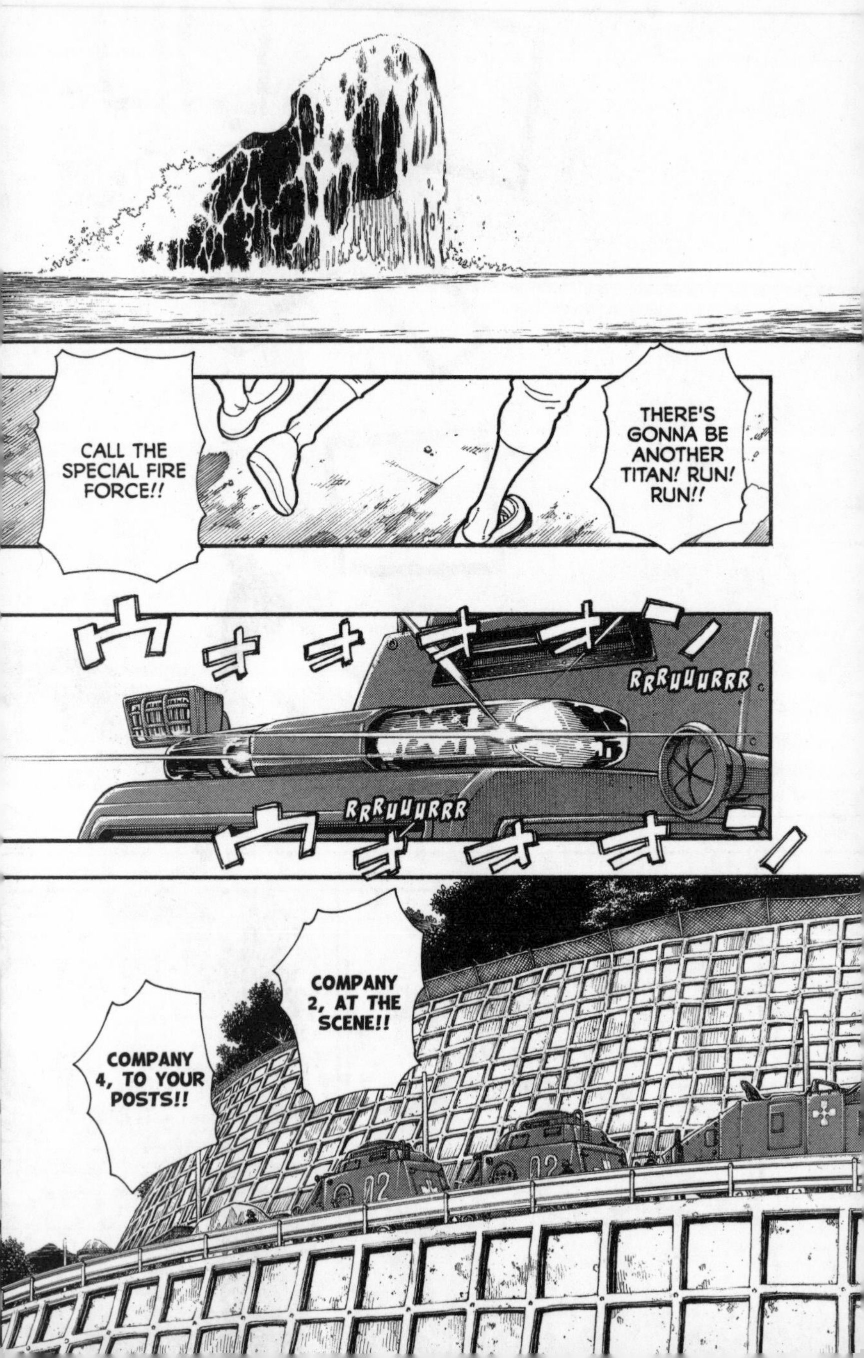
THERE'S GONNA BE ANOTHER TITAN! RUN! RUN!!
CALL THE SPECIAL FIRE FORCE!!
RRRUUURRR
RRRUUURRR
COMPANY 2, AT THE SCENE!!
COMPANY 4, TO YOUR POSTS!!

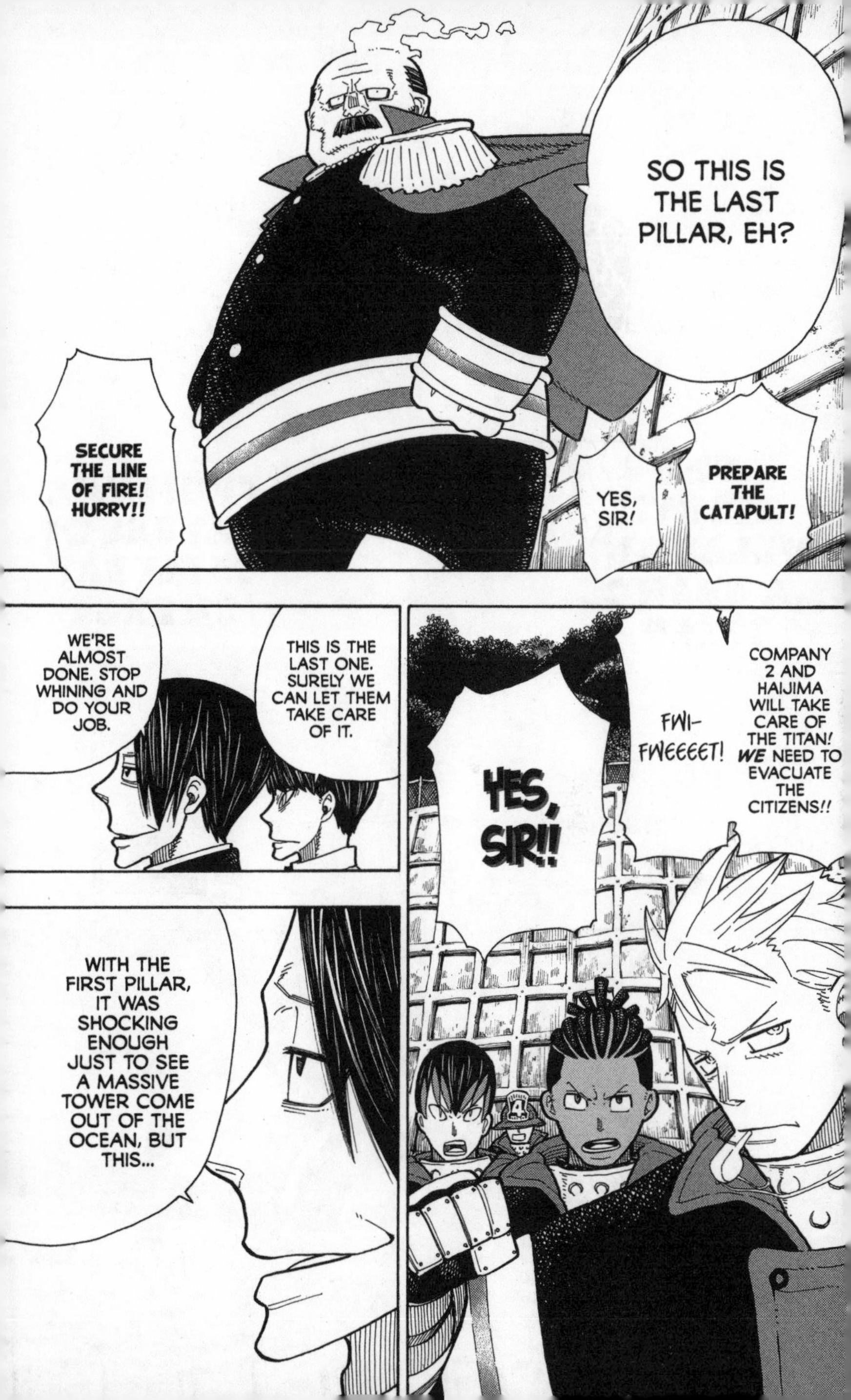
SO THIS IS THE LAST PILLAR, EH?
PREPARE THE CATAPULT!
YES, SIR!
SECURE THE LINE OF FIRE! HURRY!!
COMPANY 2 AND HAIJIMA WILL TAKE CARE OF THE TITAN! WE NEED TO EVACUATE THE CITIZENS!!
FWI-FWEEEET!
YES, SIR!!
THIS IS THE LAST ONE. SURELY WE CAN LET THEM TAKE CARE OF IT.
WE'RE ALMOST DONE. STOP WHINING AND DO YOUR JOB.
WITH THE FIRST PILLAR, IT WAS SHOCKING ENOUGH JUST TO SEE A MASSIVE TOWER COME OUT OF THE OCEAN, BUT THIS...

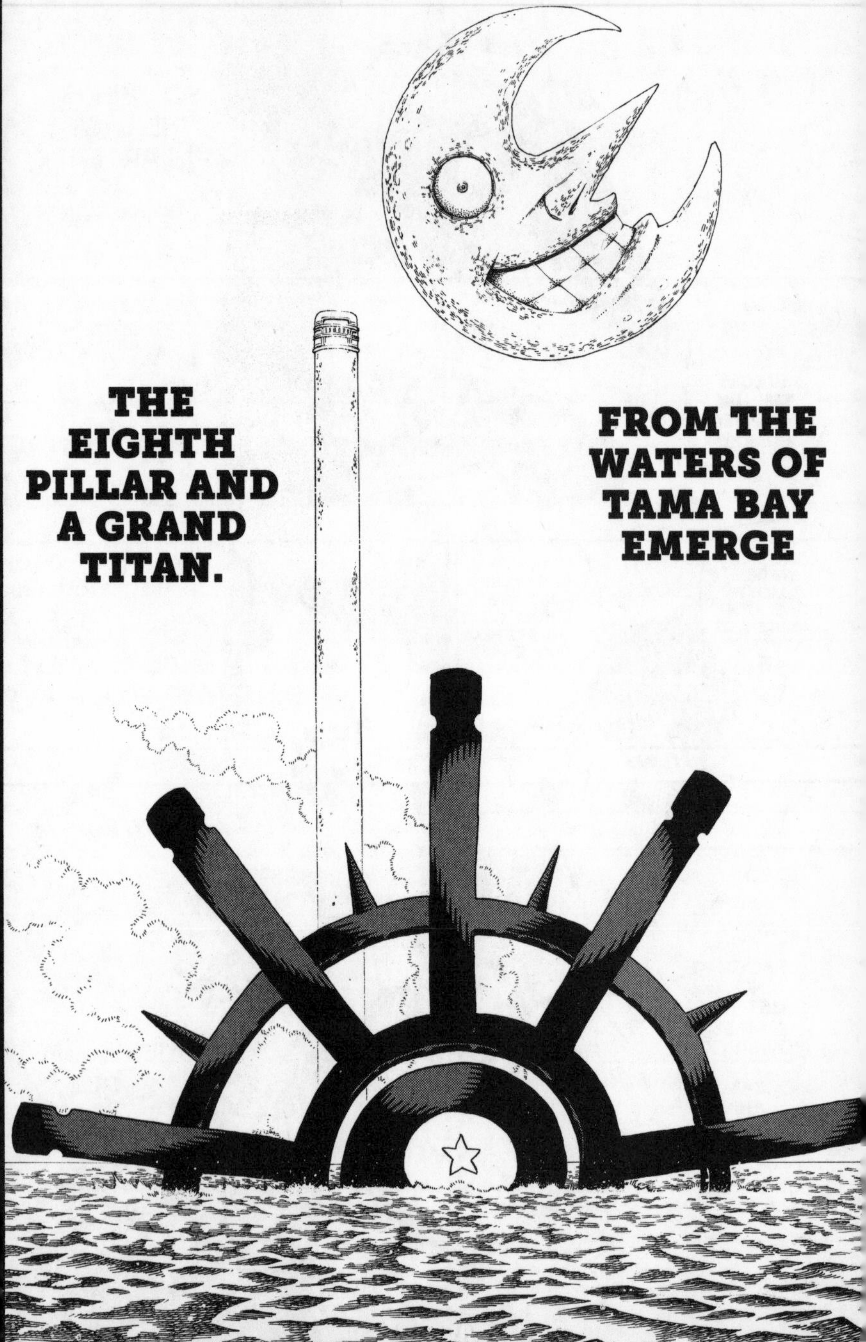
FROM THE WATERS OF TAMA BAY EMERGE
THE EIGHTH PILLAR AND A GRAND TITAN.

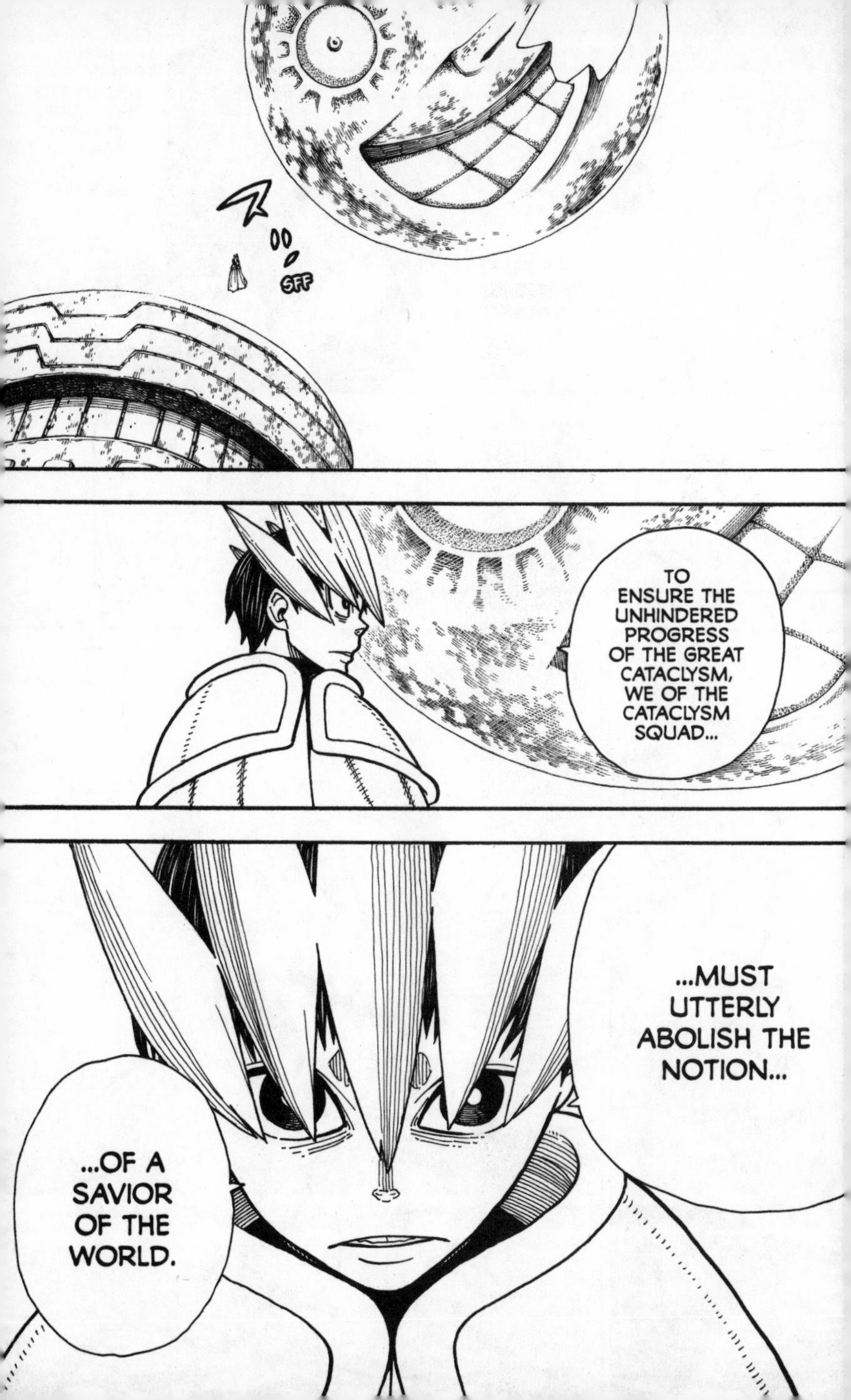
SFF
TO ENSURE THE UNHINDERED PROGRESS OF THE GREAT CATACLYSM, WE OF THE CATACLYSM SQUAD...
...MUST UTTERLY ABOLISH THE NOTION...
...OF A SAVIOR OF THE WORLD.

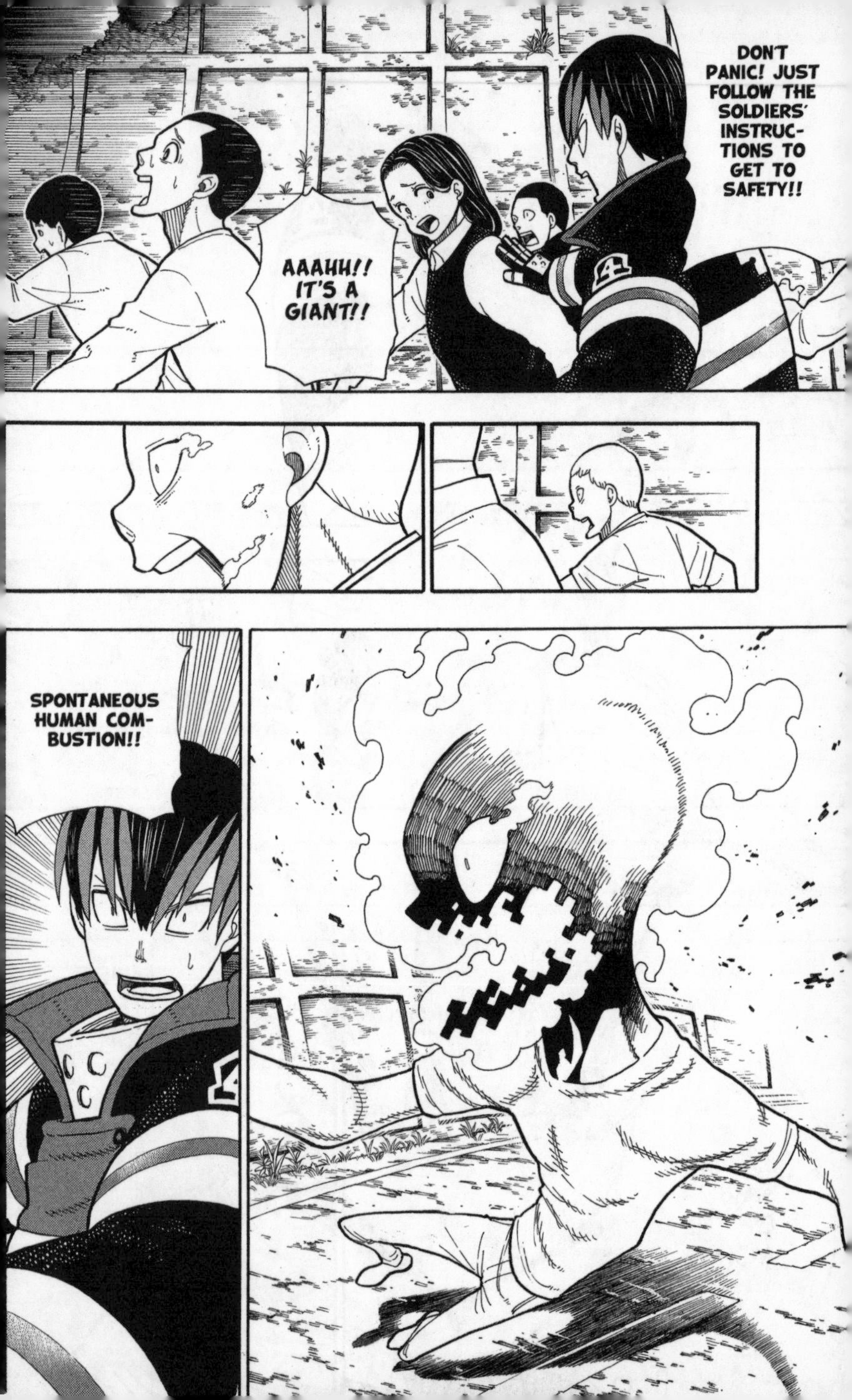
DON'T PANIC! JUST FOLLOW THE SOLDIERS' INSTRUCTIONS TO GET TO SAFETY!!
AAAHH!! IT'S A GIANT!!
SPONTANEOUS HUMAN COMBUSTION!!

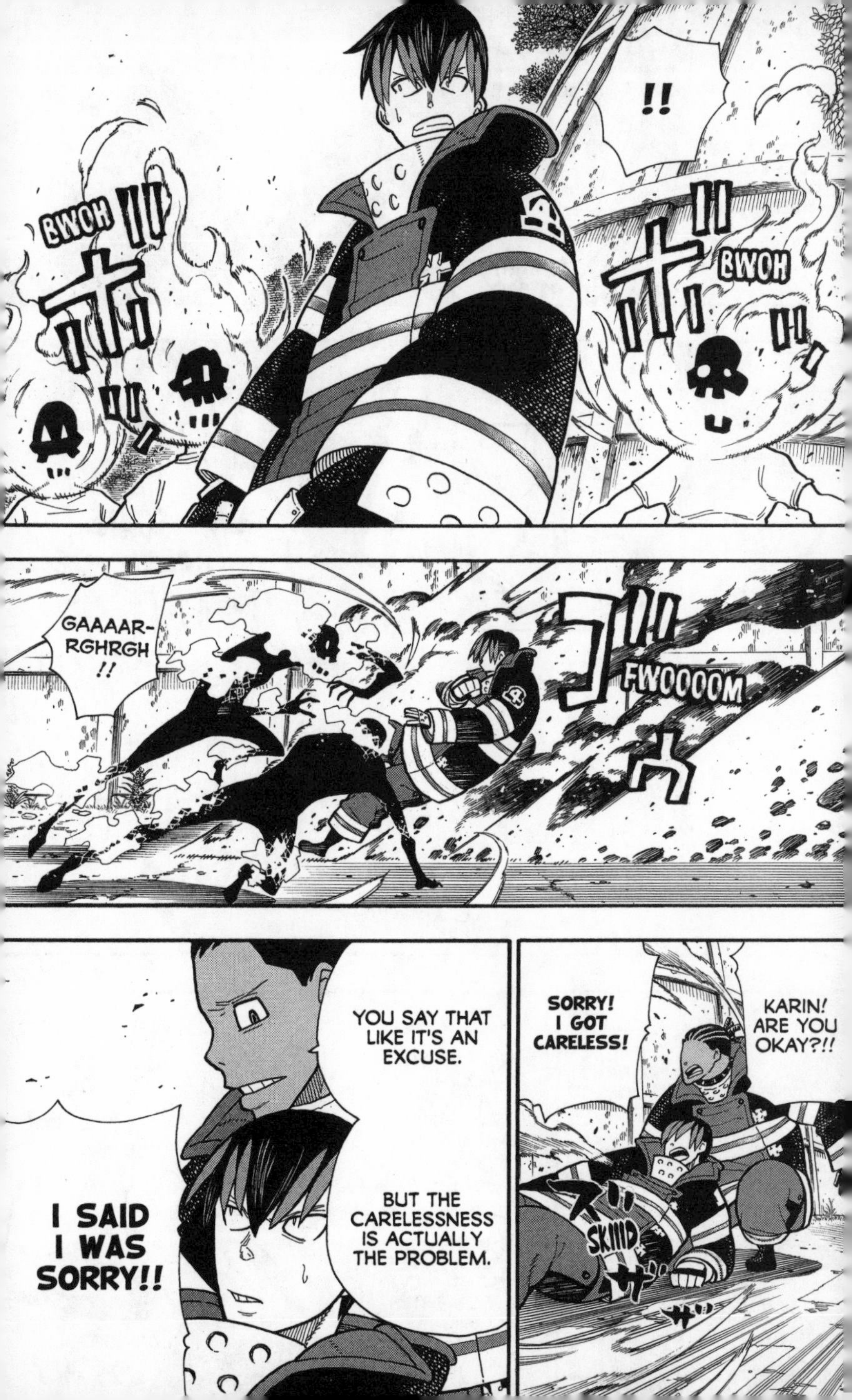
!!
BWOH
BWOH
FWOOOOM
GAAAAR-RGHRGH!!
KARIN! ARE YOU OKAY?!!
SORRY! I GOT CARELESS!
SKIIID
YOU SAY THAT LIKE IT'S AN EXCUSE.
BUT THE CARELESSNESS IS ACTUALLY THE PROBLEM.
I SAID I WAS SORRY!!

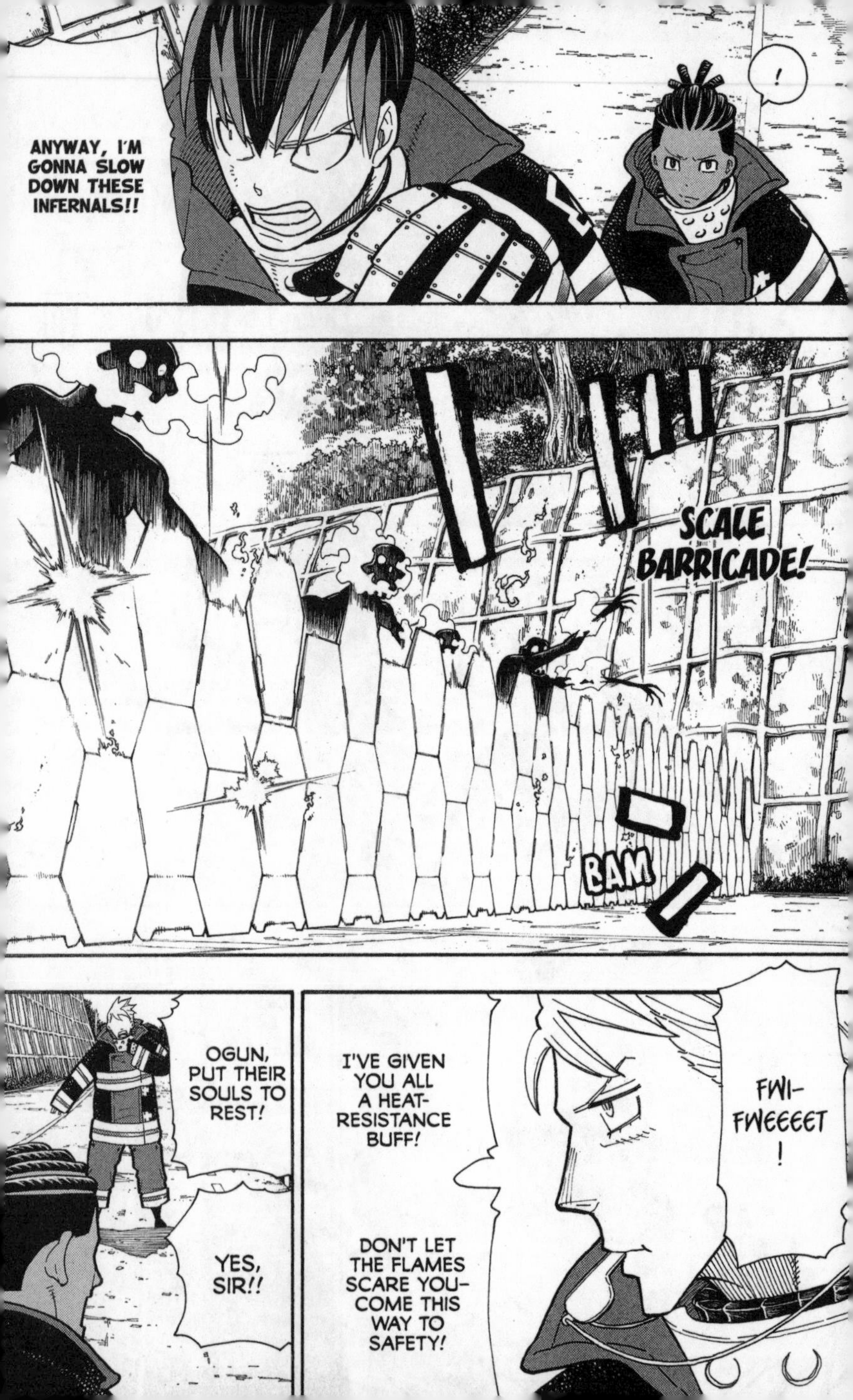
!
ANYWAY, I'M GONNA SLOW DOWN THESE INFERNALS!!
SCALE BARRICADE!
BAM
FWI-FWEEEET!
I'VE GIVEN YOU ALL A HEAT-RESISTANCE BUFF!
DON'T LET THE FLAMES SCARE YOU—COME THIS WAY TO SAFETY!
OGUN, PUT THEIR SOULS TO REST!
YES, SIR!!

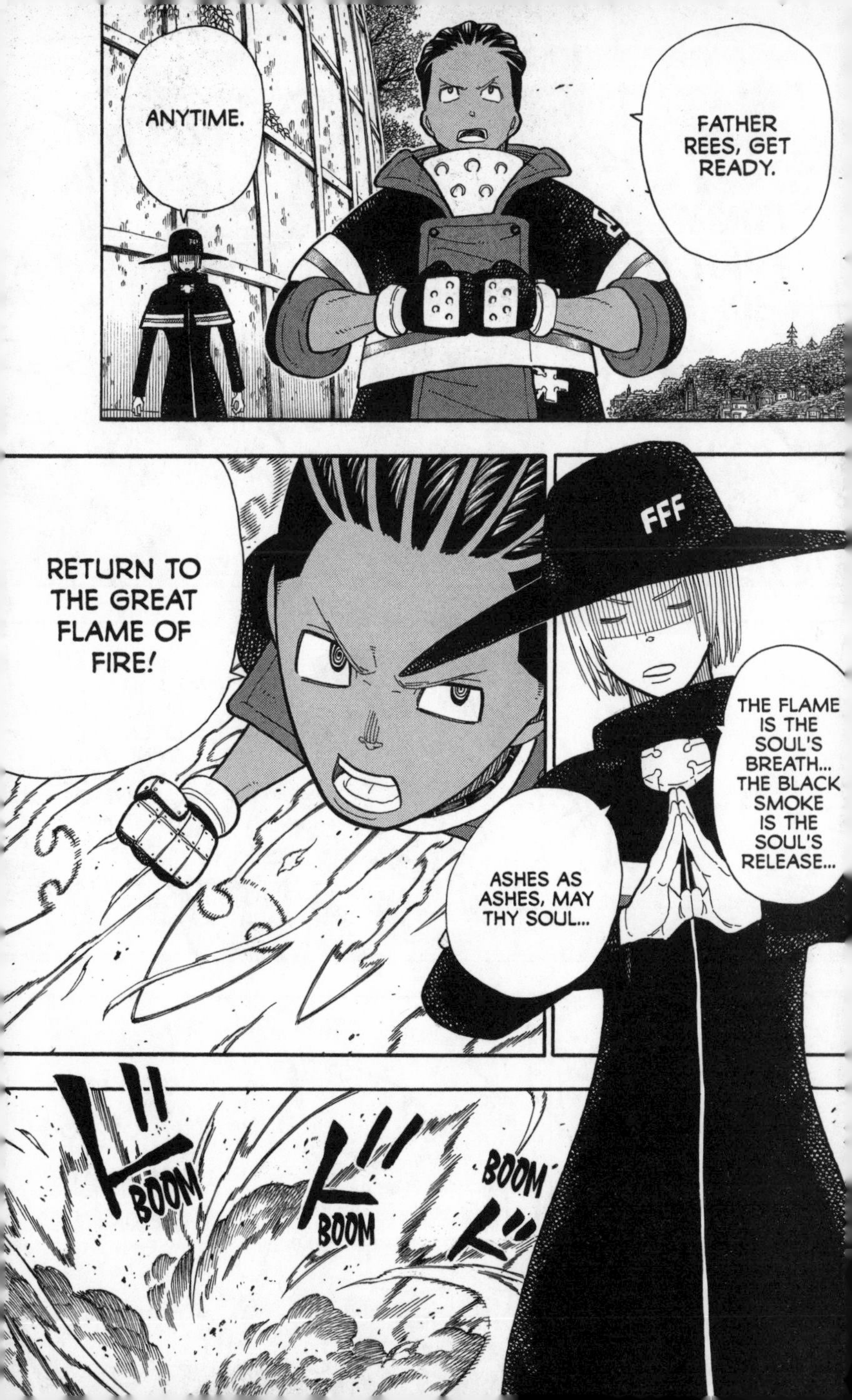
FATHER REES, GET READY.
ANYTIME.
THE FLAME IS THE SOUL'S BREATH... THE BLACK SMOKE IS THE SOUL'S RELEASE...
ASHES AS ASHES, MAY THY SOUL...
RETURN TO THE GREAT FLAME OF FIRE!
BOOM
BOOM
BOOM

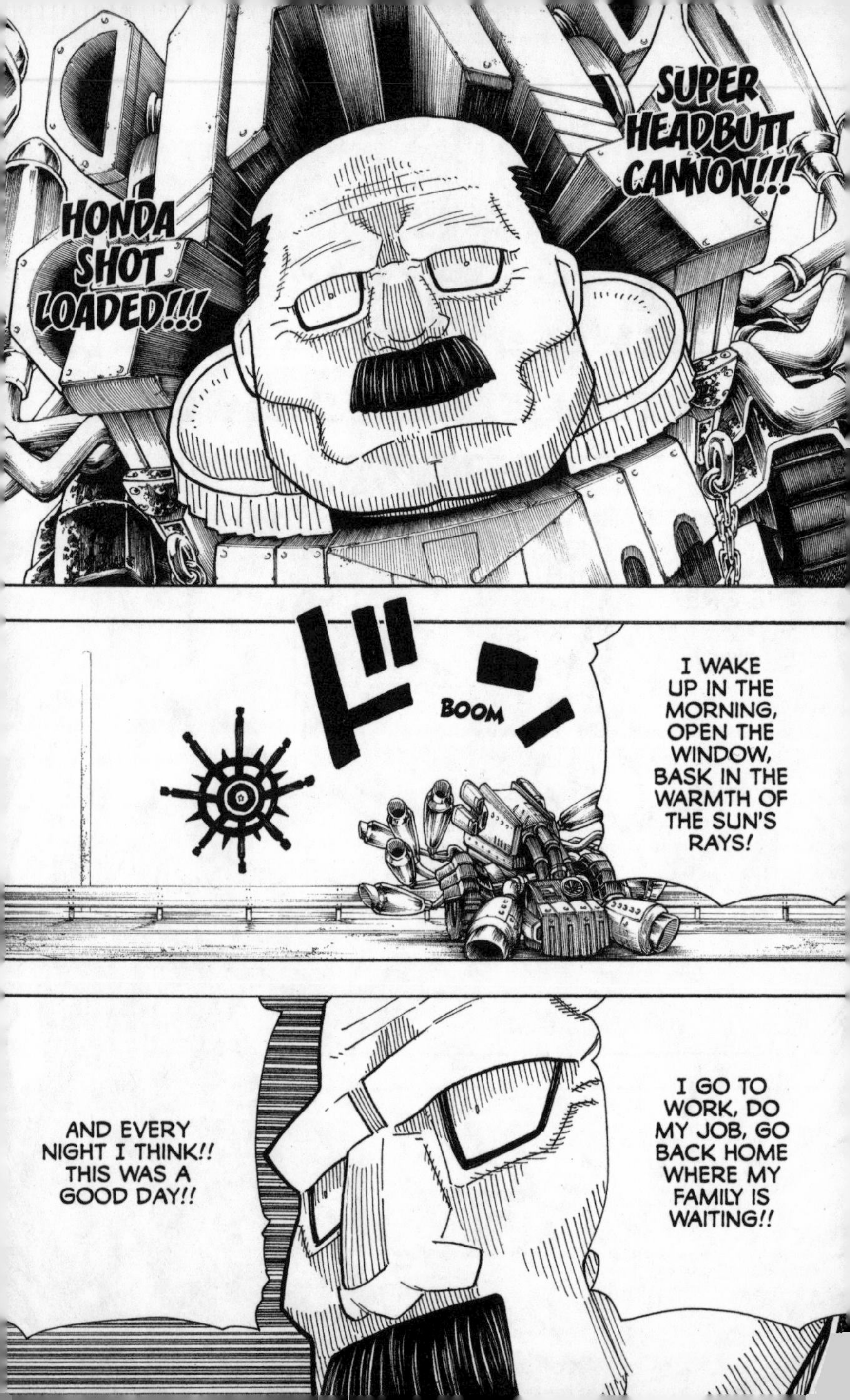
SUPER HEADBUTT CANNON!!!
HONDA SHOT LOADED!!!
I WAKE UP IN THE MORNING, OPEN THE WINDOW, BASK IN THE WARMTH OF THE SUN'S RAYS!
ドン
BOOM
I GO TO WORK, DO MY JOB, GO BACK HOME WHERE MY FAMILY IS WAITING!!
AND EVERY NIGHT I THINK!! THIS WAS A GOOD DAY!!

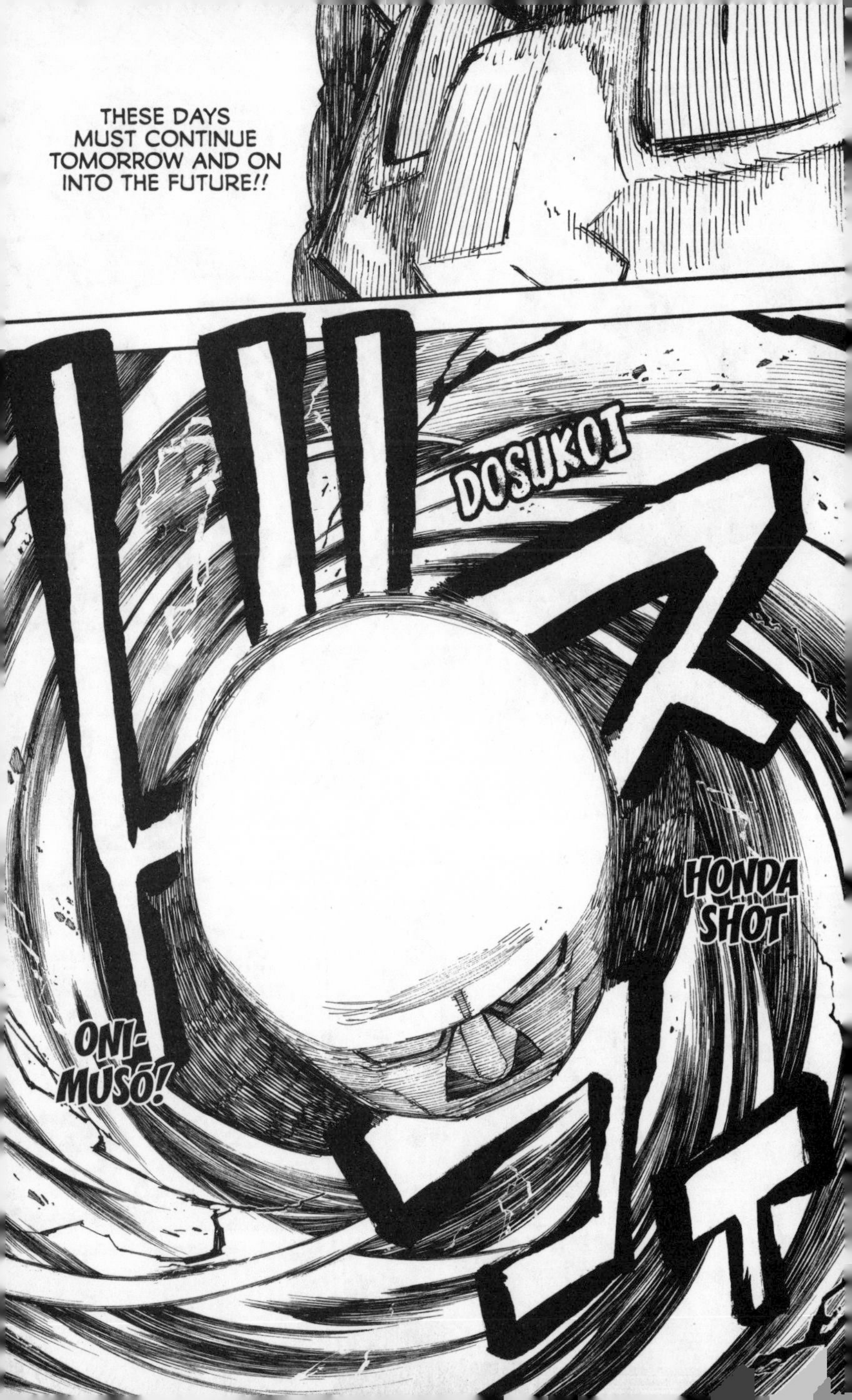
THESE DAYS MUST CONTINUE TOMORROW AND ON INTO THE FUTURE!!
DOSUKOI
HONDA SHOT
ONI-MUSŌ!

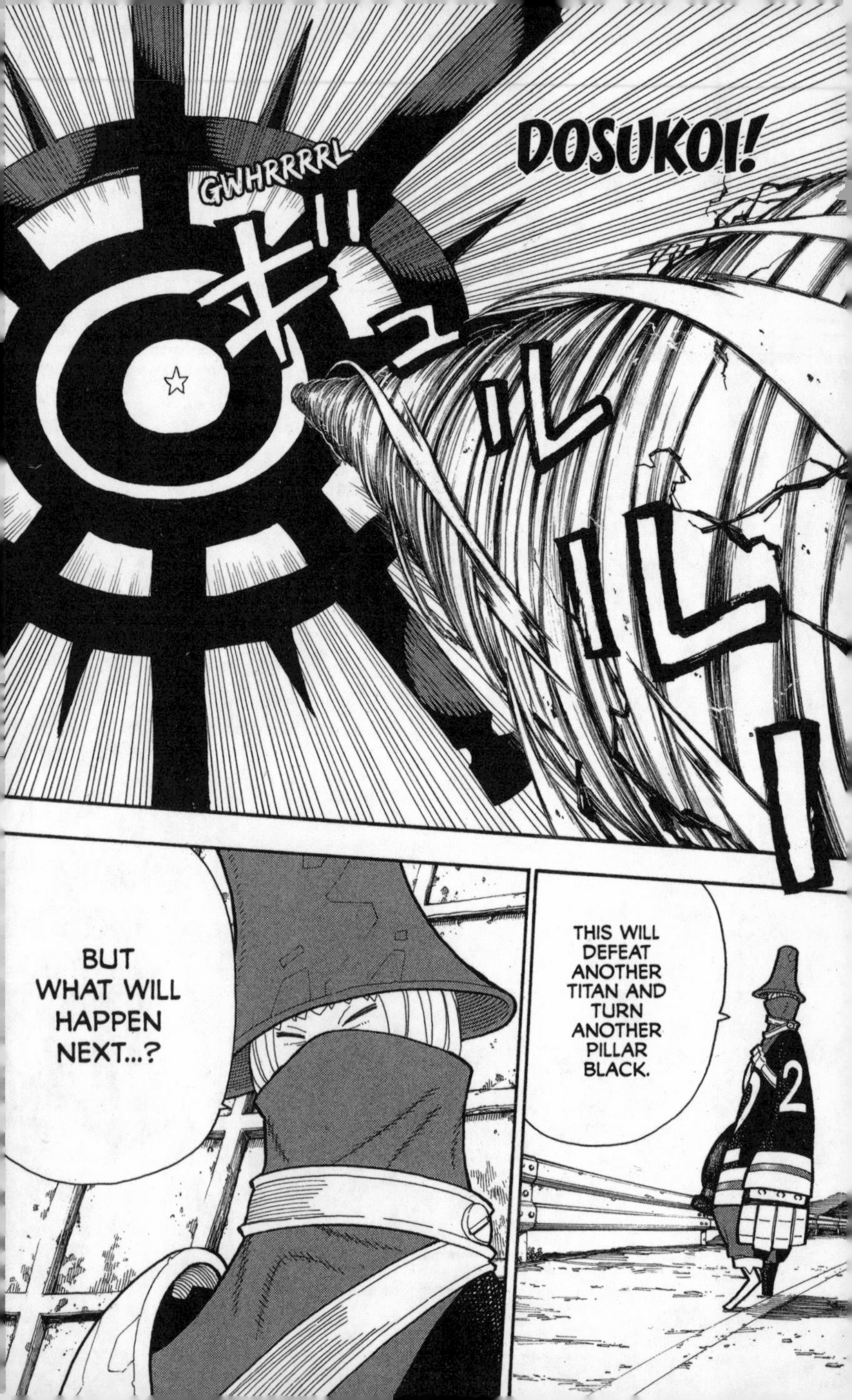
DOSUKOI!
GWHRRRL
ギュルル
THIS WILL DEFEAT ANOTHER TITAN AND TURN ANOTHER PILLAR BLACK.
BUT WHAT WILL HAPPEN NEXT...?

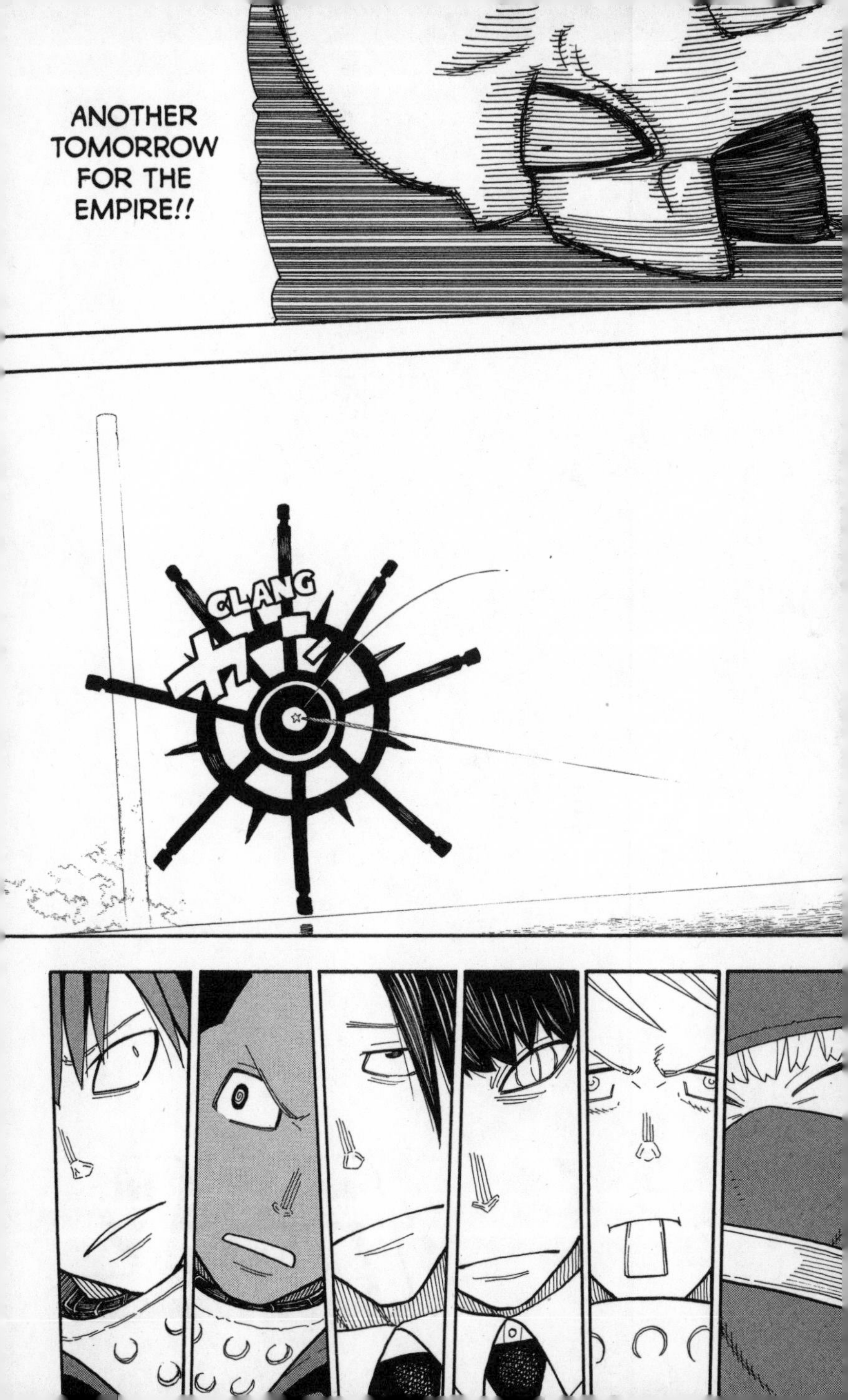
ANOTHER TOMORROW FOR THE EMPIRE!!
CLANG

FIRE FORCE

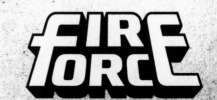

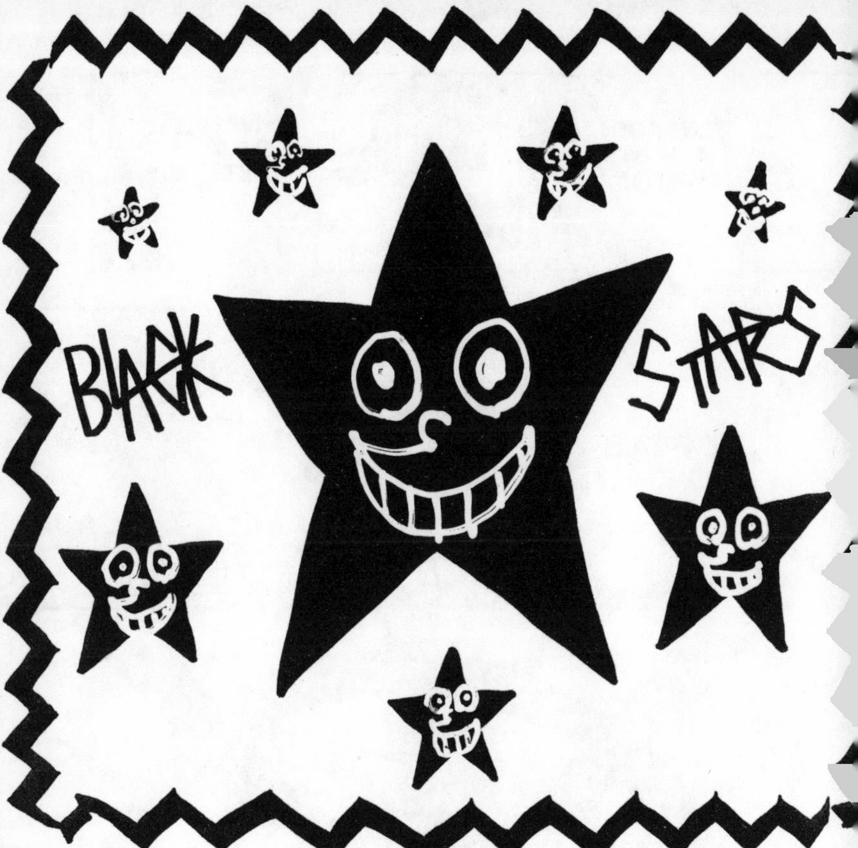
BLACK
STARS

CHAPTER CCXXXV: SAVIOR

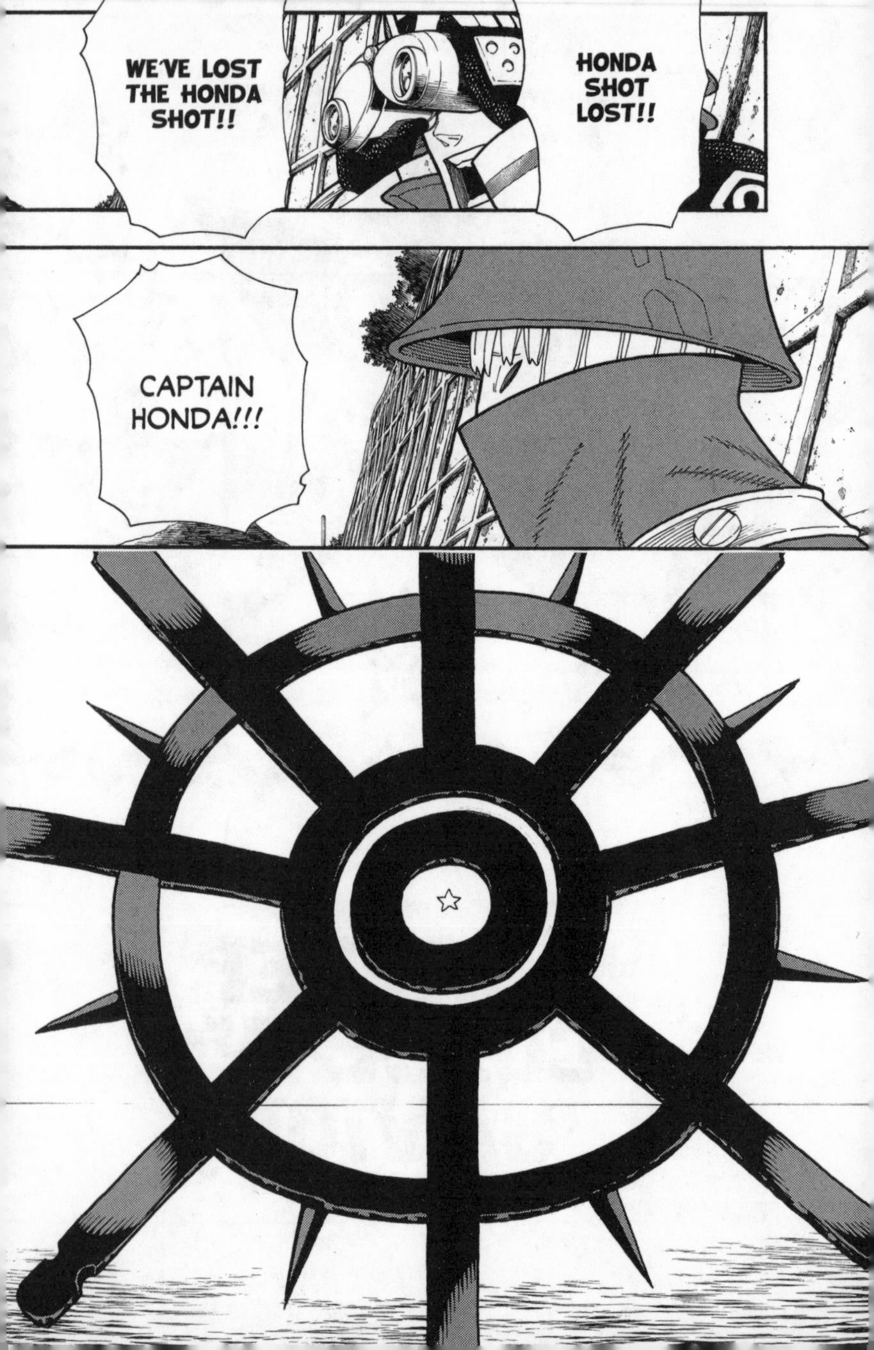
HONDA SHOT LOST!!
WE'VE LOST THE HONDA SHOT!!
CAPTAIN HONDA!!!

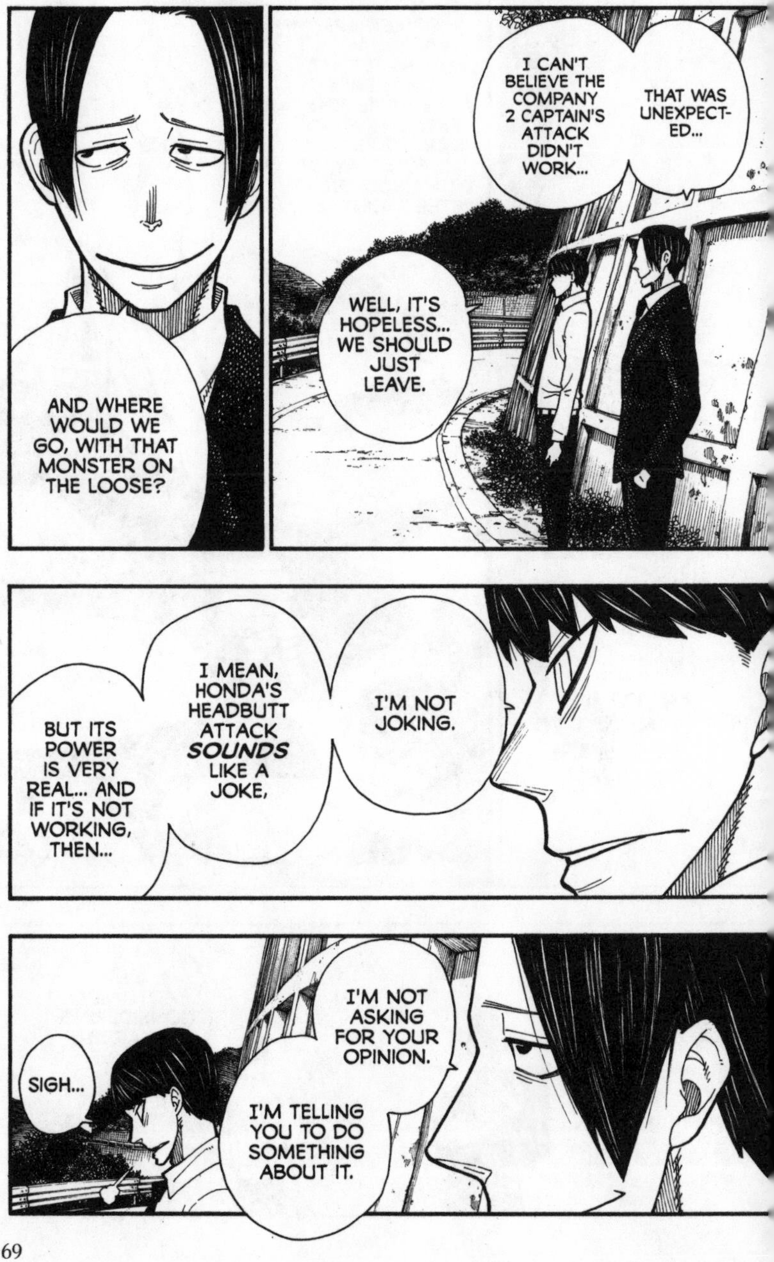
THAT WAS UNEXPECTED...
I CAN'T BELIEVE THE COMPANY 2 CAPTAIN'S ATTACK DIDN'T WORK...
WELL, IT'S HOPELESS... WE SHOULD JUST LEAVE.
AND WHERE WOULD WE GO, WITH THAT MONSTER ON THE LOOSE?
I'M NOT JOKING.
I MEAN, HONDA'S HEADBUTT ATTACK ***SOUNDS*** LIKE A JOKE,
BUT ITS POWER IS VERY REAL... AND IF IT'S NOT WORKING, THEN...
I'M NOT ASKING FOR YOUR OPINION.
I'M TELLING YOU TO DO SOMETHING ABOUT IT.
SIGH...

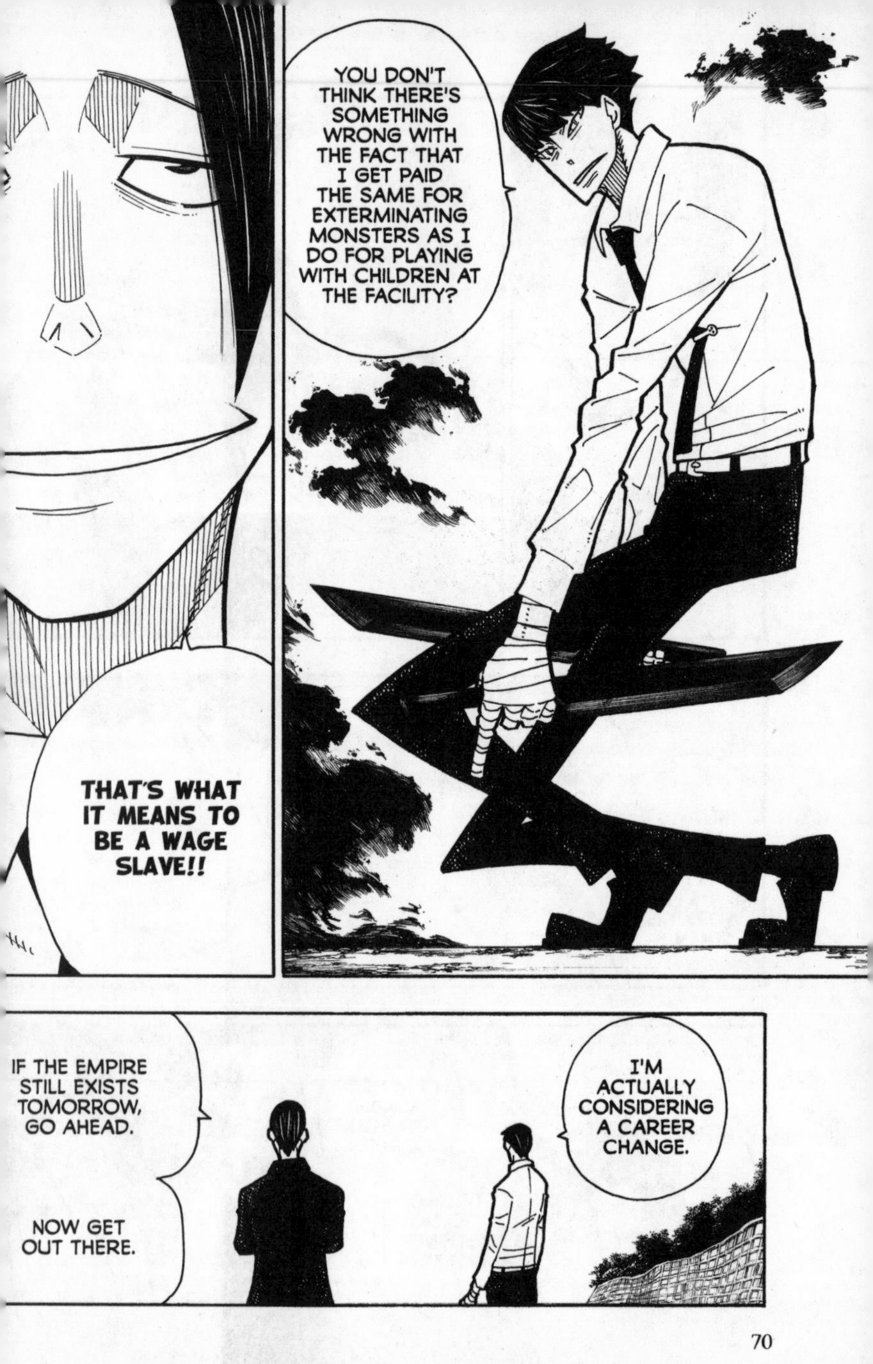
YOU DON'T THINK THERE'S SOMETHING WRONG WITH THE FACT THAT I GET PAID THE SAME FOR EXTERMINATING MONSTERS AS I DO FOR PLAYING WITH CHILDREN AT THE FACILITY?
THAT'S WHAT IT MEANS TO BE A WAGE SLAVE!!
I'M ACTUALLY CONSIDERING A CAREER CHANGE.
IF THE EMPIRE STILL EXISTS TOMORROW, GO AHEAD.
NOW GET OUT THERE.

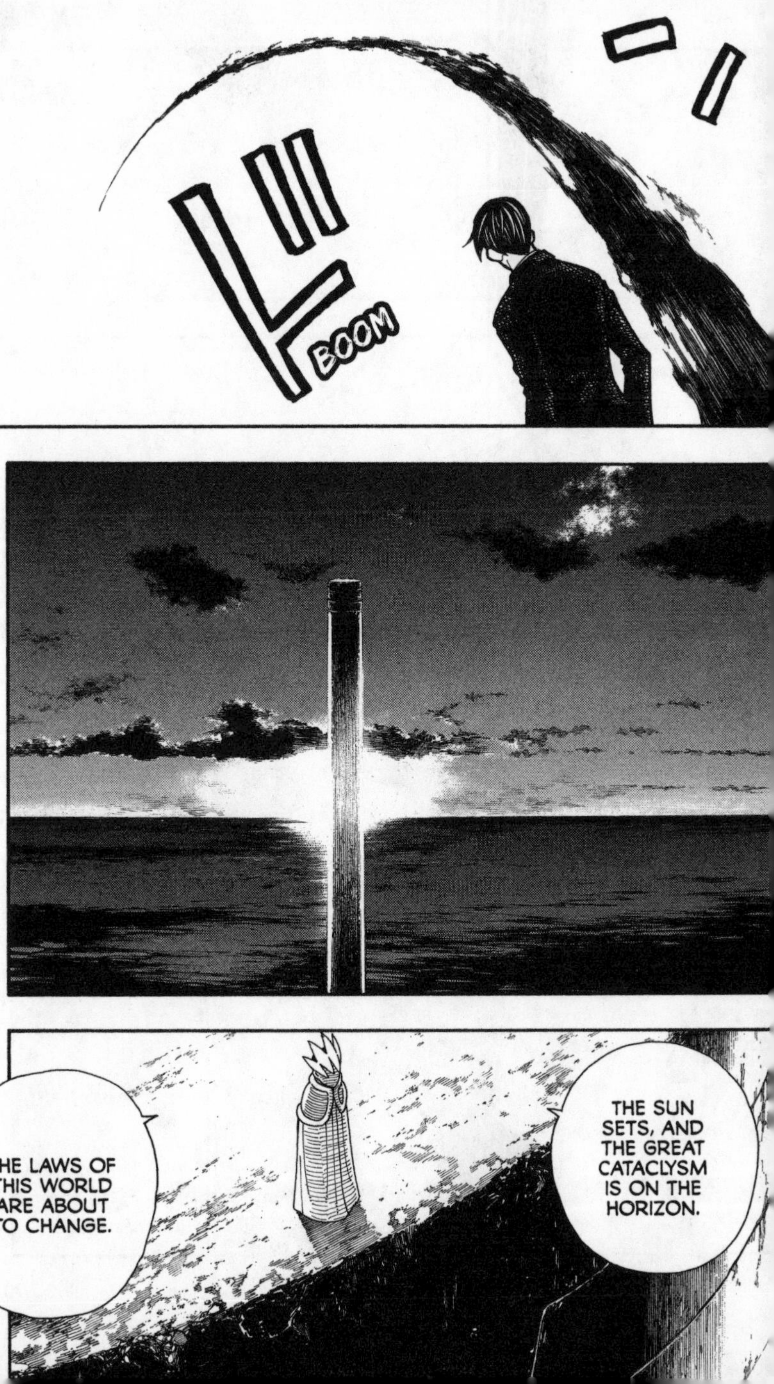
BOOM
THE SUN SETS, AND THE GREAT CATACLYSM IS ON THE HORIZON.
THE LAWS OF THIS WORLD ARE ABOUT TO CHANGE.

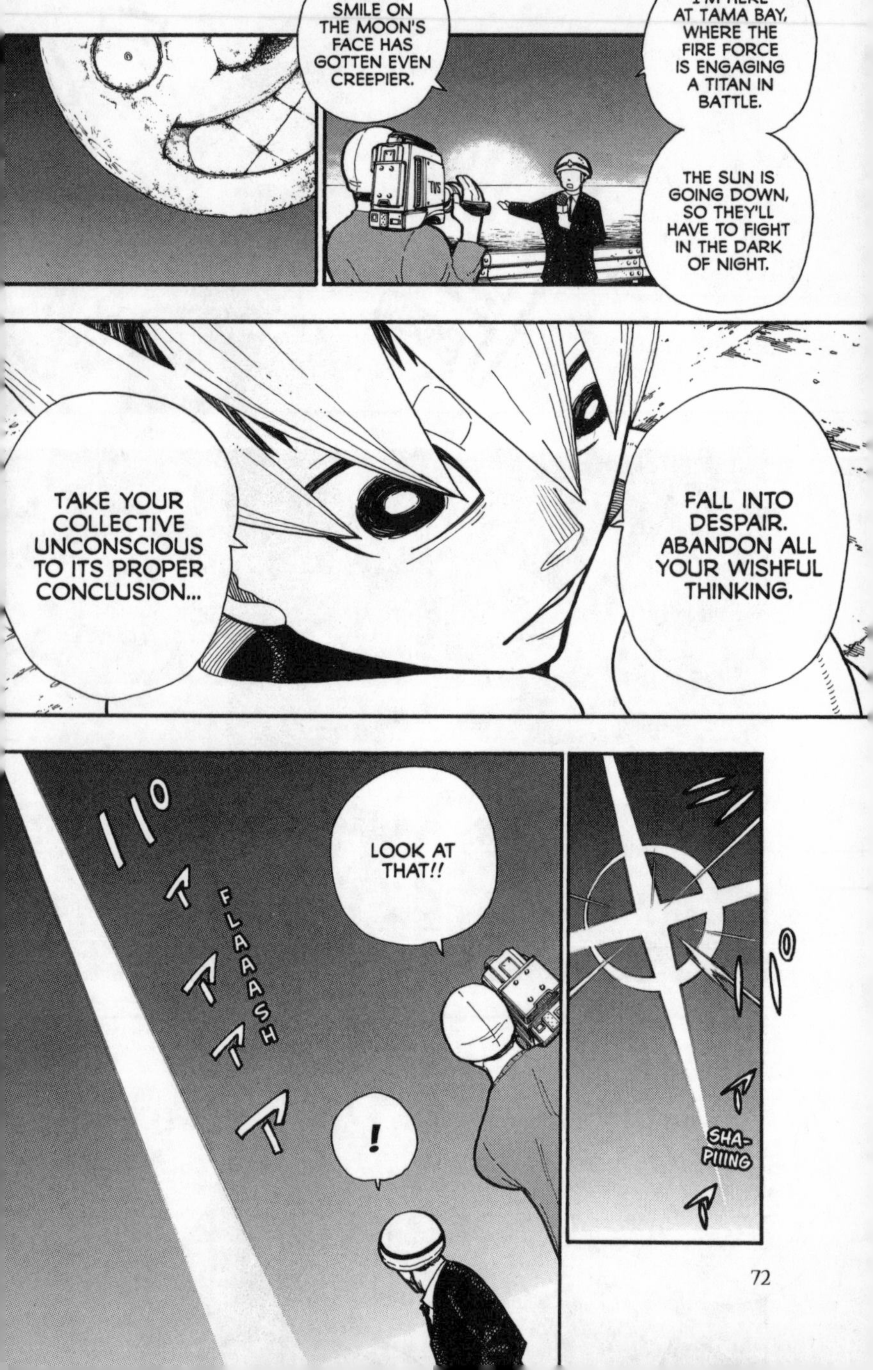
I'M HERE AT TAMA BAY, WHERE THE FIRE FORCE IS ENGAGING A TITAN IN BATTLE.
THE SUN IS GOING DOWN, SO THEY'LL HAVE TO FIGHT IN THE DARK OF NIGHT.
AND THE SMILE ON THE MOON'S FACE HAS GOTTEN EVEN CREEPIER.
FALL INTO DESPAIR. ABANDON ALL YOUR WISHFUL THINKING.
TAKE YOUR COLLECTIVE UNCONSCIOUS TO ITS PROPER CONCLUSION...
SHA-PIIING
FLAAASH
LOOK AT THAT!!
!

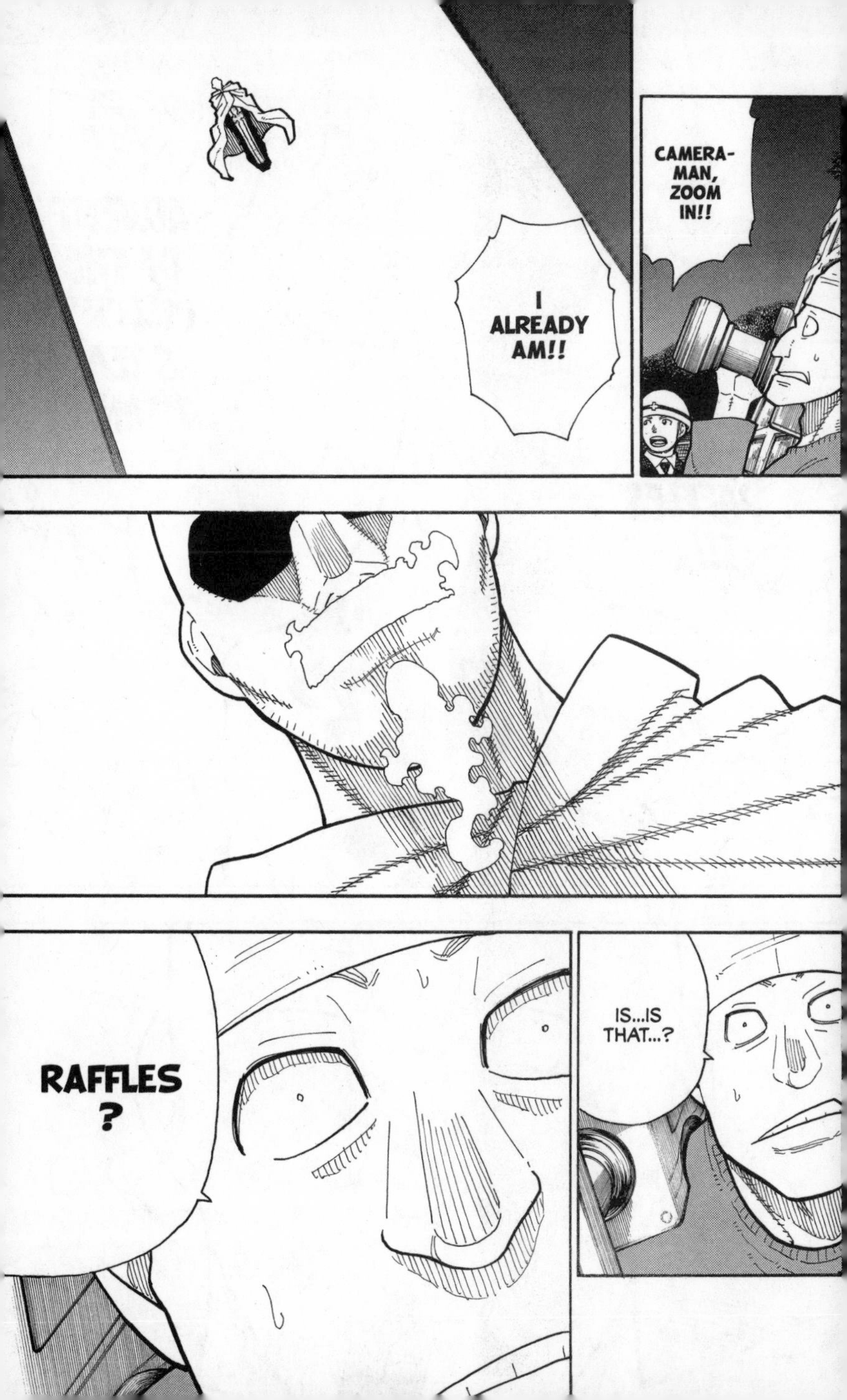
CAMERA-MAN, ZOOM IN!!
I ALREADY AM!!
IS...IS THAT...?
RAFFLES?

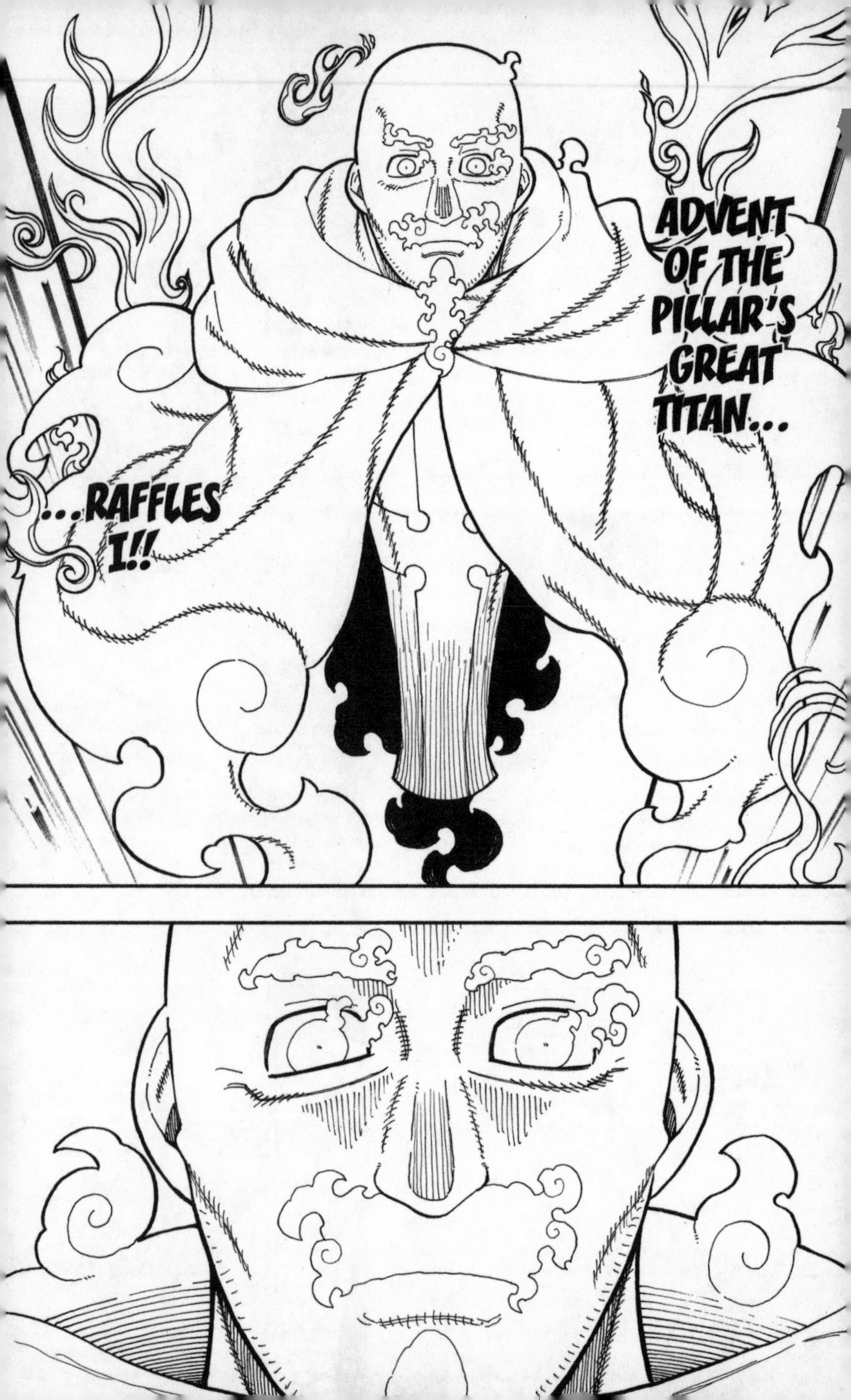
ADVENT OF THE PILLAR'S GREAT TITAN...
...RAFFLES I!!

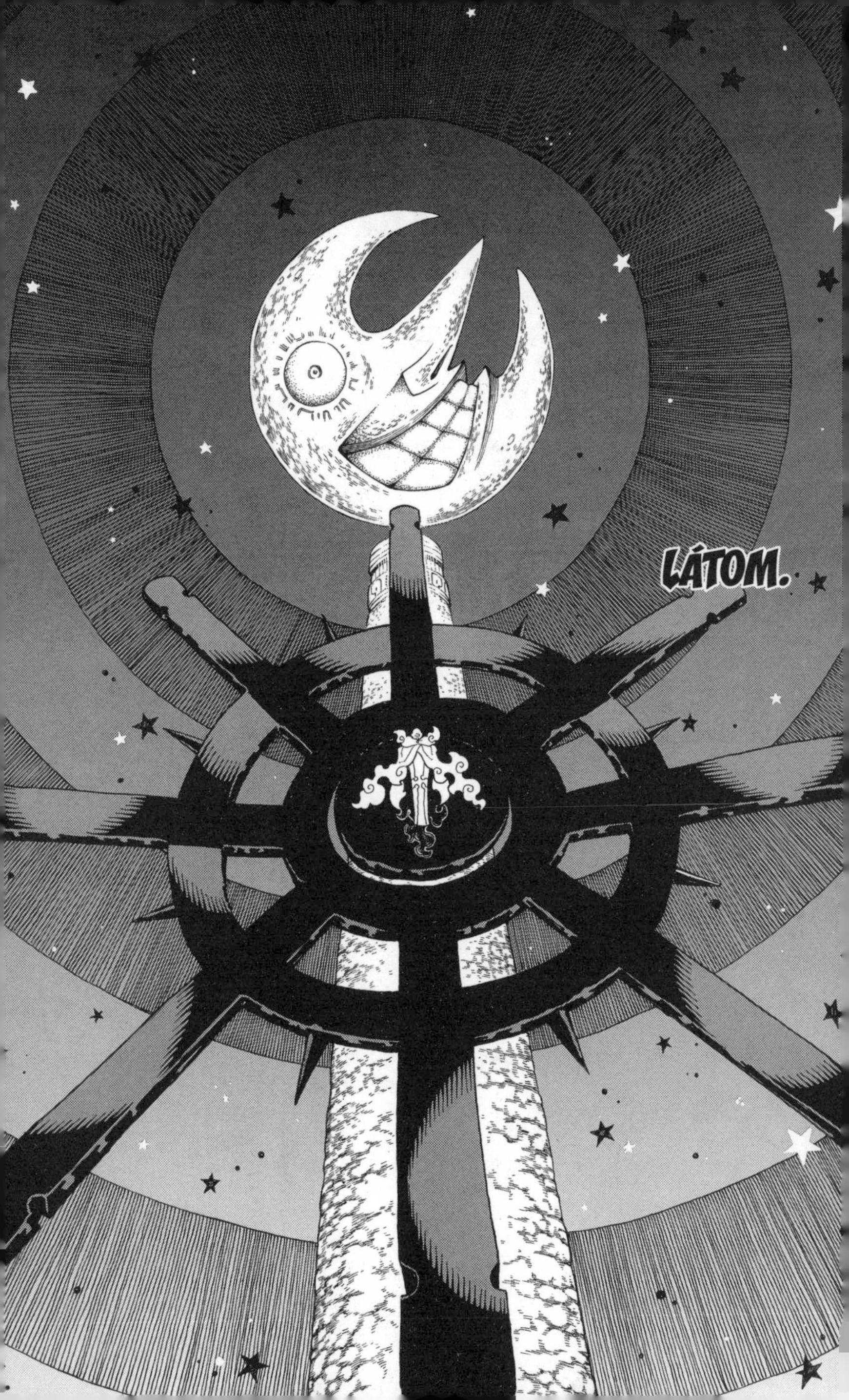
LÁTOM.

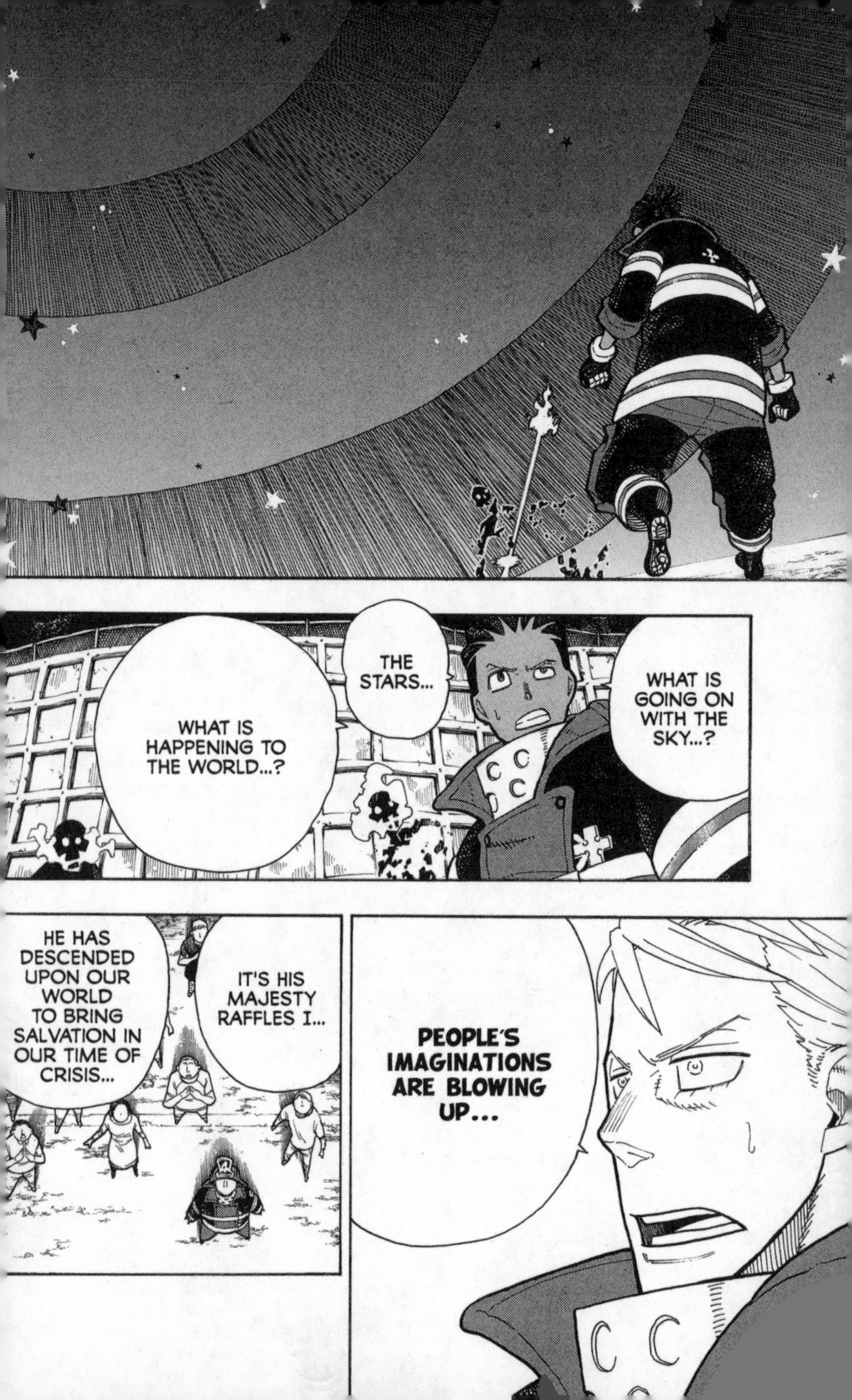
WHAT IS GOING ON WITH THE SKY...?
THE STARS...
WHAT IS HAPPENING TO THE WORLD...?
PEOPLE'S IMAGINATIONS ARE BLOWING UP...
IT'S HIS MAJESTY RAFFLES I...
HE HAS DESCENDED UPON OUR WORLD TO BRING SALVATION IN OUR TIME OF CRISIS...

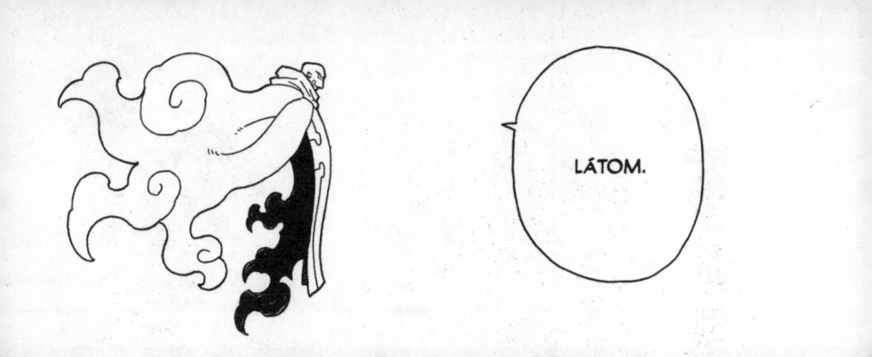
LÁTOM.
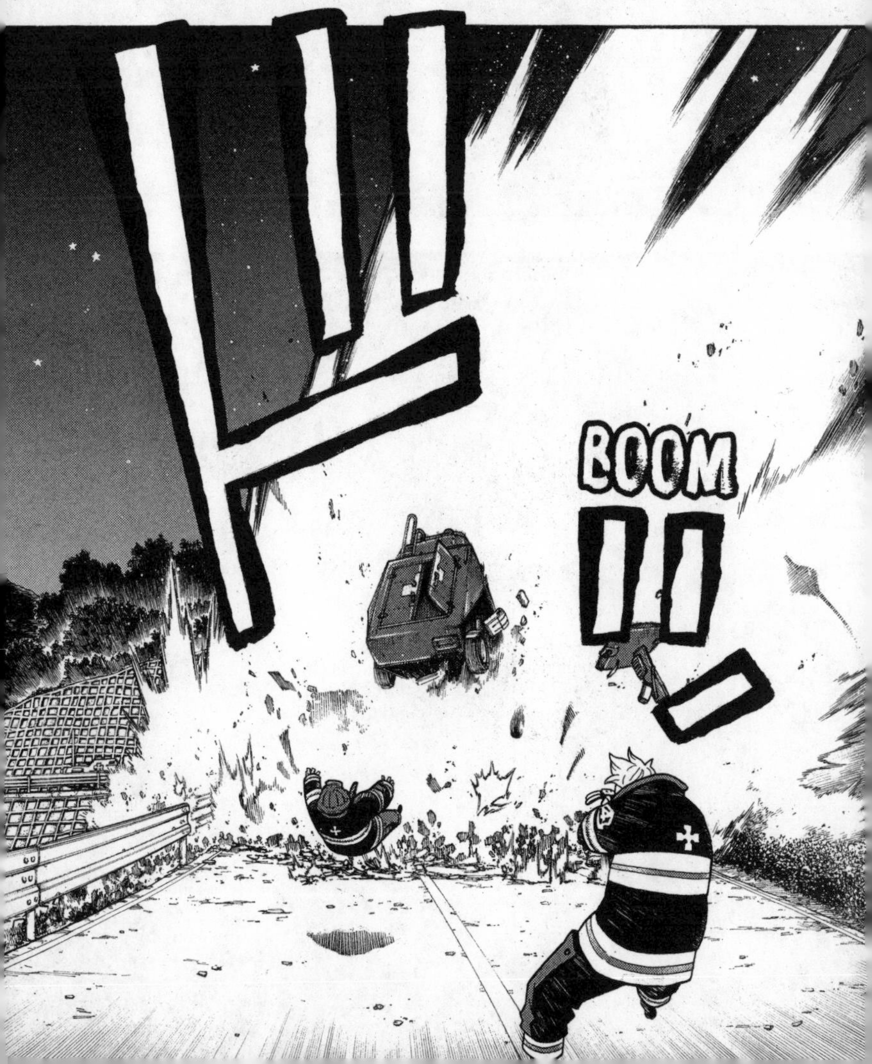
BOOM

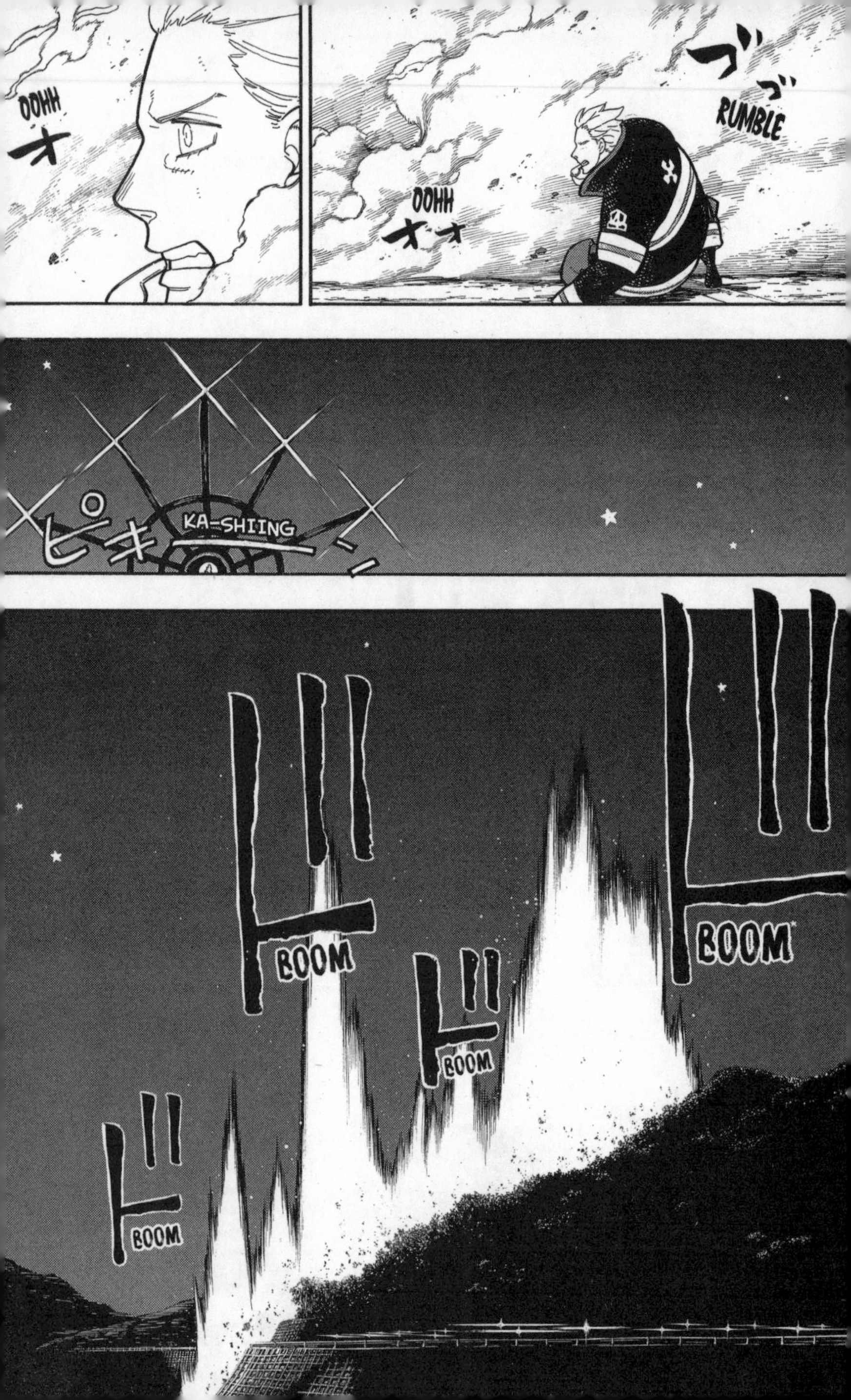
ゴゴ
RUMBLE
オオ
OOHH
オ
OOHH
ピキーン
KA-SHIING
ド
BOOM
ド
BOOM
ド
BOOM
ド
BOOM

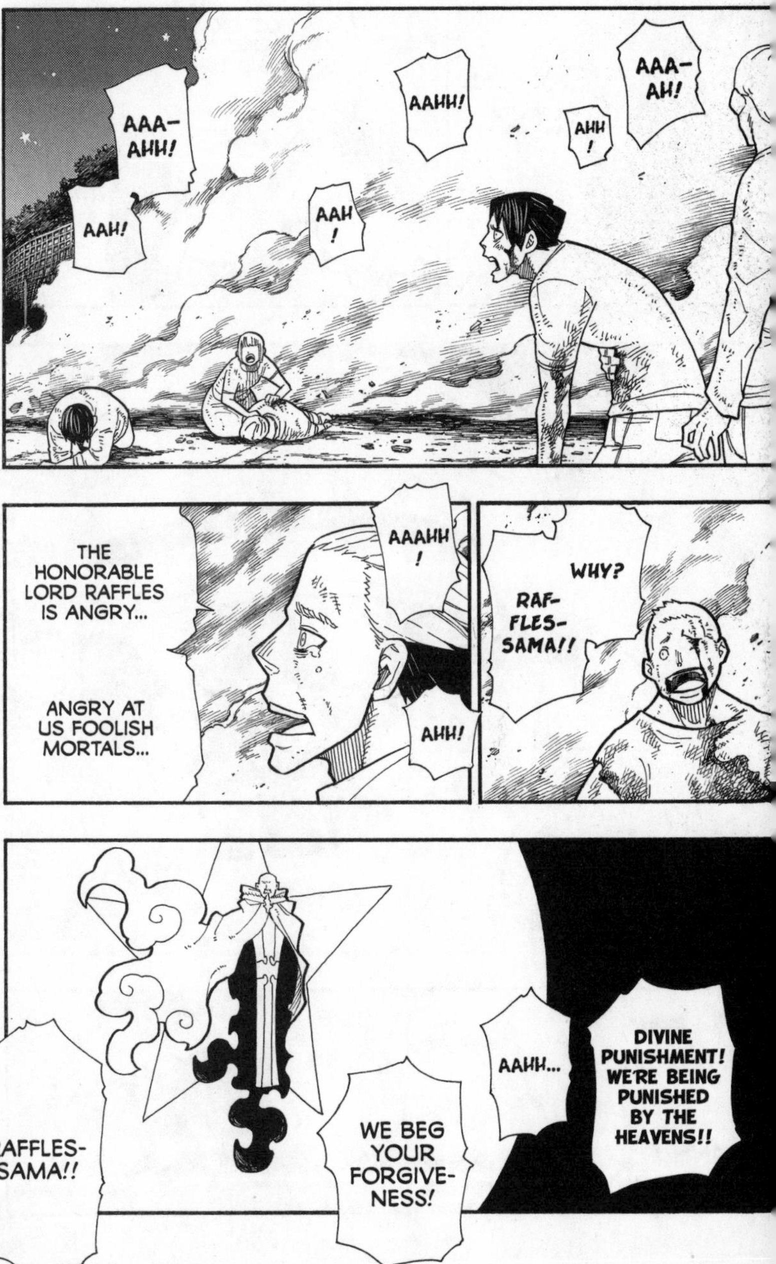
AAA-AH!
AHH!
AAHH!
AAH!
AAA-AHH!
AAH!
WHY?
RAF-FLES-SAMA!!
AAAHH!
THE HONORABLE LORD RAFFLES IS ANGRY...
ANGRY AT US FOOLISH MORTALS...
AHH!
DIVINE PUNISHMENT! WE'RE BEING PUNISHED BY THE HEAVENS!!
AAHH...
WE BEG YOUR FORGIVE-NESS!
RAFFLES-SAMA!!

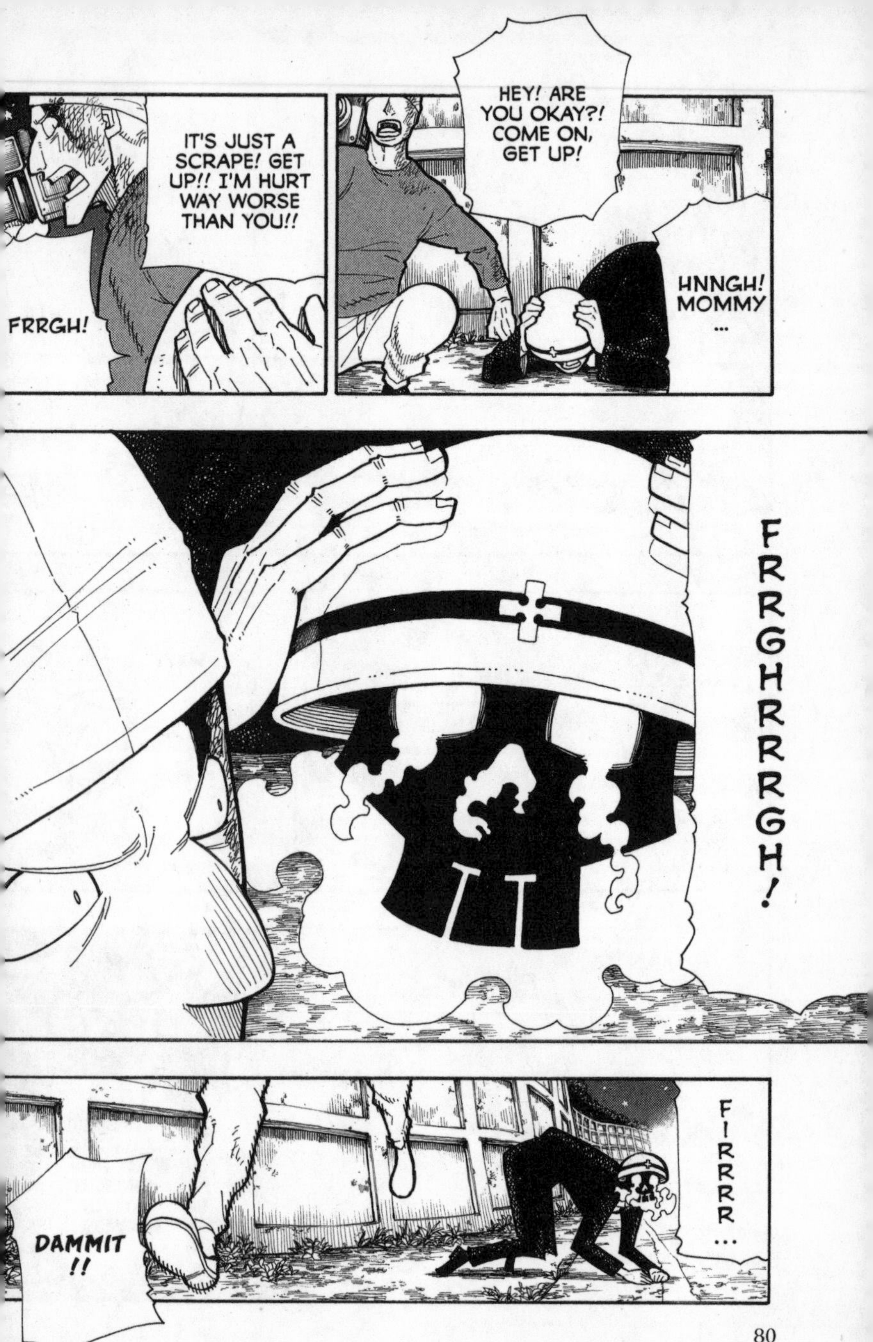
HEY! ARE YOU OKAY?! COME ON, GET UP!
HNNGH! MOMMY ...
IT'S JUST A SCRAPE! GET UP!! I'M HURT WAY WORSE THAN YOU!!
FRRGH!
FRRGHRRRRGH!
FIRRRR ...
DAMMIT !!

WHY DID YOU HAVE TO GO INFERNAL *NOW* OF ALL TIMES?! YOU NEVER DID MANAGE TO MAKE YOURSELF USEFUL!!

BUT I DON'T NEED SOME SORRY EXCUSE FOR AN ANCHOR TO REPORT THE NEWS!!

I GOT MY CAMERA, AND THAT'S GOOD ENOUGH!!

IS THAT A BIRD...?

IS IT A PLANE...?!

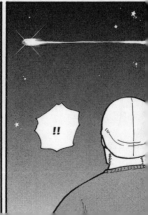

!!

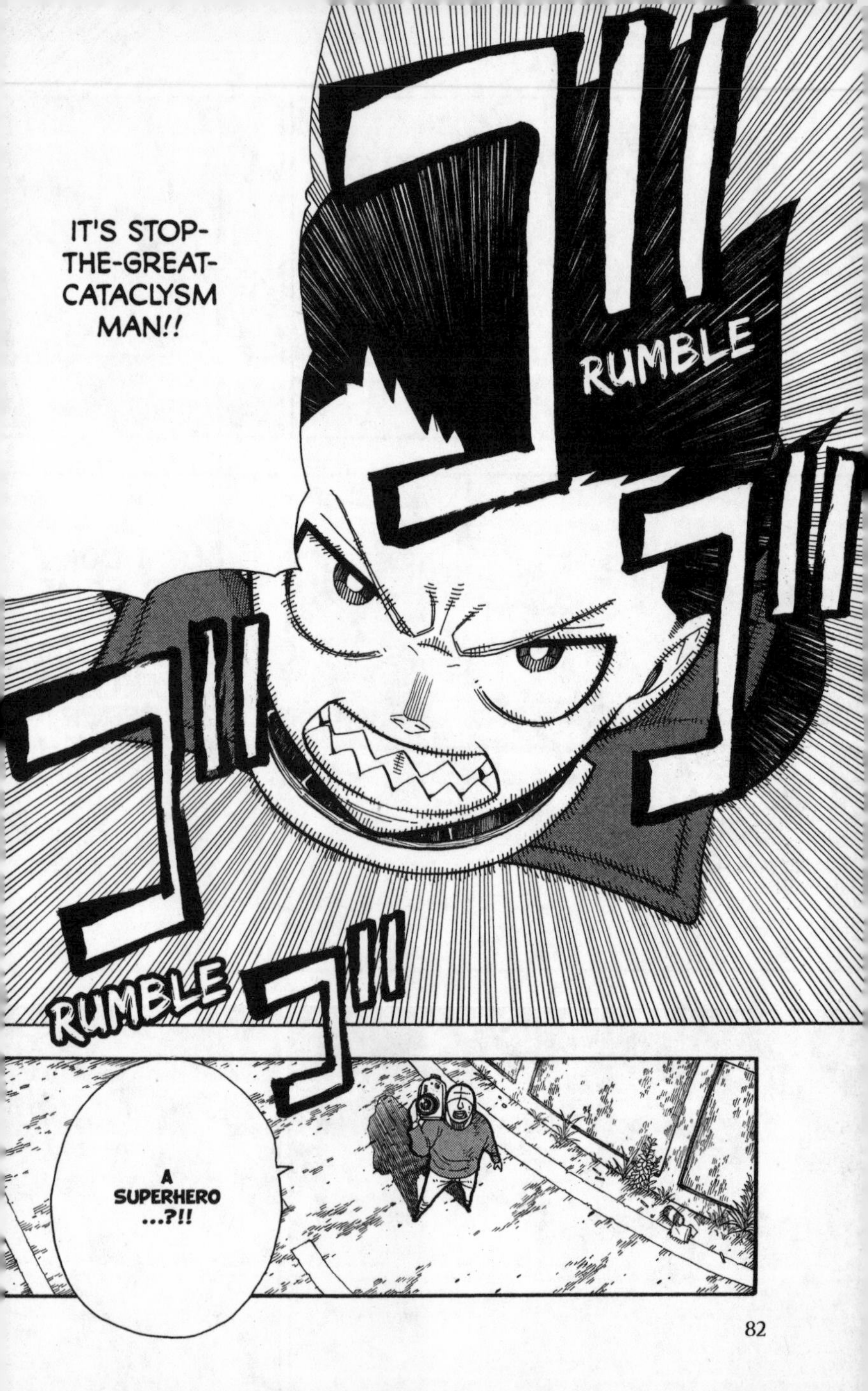

IT'S STOP-THE-GREAT-CATACLYSM MAN!!
RUMBLE
RUMBLE
A SUPERHERO ...?!!

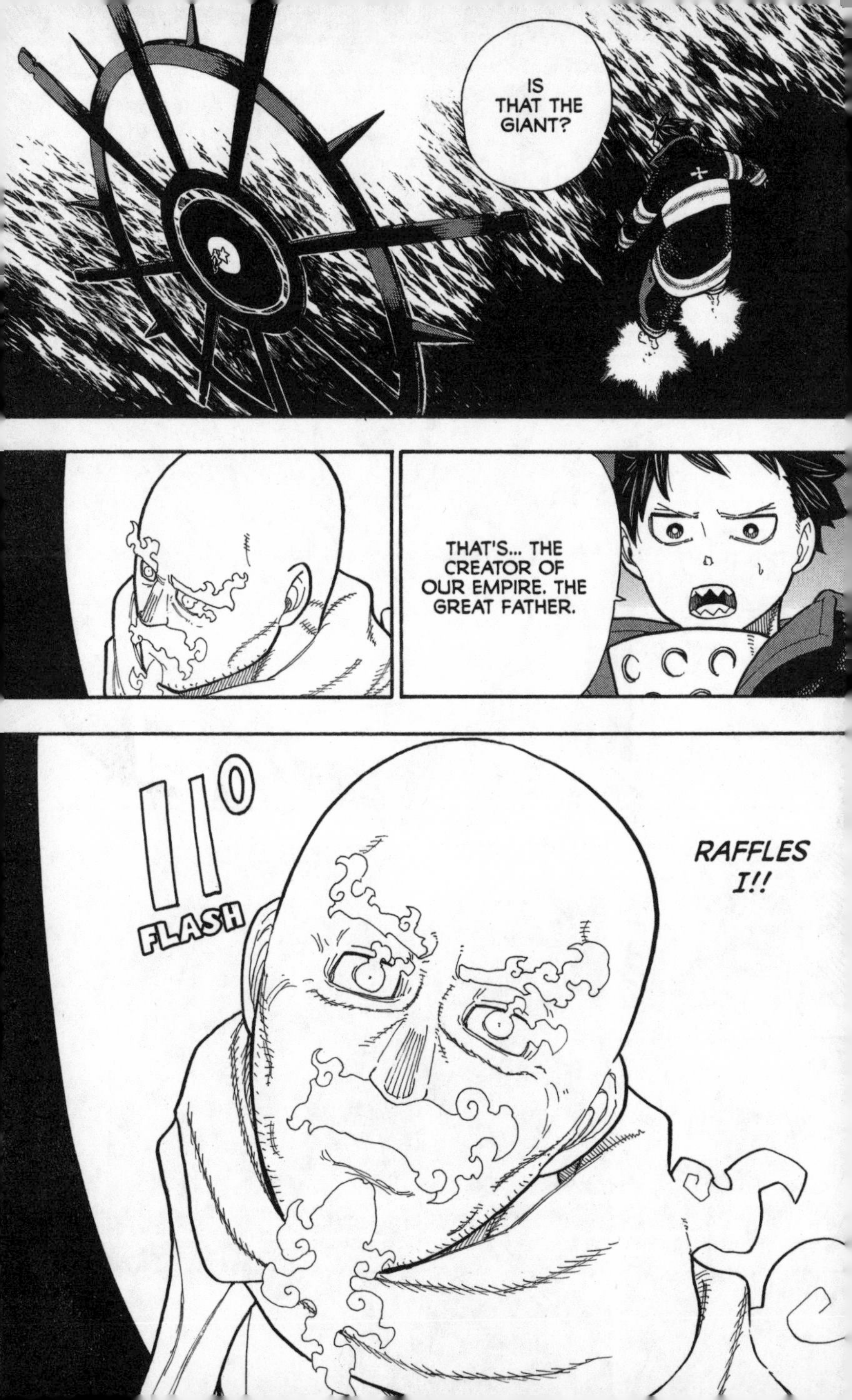
IS THAT THE GIANT?
THAT'S... THE CREATOR OF OUR EMPIRE. THE GREAT FATHER.
RAFFLES I!!
FLASH

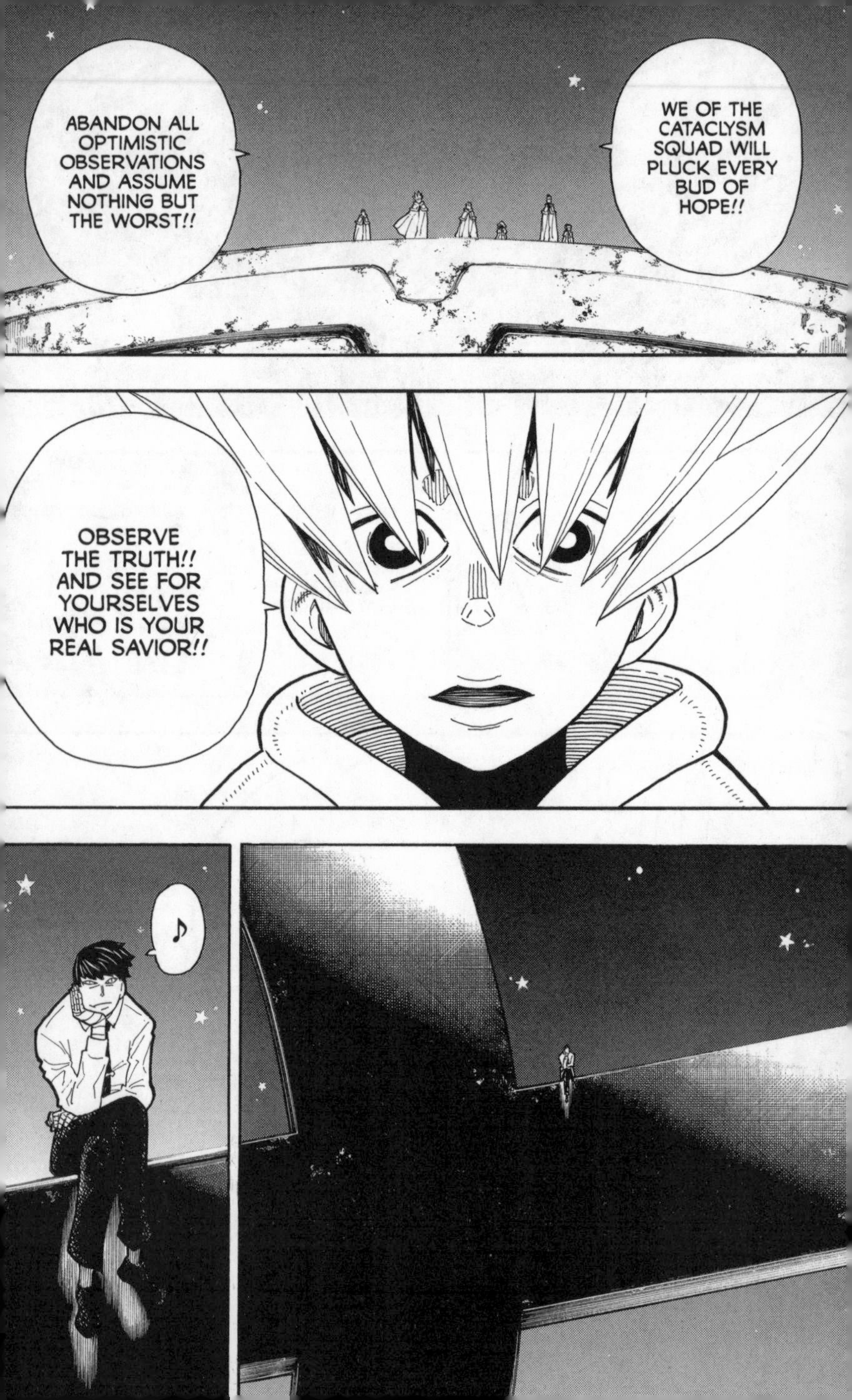
WE OF THE CATACLYSM SQUAD WILL PLUCK EVERY BUD OF HOPE!!
ABANDON ALL OPTIMISTIC OBSERVATIONS AND ASSUME NOTHING BUT THE WORST!!
OBSERVE THE TRUTH!! AND SEE FOR YOURSELVES WHO IS YOUR REAL SAVIOR!!
♪

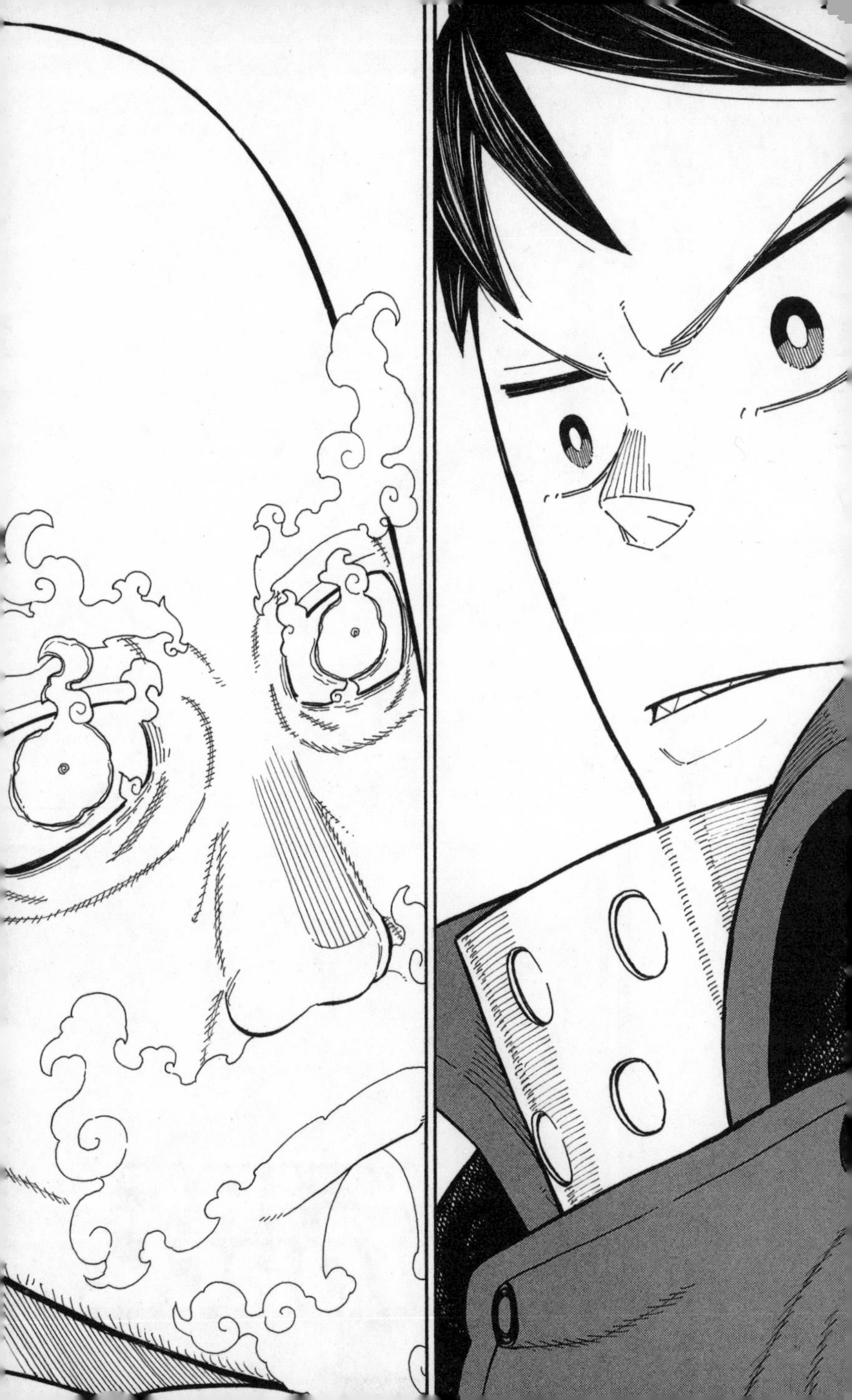

FIRE FORCE

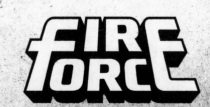

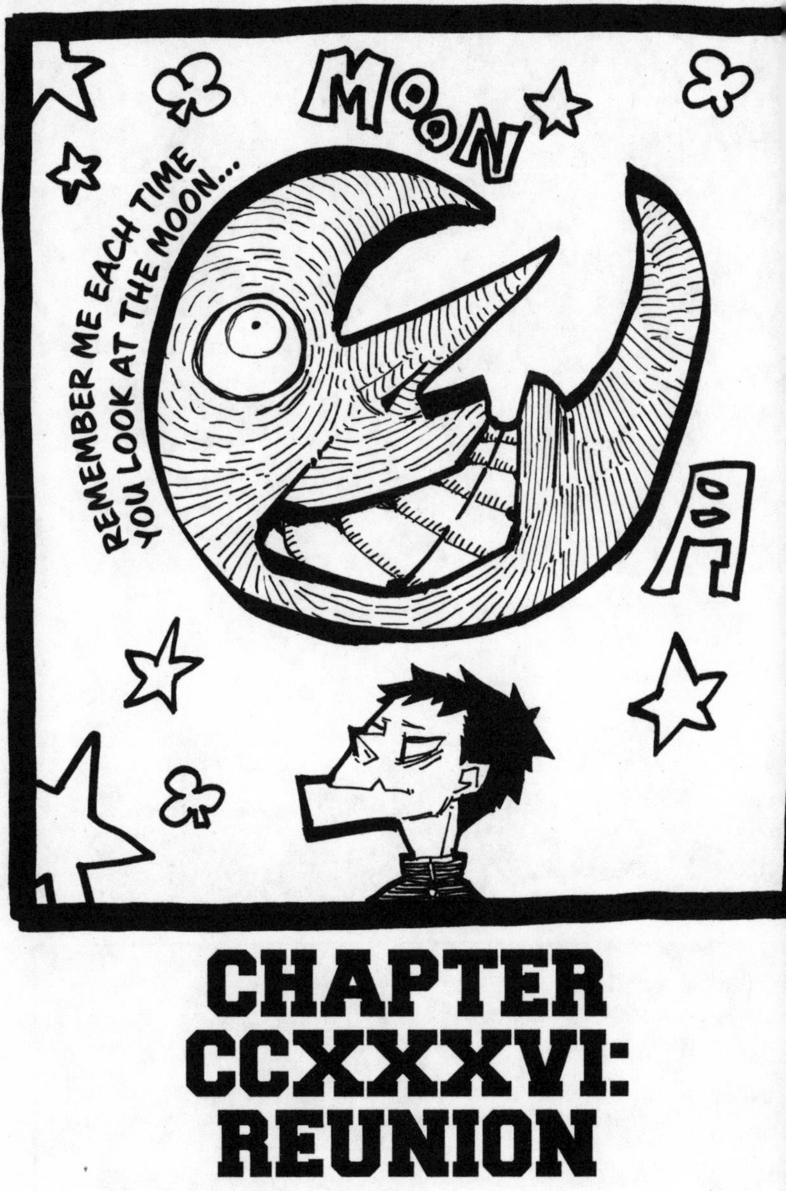
MOON
REMEMBER ME EACH TIME YOU LOOK AT THE MOON...

CHAPTER CCXXXVI: REUNION

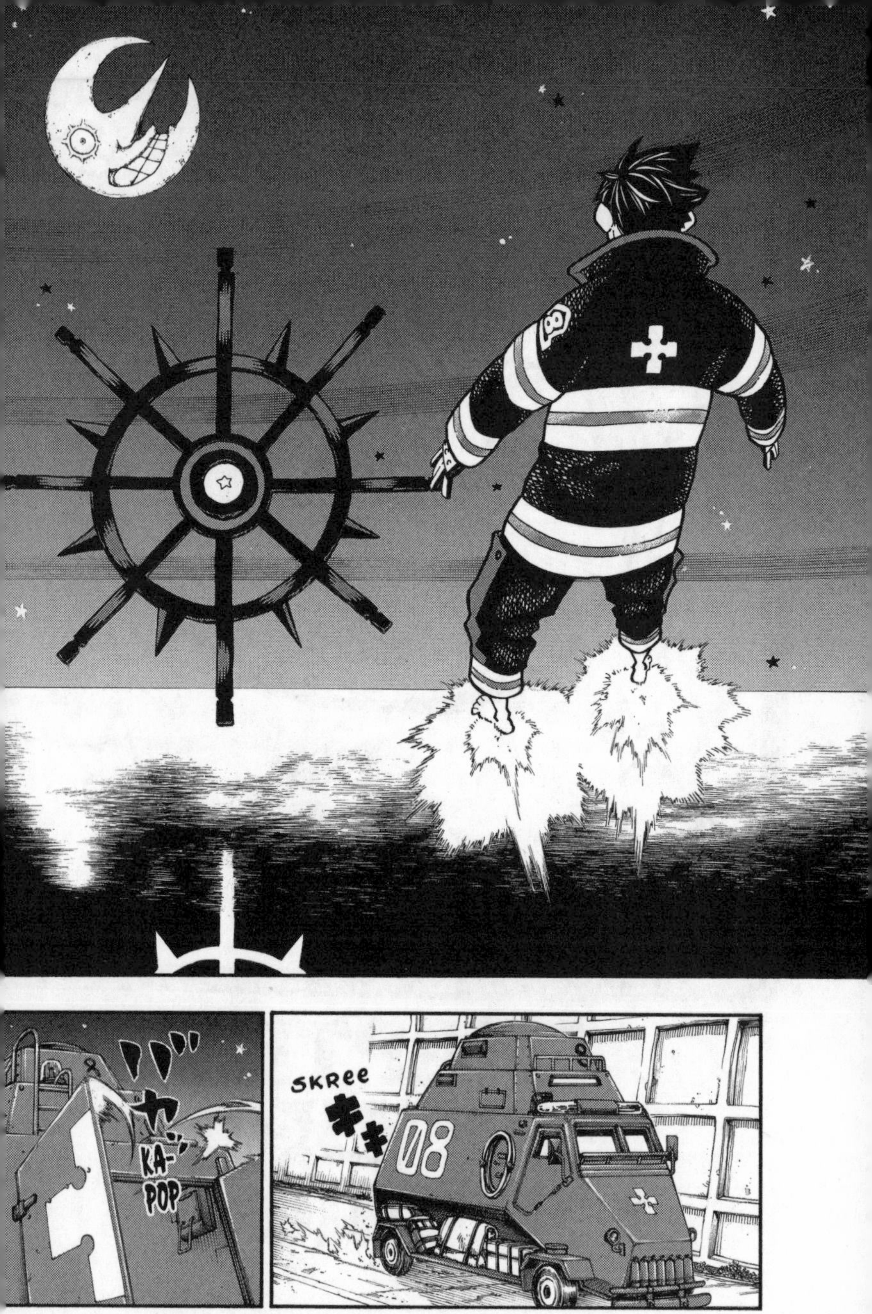
SKREE
KA-POP

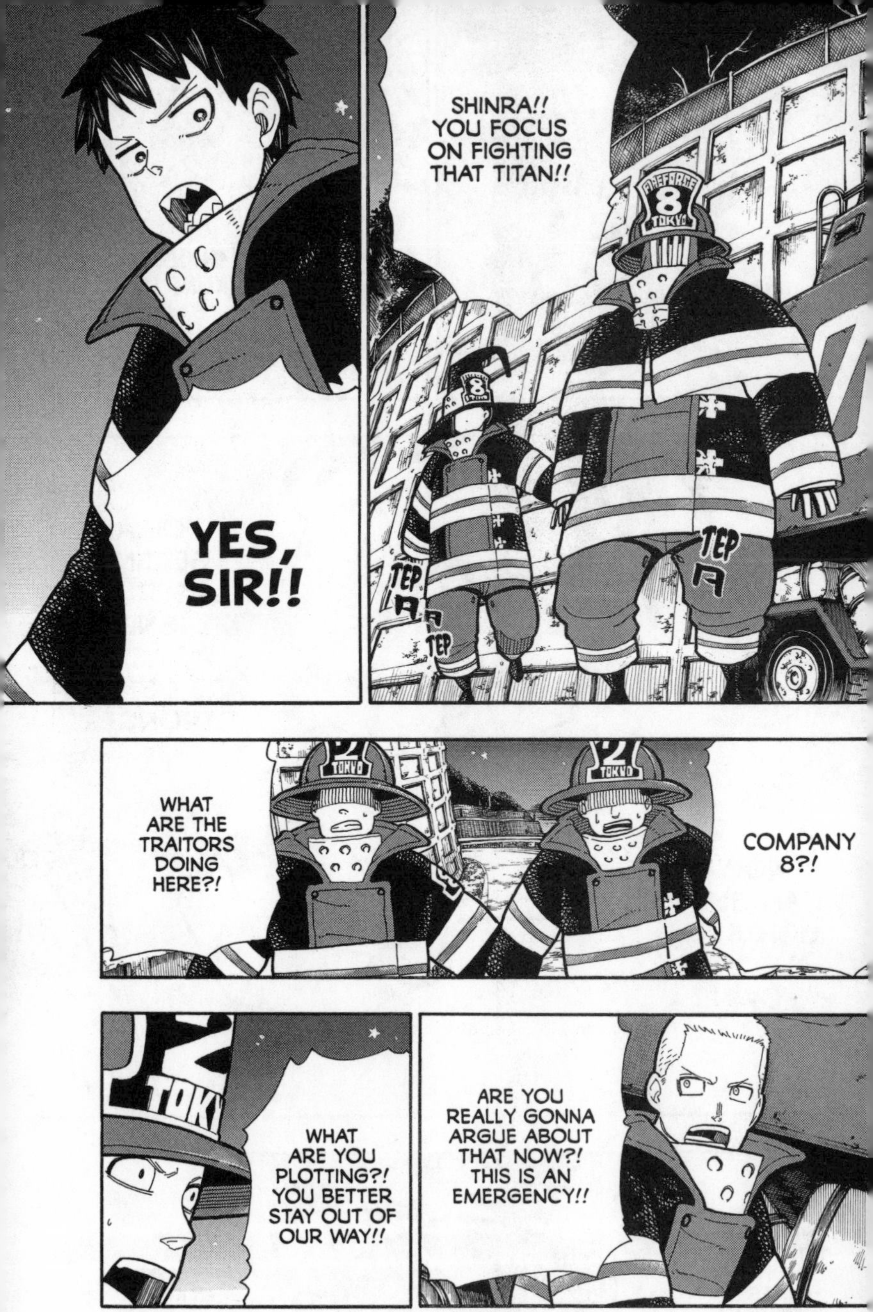
SHINRA!! YOU FOCUS ON FIGHTING THAT TITAN!!
TEP
TEP
TEP
YES, SIR!!
COMPANY 8?!
WHAT ARE THE TRAITORS DOING HERE?!
ARE YOU REALLY GONNA ARGUE ABOUT THAT NOW?! THIS IS AN EMERGENCY!!
WHAT ARE YOU PLOTTING?! YOU BETTER STAY OUT OF OUR WAY!!

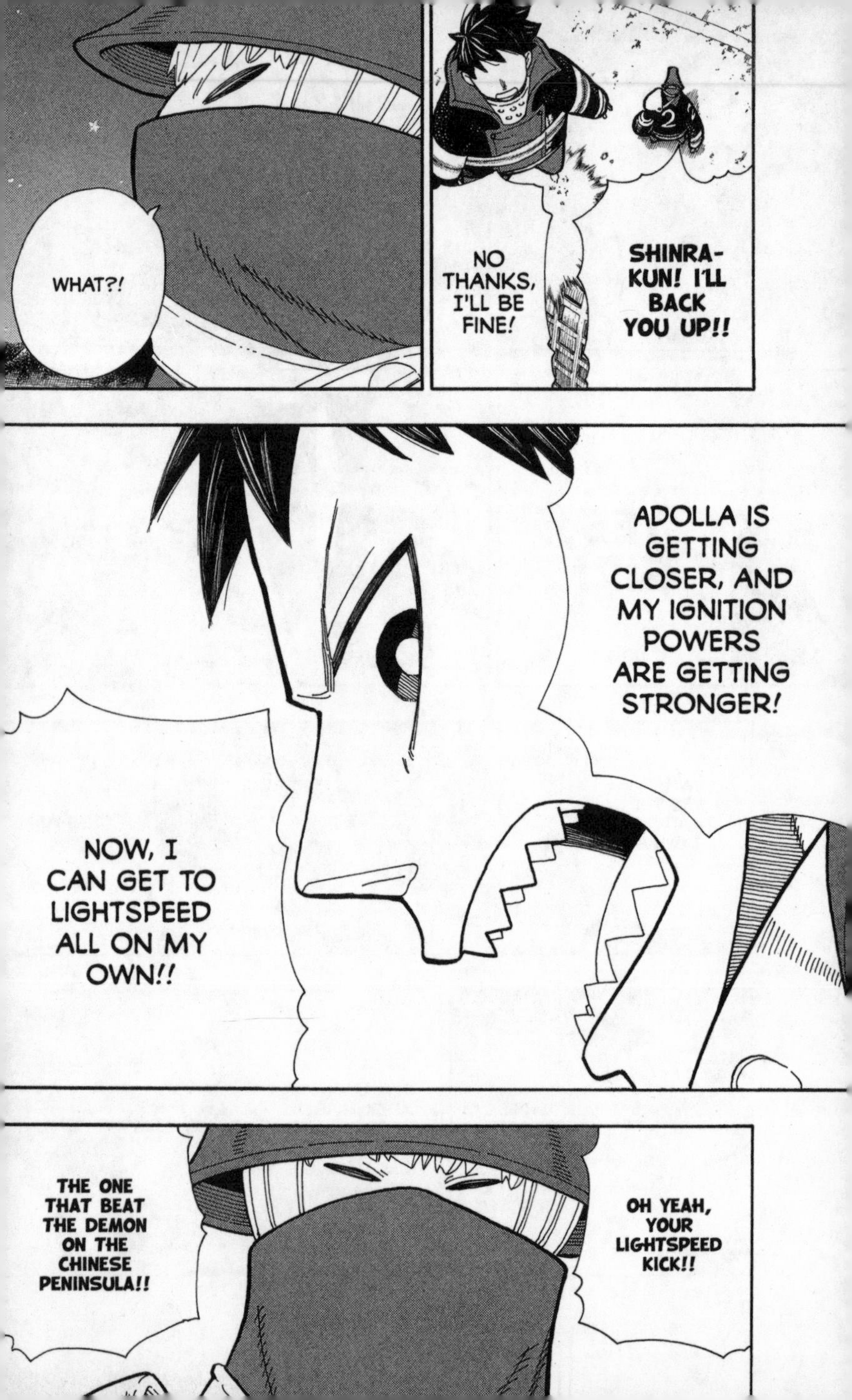
SHINRA-KUN! I'LL BACK YOU UP!!
NO THANKS, I'LL BE FINE!
WHAT?!
ADOLLA IS GETTING CLOSER, AND MY IGNITION POWERS ARE GETTING STRONGER!
NOW, I CAN GET TO LIGHTSPEED ALL ON MY OWN!!
OH YEAH, YOUR LIGHTSPEED KICK!!
THE ONE THAT BEAT THE DEMON ON THE CHINESE PENINSULA!!

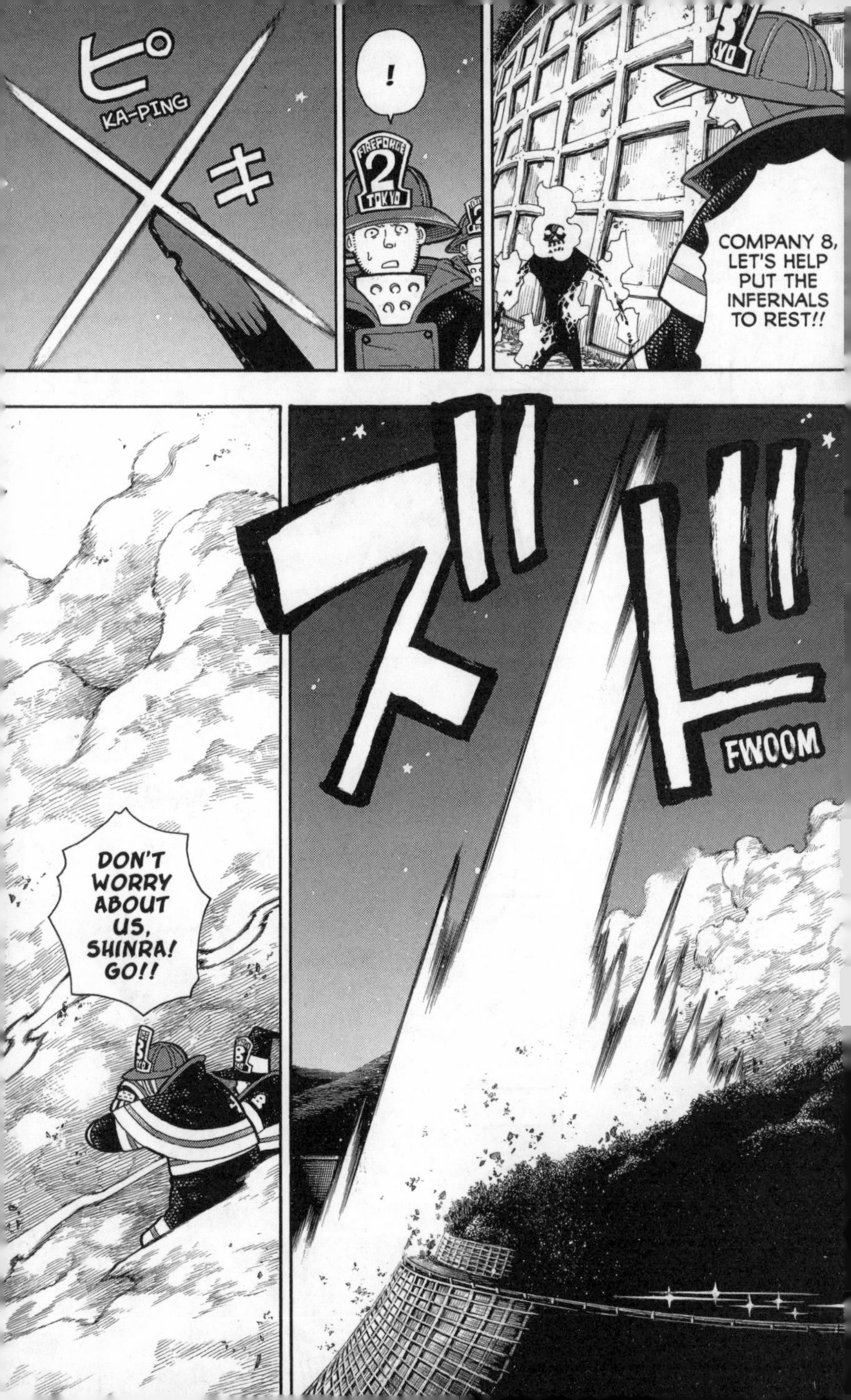
COMPANY 8, LET'S HELP PUT THE INFERNALS TO REST!!
!
ピキ
KA-PING
ズド
FWOOM
DON'T WORRY ABOUT US, SHINRA! GO!!

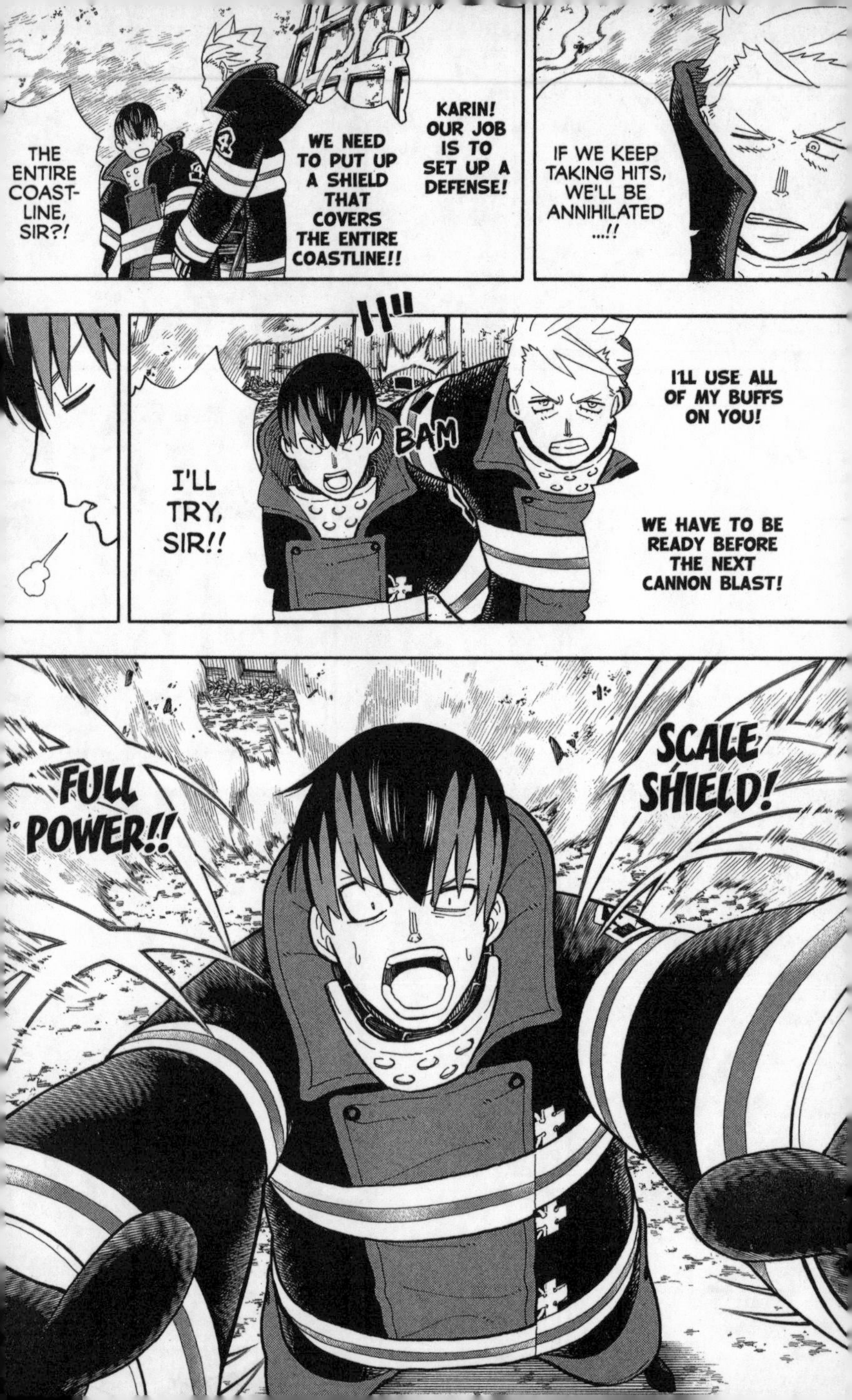
IF WE KEEP TAKING HITS, WE'LL BE ANNIHILATED ...!!
KARIN! OUR JOB IS TO SET UP A DEFENSE!
WE NEED TO PUT UP A SHIELD THAT COVERS THE ENTIRE COASTLINE!!
THE ENTIRE COASTLINE, SIR?!
I'LL USE ALL OF MY BUFFS ON YOU!
WE HAVE TO BE READY BEFORE THE NEXT CANNON BLAST!
BAM
I'LL TRY, SIR!!
SCALE SHIELD!
FULL POWER!!

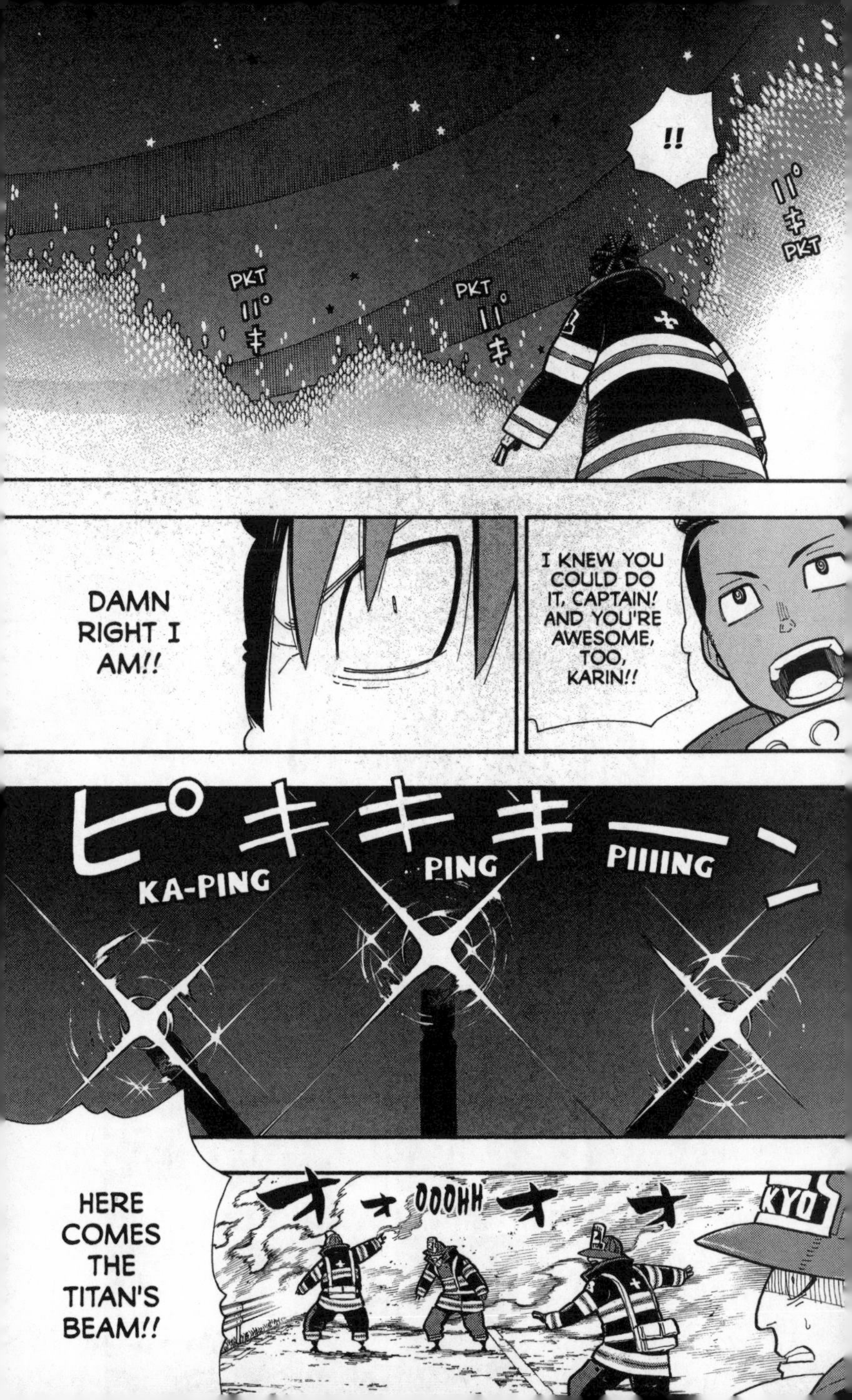
!!
パキ PKT
PKT パキ
PKT パキ
I KNEW YOU COULD DO IT, CAPTAIN! AND YOU'RE AWESOME, TOO, KARIN!!
DAMN RIGHT I AM!!
ピキキキーン
KA-PING
PING
PIIIING
KYO
オォ OOOHH オオ
HERE COMES THE TITAN'S BEAM!!

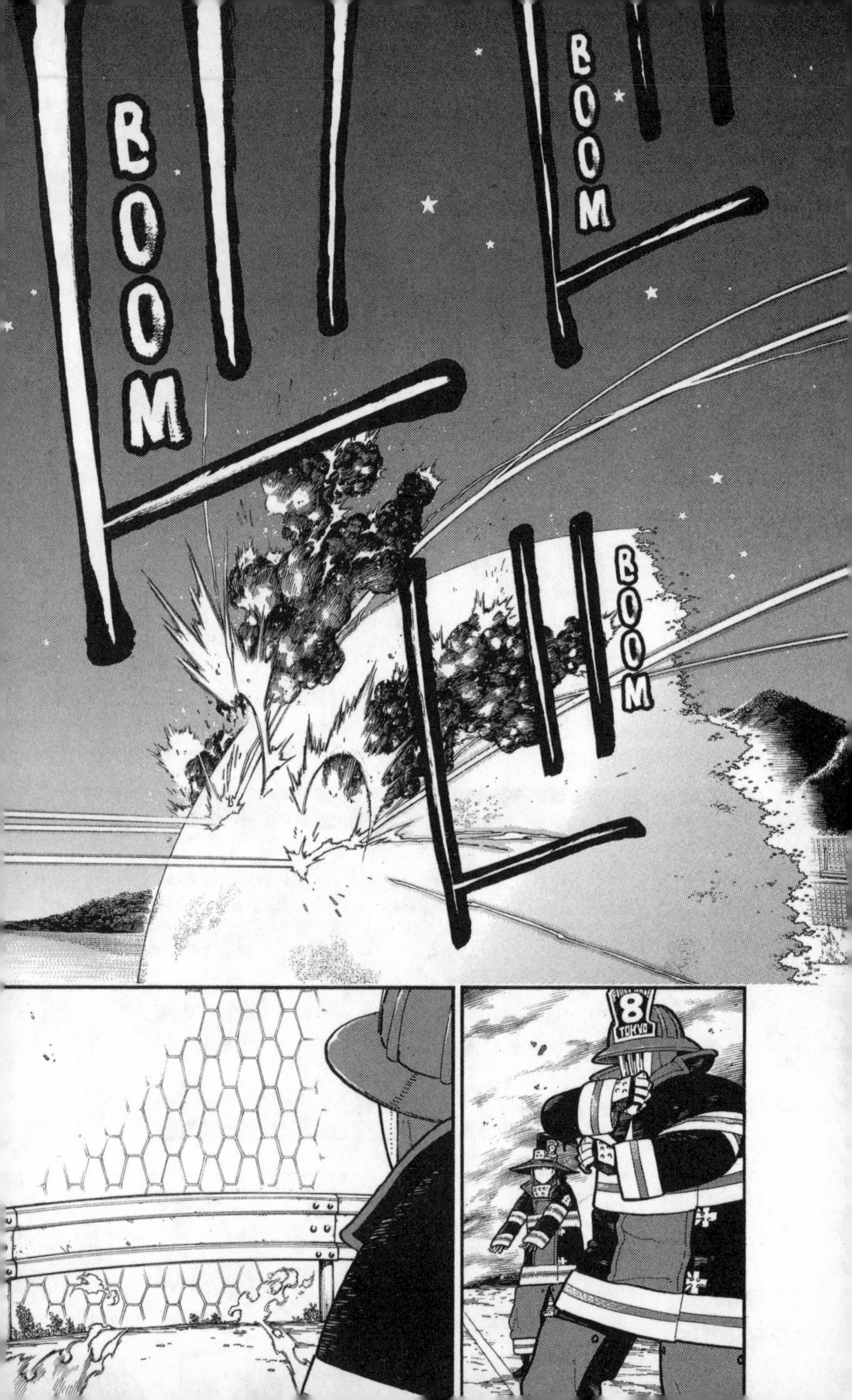
BOOM BOOM
BOOM
BOOM BOOM
8
TOKYO

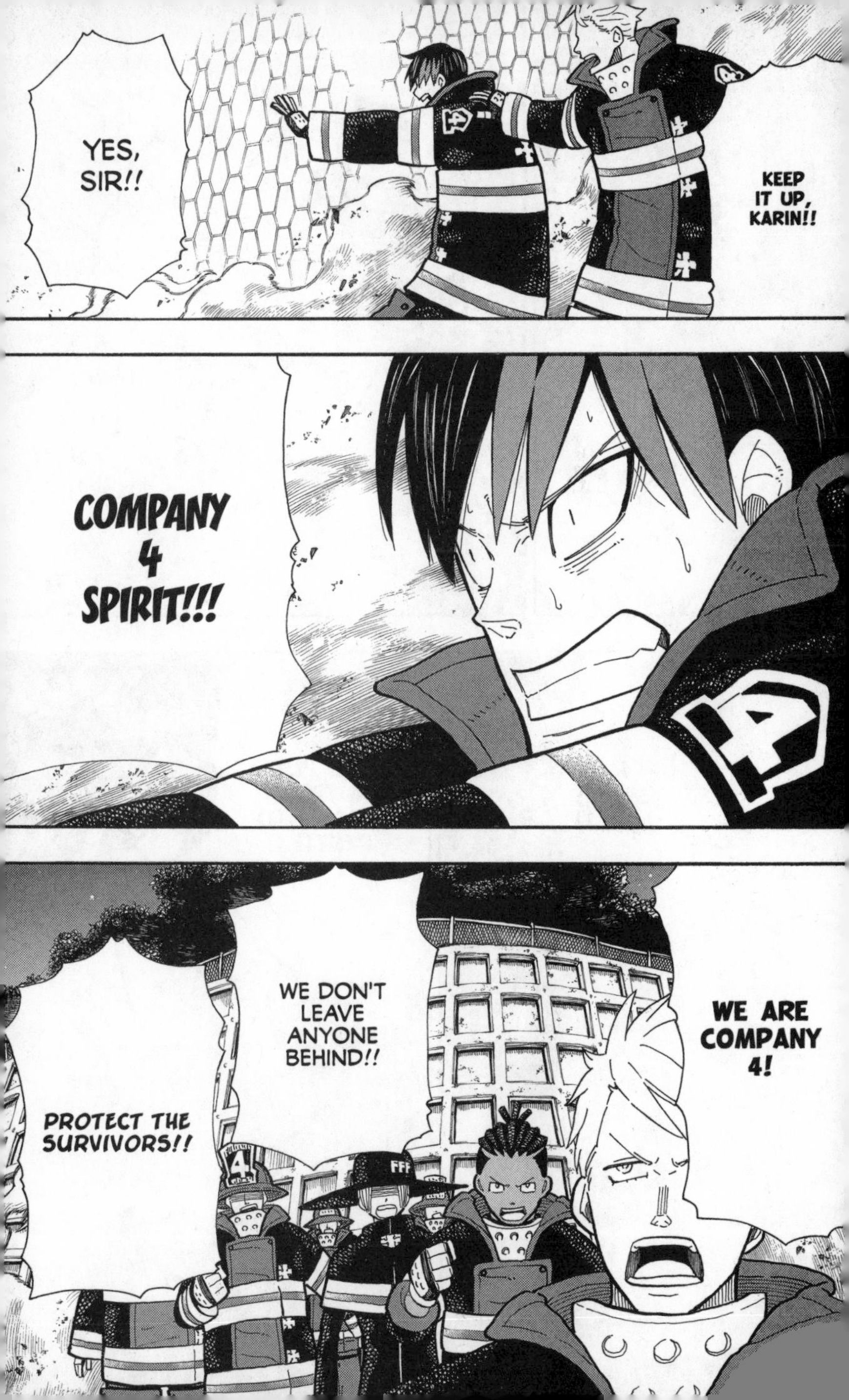
KEEP IT UP, KARIN!!
YES, SIR!!
COMPANY 4 SPIRIT!!!
WE ARE COMPANY 4!
WE DON'T LEAVE ANYONE BEHIND!!
PROTECT THE SURVIVORS!!

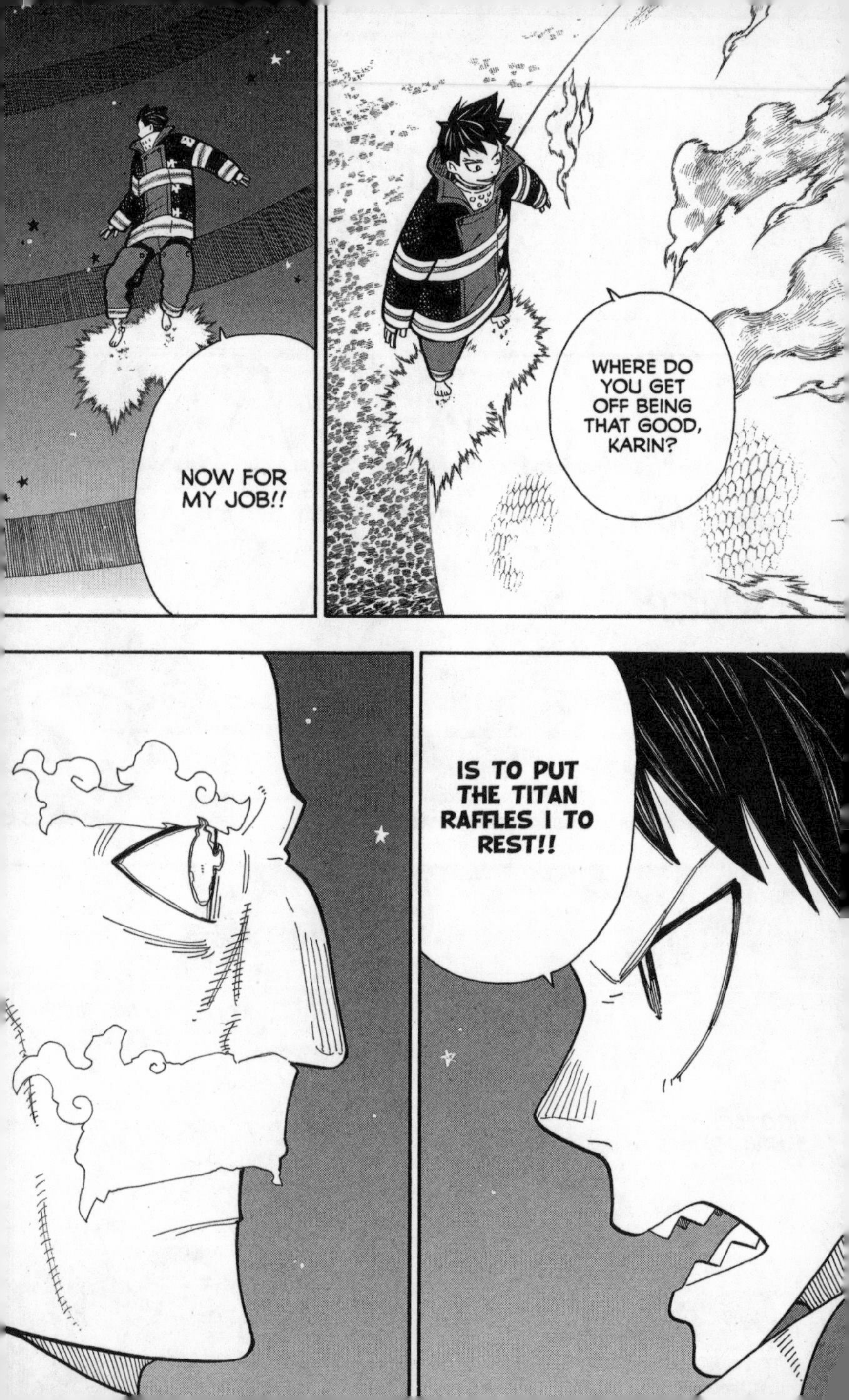
WHERE DO YOU GET OFF BEING THAT GOOD, KARIN?
NOW FOR MY JOB!!
IS TO PUT THE TITAN RAFFLES I TO REST!!

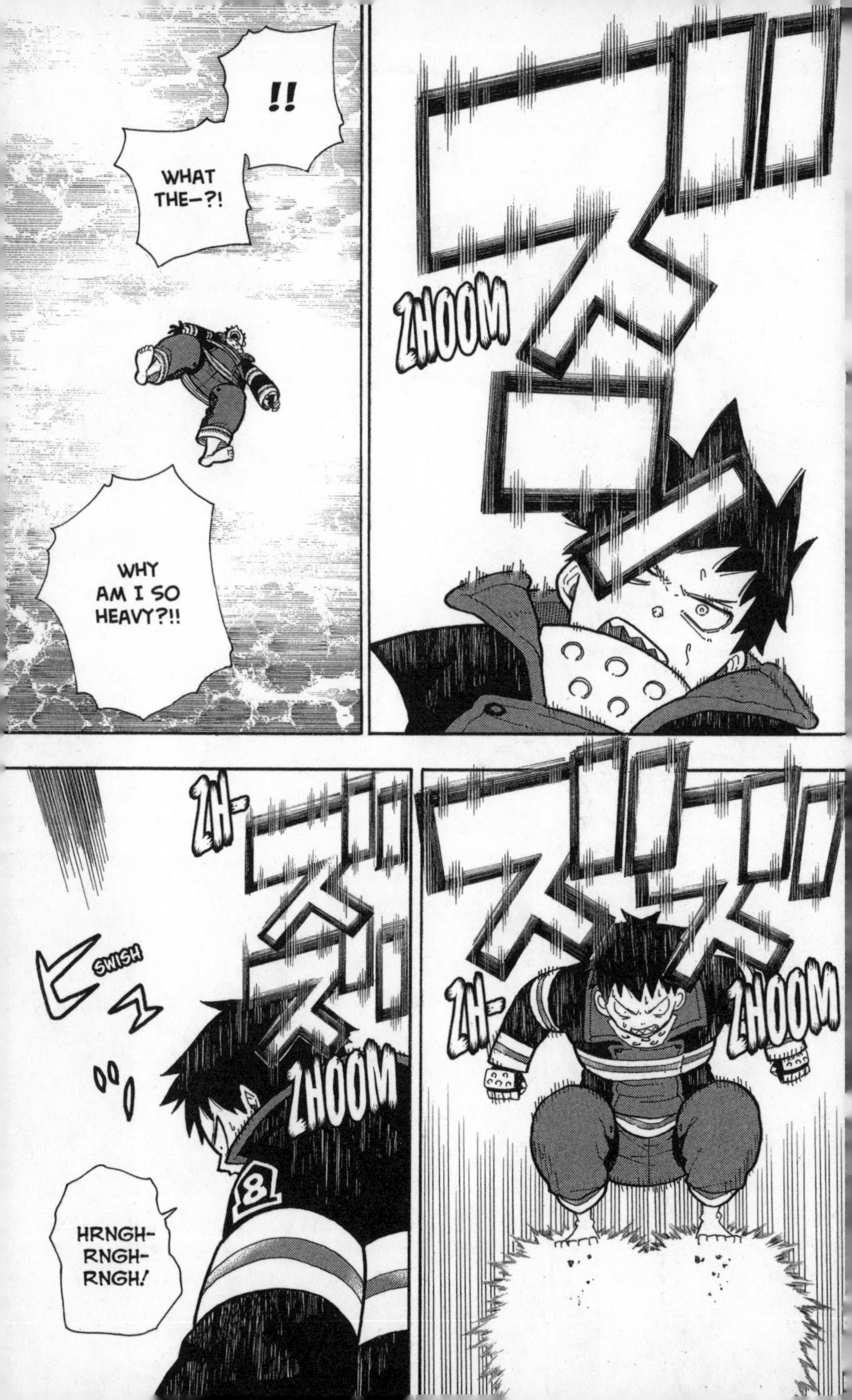
ZHOOM
!!
WHAT THE-?!
WHY AM I SO HEAVY?!!
ZH-
ZHOOM
ZH-
SWISH
ZHOOM
HRNGH-RNGH-RNGH!

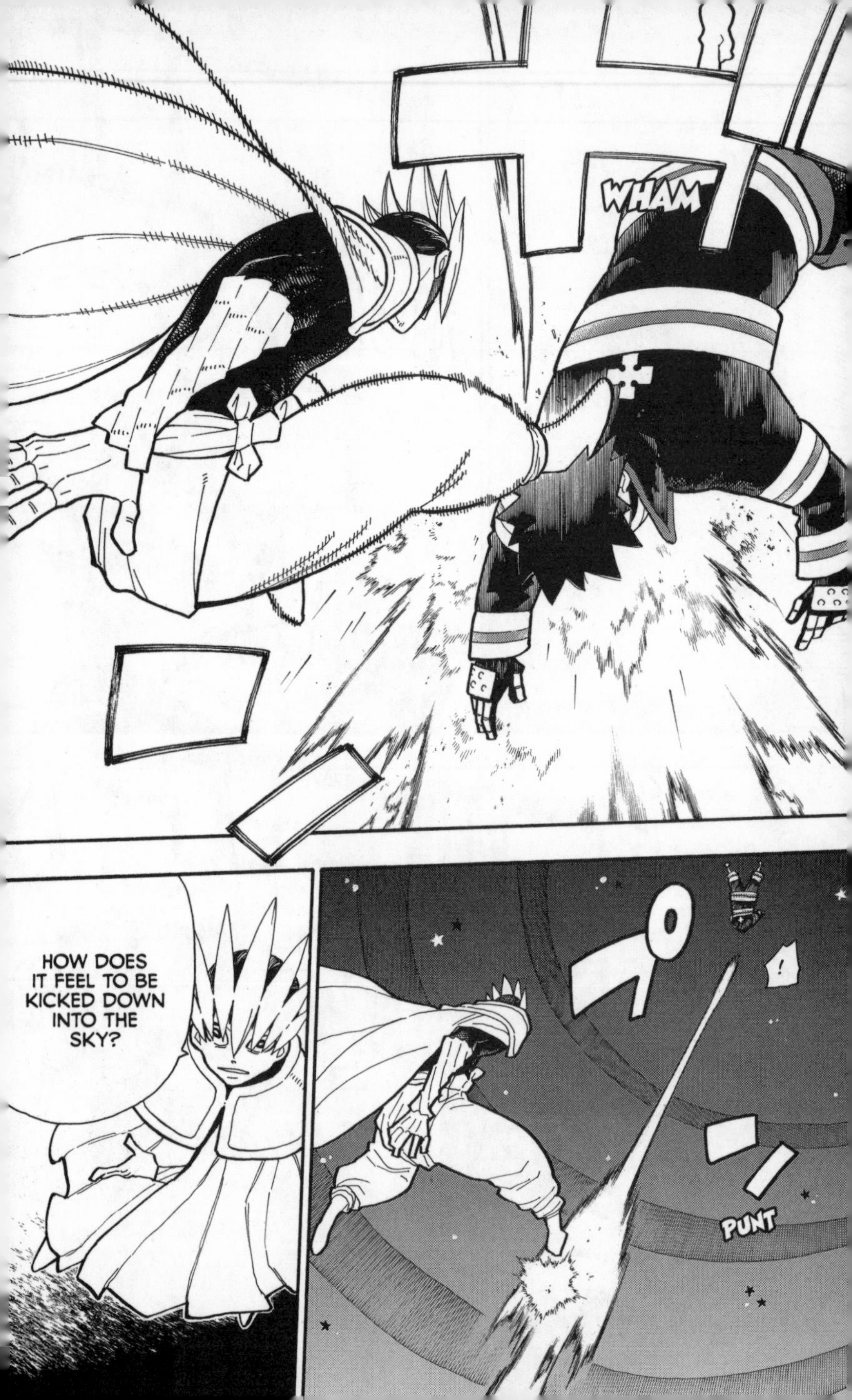
WHAM
!
PUNT
HOW DOES IT FEEL TO BE KICKED DOWN INTO THE SKY?

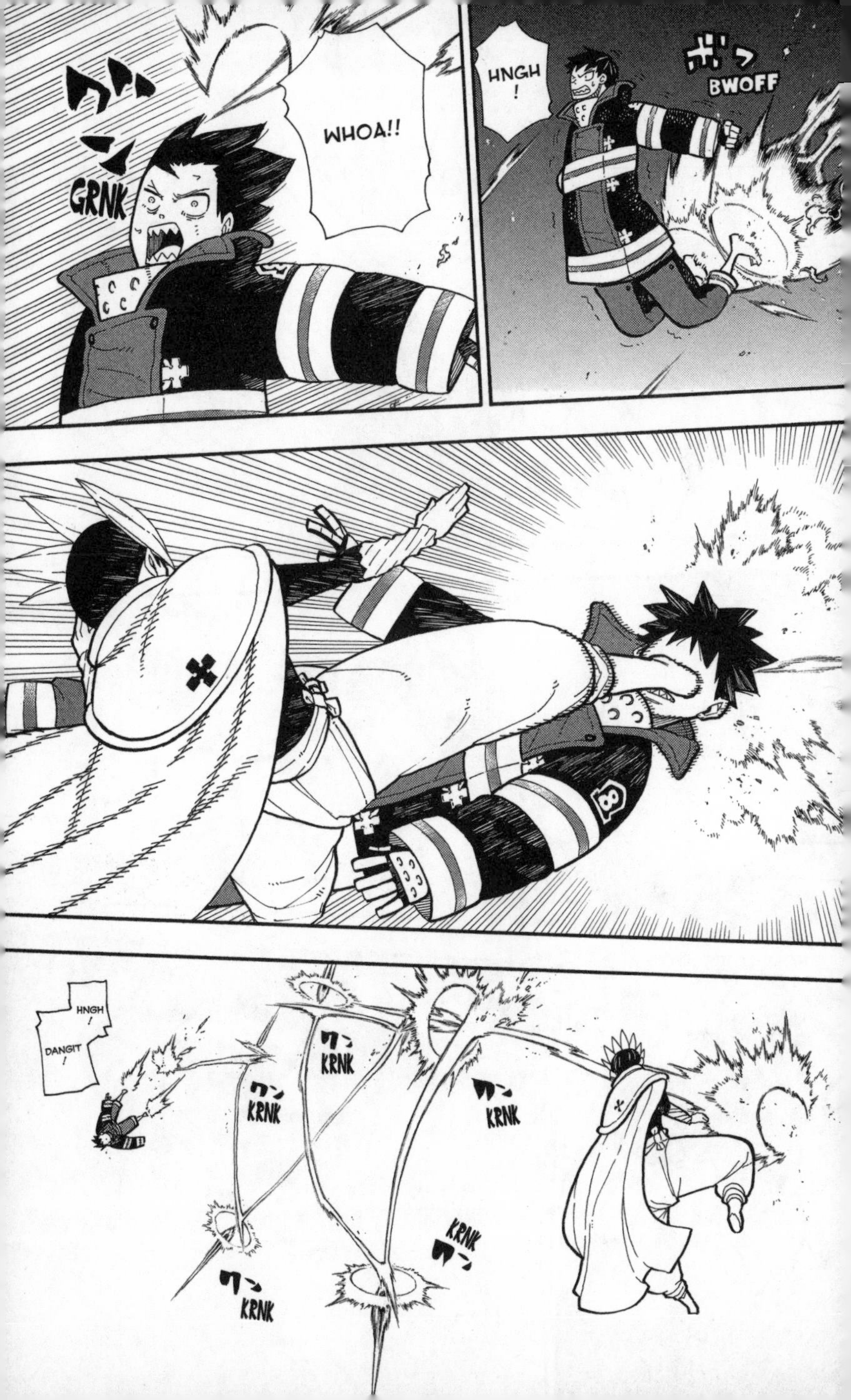

HNGH!
ボッ
BWOFF
WHOA!!
GRNK
KRNK
KRNK
KRNK
KRNK
HNGH!
DANGIT!
KRNK

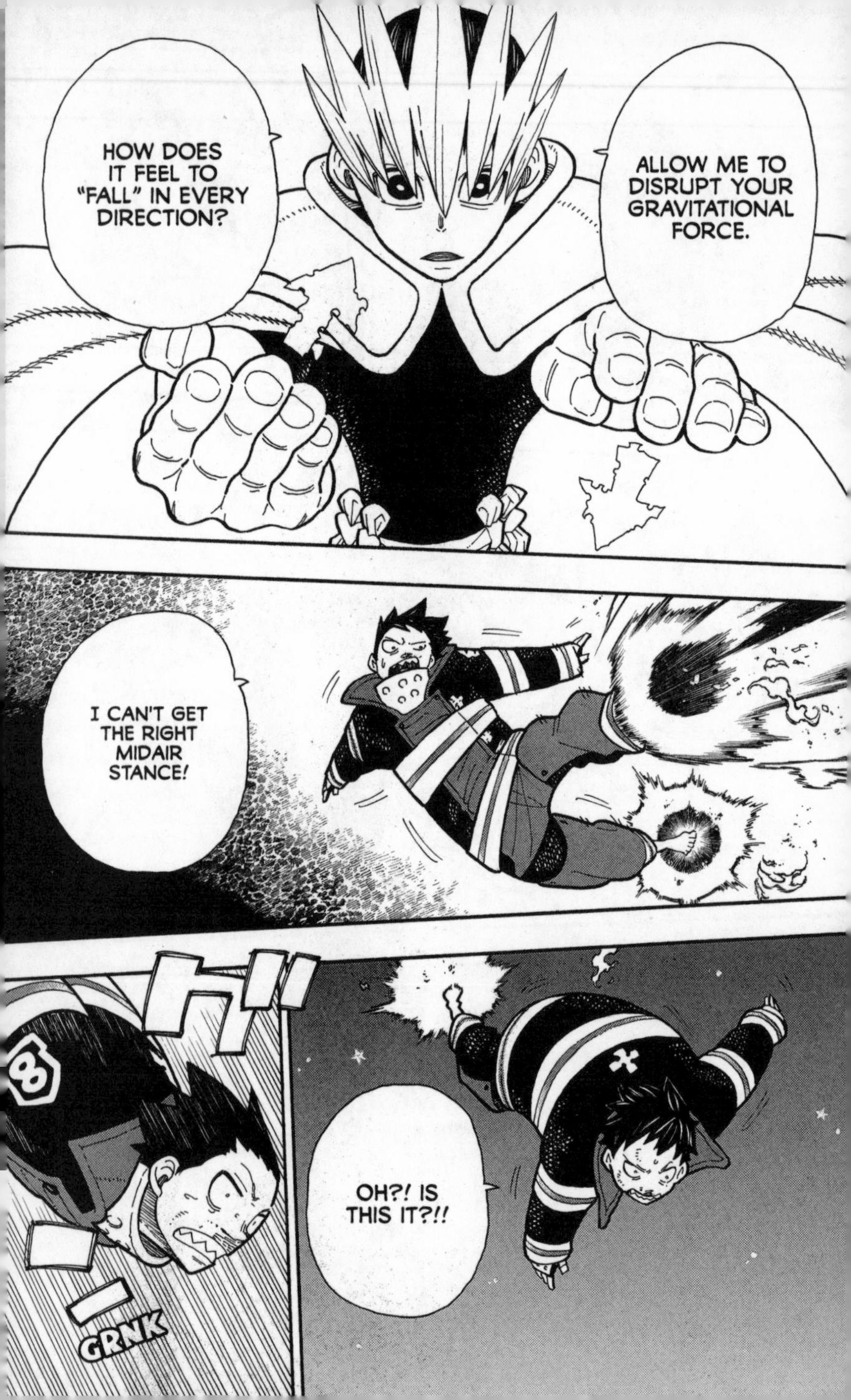
ALLOW ME TO DISRUPT YOUR GRAVITATIONAL FORCE.
HOW DOES IT FEEL TO "FALL" IN EVERY DIRECTION?
I CAN'T GET THE RIGHT MIDAIR STANCE!
OH?! IS THIS IT?!!
GRNK

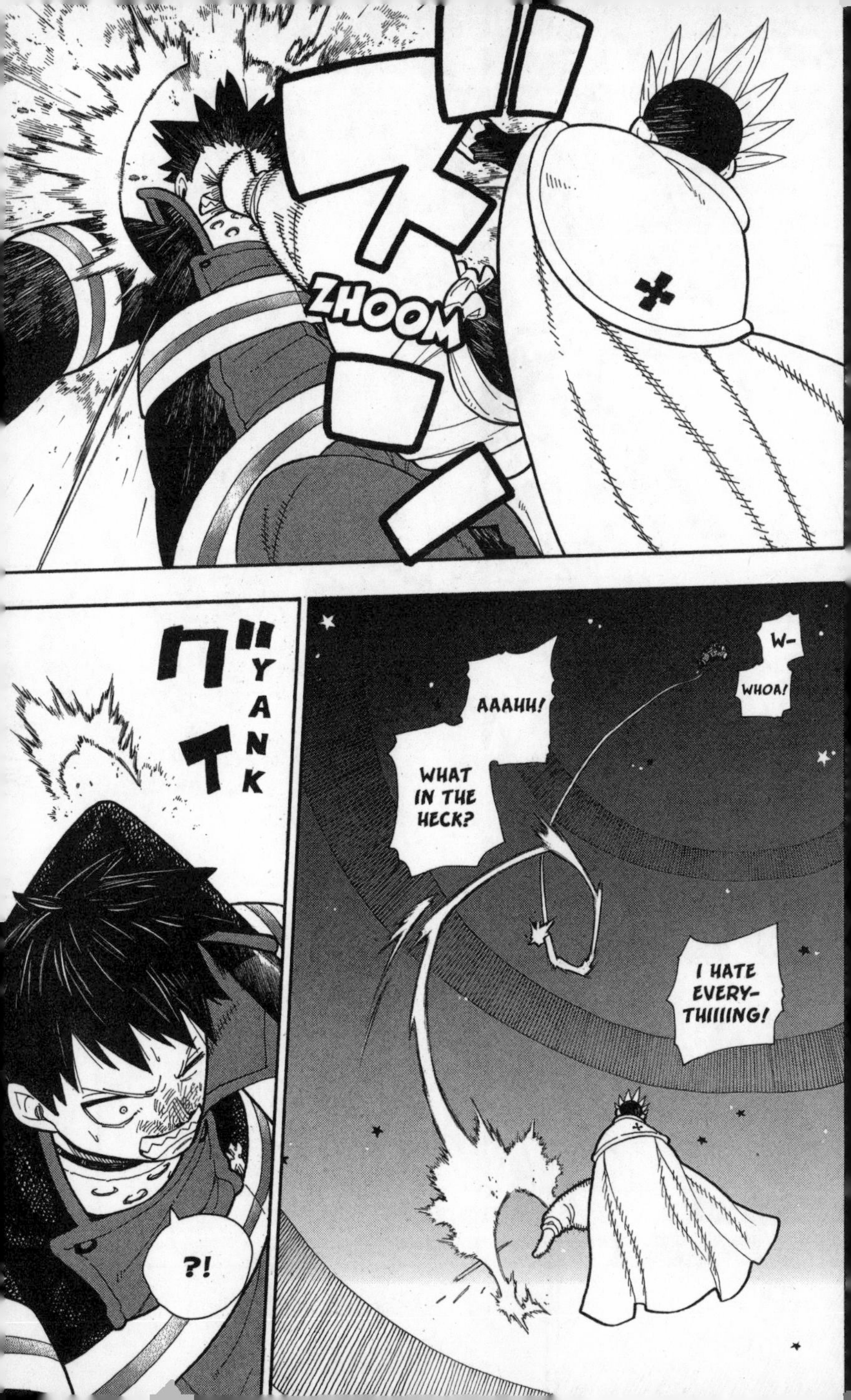
ZHOOM
W-
WHOA!
AAAHH!
WHAT IN THE HECK?
I HATE EVERY-THIIIING!
YANK
?!

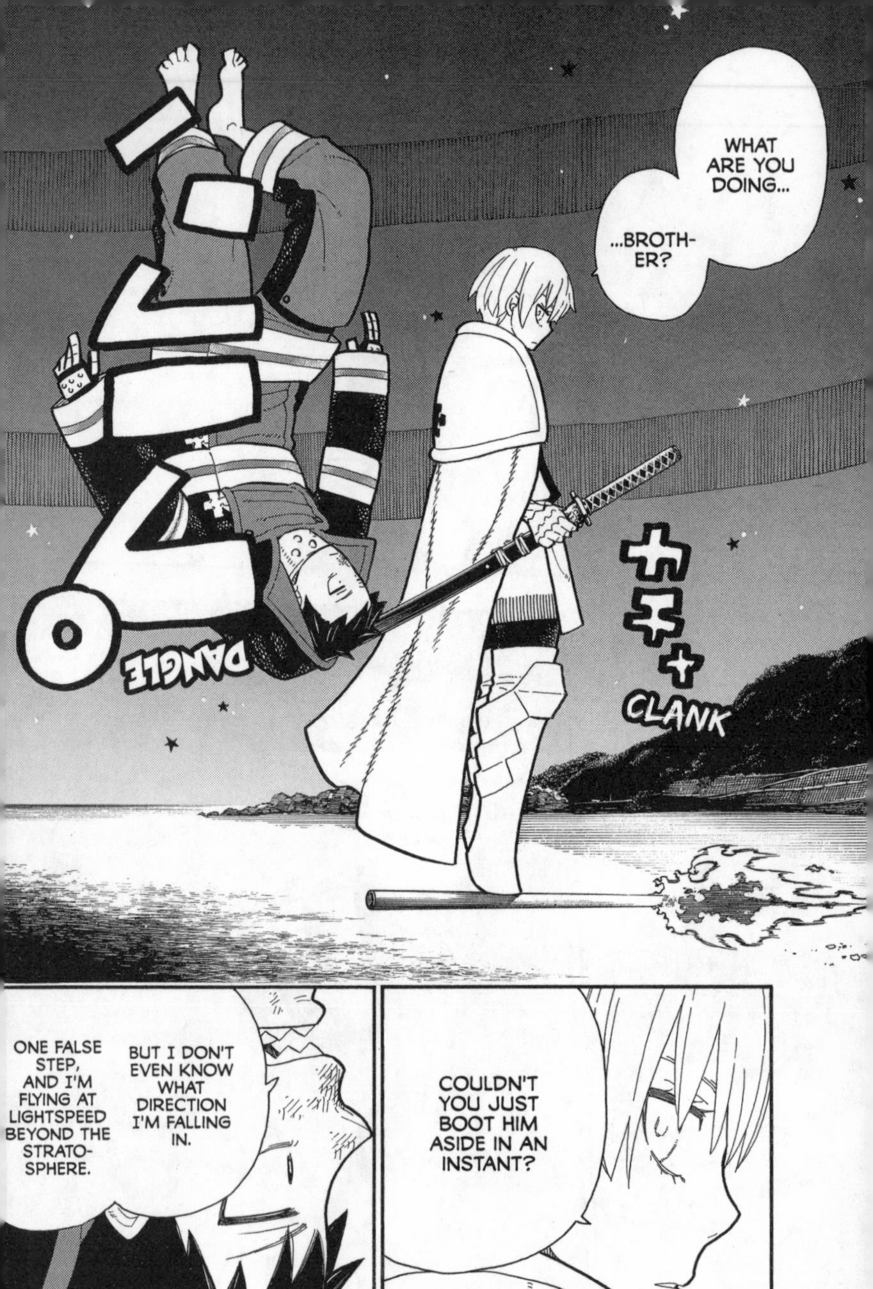
WHAT ARE YOU DOING...
...BROTHER?
DANGLE
CLANK
COULDN'T YOU JUST BOOT HIM ASIDE IN AN INSTANT?
BUT I DON'T EVEN KNOW WHAT DIRECTION I'M FALLING IN.
ONE FALSE STEP, AND I'M FLYING AT LIGHTSPEED BEYOND THE STRATOSPHERE.

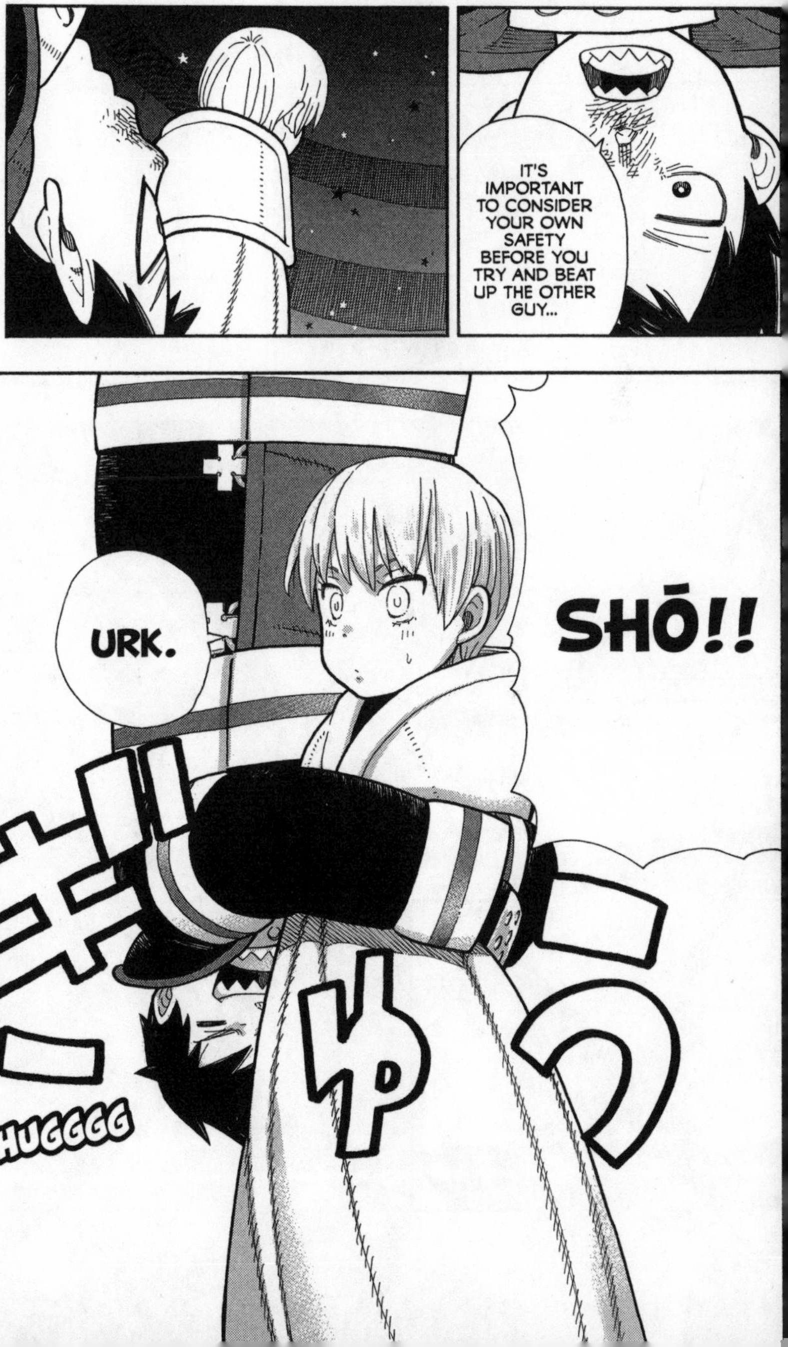
IT'S IMPORTANT TO CONSIDER YOUR OWN SAFETY BEFORE YOU TRY AND BEAT UP THE OTHER GUY...
SHŌ!!
URK.
HUGGGG

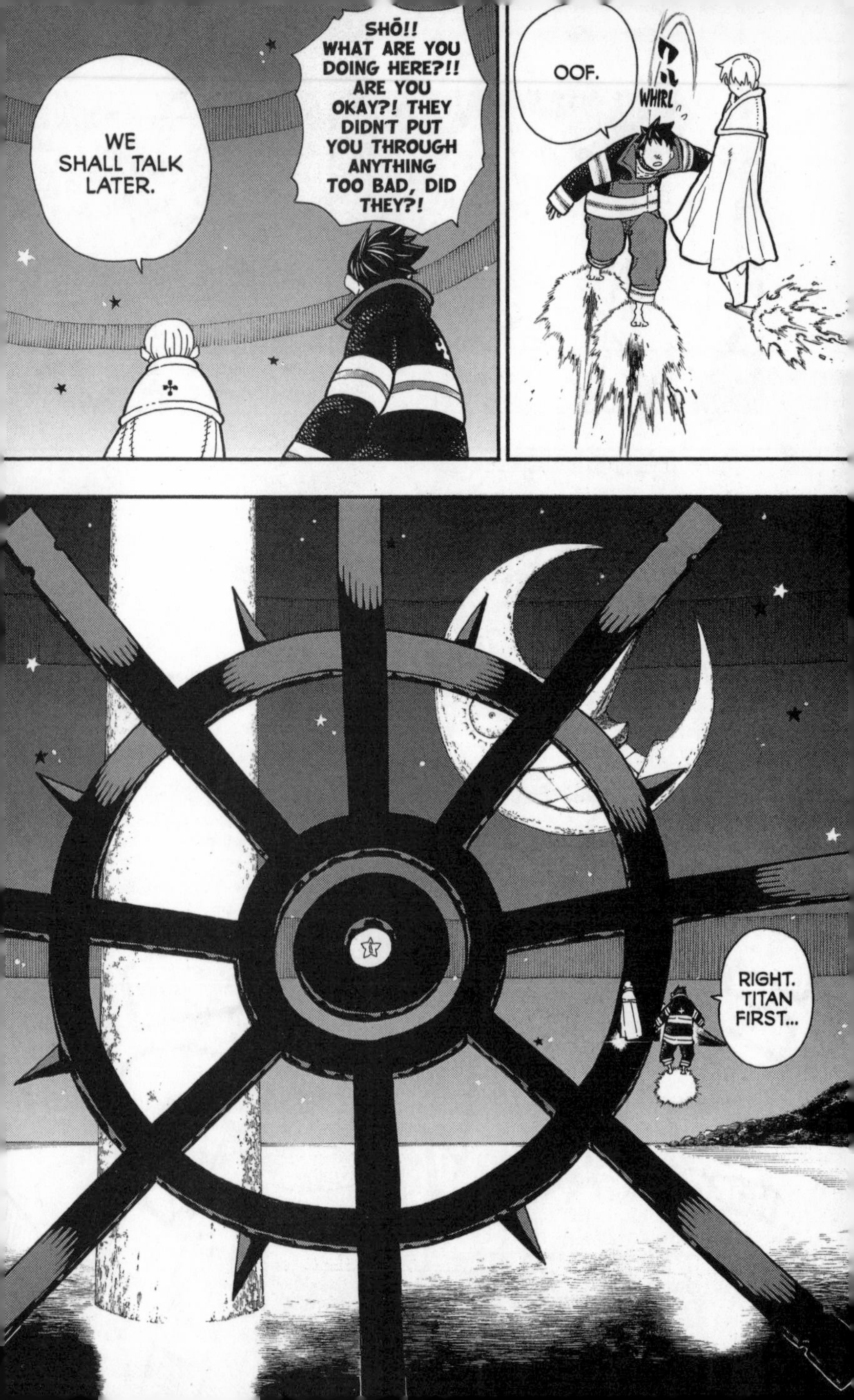
OOF.
WHIRL
SHŌ!! WHAT ARE YOU DOING HERE?!! ARE YOU OKAY?! THEY DIDN'T PUT YOU THROUGH ANYTHING TOO BAD, DID THEY?!
WE SHALL TALK LATER.
RIGHT. TITAN FIRST...

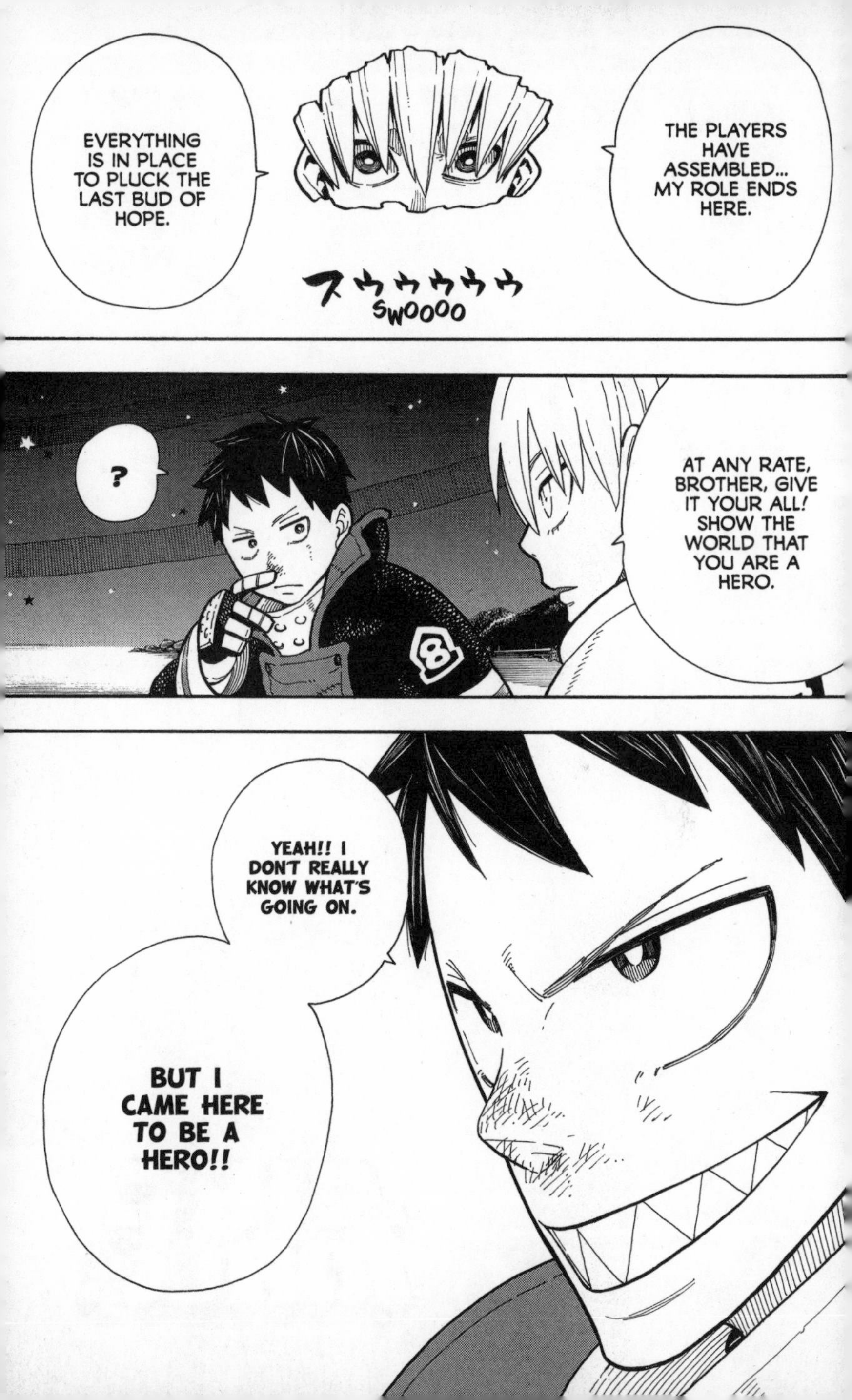
THE PLAYERS HAVE ASSEMBLED... MY ROLE ENDS HERE.
EVERYTHING IS IN PLACE TO PLUCK THE LAST BUD OF HOPE.
スウウウウウ
SWOOOO
AT ANY RATE, BROTHER, GIVE IT YOUR ALL! SHOW THE WORLD THAT YOU ARE A HERO.
?
YEAH!! I DON'T REALLY KNOW WHAT'S GOING ON.
BUT I CAME HERE TO BE A HERO!!

FIRE FORCE

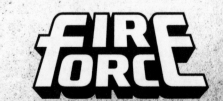

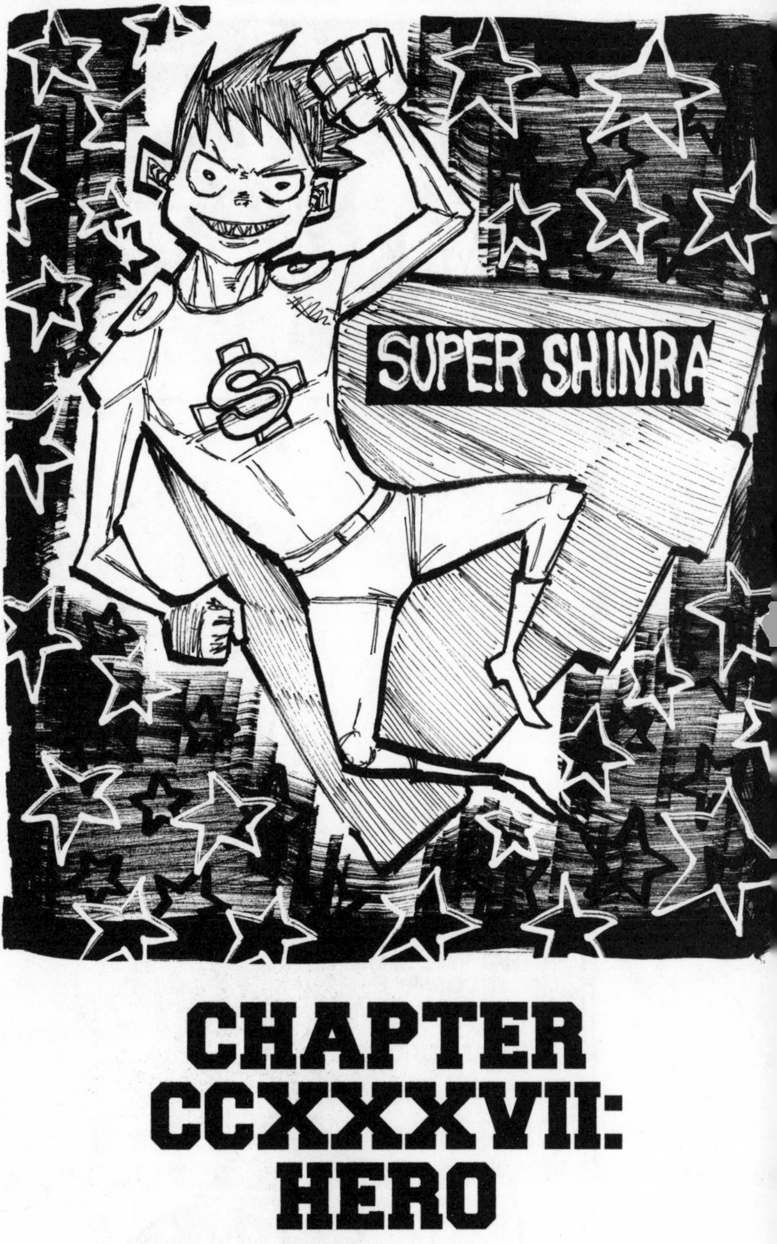
SUPER SHINRA

CHAPTER CCXXXVII: HERO

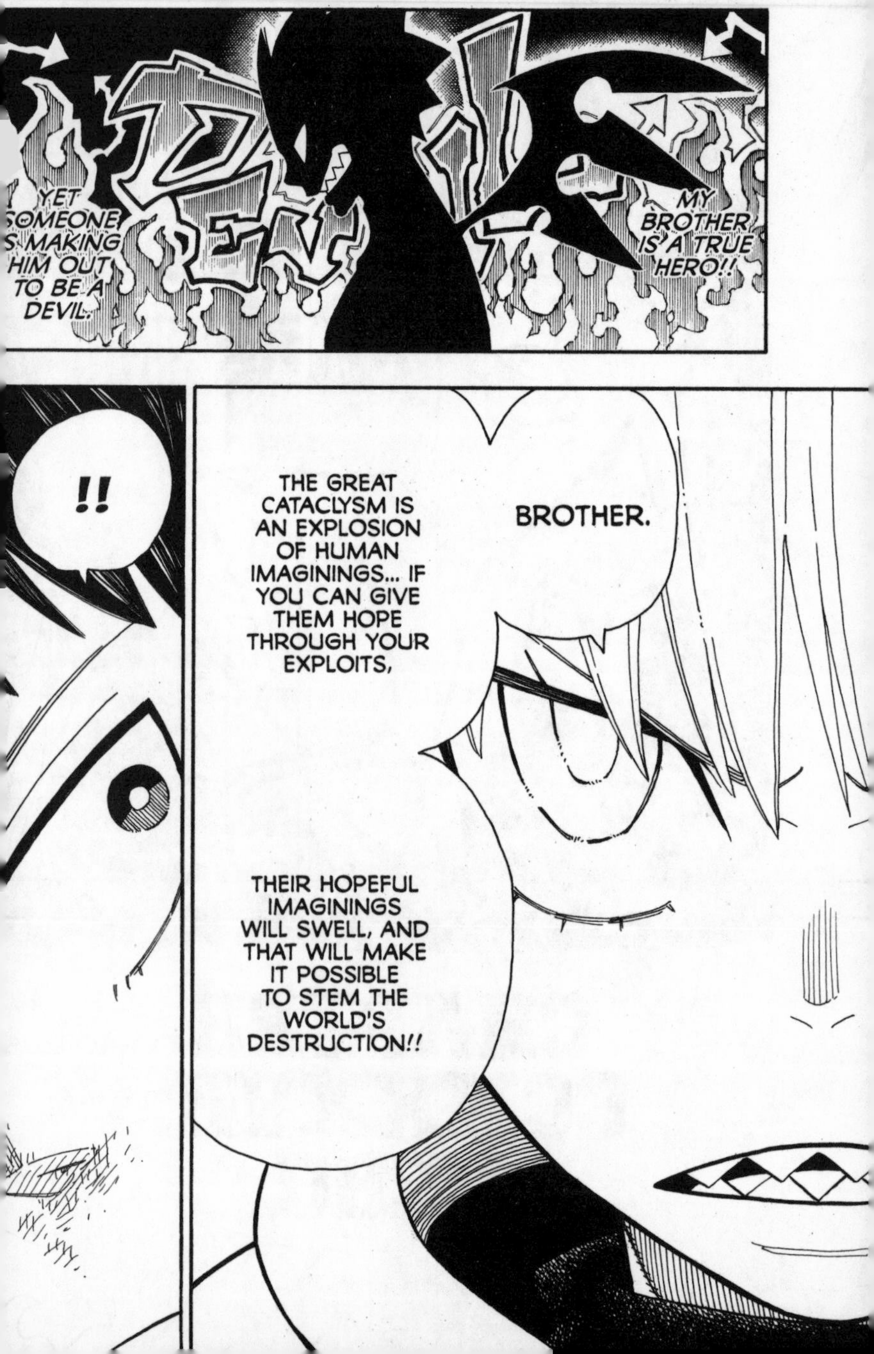
MY BROTHER IS A TRUE HERO!!
YET SOMEONE S MAKING HIM OUT TO BE A DEVIL.
BROTHER.
THE GREAT CATACLYSM IS AN EXPLOSION OF HUMAN IMAGININGS... IF YOU CAN GIVE THEM HOPE THROUGH YOUR EXPLOITS,
THEIR HOPEFUL IMAGININGS WILL SWELL, AND THAT WILL MAKE IT POSSIBLE TO STEM THE WORLD'S DESTRUCTION!!
!!

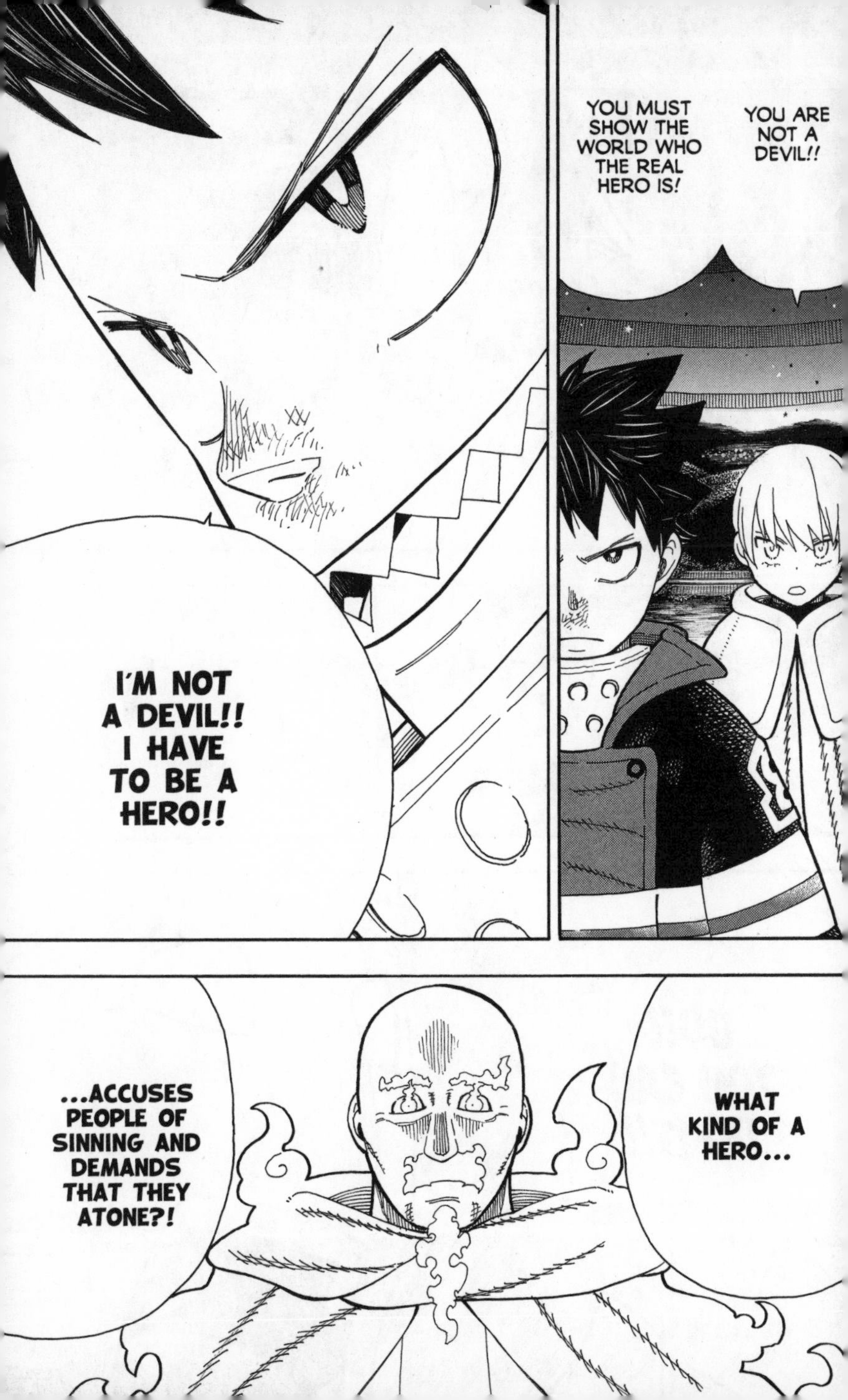
YOU ARE NOT A DEVIL!!
YOU MUST SHOW THE WORLD WHO THE REAL HERO IS!
I'M NOT A DEVIL!! I HAVE TO BE A HERO!!
WHAT KIND OF A HERO...
...ACCUSES PEOPLE OF SINNING AND DEMANDS THAT THEY ATONE?!

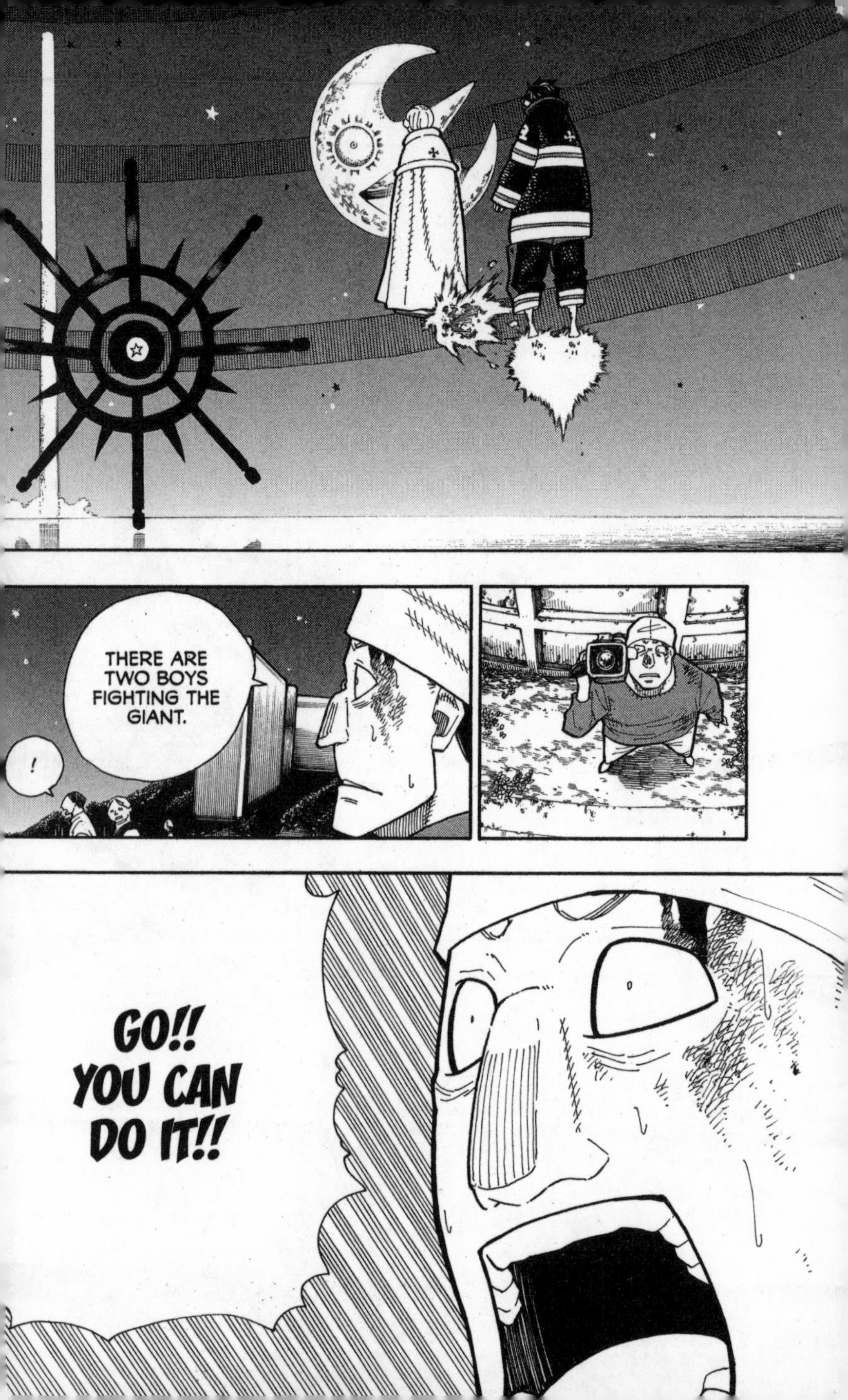
THERE ARE TWO BOYS FIGHTING THE GIANT.
!
GO!! YOU CAN DO IT!!

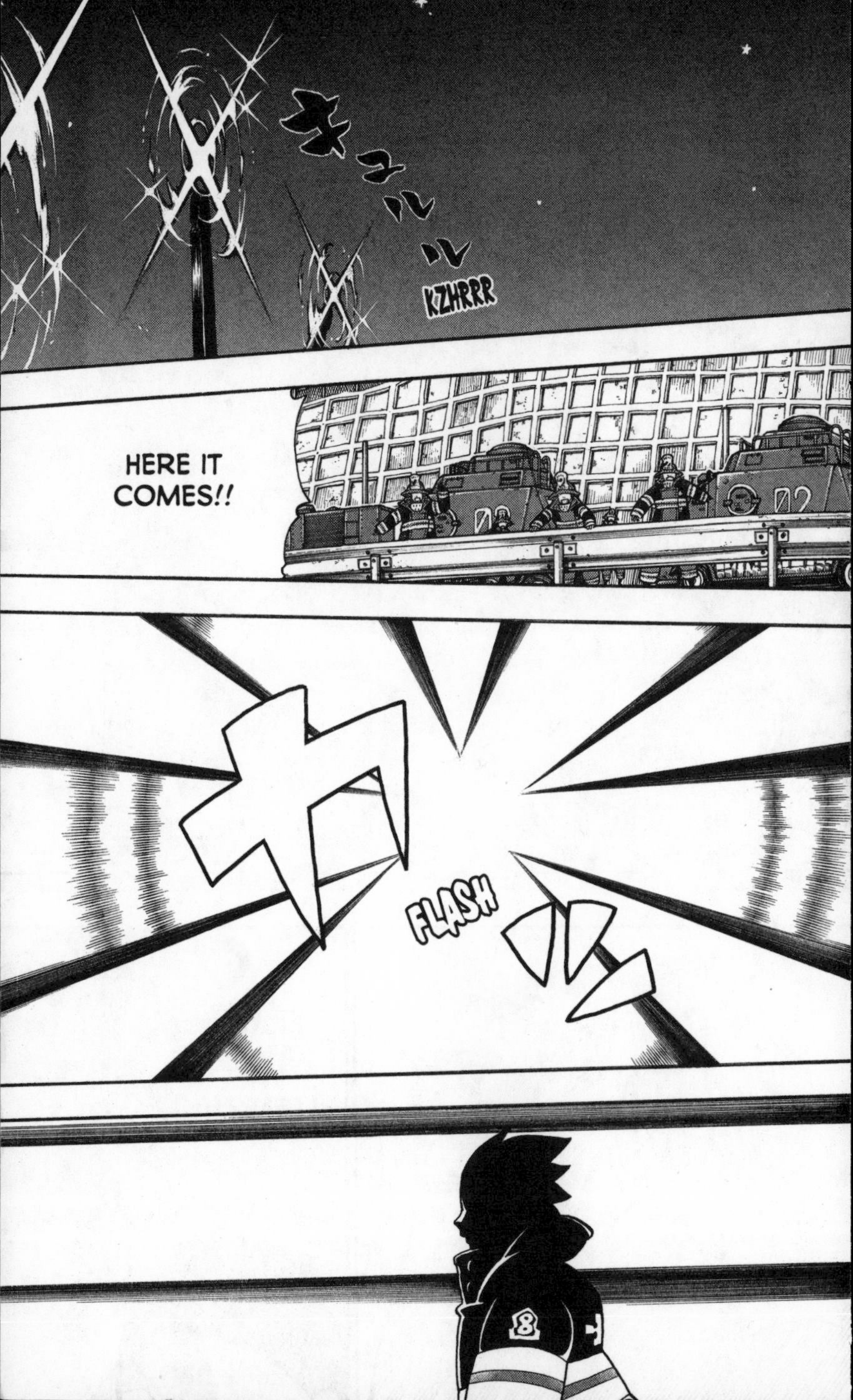
KZHRRR
HERE IT COMES!!
FLASH

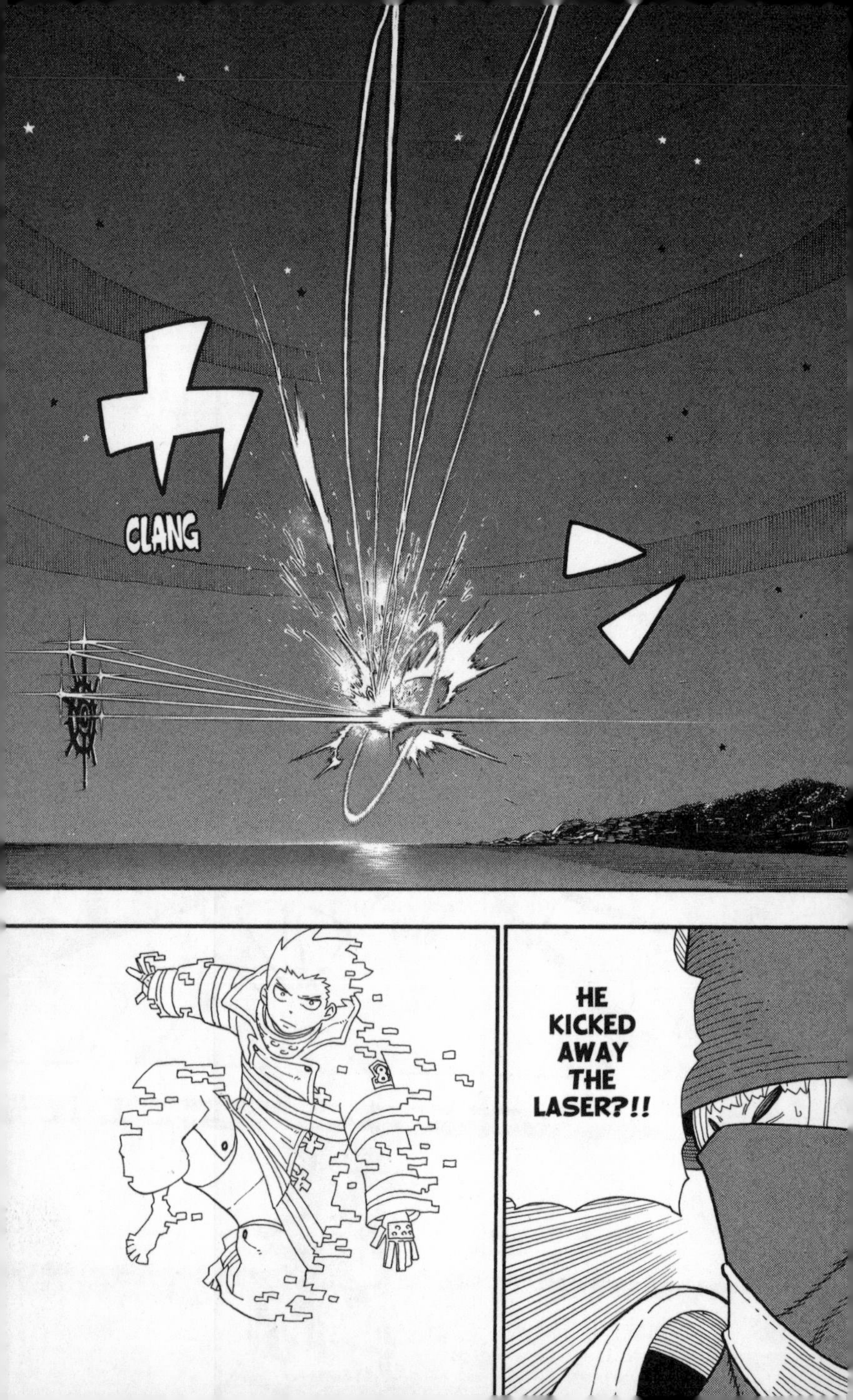
CLANG
HE KICKED AWAY THE LASER?!!

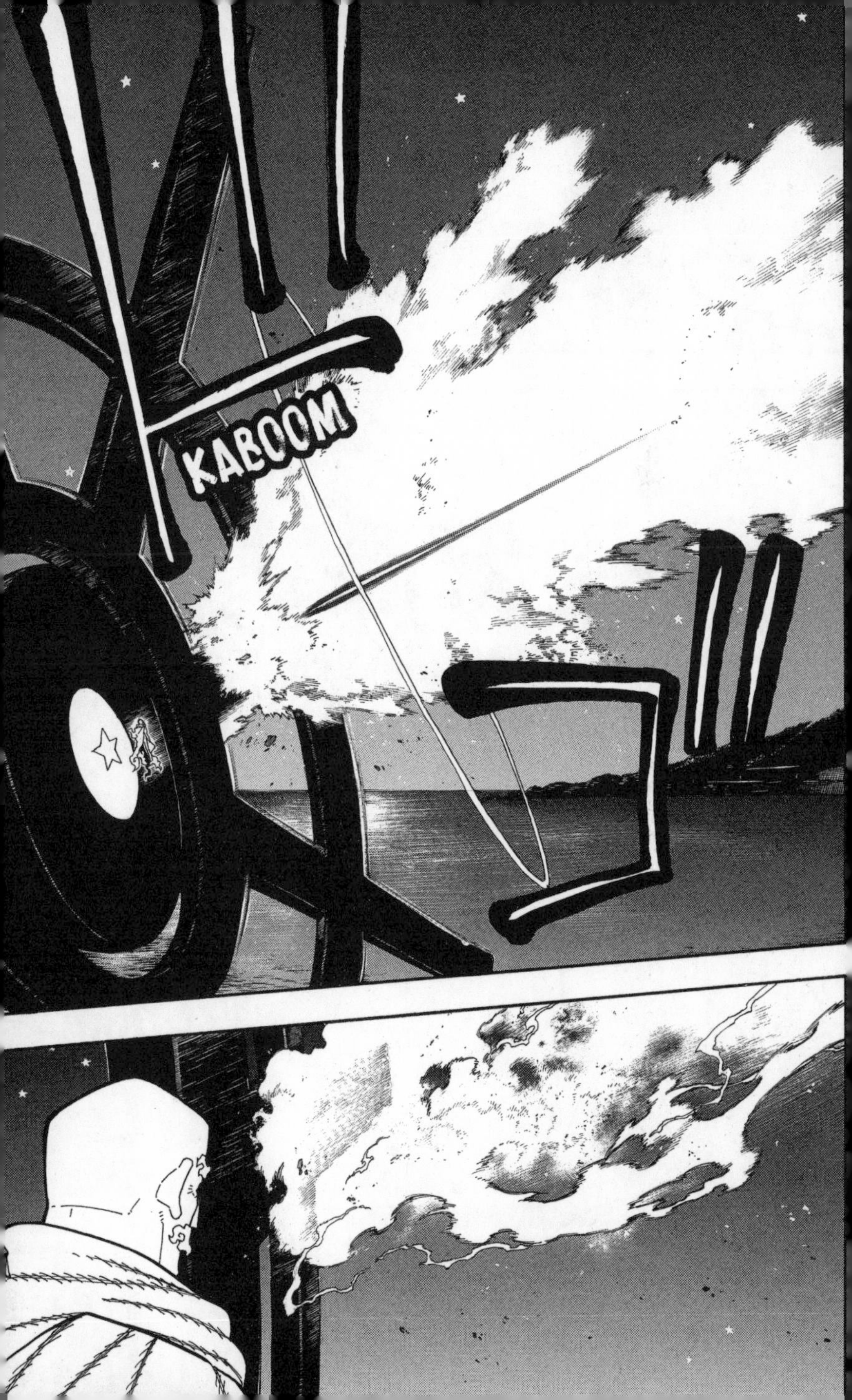
KABOOM

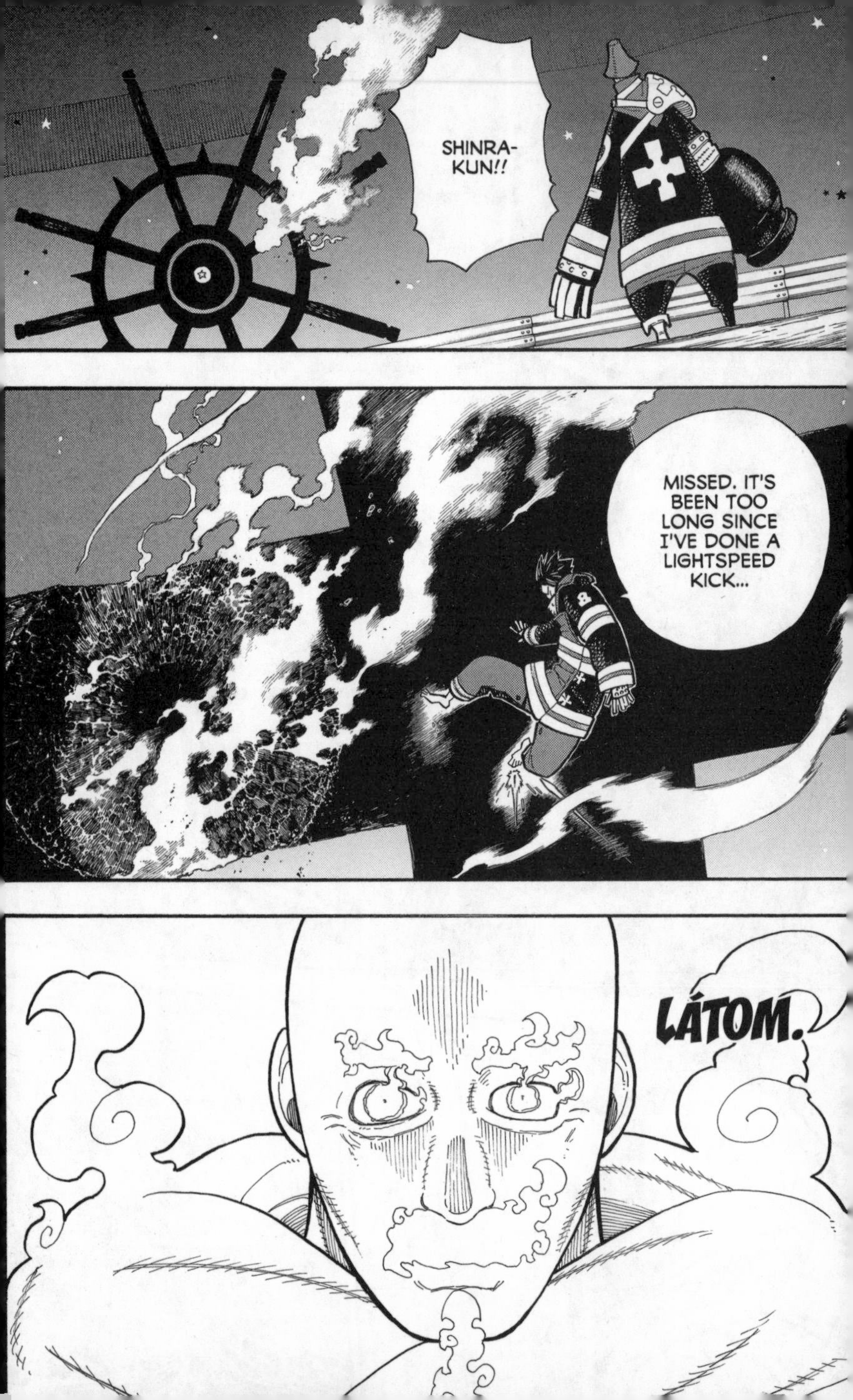
SHINRA-KUN!!
MISSED. IT'S BEEN TOO LONG SINCE I'VE DONE A LIGHTSPEED KICK...
LÁTOM.

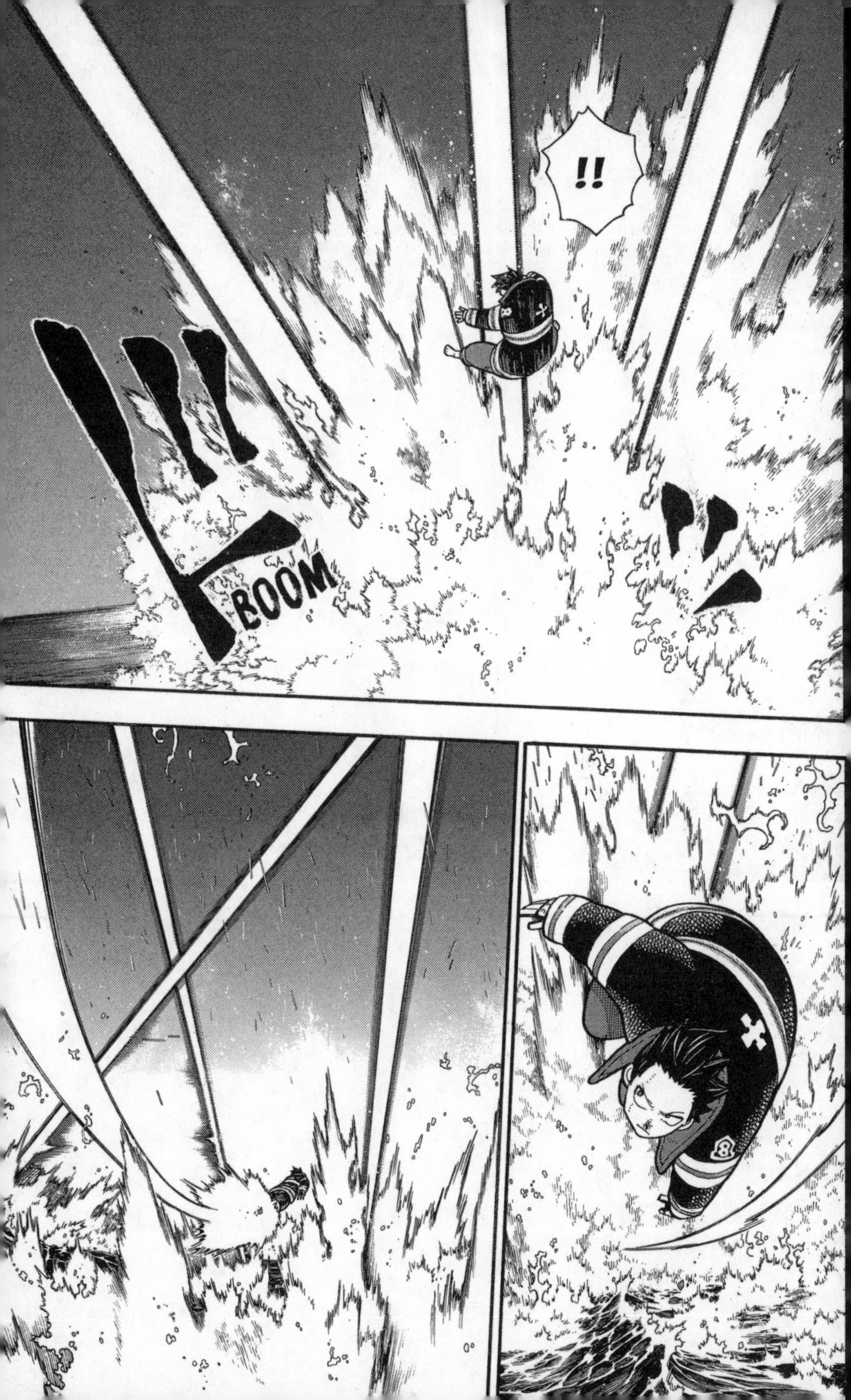
!!
BOOM

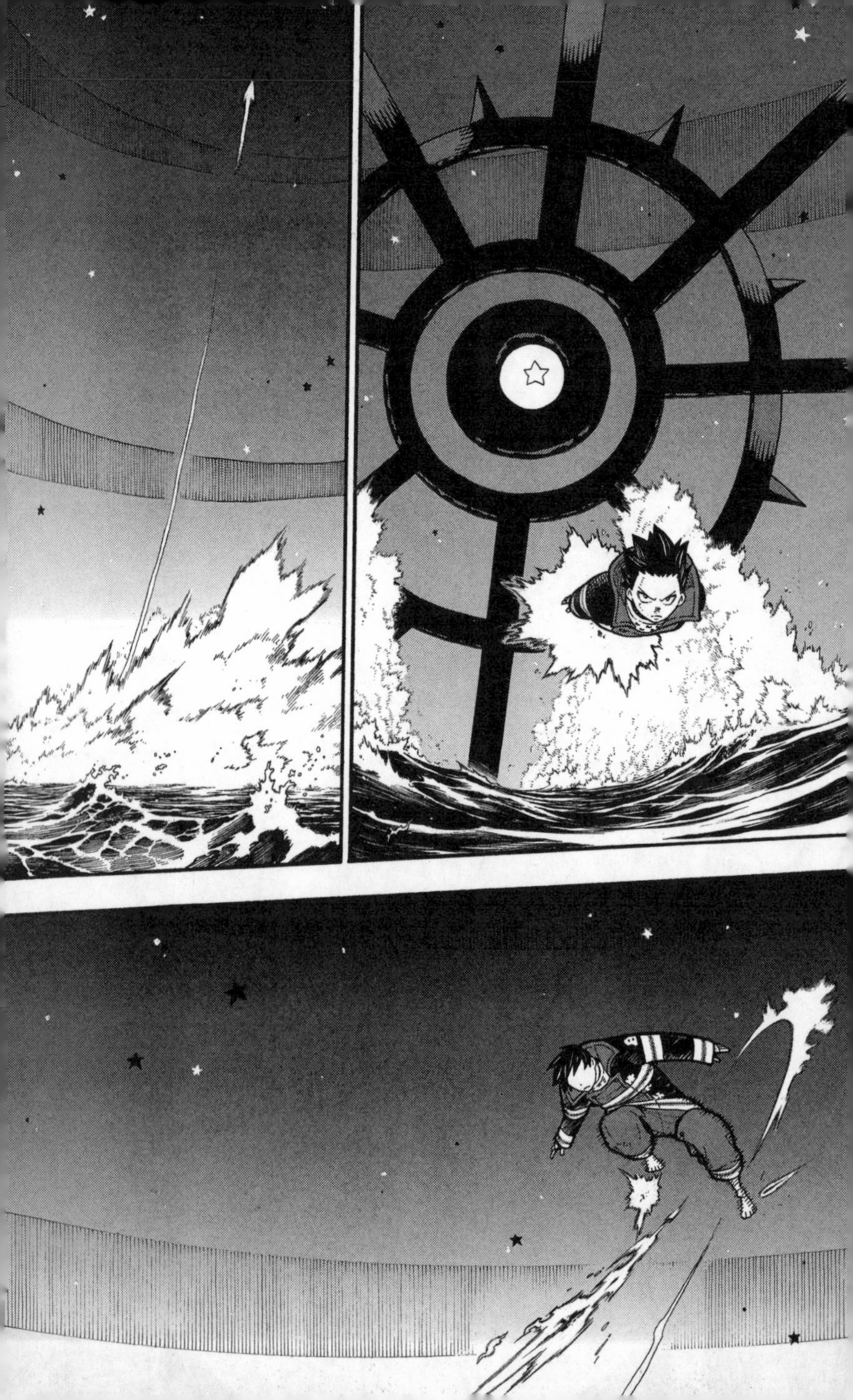

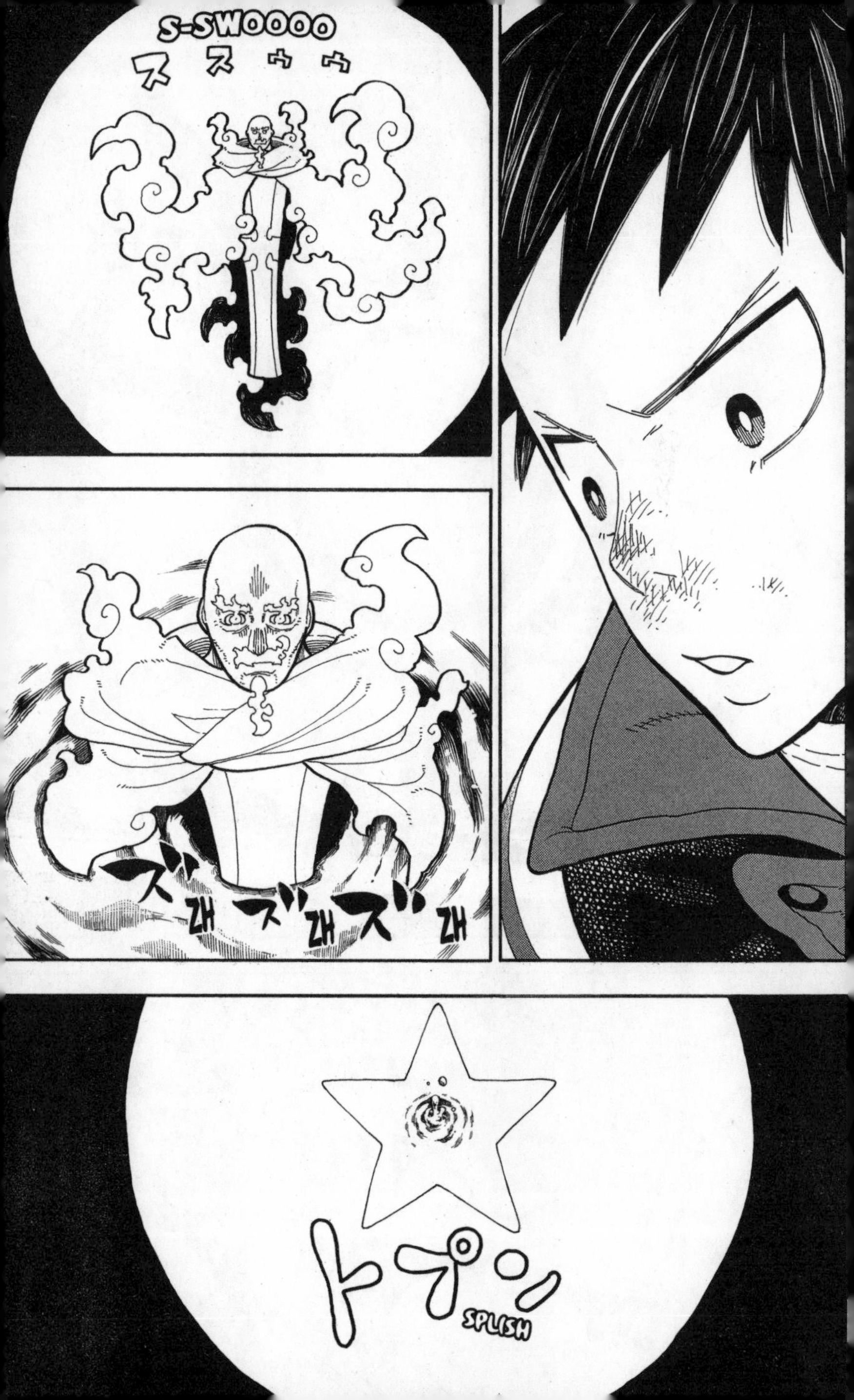
S-SWOOOO
ススウウ
ズ ZH ズ ZH ズ ZH
トプン
SPLISH

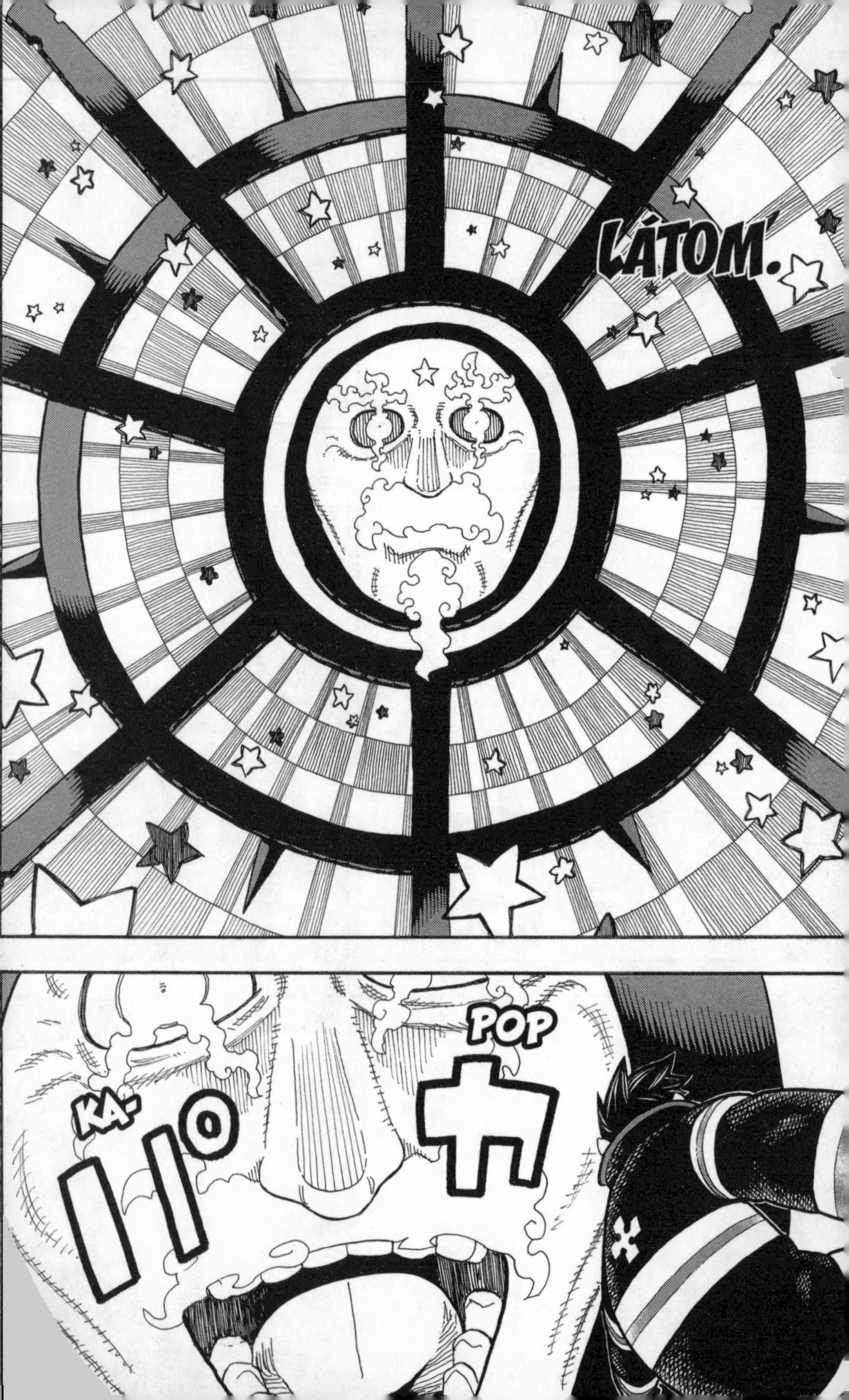
LÁTOM.
POP
KA-

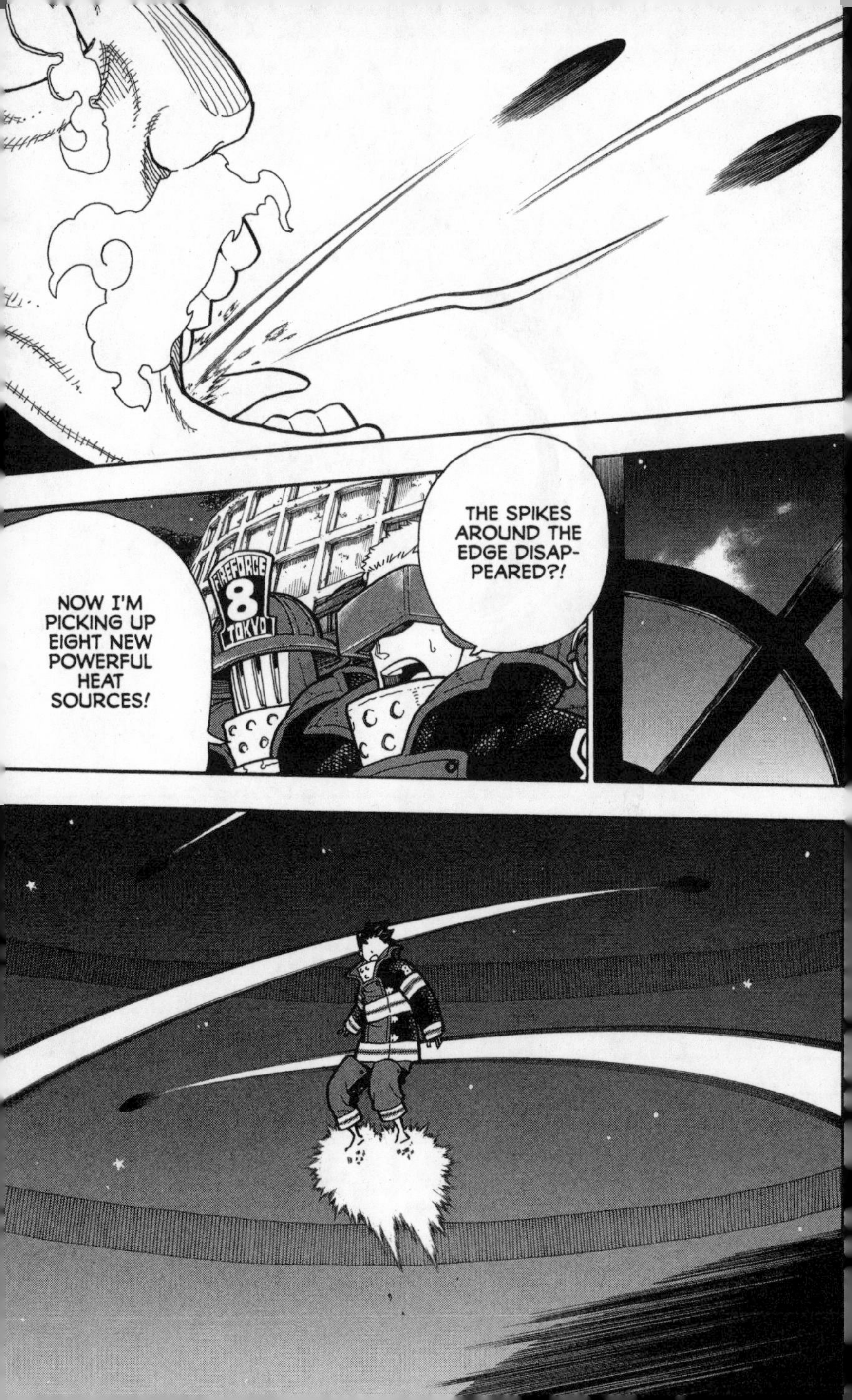
THE SPIKES AROUND THE EDGE DISAP-PEARED?!
FIREFORCE 8 TOKYO
NOW I'M PICKING UP EIGHT NEW POWERFUL HEAT SOURCES!

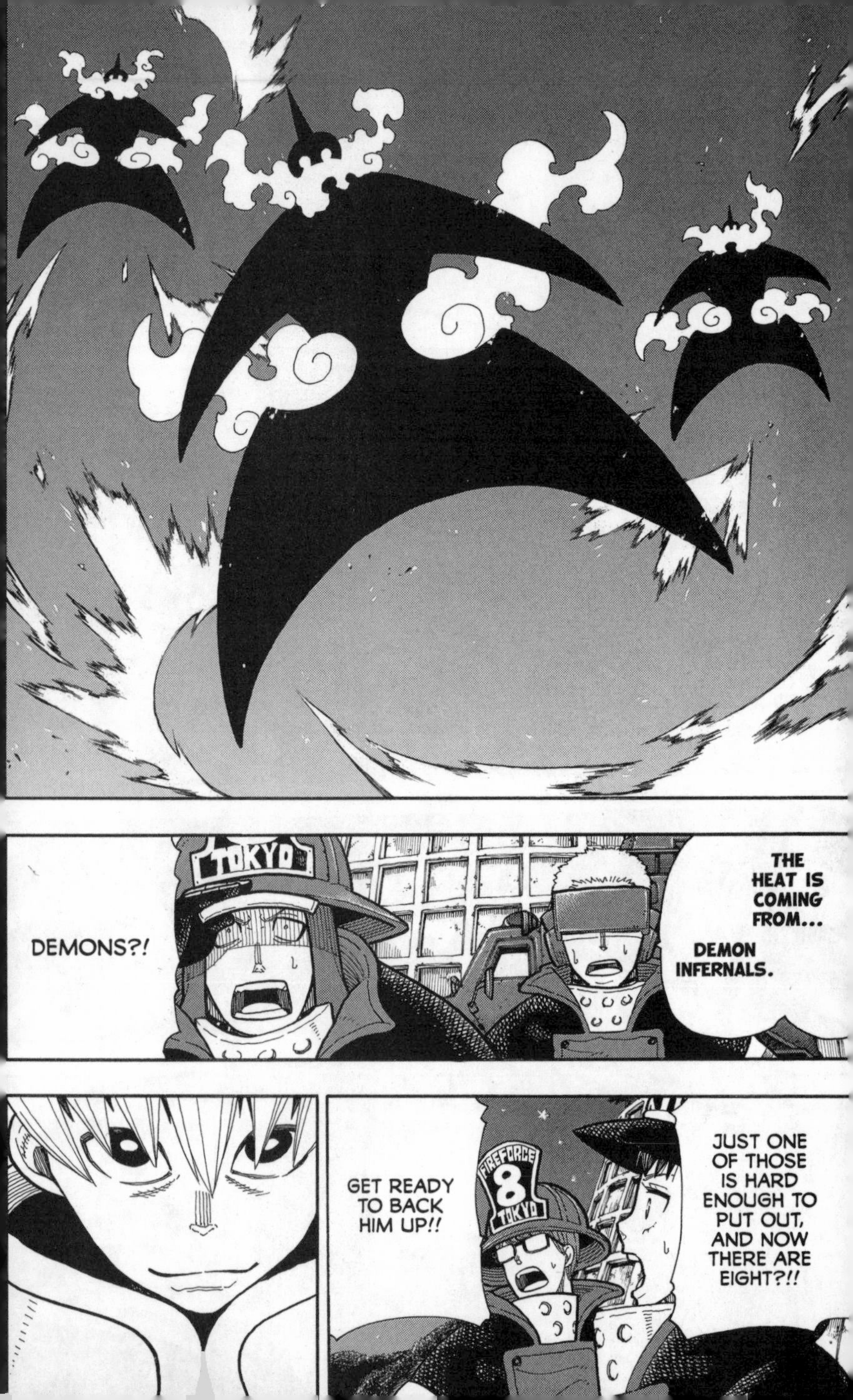
THE HEAT IS COMING FROM...
DEMON INFERNALS.
TOKYO
DEMONS?!
JUST ONE OF THOSE IS HARD ENOUGH TO PUT OUT, AND NOW THERE ARE EIGHT?!!
FIREFORCE 8 TOKYO
GET READY TO BACK HIM UP!!

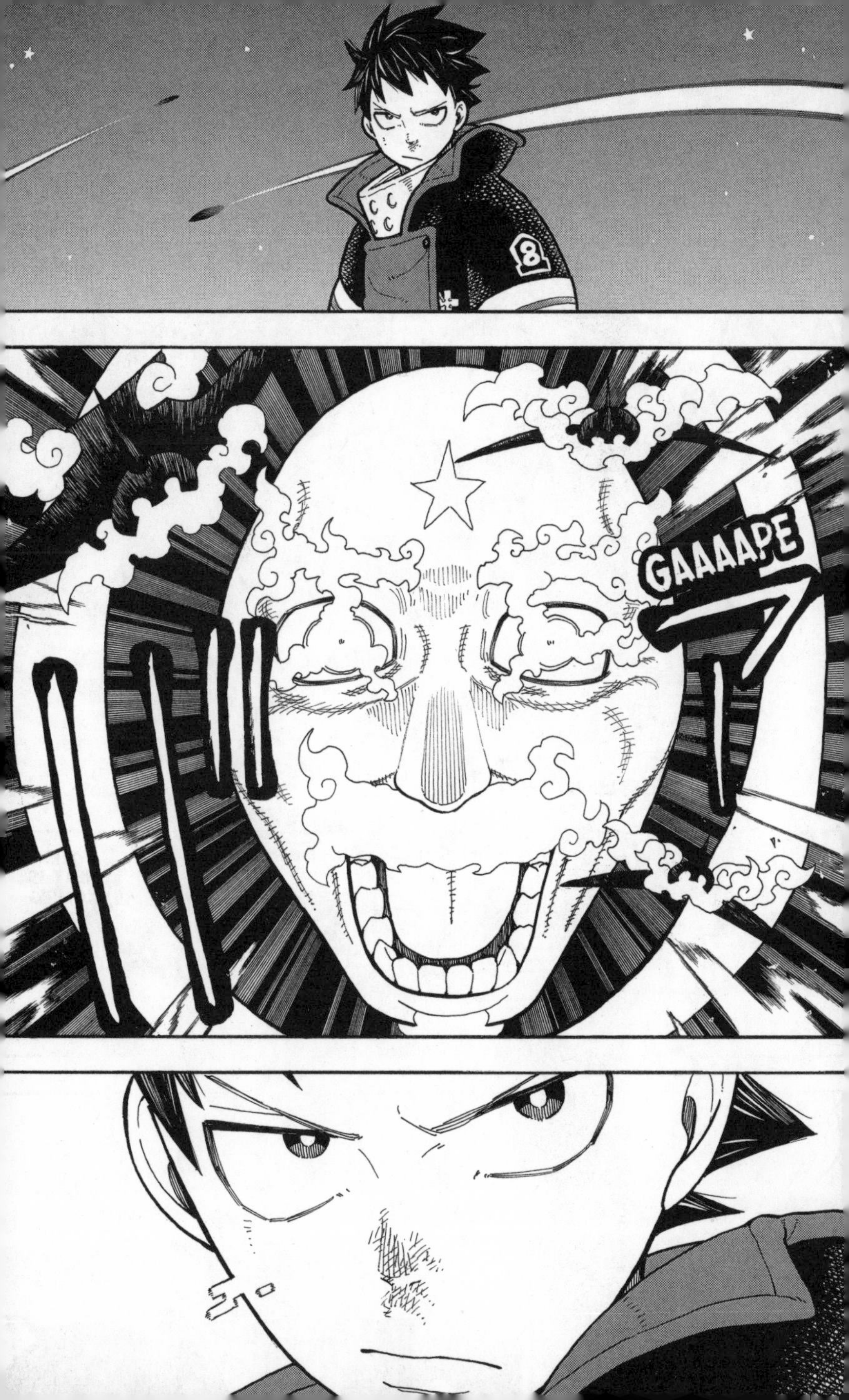
GAAAAPE

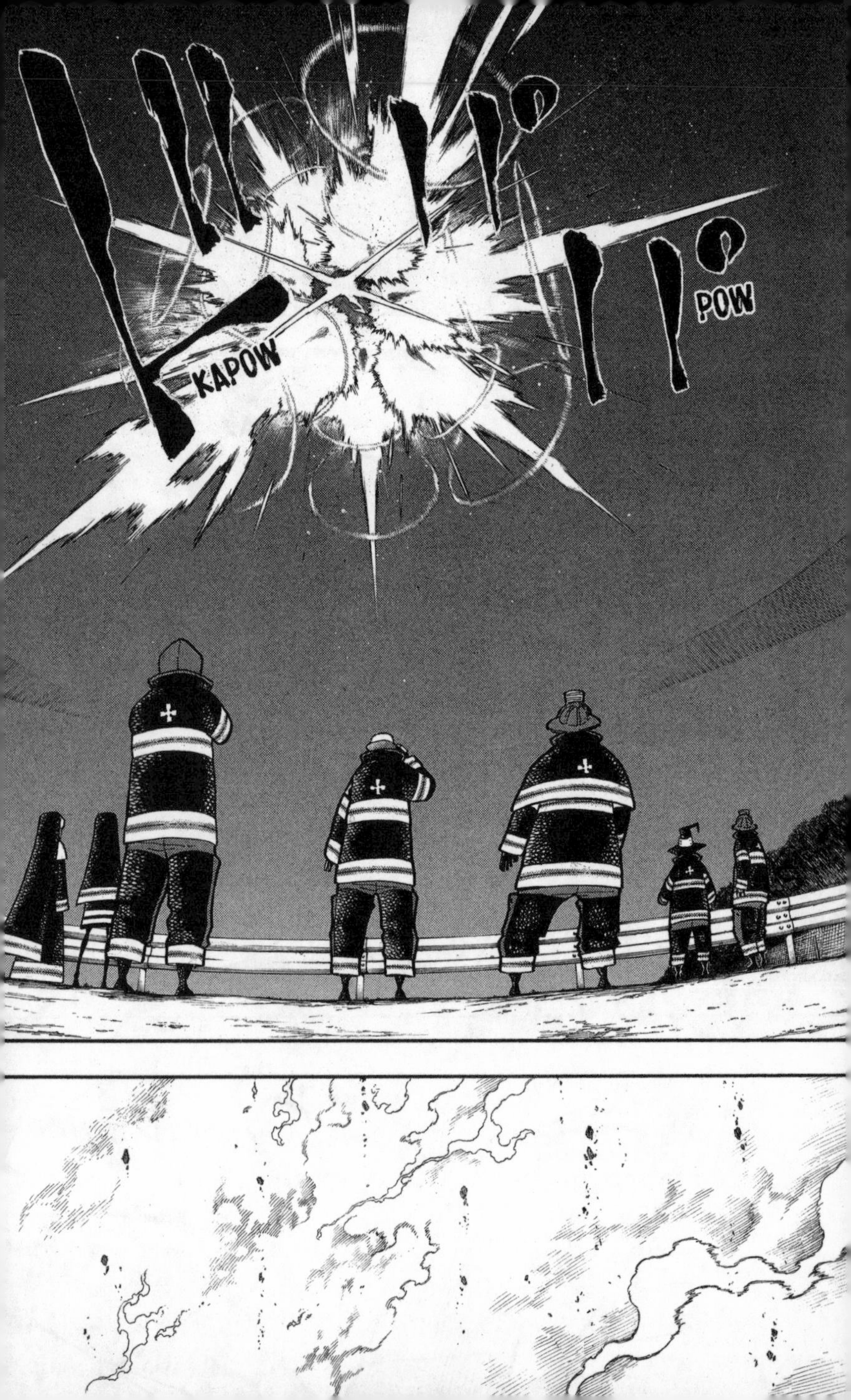
POW
KAPOW

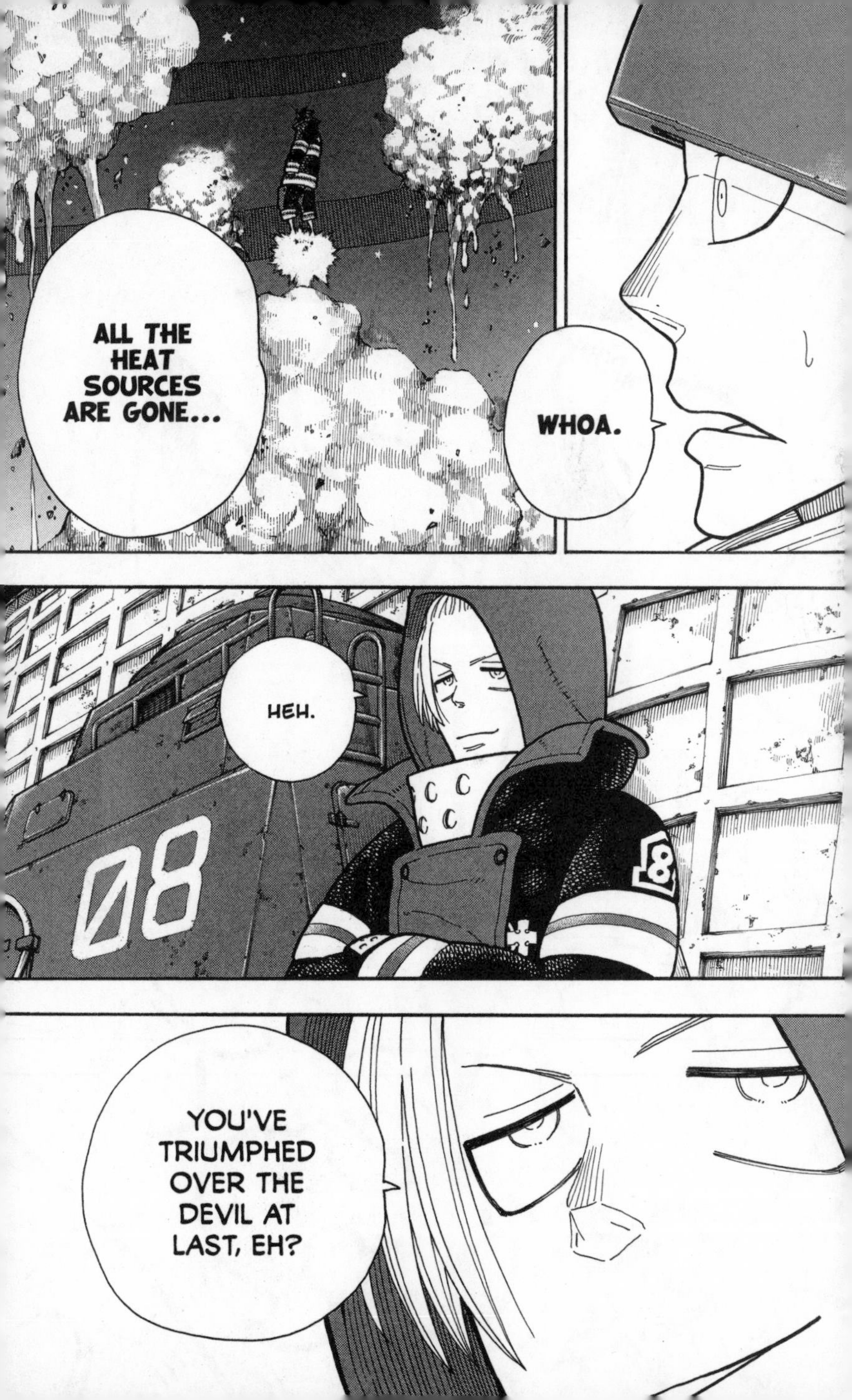
WHOA.
ALL THE HEAT SOURCES ARE GONE...
HEH.
08
YOU'VE TRIUMPHED OVER THE DEVIL AT LAST, EH?

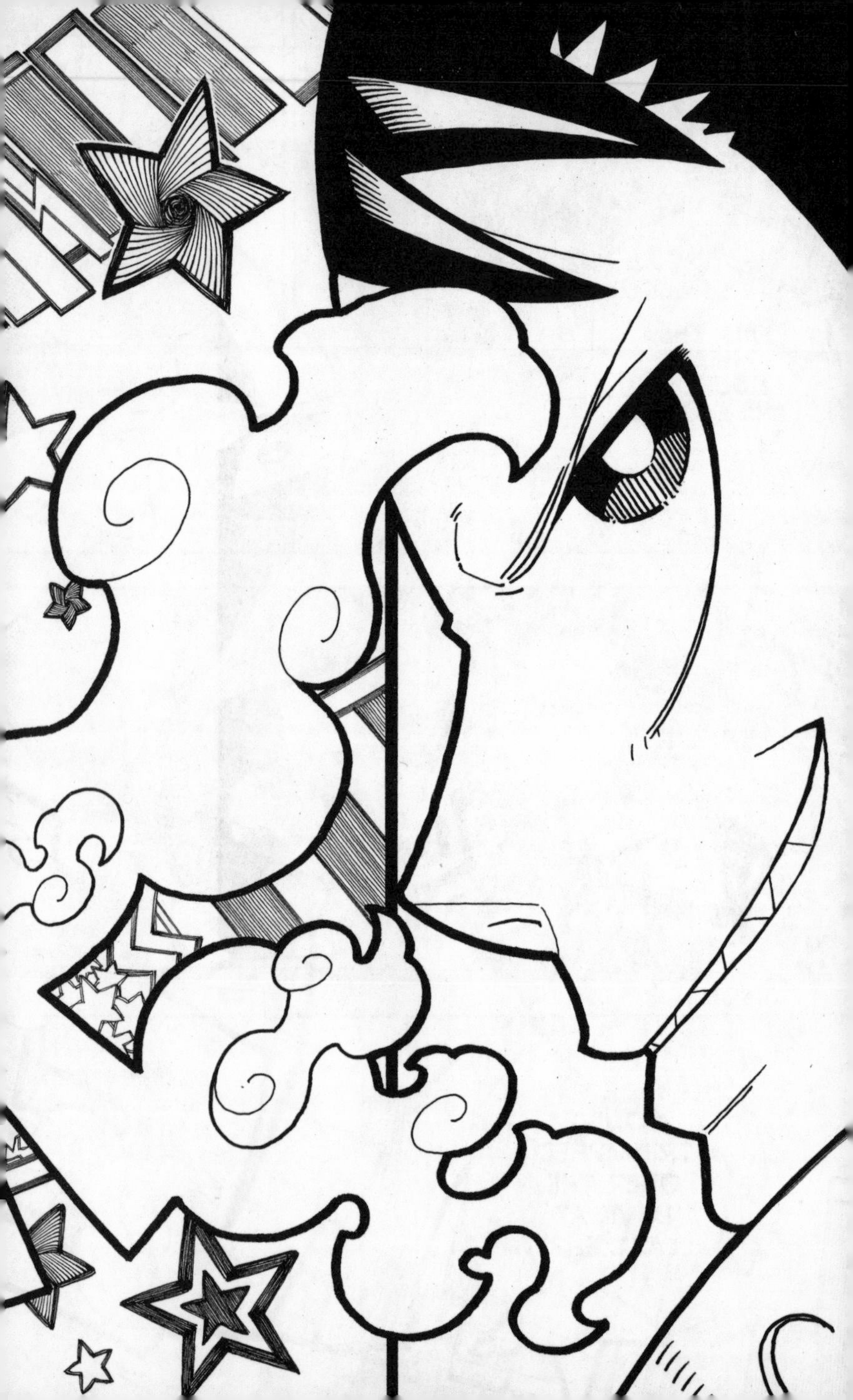

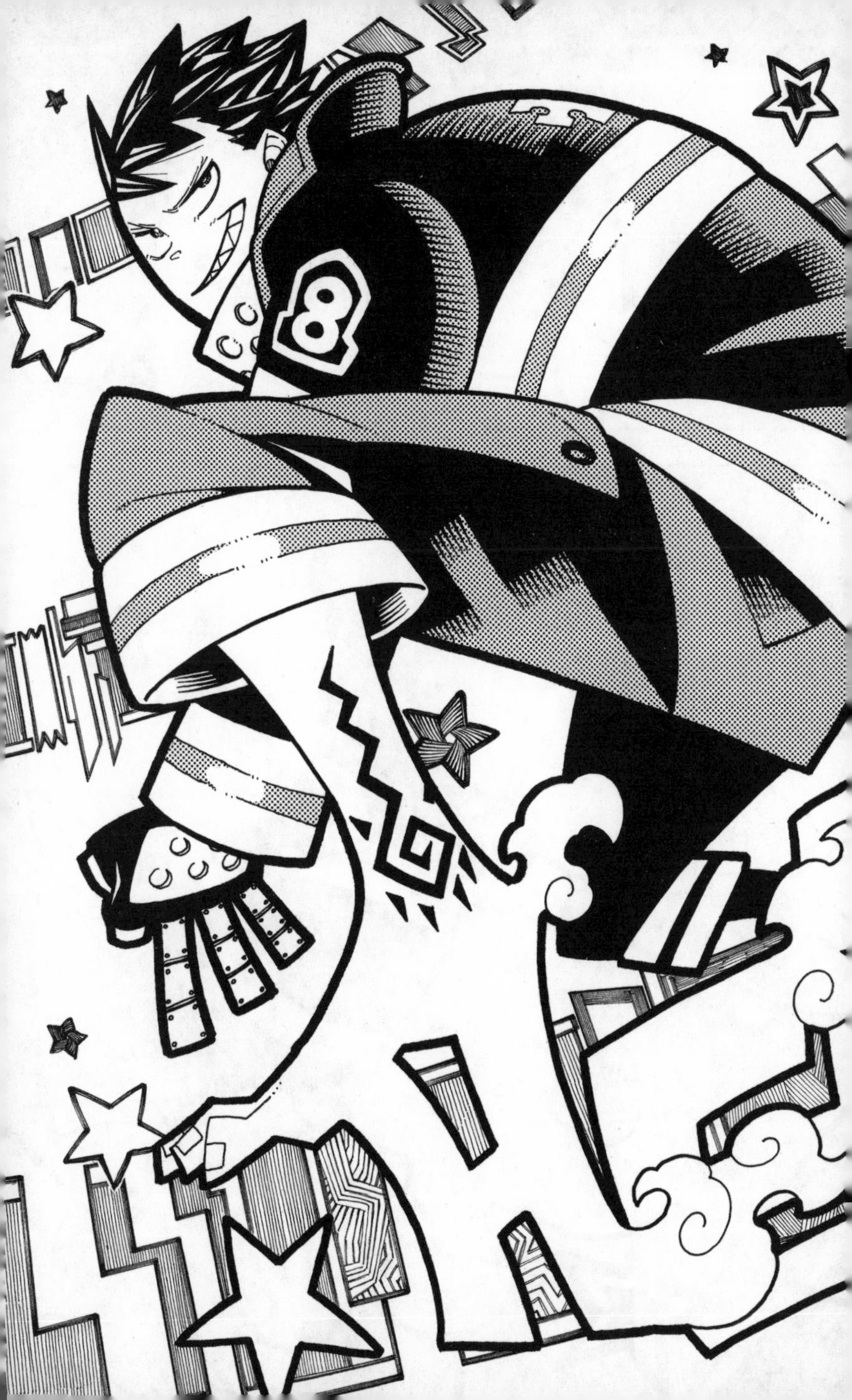

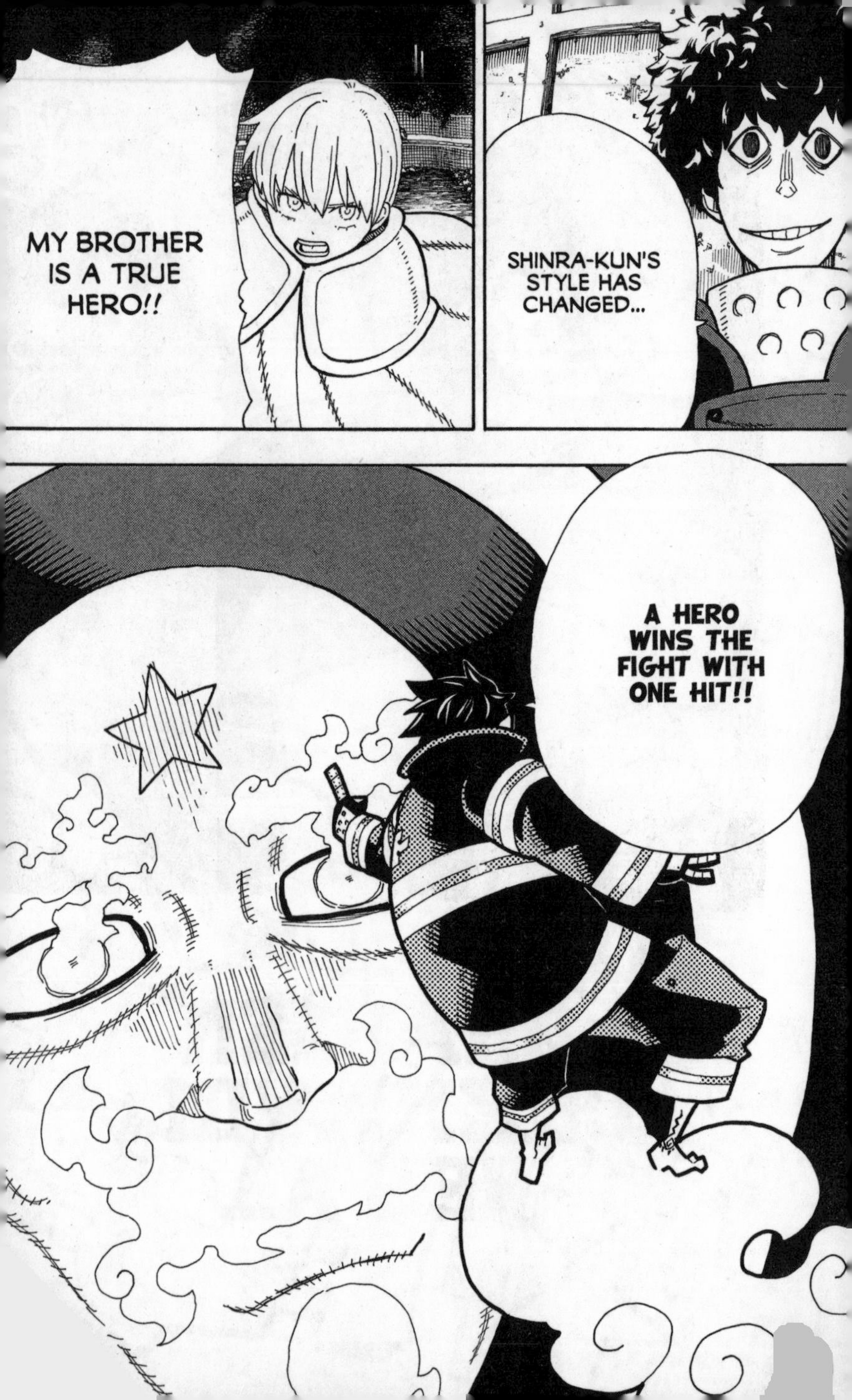
SHINRA-KUN'S STYLE HAS CHANGED...
MY BROTHER IS A TRUE HERO!!
A HERO WINS THE FIGHT WITH ONE HIT!!

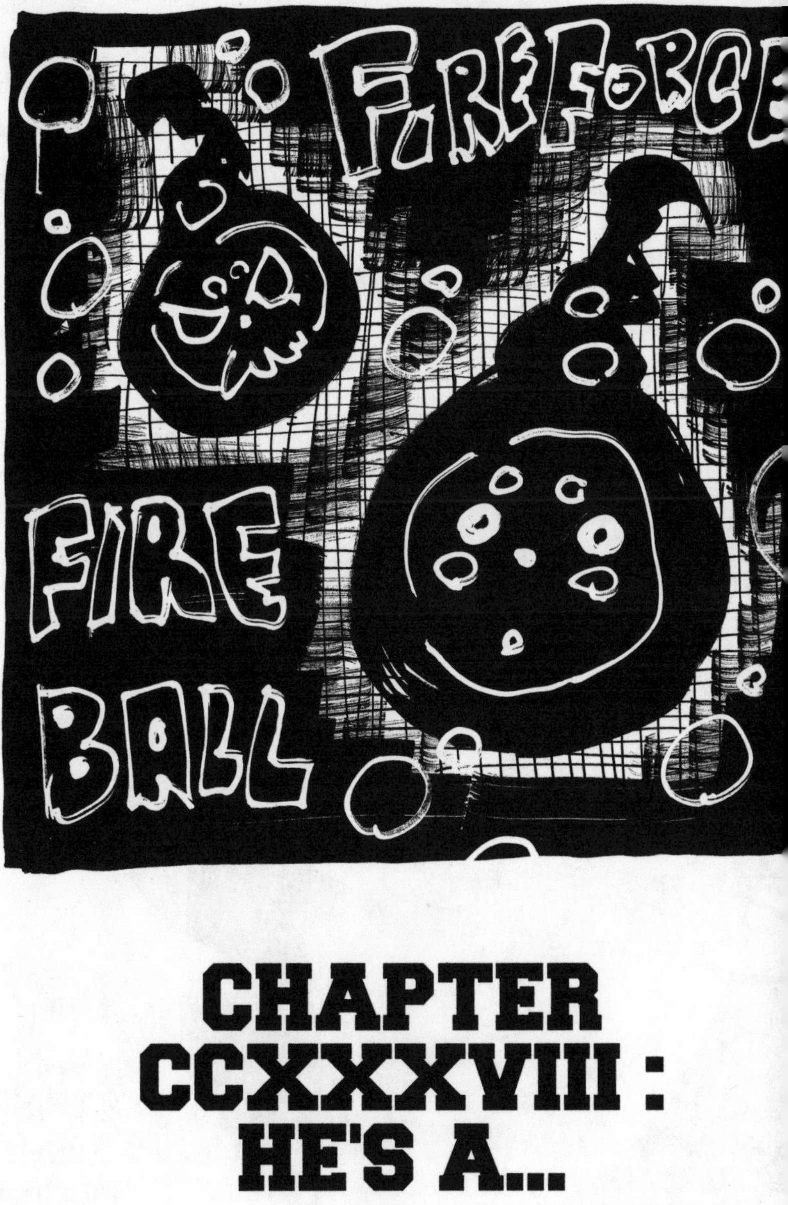
FIRE FORCE
FIRE
BALL

CHAPTER CCXXXVIII: HE'S A...

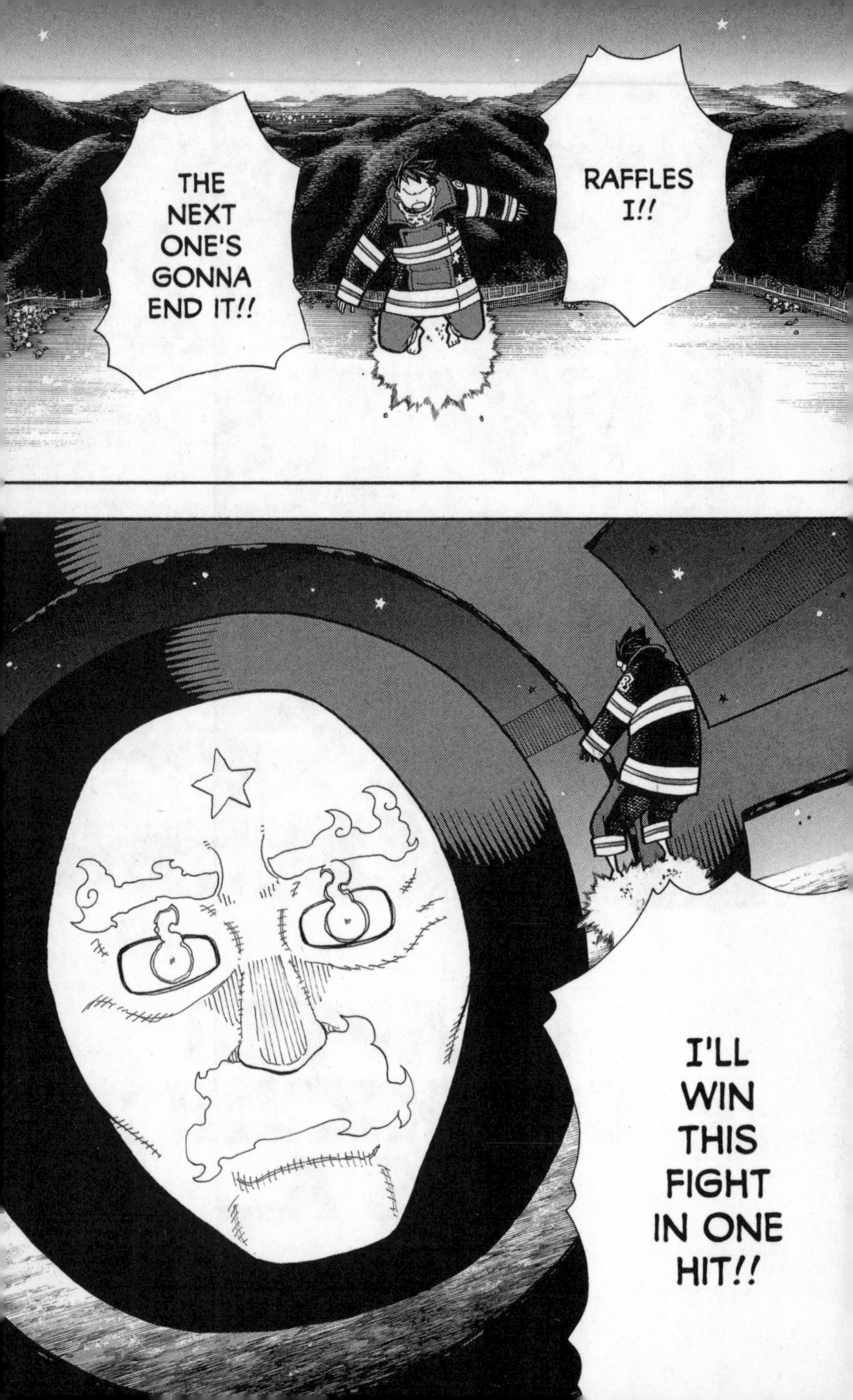
RAFFLES I!!
THE NEXT ONE'S GONNA END IT!!
I'LL WIN THIS FIGHT IN ONE HIT!!

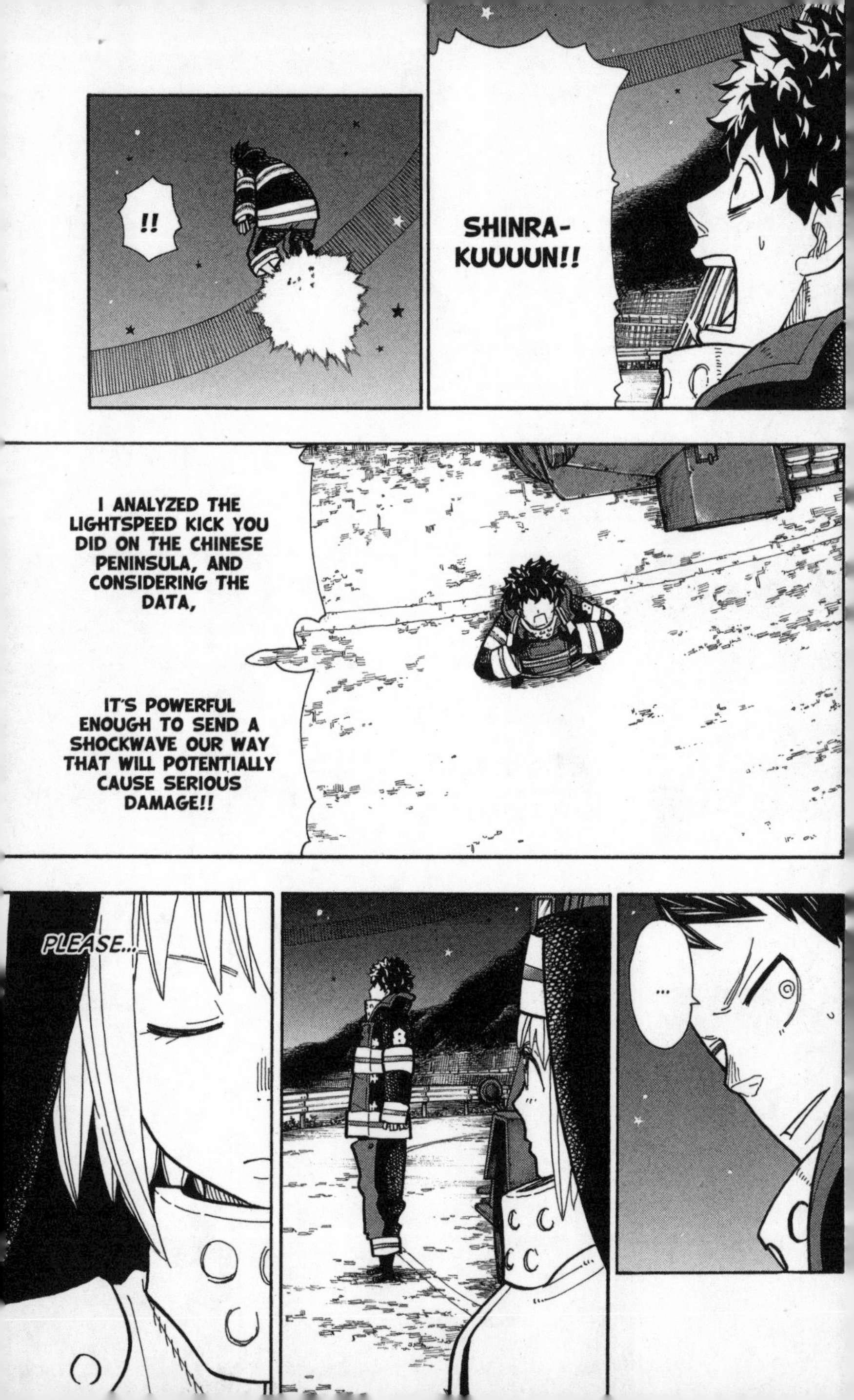
SHINRA-KUUUUN!!
!!
I ANALYZED THE LIGHTSPEED KICK YOU DID ON THE CHINESE PENINSULA, AND CONSIDERING THE DATA,
IT'S POWERFUL ENOUGH TO SEND A SHOCKWAVE OUR WAY THAT WILL POTENTIALLY CAUSE SERIOUS DAMAGE!!
...
PLEASE...

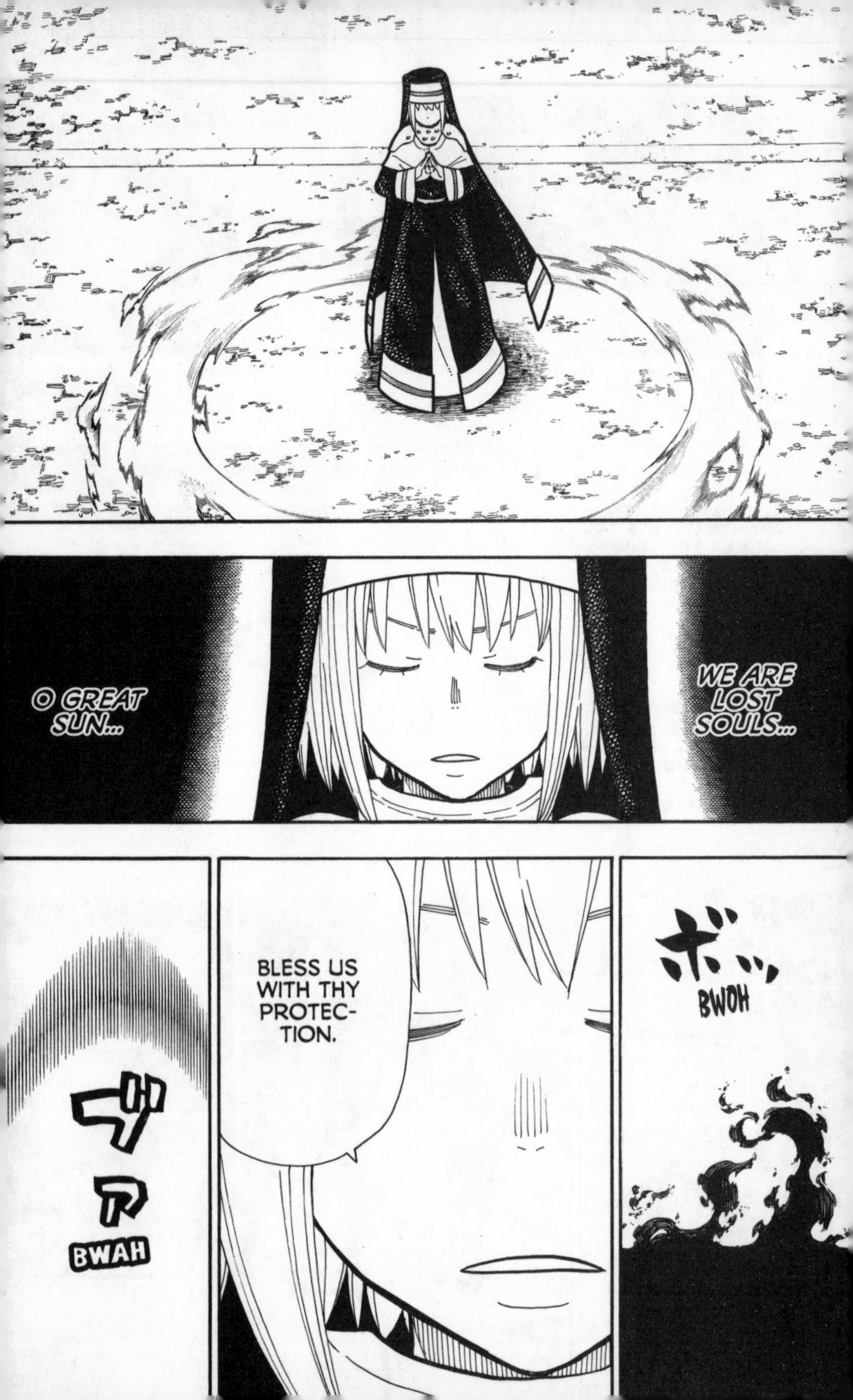
WE ARE LOST SOULS...
O GREAT SUN...
ボッ
BWOH
BLESS US WITH THY PROTECTION.
ブワァ
BWAH

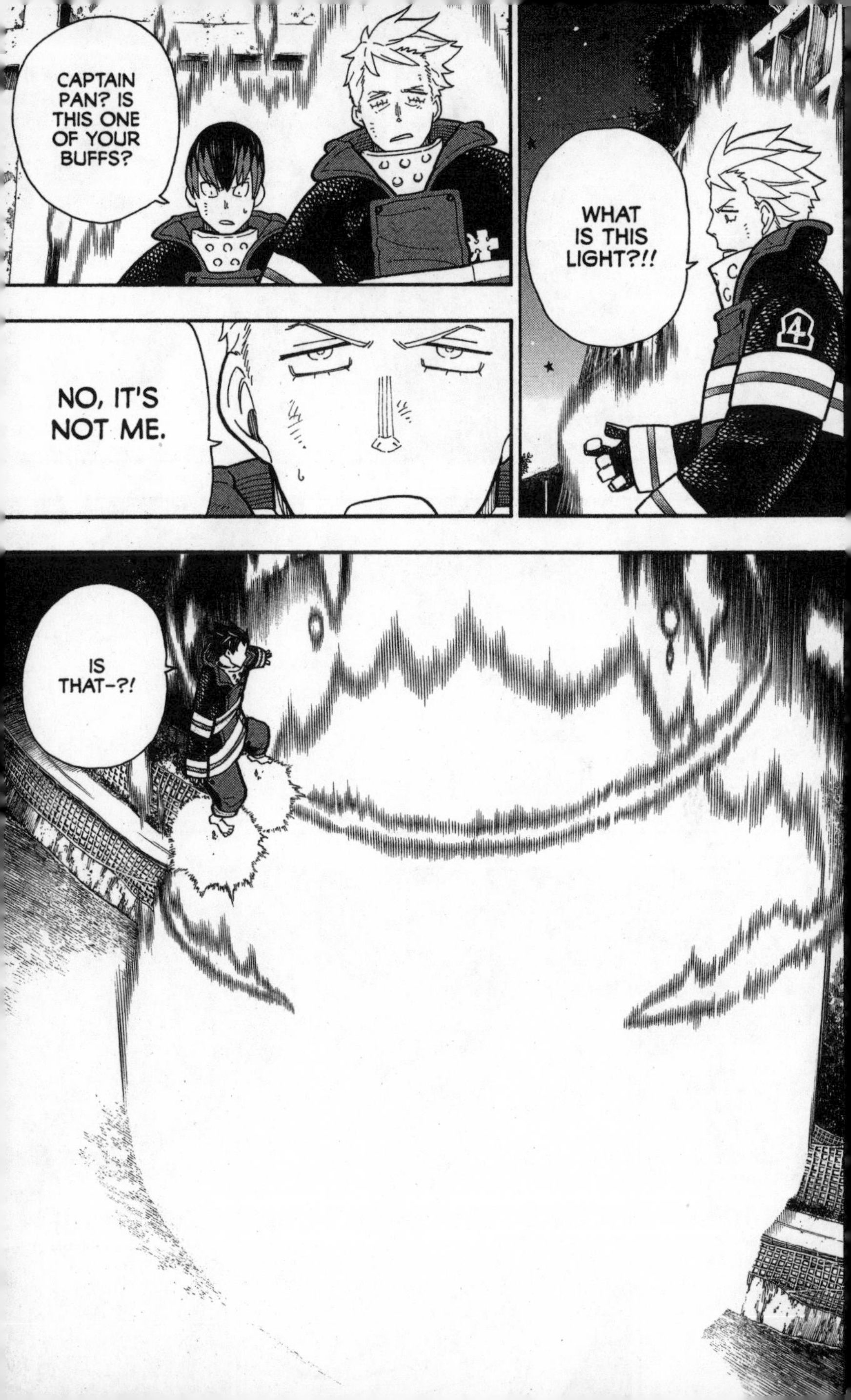
WHAT IS THIS LIGHT?!!
CAPTAIN PAN? IS THIS ONE OF YOUR BUFFS?
NO, IT'S NOT ME.
IS THAT-?!

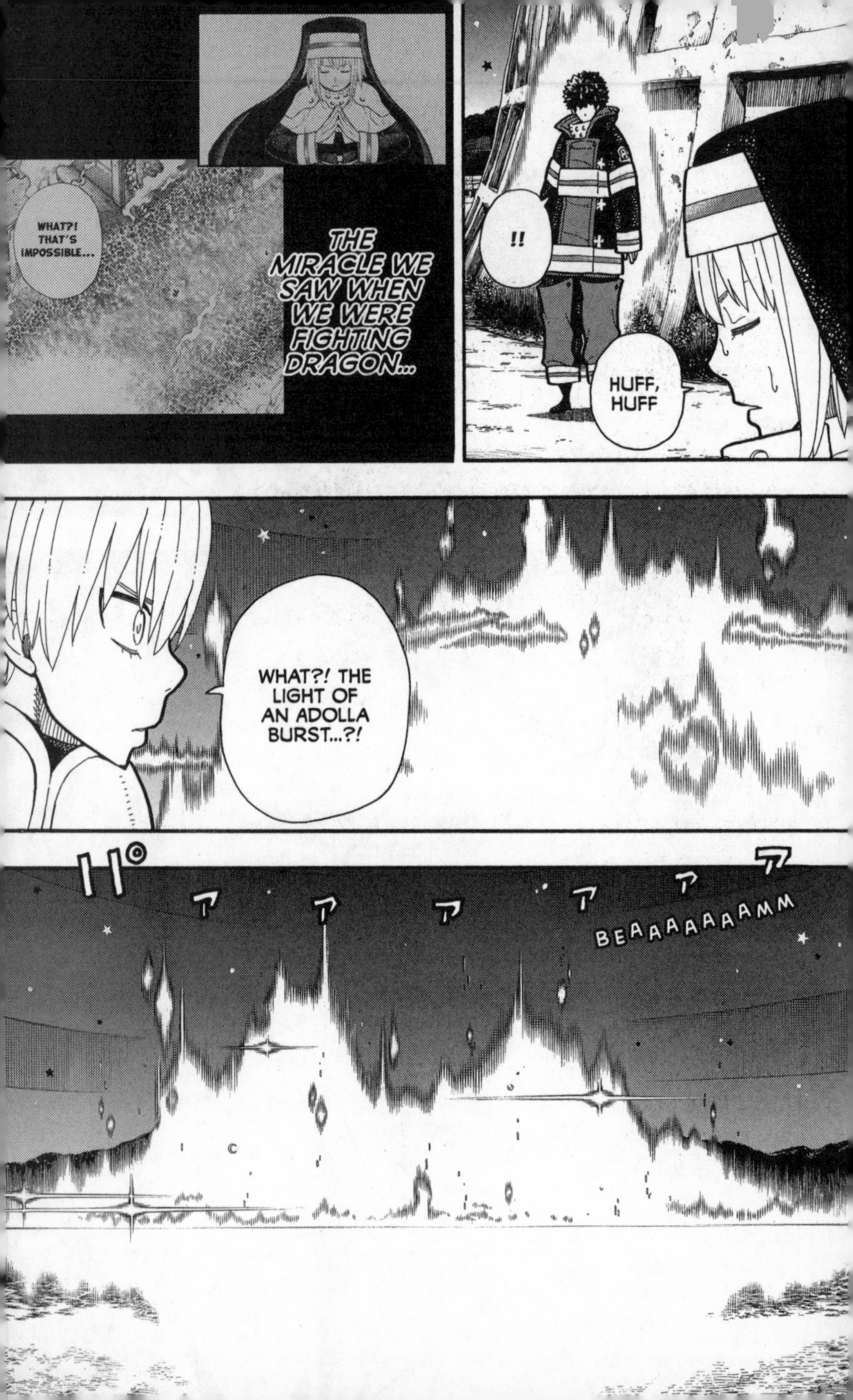
HUFF, HUFF
!!
THE MIRACLE WE SAW WHEN WE WERE FIGHTING DRAGON...
WHAT?! THAT'S IMPOSSIBLE...
WHAT?! THE LIGHT OF AN ADOLLA BURST...?!
パアアアアアア
BEAAAAAAAAMM

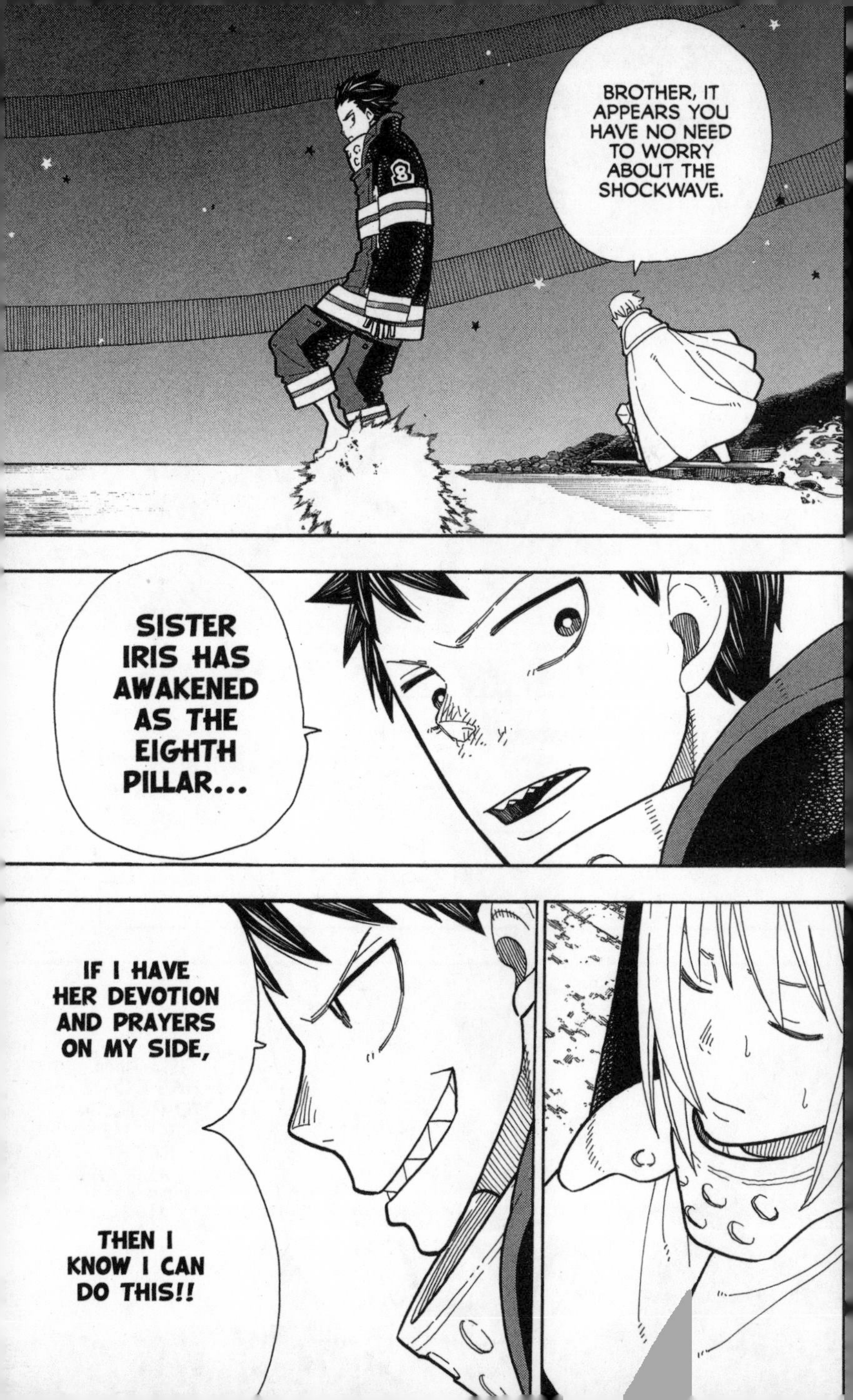
BROTHER, IT APPEARS YOU HAVE NO NEED TO WORRY ABOUT THE SHOCKWAVE.
SISTER IRIS HAS AWAKENED AS THE EIGHTH PILLAR...
IF I HAVE HER DEVOTION AND PRAYERS ON MY SIDE,
THEN I KNOW I CAN DO THIS!!

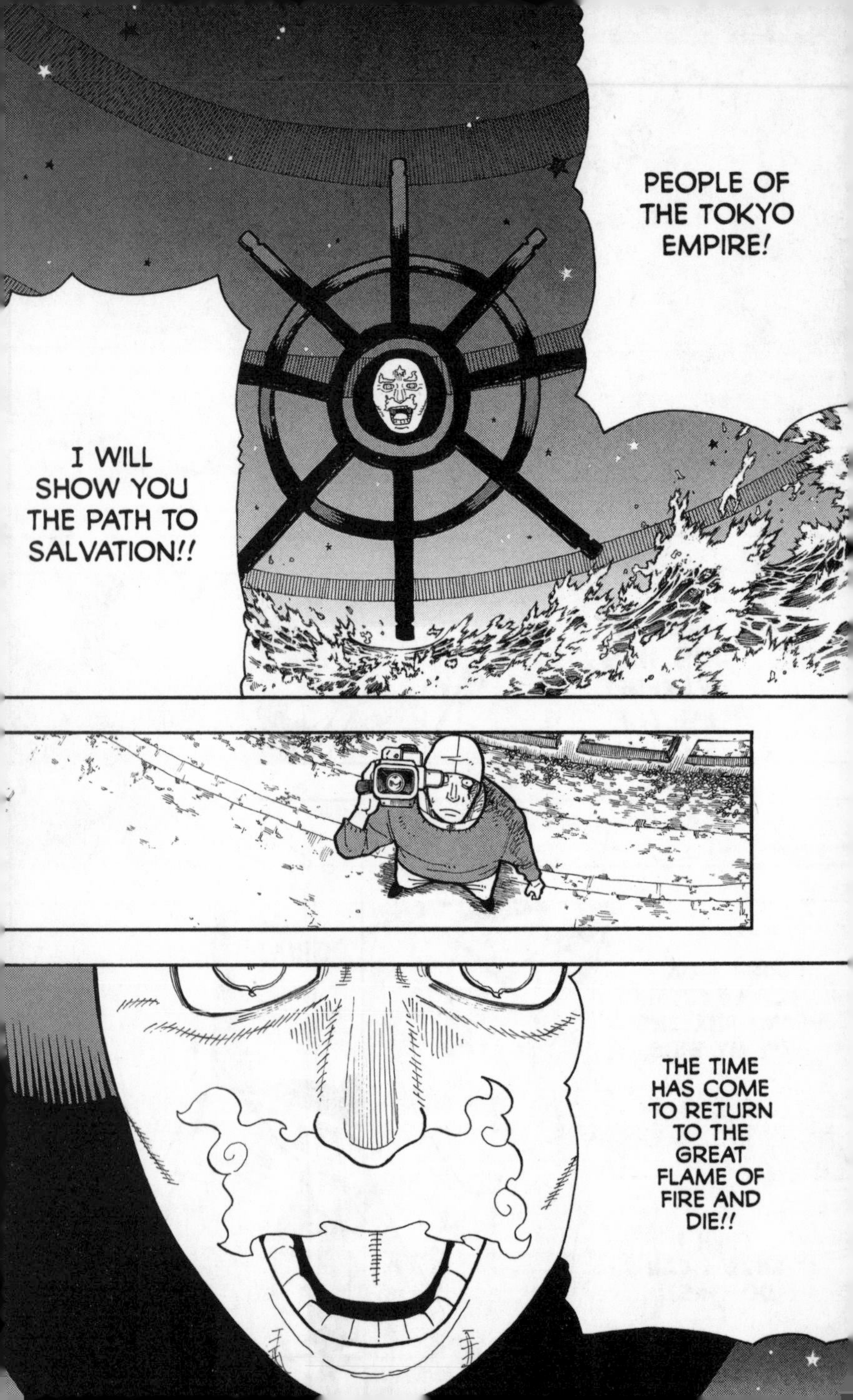
PEOPLE OF THE TOKYO EMPIRE!
I WILL SHOW YOU THE PATH TO SALVATION!!
THE TIME HAS COME TO RETURN TO THE GREAT FLAME OF FIRE AND DIE!!

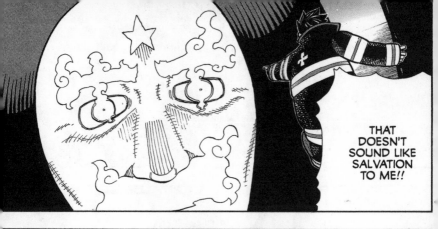

THAT DOESN'T SOUND LIKE SALVATION TO ME!!

A SAVIOR IS A SAVIOR BECAUSE HE *SAVES* THE WORLD!!

YOU CAN DO IT, SHINRA-KUN!!

GO, SHINRA!!

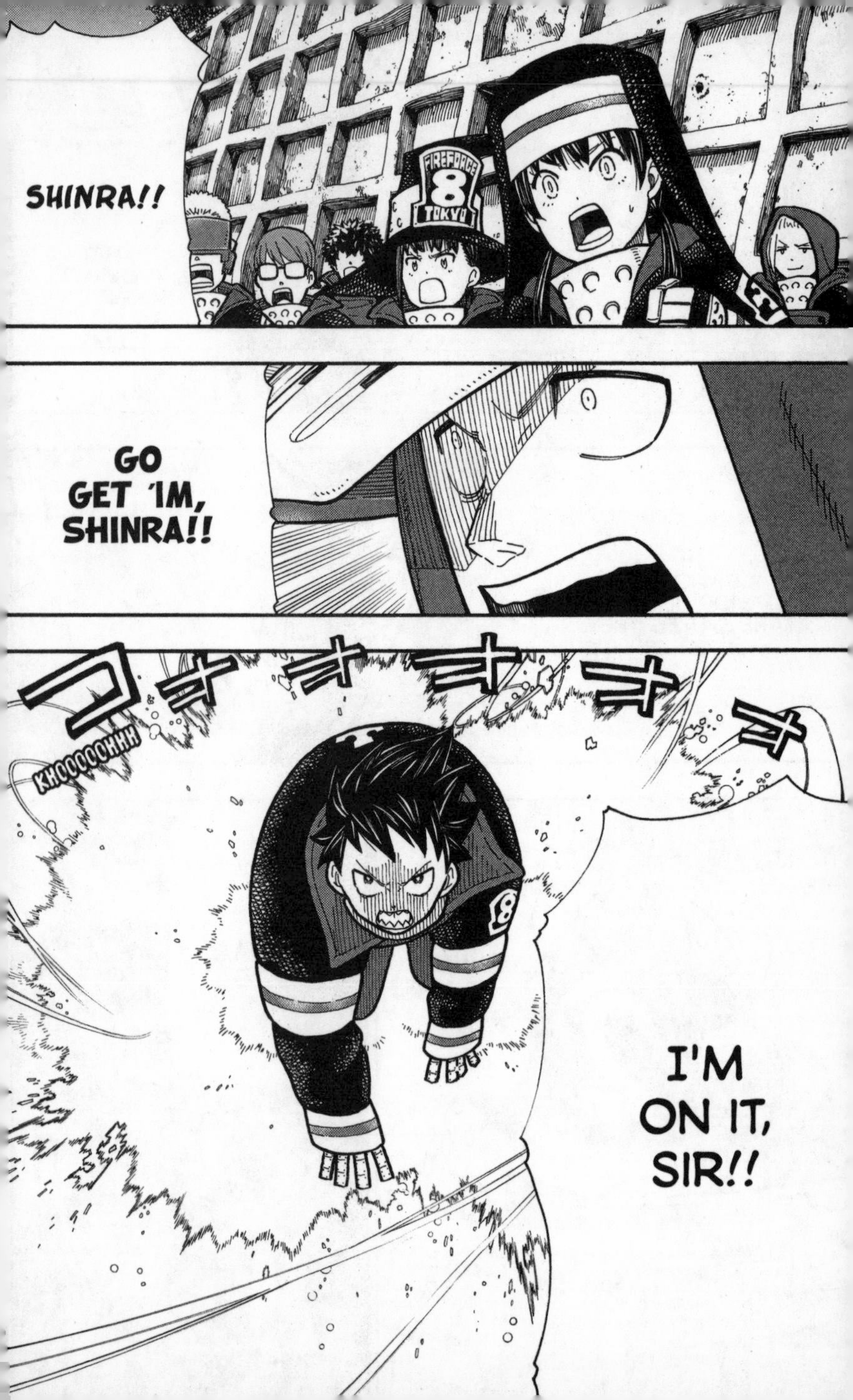
SHINRA!!
GO GET 'IM, SHINRA!!
コォォォォォ
KHOOOOOOHHH
I'M ON IT, SIR!!

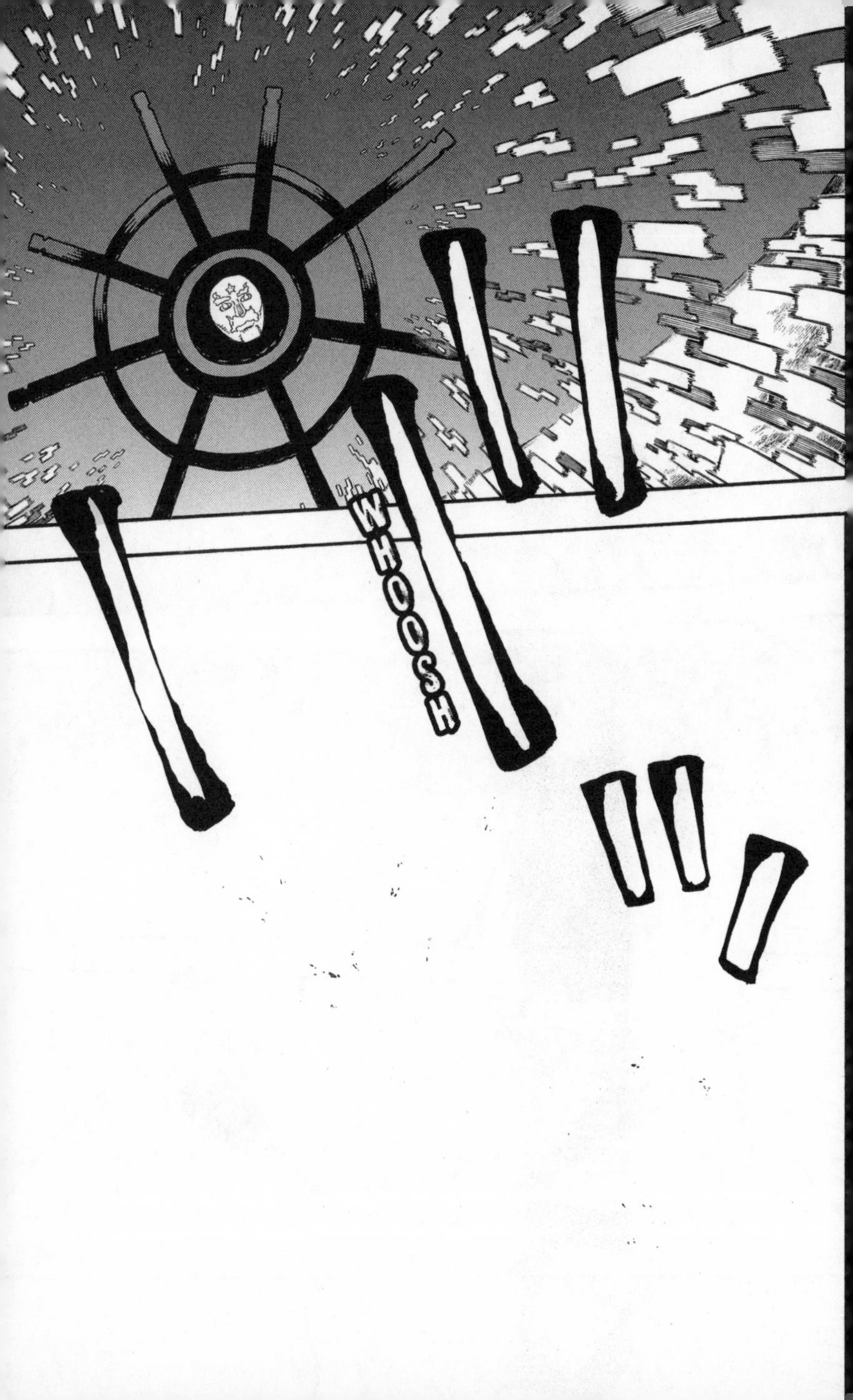
WHOOSH

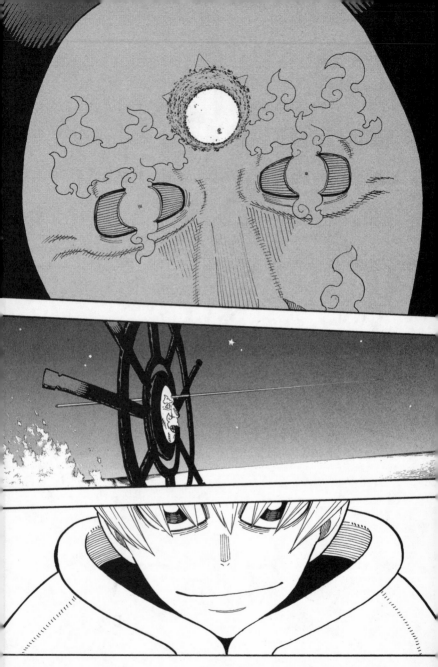

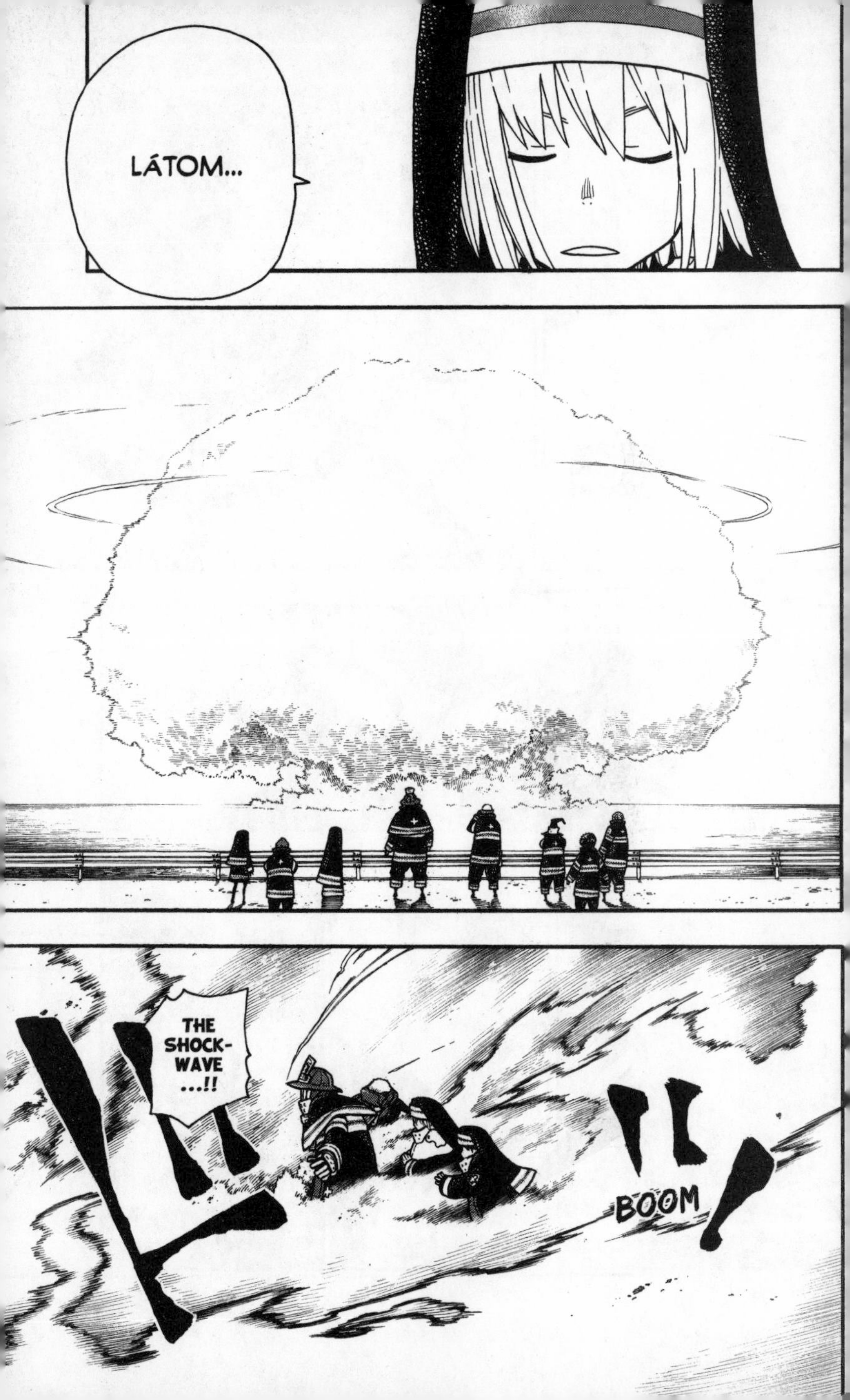
LÁTOM...
THE SHOCK-WAVE ...!!
BOOM

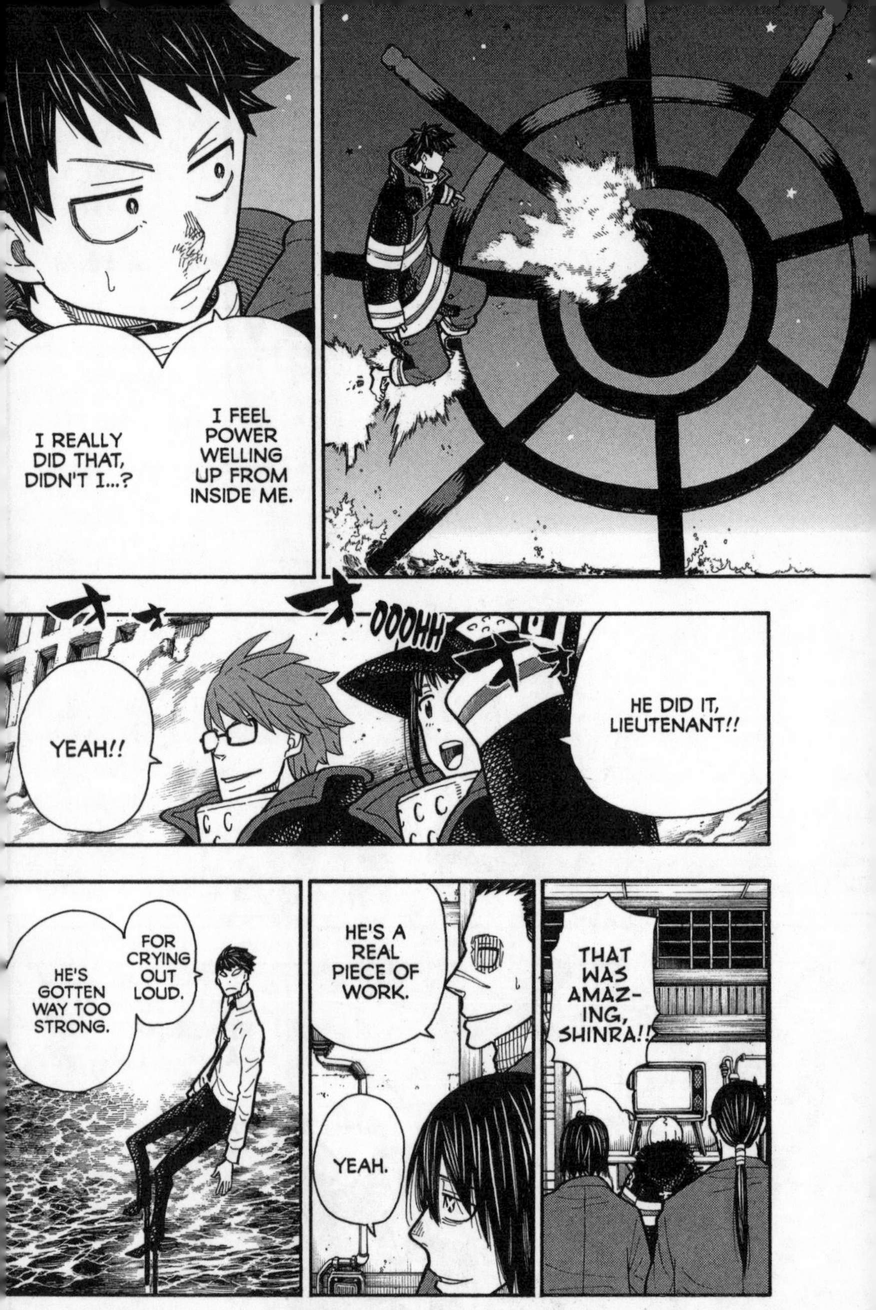
I FEEL POWER WELLING UP FROM INSIDE ME.
I REALLY DID THAT, DIDN'T I...?
HE DID IT, LIEUTENANT!!
OOOHH
YEAH!!
THAT WAS AMAZ-ING, SHINRA!!
HE'S A REAL PIECE OF WORK.
YEAH.
FOR CRYING OUT LOUD.
HE'S GOTTEN WAY TOO STRONG.

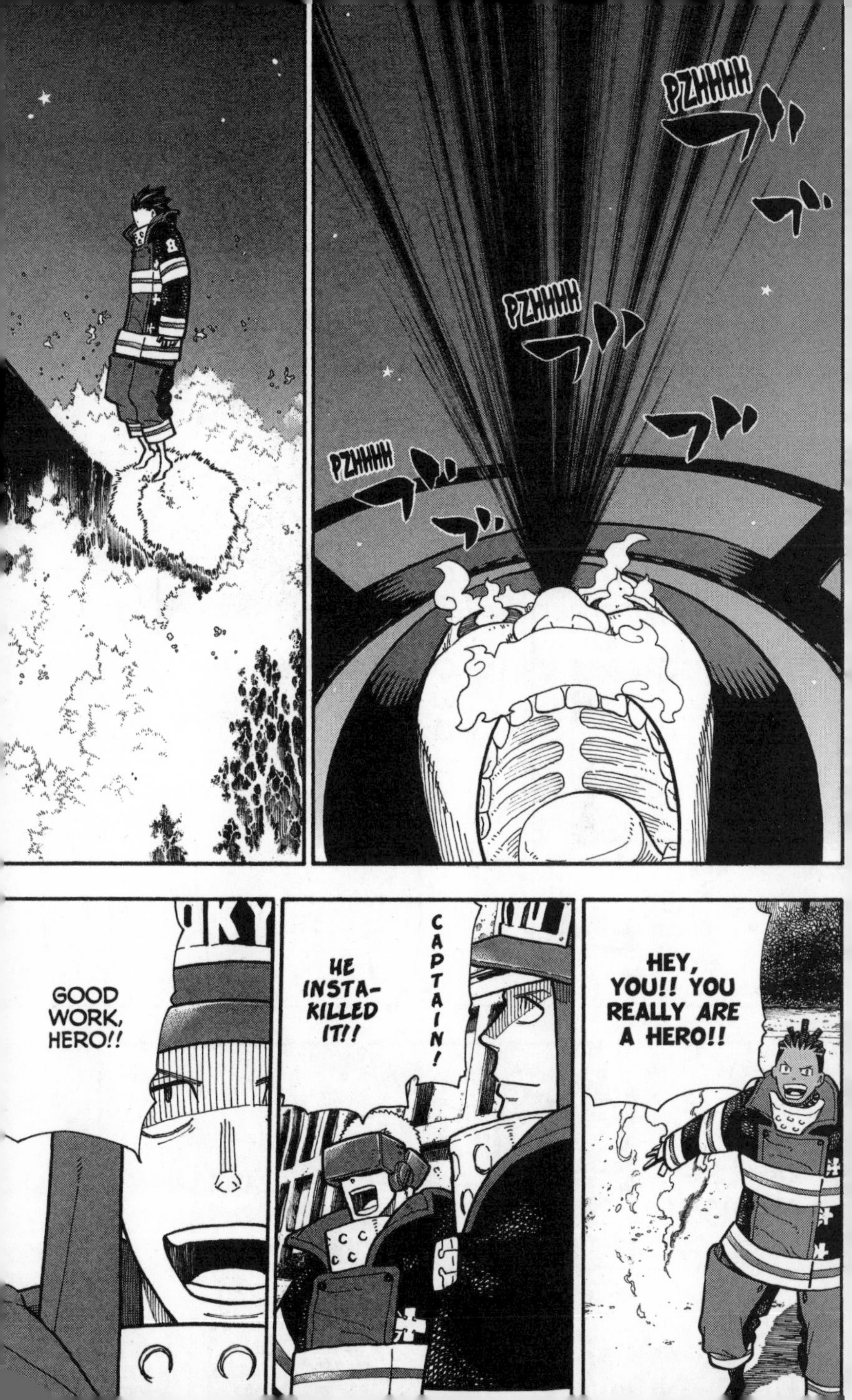
PZHHHH
PZHHHH
PZHHHH
HEY, YOU!! YOU REALLY ARE A HERO!!
CAPTAIN!
HE INSTA-KILLED IT!!
GOOD WORK, HERO!!

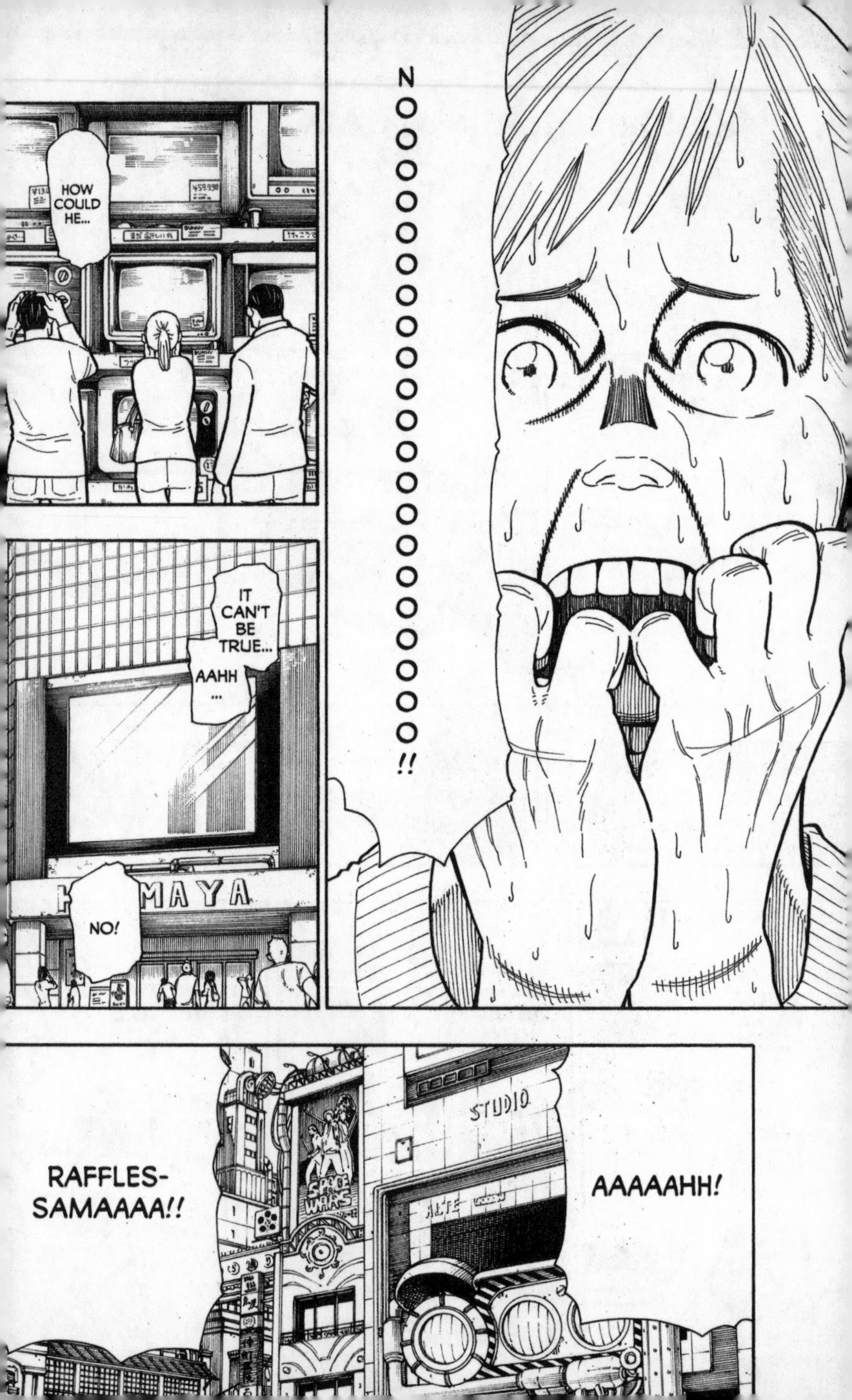
NOOOOOOOOOOOOOOOOOOOOO!!
HOW COULD HE...
IT CAN'T BE TRUE...
AAHH ...
NO!
STUDIO
AAAAAHH!
RAFFLES-SAMAAAA!!

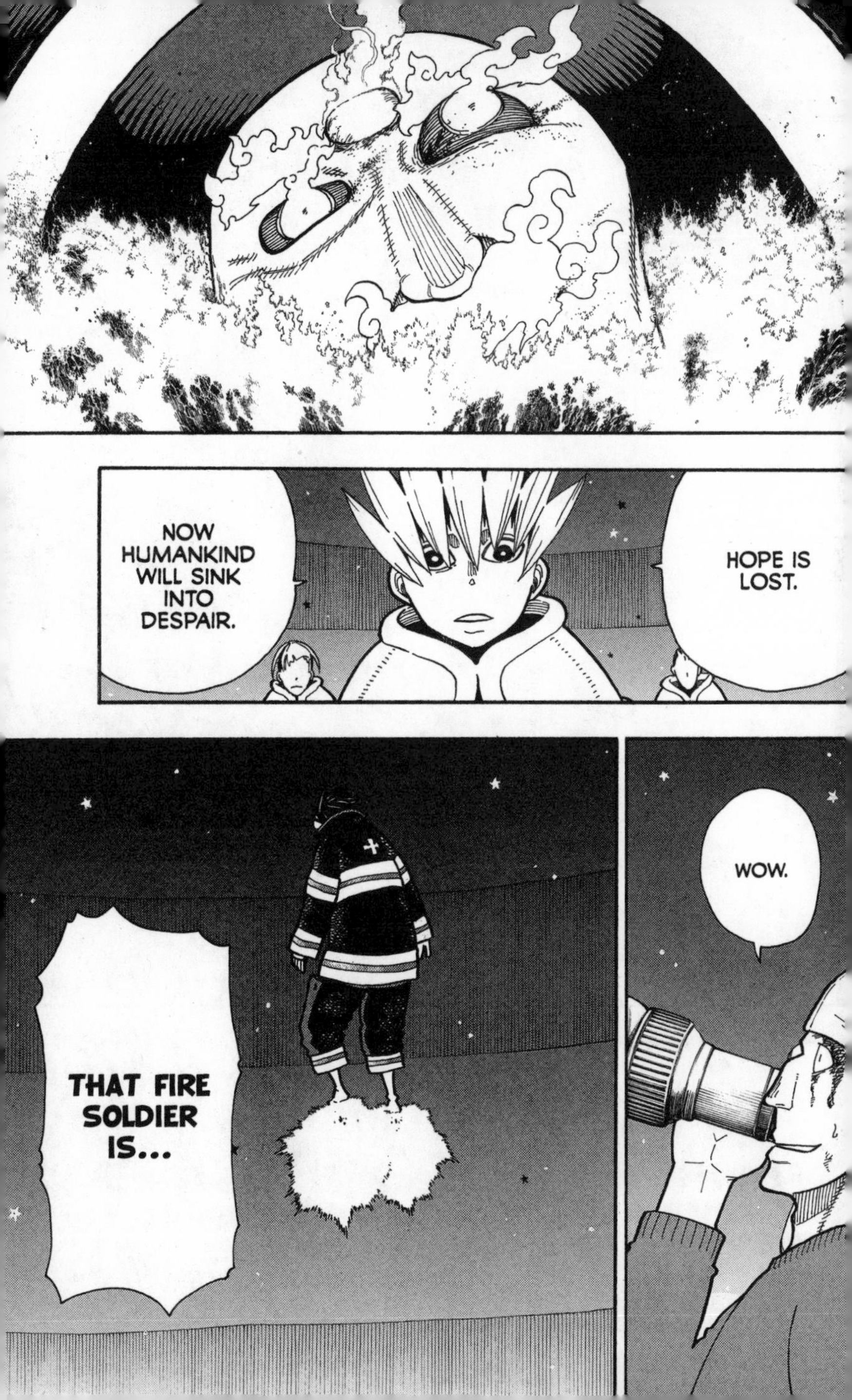
HOPE IS LOST.
NOW HUMANKIND WILL SINK INTO DESPAIR.
WOW.
THAT FIRE SOLDIER IS...

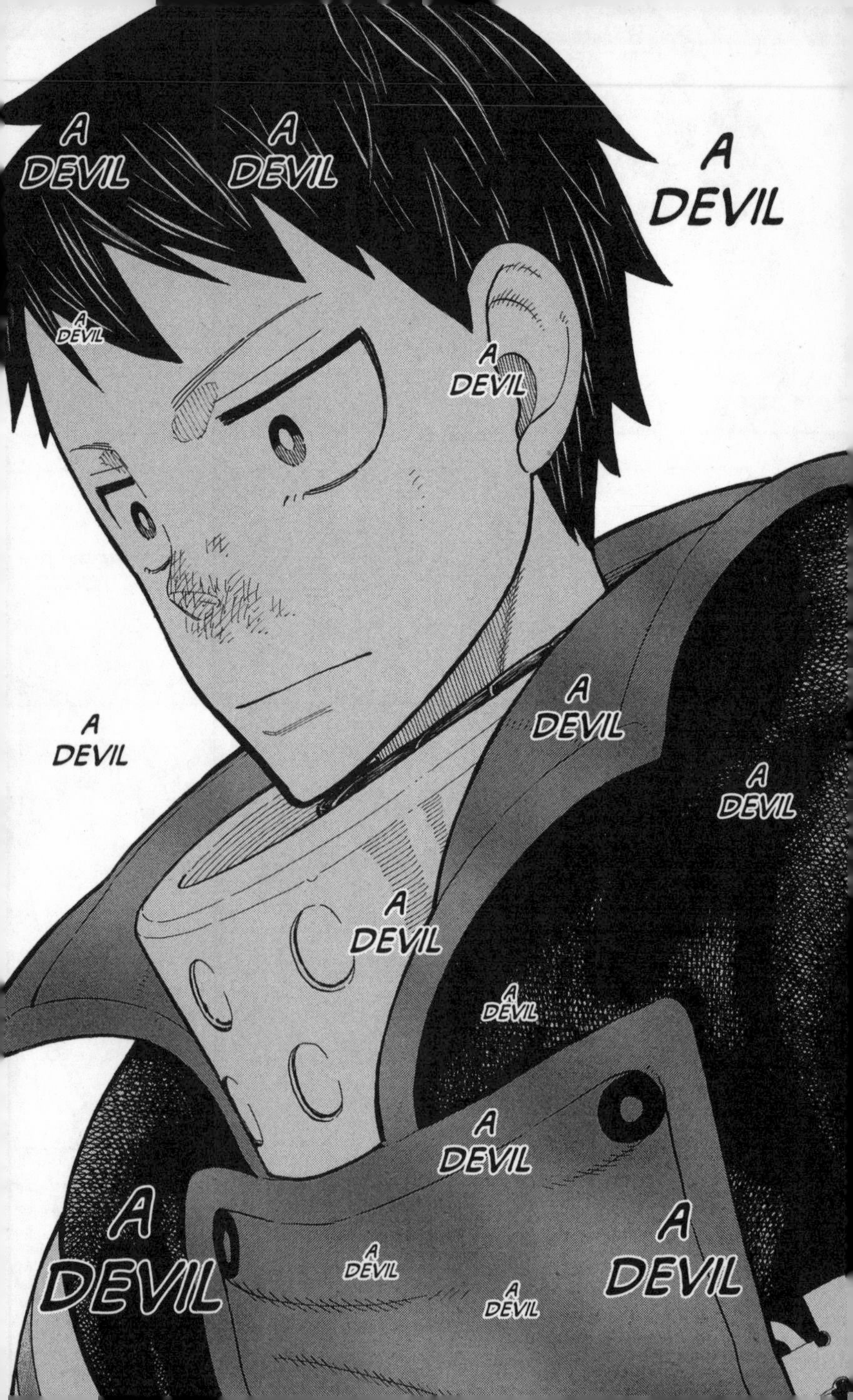
A DEVIL
A DEVIL
A DEVIL
A DEVIL
A DEVIL
A DEVIL
A DEVIL
A DEVIL
A DEVIL
A DEVIL
A DEVIL
A DEVIL
A DEVIL
A DEVIL
A DEVIL

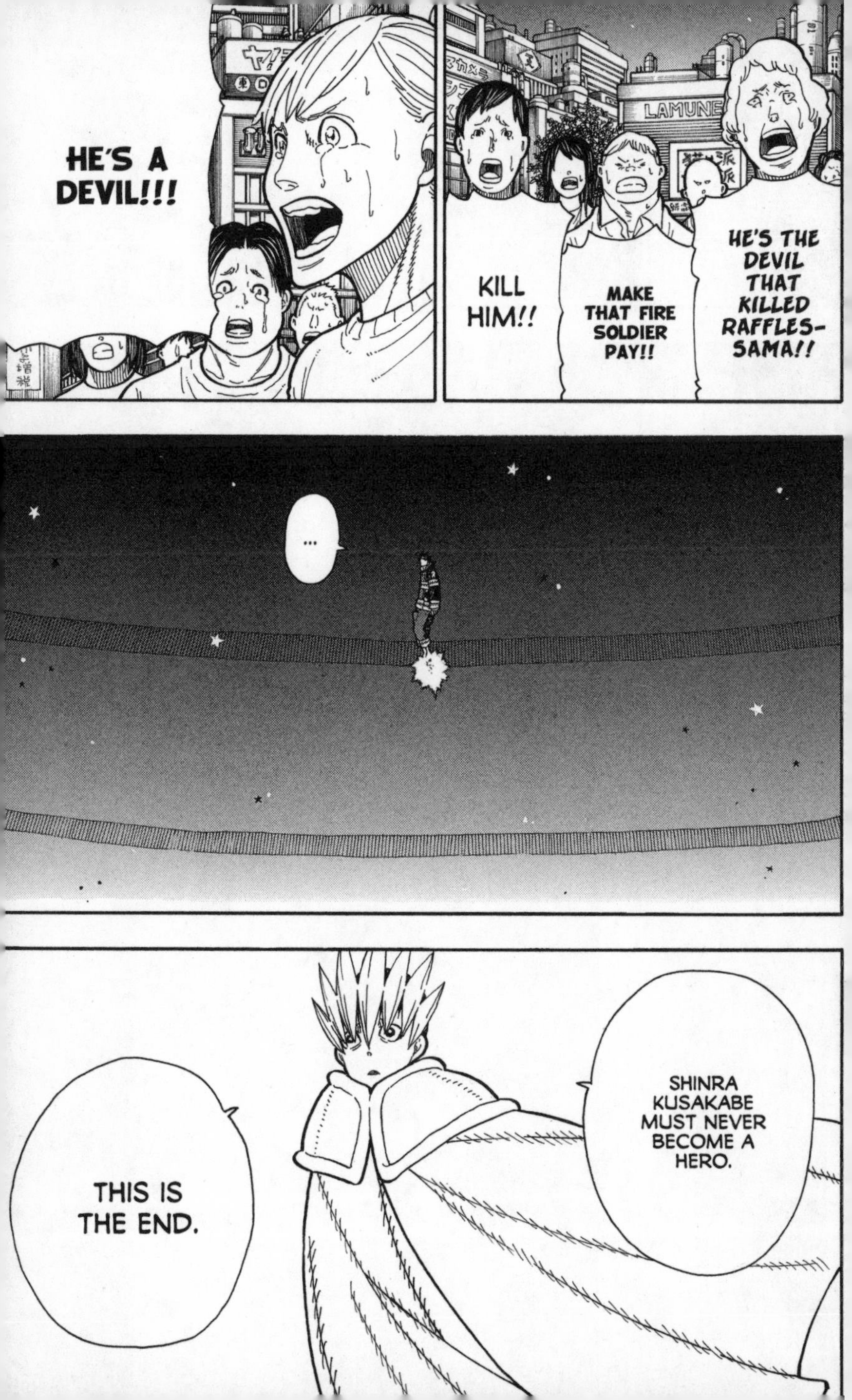
LAMUNE
HE'S THE DEVIL THAT KILLED RAFFLES-SAMA!!
MAKE THAT FIRE SOLDIER PAY!!
KILL HIM!!
HE'S A DEVIL!!!
...
SHINRA KUSAKABE MUST NEVER BECOME A HERO.
THIS IS THE END.

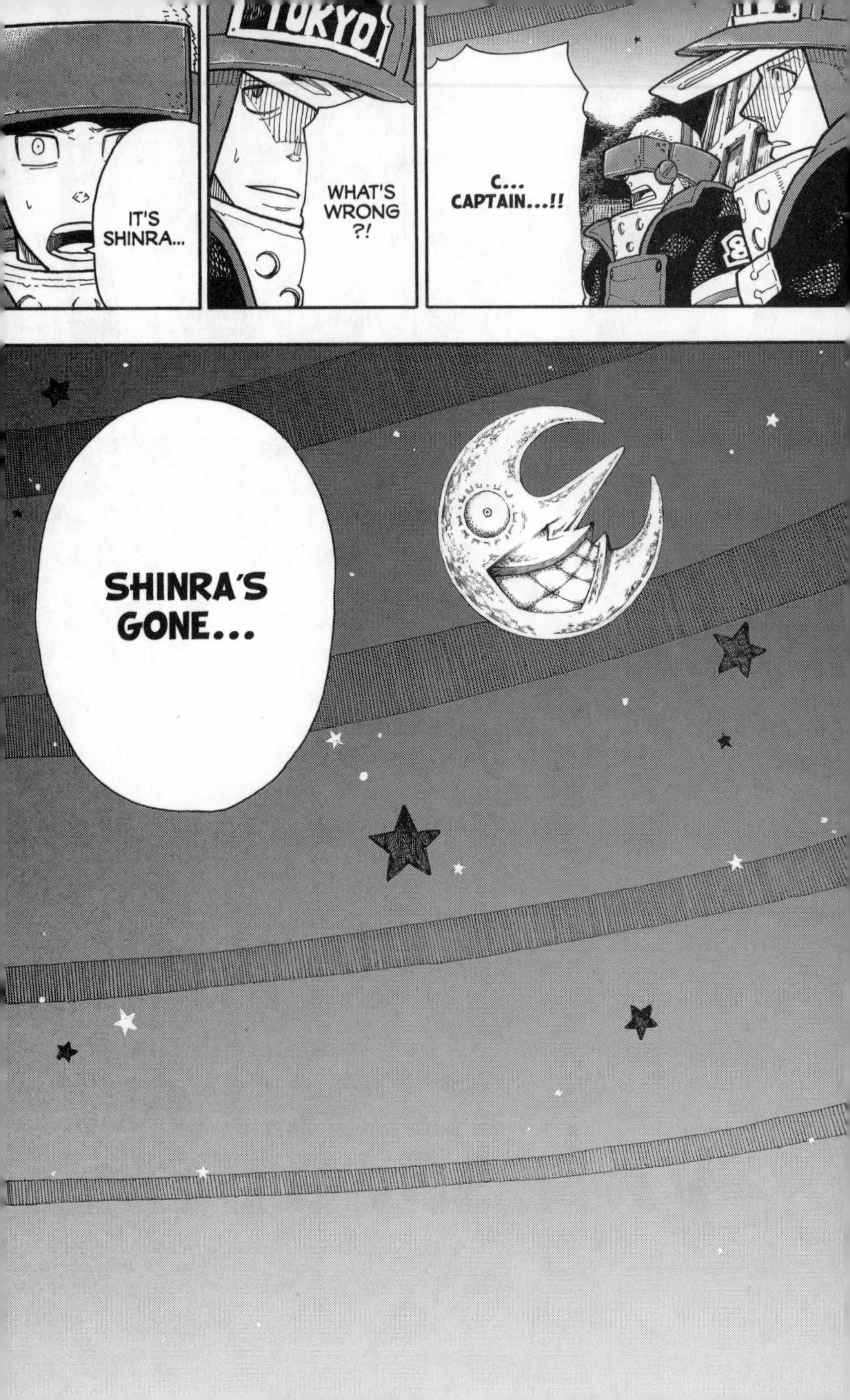
C... CAPTAIN...!!
WHAT'S WRONG ?!
IT'S SHINRA...
SHINRA'S GONE...

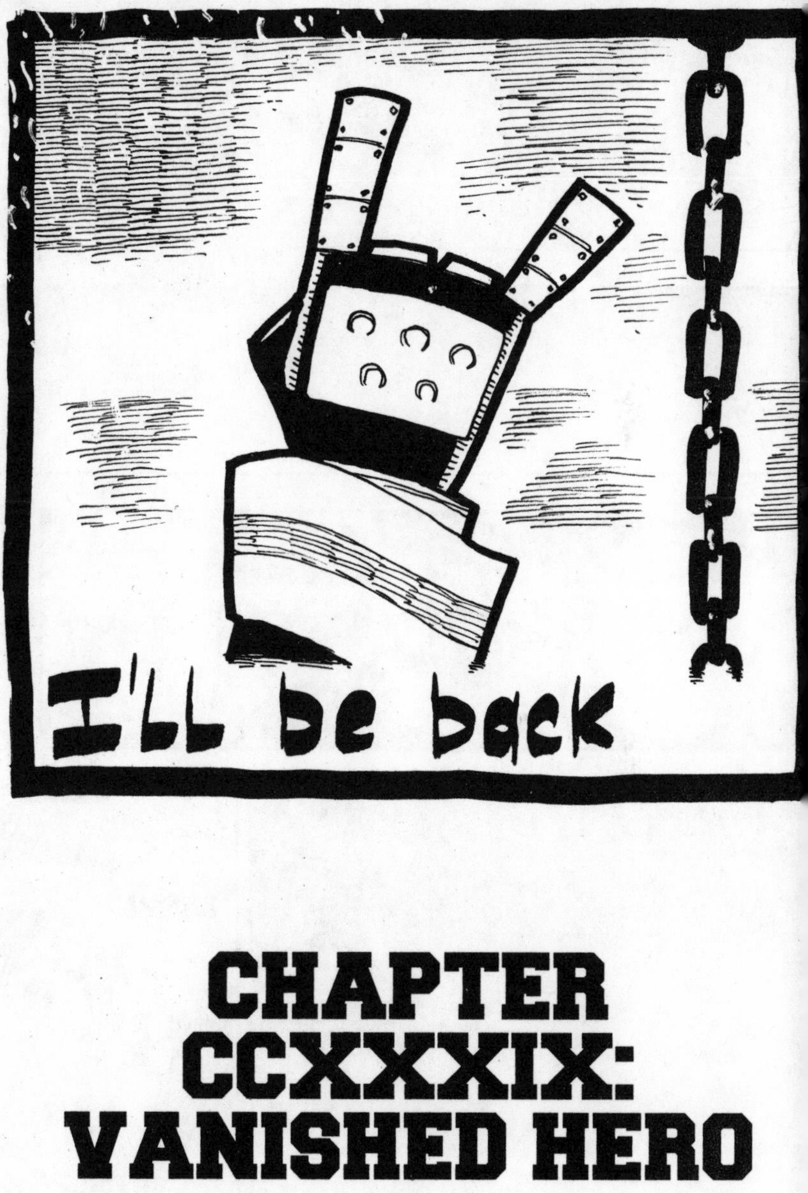
I'LL be back

CHAPTER CCXXXIX: VANISHED HERO

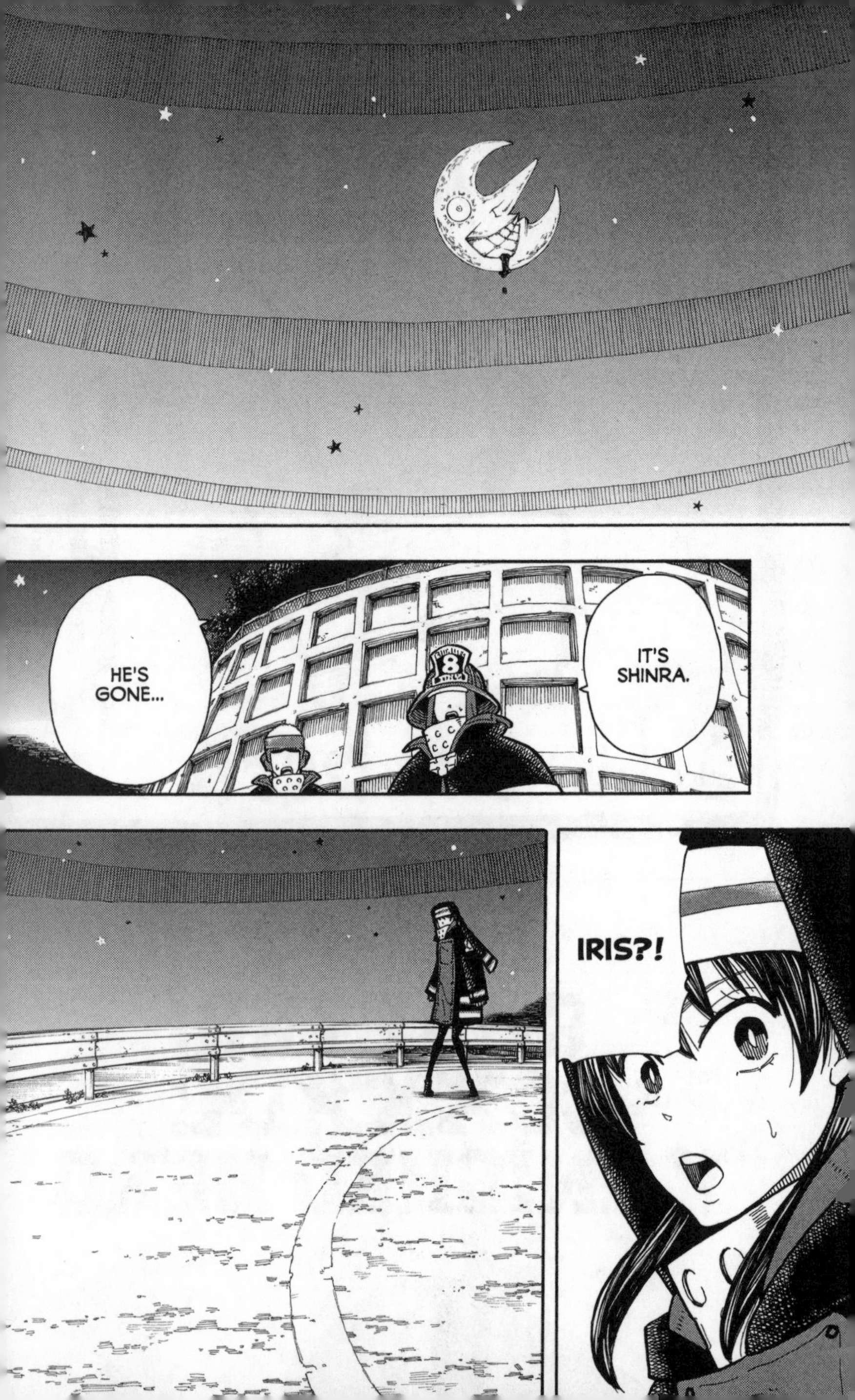
IT'S SHINRA.
HE'S GONE...
IRIS?!

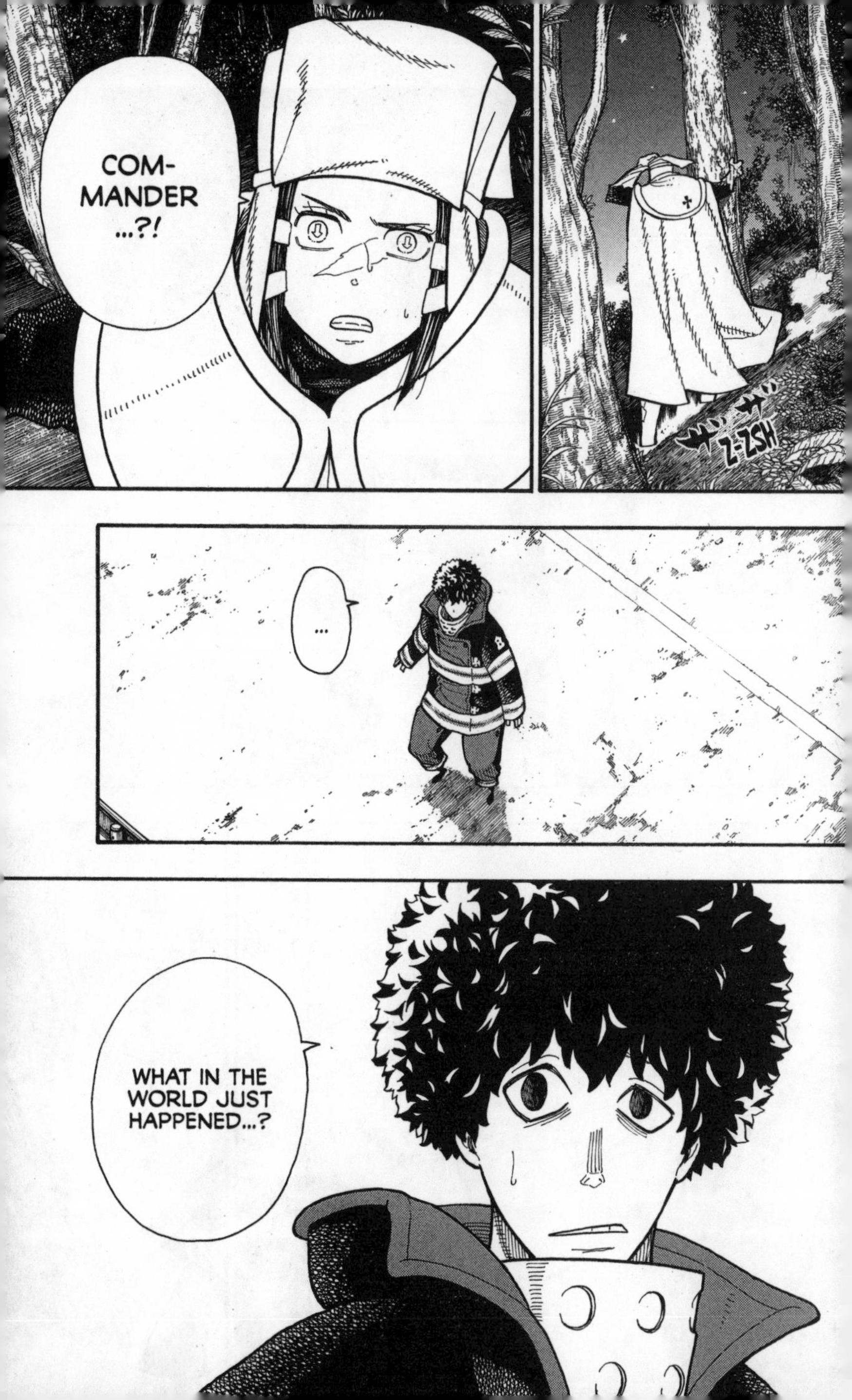
Z-ZSH
COM-MANDER ...?!
...
WHAT IN THE WORLD JUST HAPPENED...?

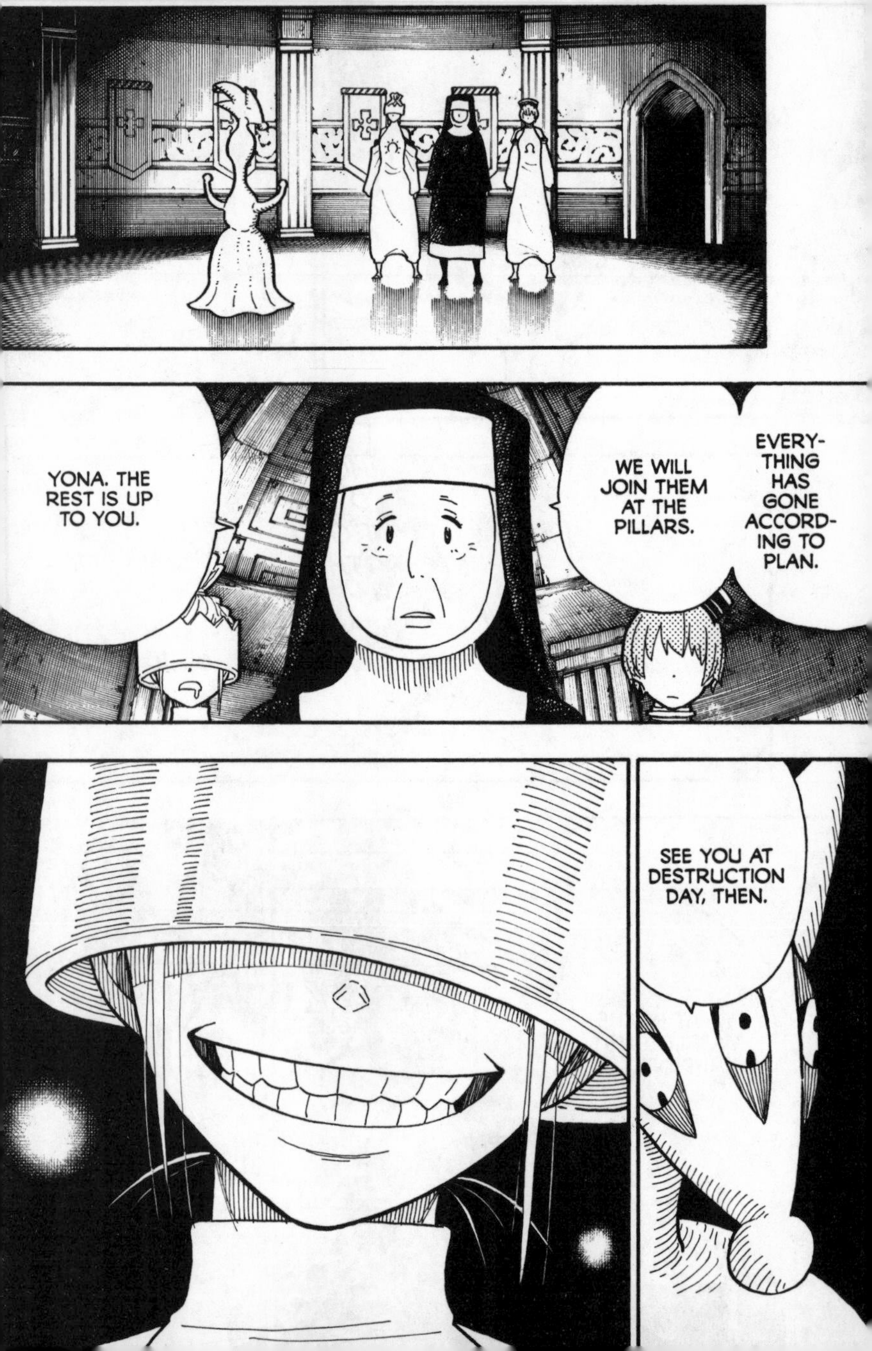
EVERY-THING HAS GONE ACCORD-ING TO PLAN.
WE WILL JOIN THEM AT THE PILLARS.
YONA. THE REST IS UP TO YOU.
SEE YOU AT DESTRUCTION DAY, THEN.

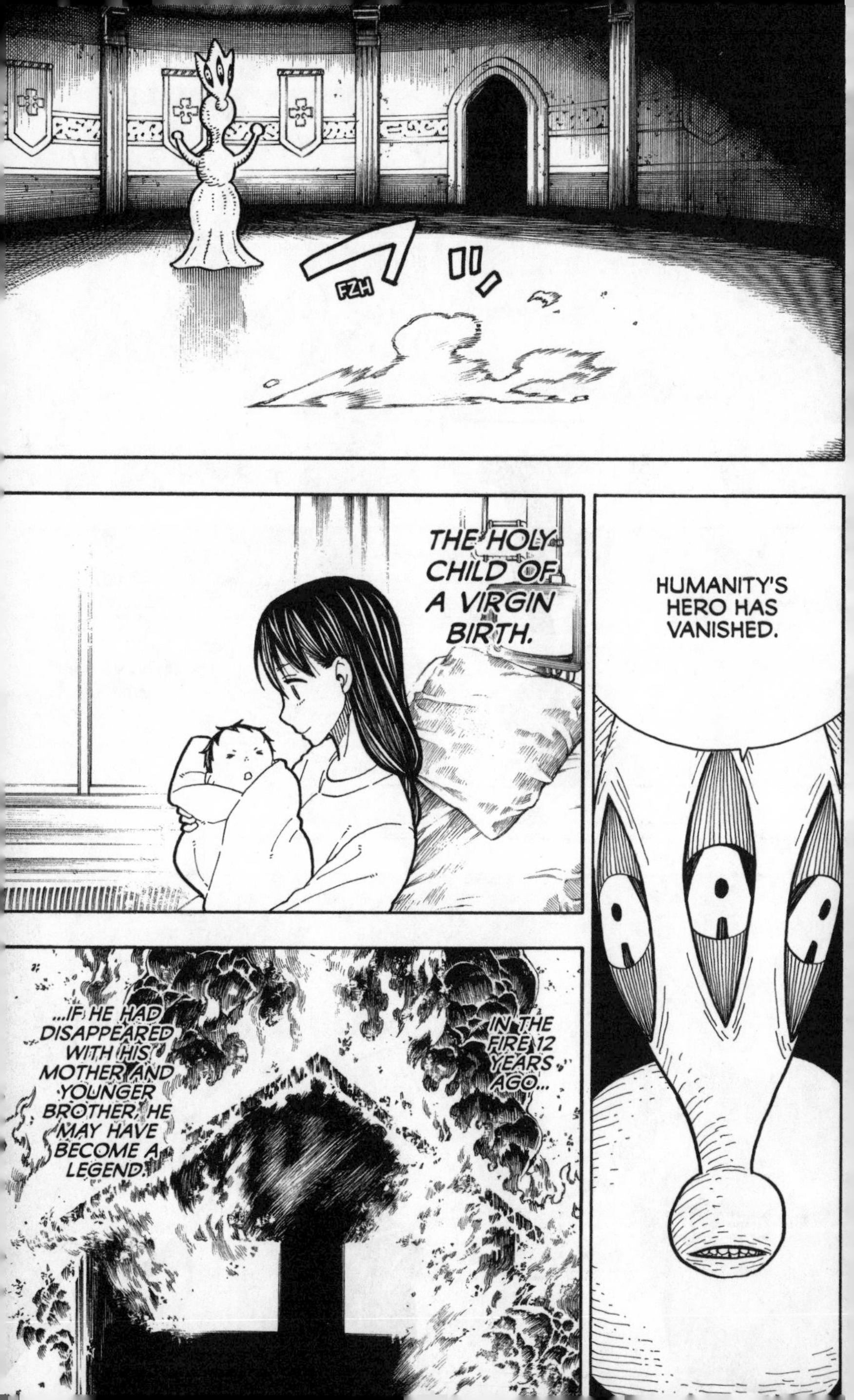
FZH
HUMANITY'S HERO HAS VANISHED.
THE HOLY CHILD OF A VIRGIN BIRTH.
IN THE FIRE 12 YEARS AGO...
...IF HE HAD DISAPPEARED WITH HIS MOTHER AND YOUNGER BROTHER, HE MAY HAVE BECOME A LEGEND.

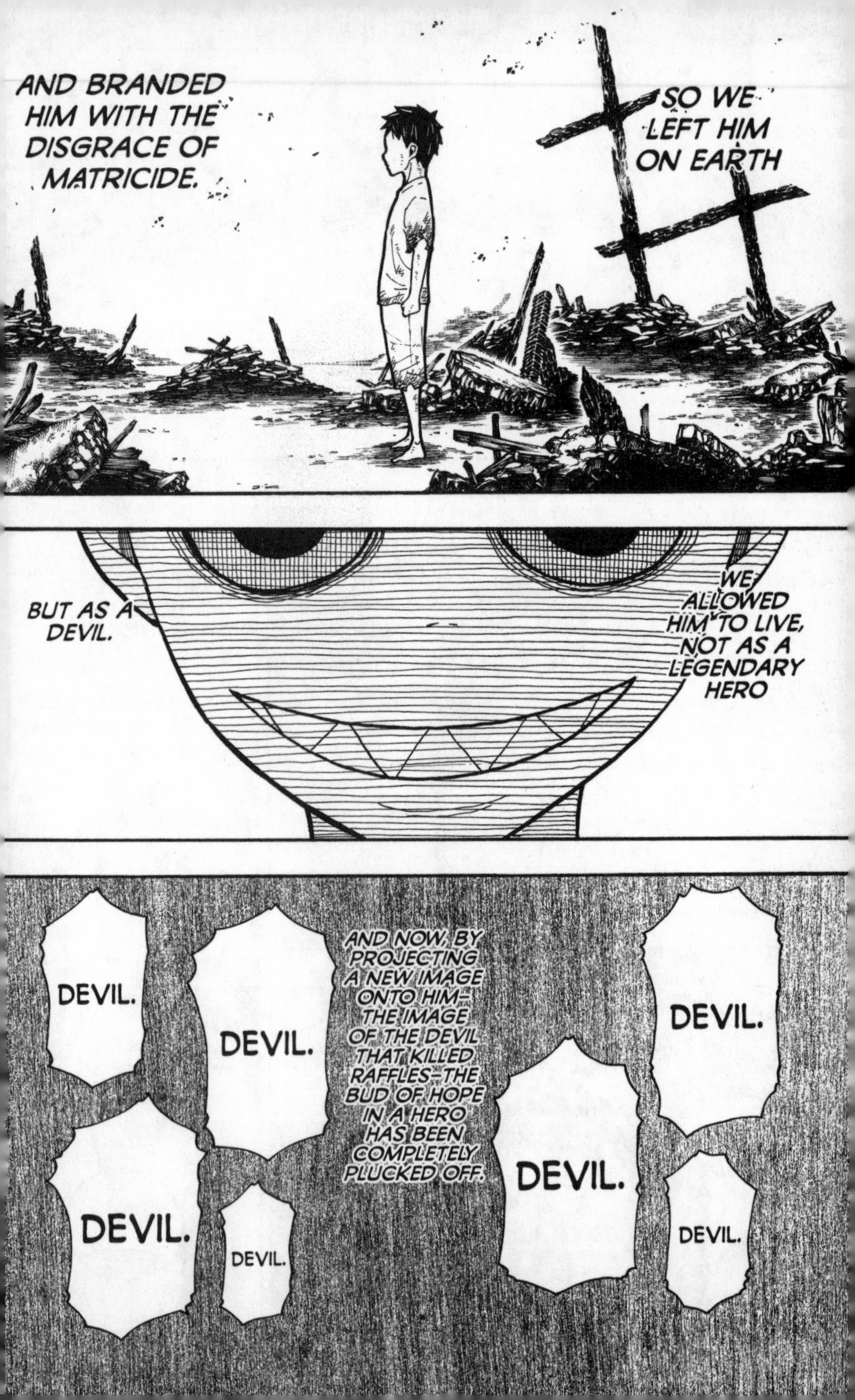
SO WE LEFT HIM ON EARTH
AND BRANDED HIM WITH THE DISGRACE OF MATRICIDE.
WE ALLOWED HIM TO LIVE, NOT AS A LEGENDARY HERO
BUT AS A DEVIL.
DEVIL.
DEVIL.
DEVIL.
AND NOW, BY PROJECTING A NEW IMAGE ONTO HIM—THE IMAGE OF THE DEVIL THAT KILLED RAFFLES—THE BUD OF HOPE IN A HERO HAS BEEN COMPLETELY PLUCKED OFF.
DEVIL.
DEVIL.
DEVIL.
DEVIL.

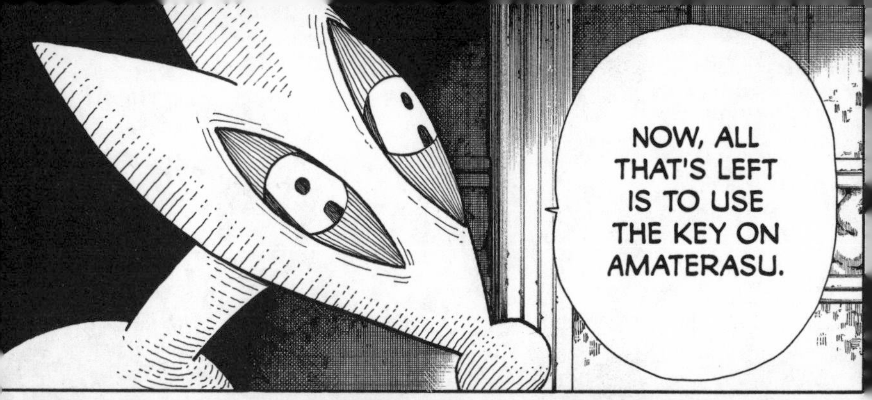
NOW, ALL THAT'S LEFT IS TO USE THE KEY ON AMATERASU.

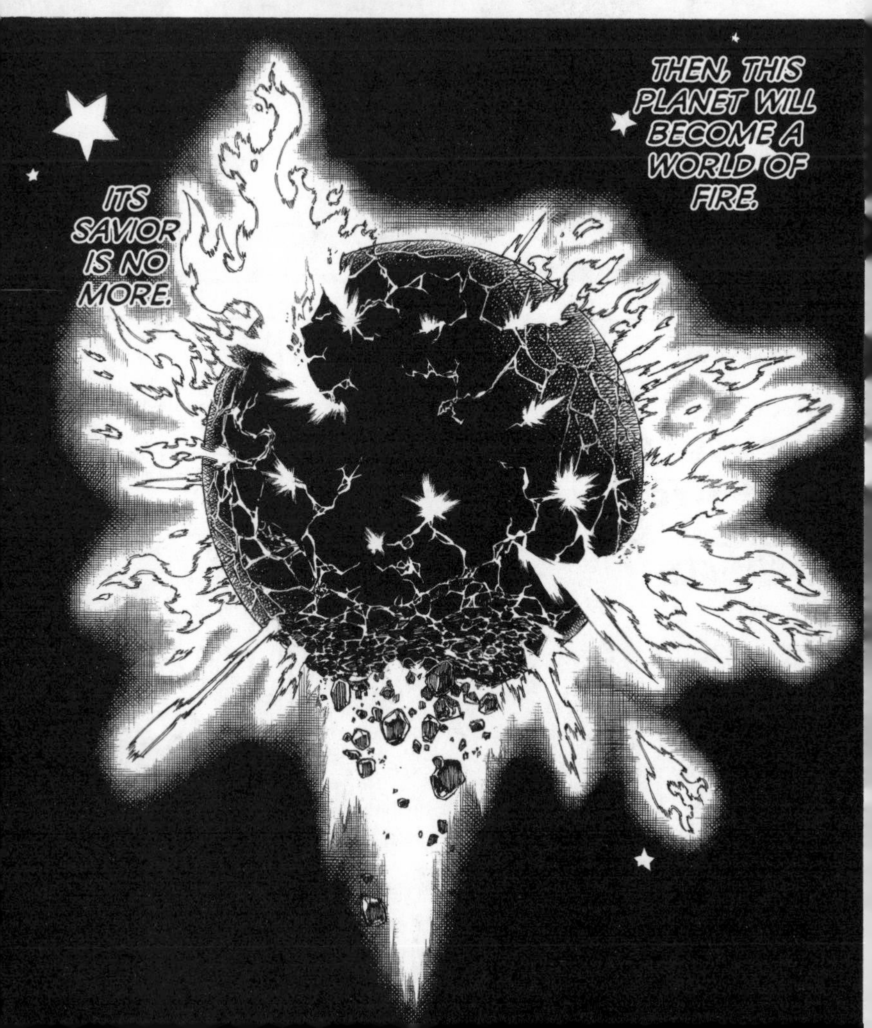
THEN, THIS PLANET WILL BECOME A WORLD OF FIRE.
ITS SAVIOR IS NO MORE.

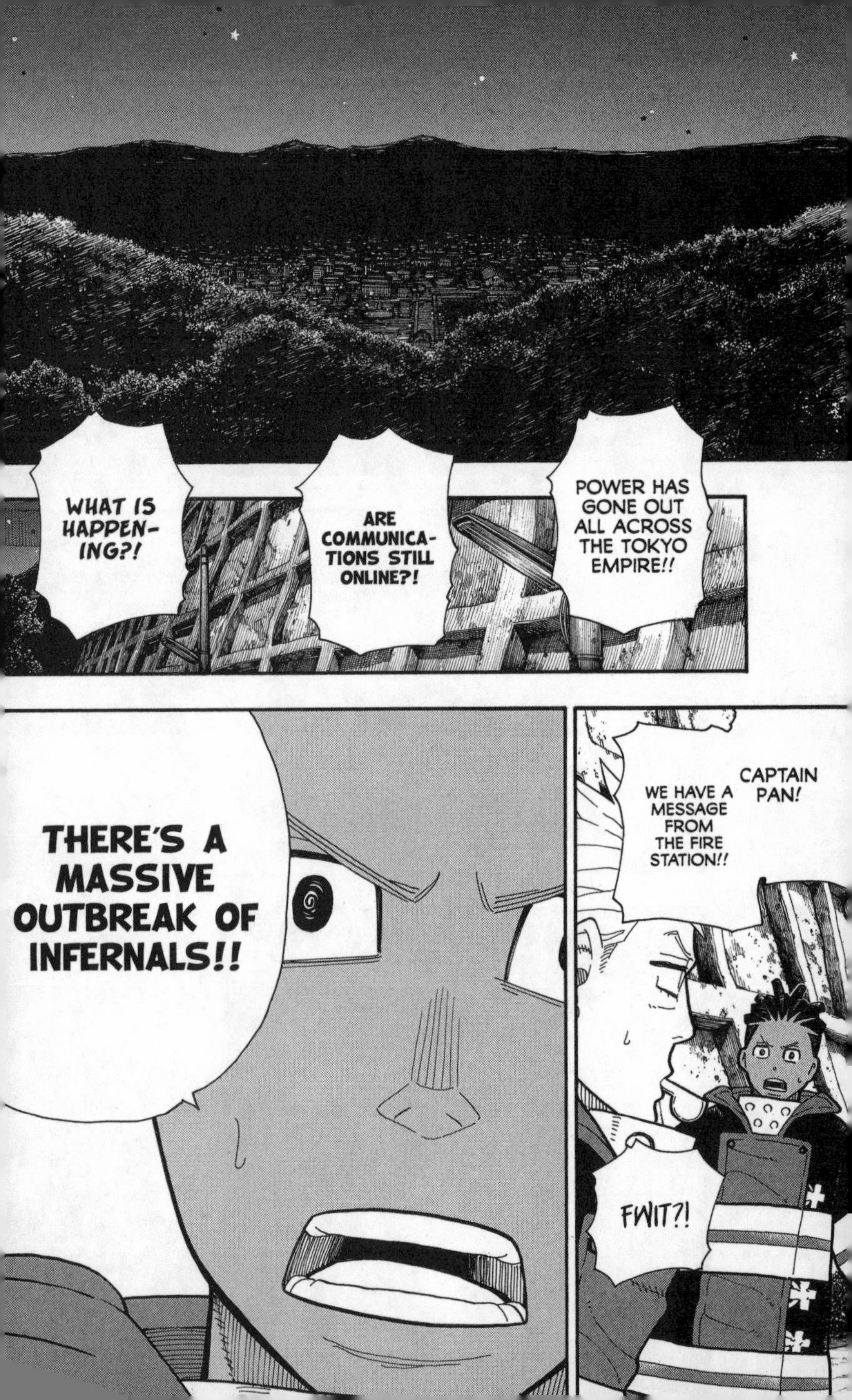
POWER HAS GONE OUT ALL ACROSS THE TOKYO EMPIRE!!
ARE COMMUNICATIONS STILL ONLINE?!
WHAT IS HAPPENING?!
CAPTAIN PAN!
WE HAVE A MESSAGE FROM THE FIRE STATION!!
FWIT?!
THERE'S A MASSIVE OUTBREAK OF INFERNALS!!

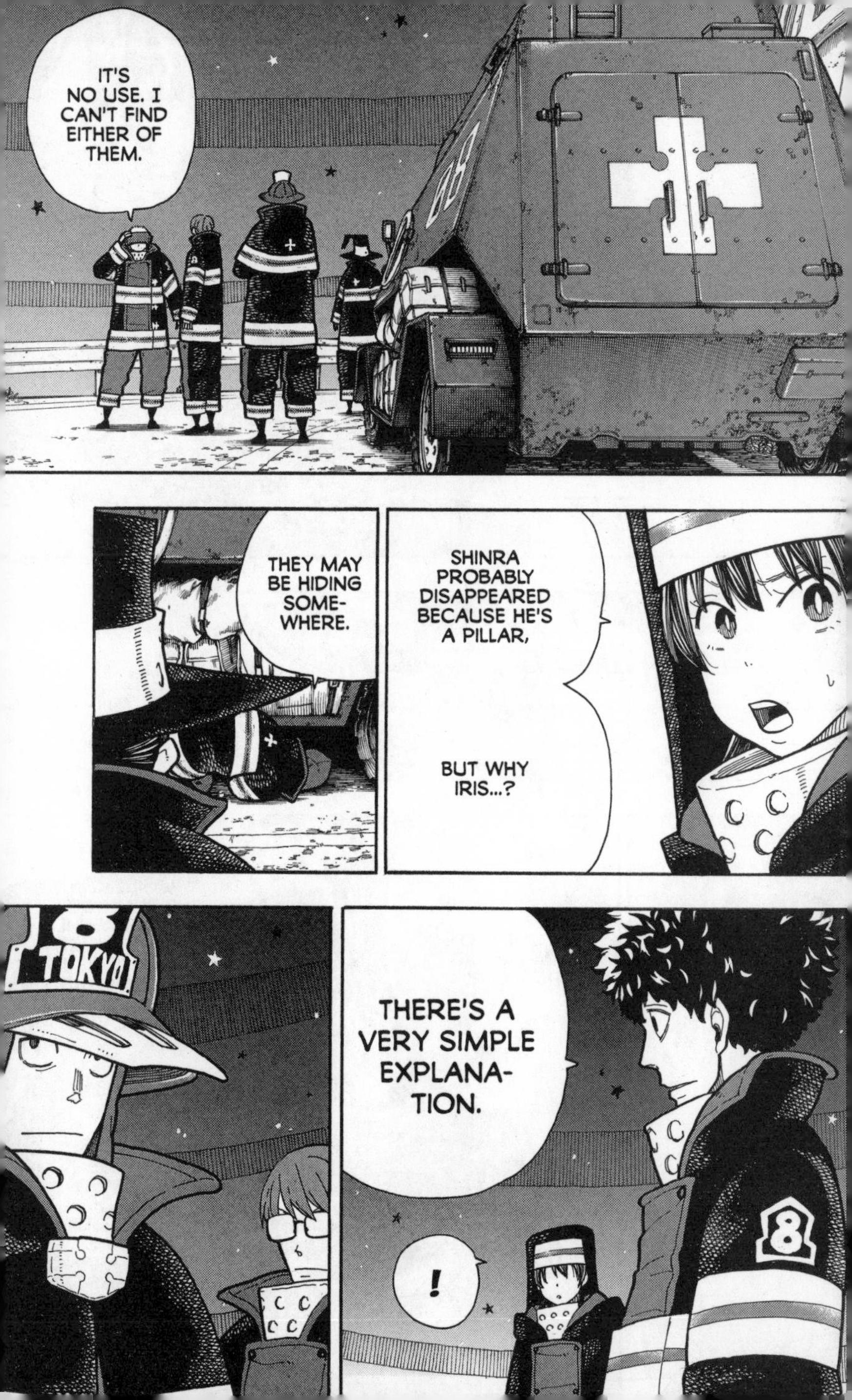
IT'S NO USE. I CAN'T FIND EITHER OF THEM.
SHINRA PROBABLY DISAPPEARED BECAUSE HE'S A PILLAR,
BUT WHY IRIS...?
THEY MAY BE HIDING SOME-WHERE.
THERE'S A VERY SIMPLE EXPLANA-TION.
!

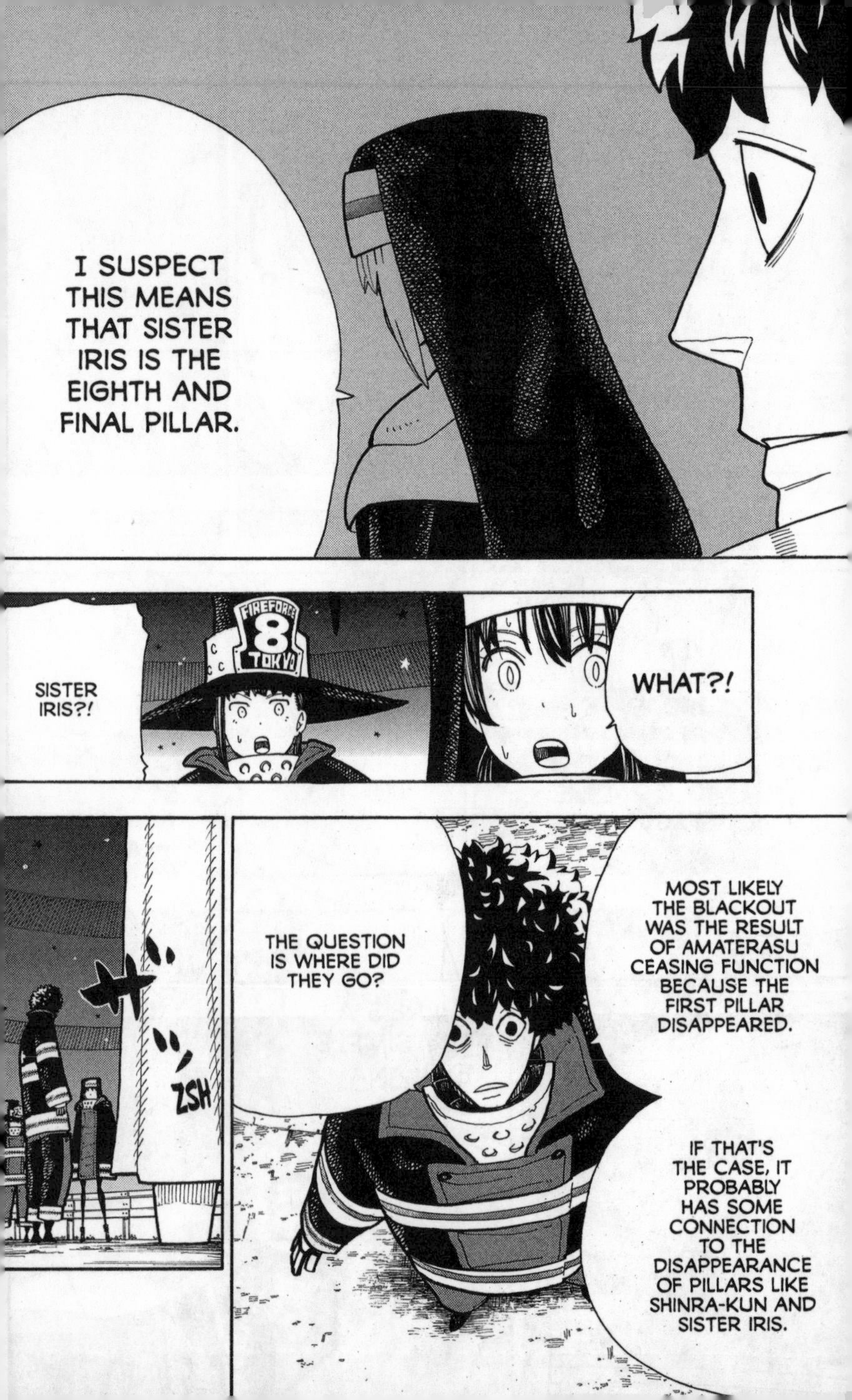
I SUSPECT THIS MEANS THAT SISTER IRIS IS THE EIGHTH AND FINAL PILLAR.
WHAT?!
FIREFORCE 8 TOKYO
SISTER IRIS?!
MOST LIKELY THE BLACKOUT WAS THE RESULT OF AMATERASU CEASING FUNCTION BECAUSE THE FIRST PILLAR DISAPPEARED.
IF THAT'S THE CASE, IT PROBABLY HAS SOME CONNECTION TO THE DISAPPEARANCE OF PILLARS LIKE SHINRA-KUN AND SISTER IRIS.
THE QUESTION IS WHERE DID THEY GO?
ZSH

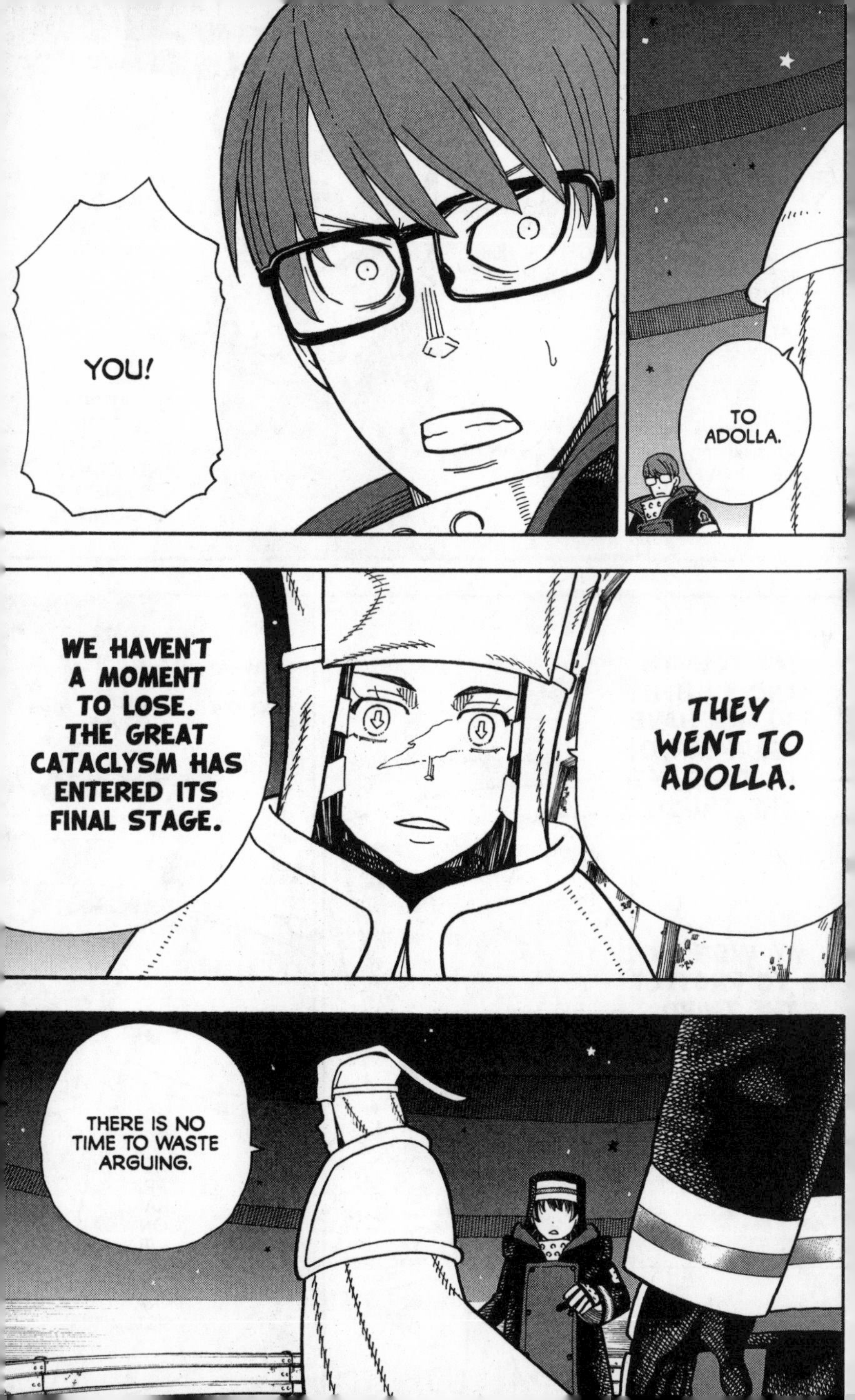
TO ADOLLA.
YOU!
THEY WENT TO ADOLLA.
WE HAVEN'T A MOMENT TO LOSE. THE GREAT CATACLYSM HAS ENTERED ITS FINAL STAGE.
THERE IS NO TIME TO WASTE ARGUING.

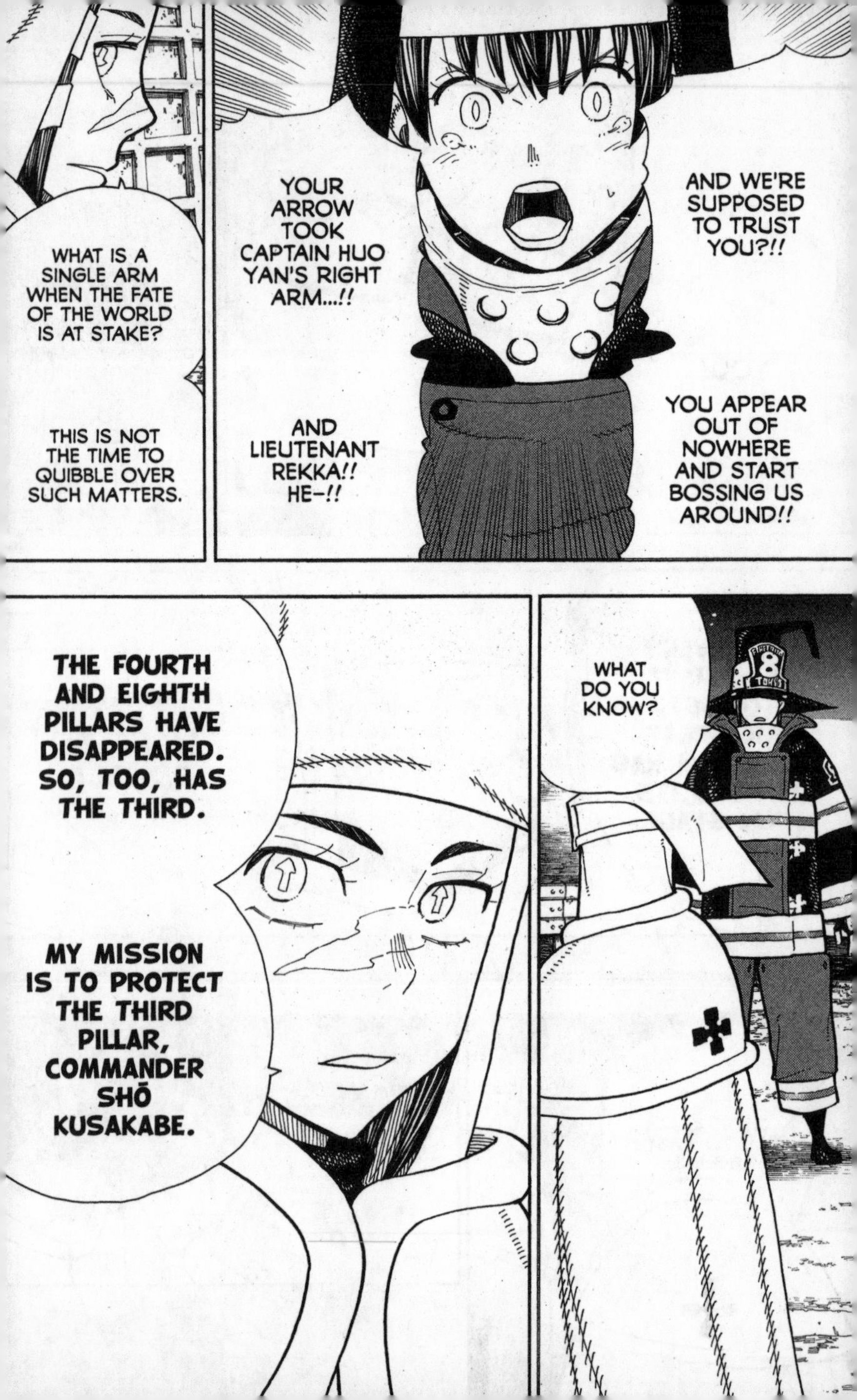
AND WE'RE SUPPOSED TO TRUST YOU?!!
YOU APPEAR OUT OF NOWHERE AND START BOSSING US AROUND!!
YOUR ARROW TOOK CAPTAIN HUO YAN'S RIGHT ARM...!!
AND LIEUTENANT REKKA!! HE-!!
WHAT IS A SINGLE ARM WHEN THE FATE OF THE WORLD IS AT STAKE?
THIS IS NOT THE TIME TO QUIBBLE OVER SUCH MATTERS.
WHAT DO YOU KNOW?
THE FOURTH AND EIGHTH PILLARS HAVE DISAPPEARED. SO, TOO, HAS THE THIRD.
MY MISSION IS TO PROTECT THE THIRD PILLAR, COMMANDER SHŌ KUSAKABE.

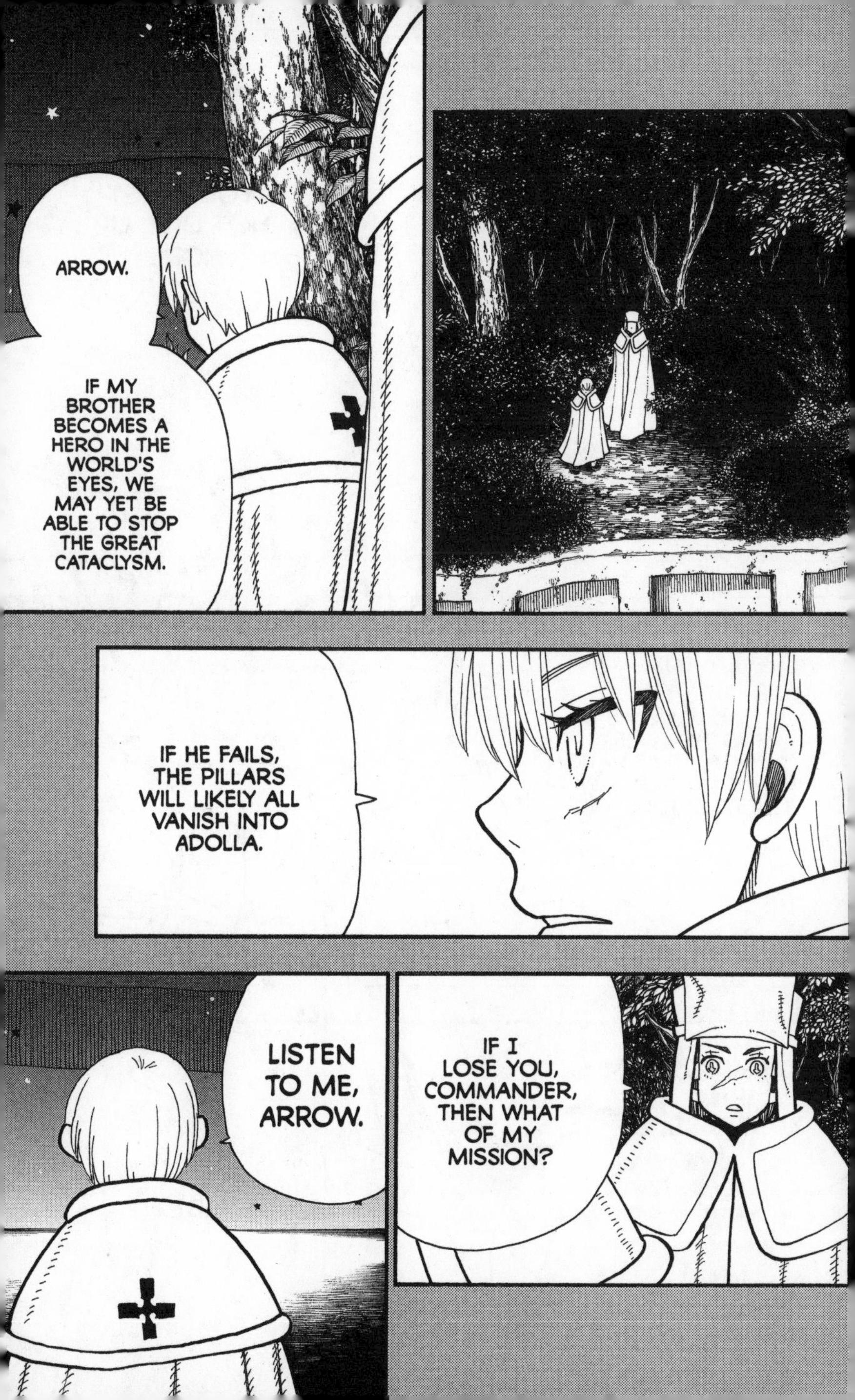
ARROW.
IF MY BROTHER BECOMES A HERO IN THE WORLD'S EYES, WE MAY YET BE ABLE TO STOP THE GREAT CATACLYSM.
IF HE FAILS, THE PILLARS WILL LIKELY ALL VANISH INTO ADOLLA.
IF I LOSE YOU, COMMANDER, THEN WHAT OF MY MISSION?
LISTEN TO ME, ARROW.

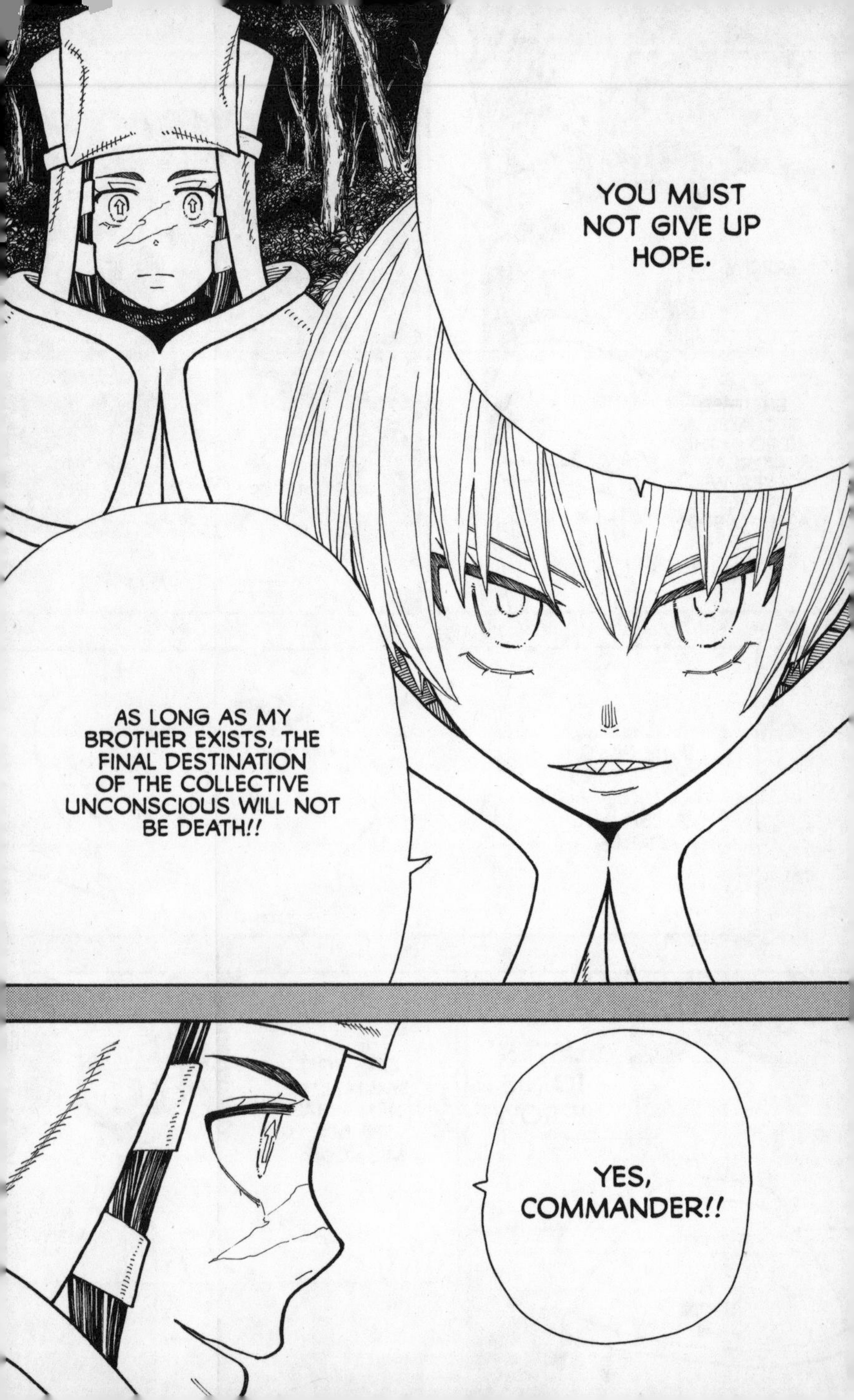
YOU MUST NOT GIVE UP HOPE.
AS LONG AS MY BROTHER EXISTS, THE FINAL DESTINATION OF THE COLLECTIVE UNCONSCIOUS WILL NOT BE DEATH!!
YES, COMMANDER!!

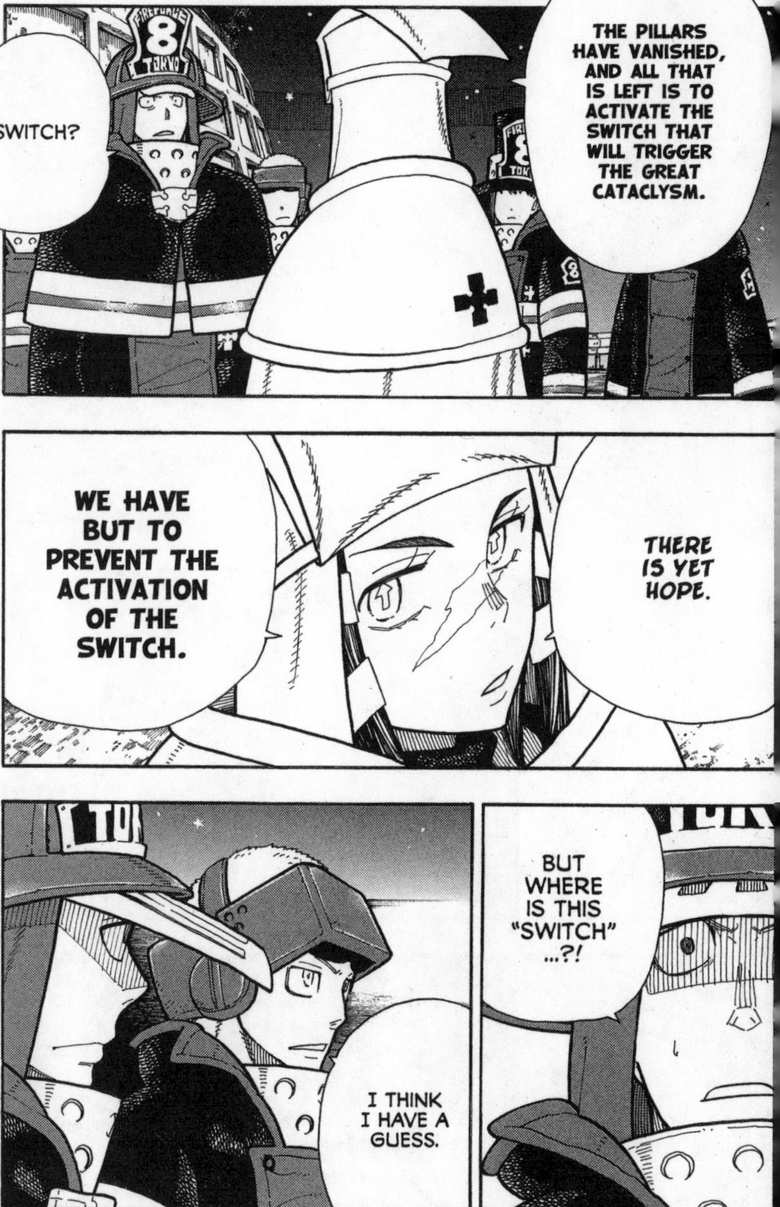
THE PILLARS HAVE VANISHED, AND ALL THAT IS LEFT IS TO ACTIVATE THE SWITCH THAT WILL TRIGGER THE GREAT CATACLYSM.
SWITCH?
THERE IS YET HOPE.
WE HAVE BUT TO PREVENT THE ACTIVATION OF THE SWITCH.
BUT WHERE IS THIS "SWITCH" ...?!
I THINK I HAVE A GUESS.

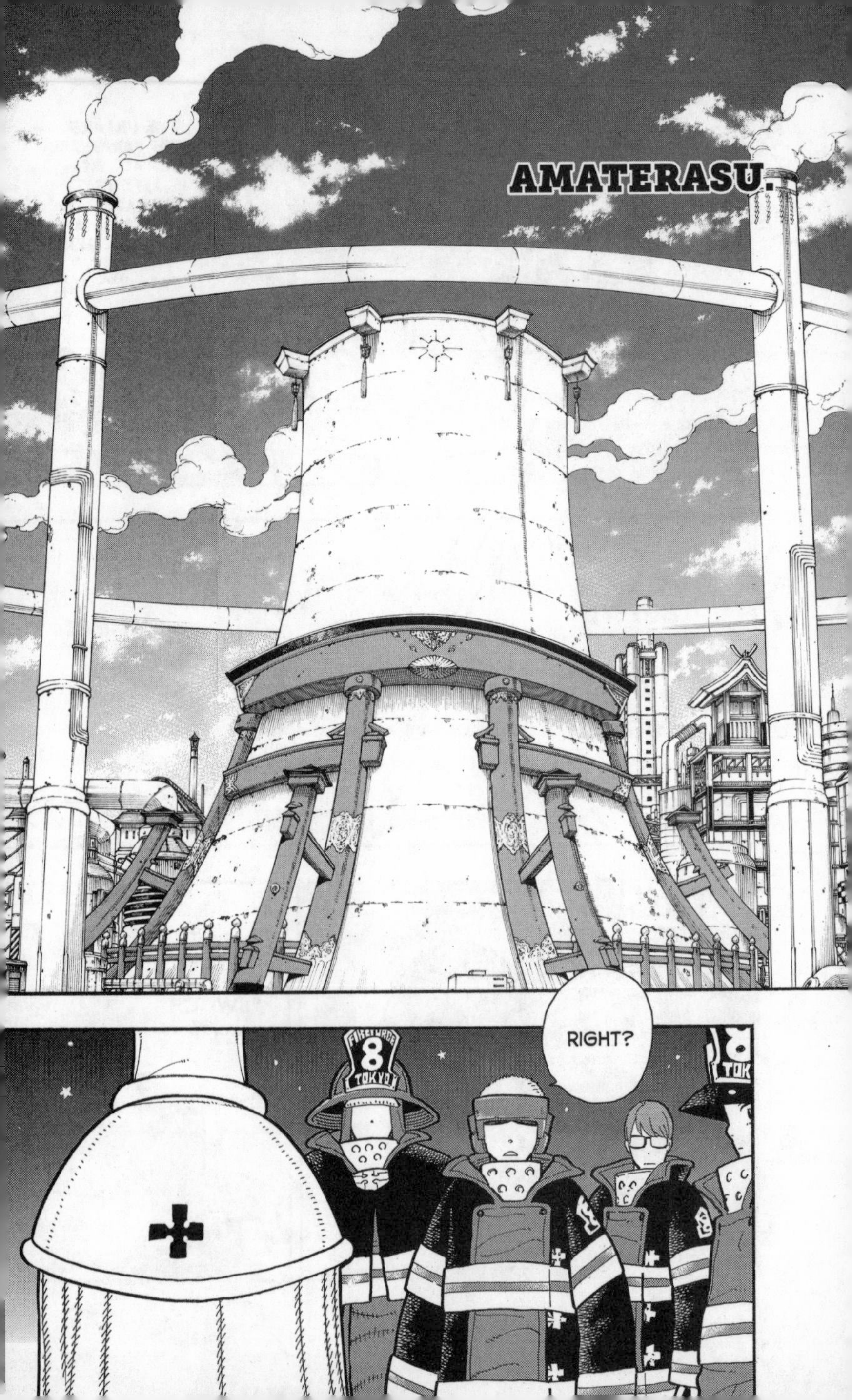
AMATERASU.
FIRE FORCE 8 TOKYO
RIGHT?

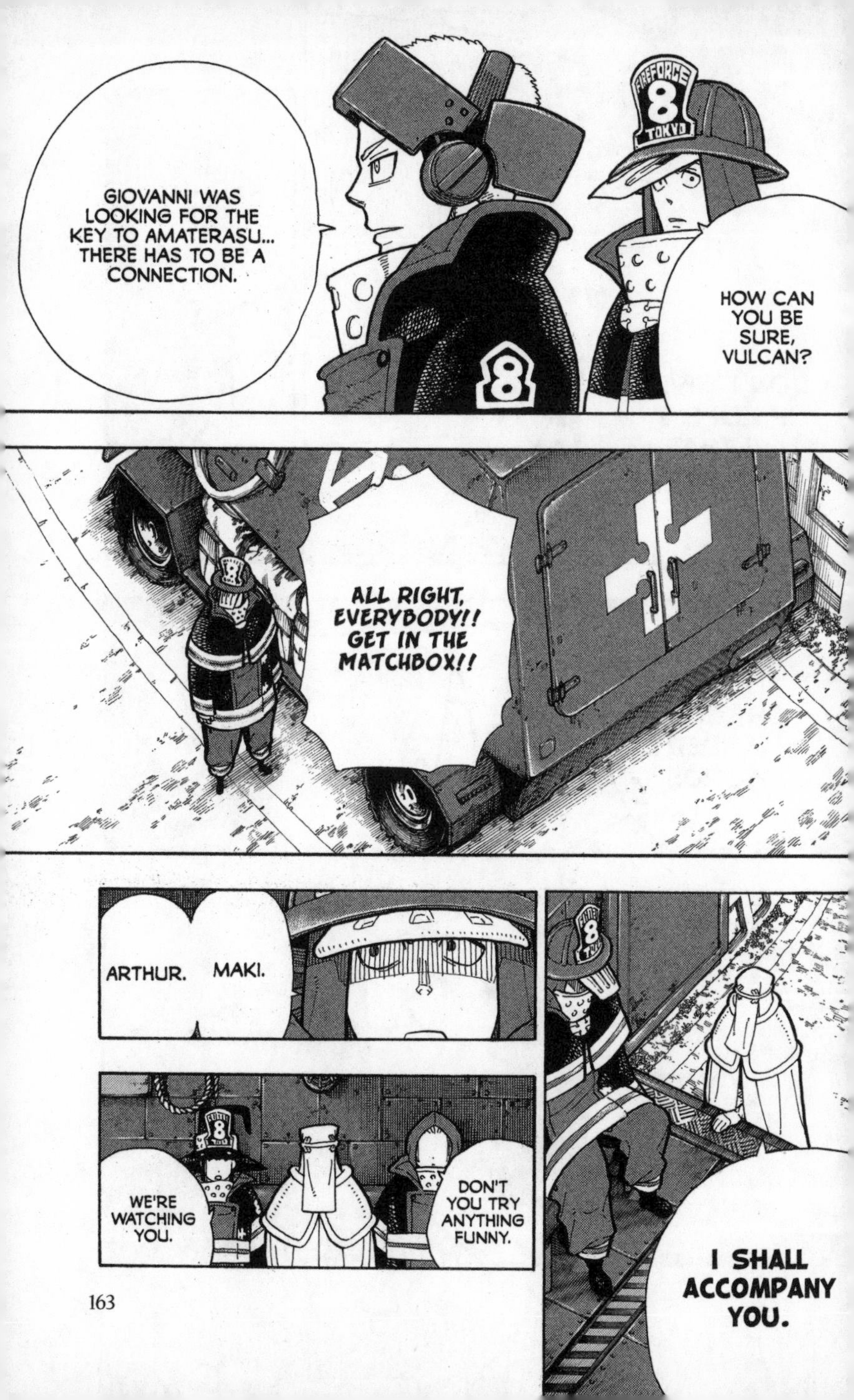
HOW CAN YOU BE SURE, VULCAN?
GIOVANNI WAS LOOKING FOR THE KEY TO AMATERASU... THERE HAS TO BE A CONNECTION.
ALL RIGHT, EVERYBODY!! GET IN THE MATCHBOX!!
I SHALL ACCOMPANY YOU.
MAKI.
ARTHUR.
DON'T YOU TRY ANYTHING FUNNY.
WE'RE WATCHING YOU.

WHAT YOU SAID EARLIER.

DON'T GIVE UP HOPE. I LIKE THAT.

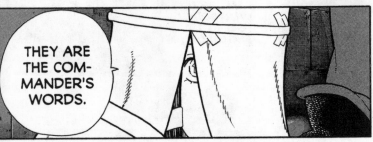

THEY ARE THE COMMANDER'S WORDS.

SHŌ-KUN'S WORDS, EH?

AS LONG AS OUR WORLD IS STILL AROUND, WE WON'T GIVE UP HOPE.

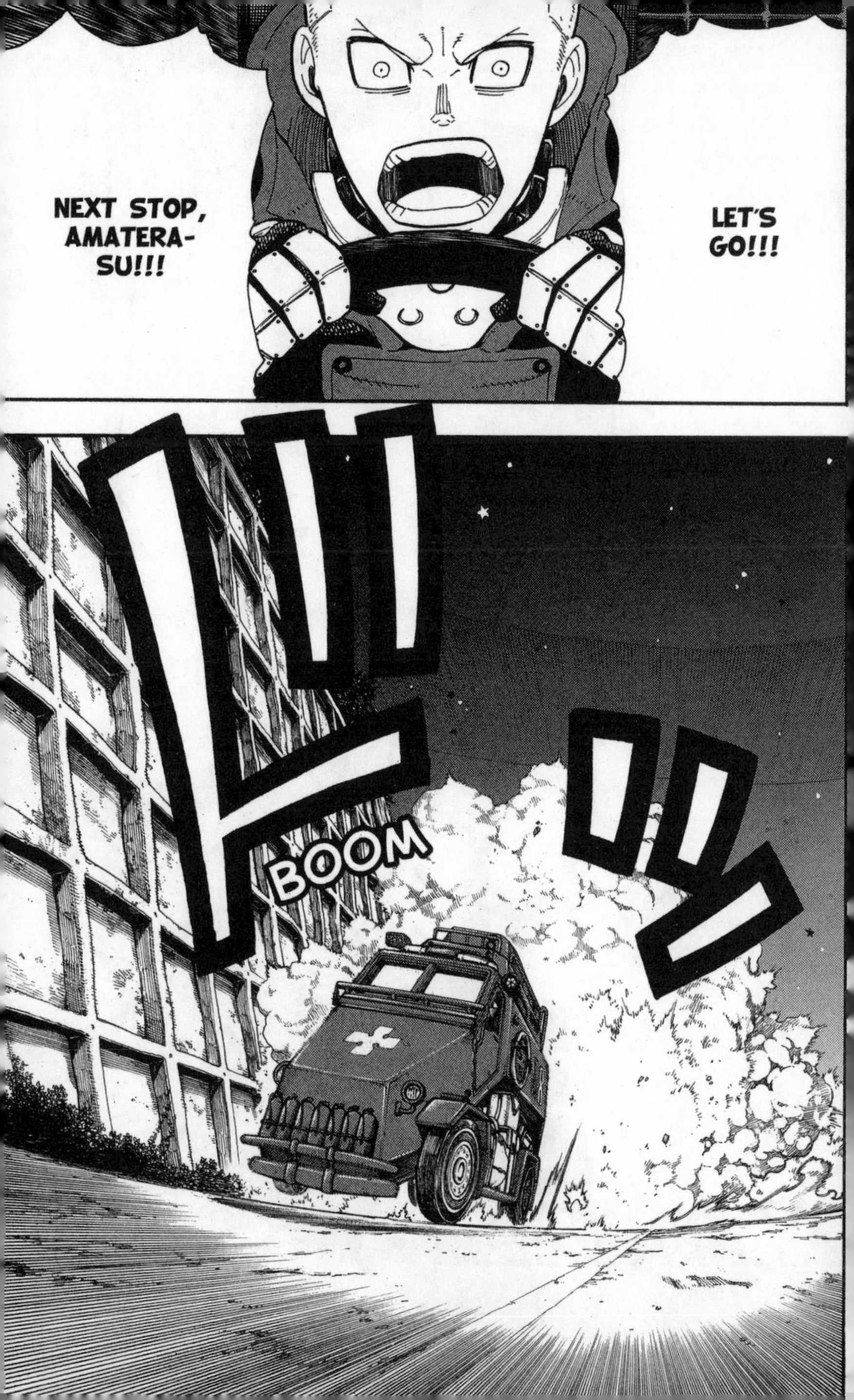
LET'S GO!!!
NEXT STOP, AMATERA-SU!!!
BOOM

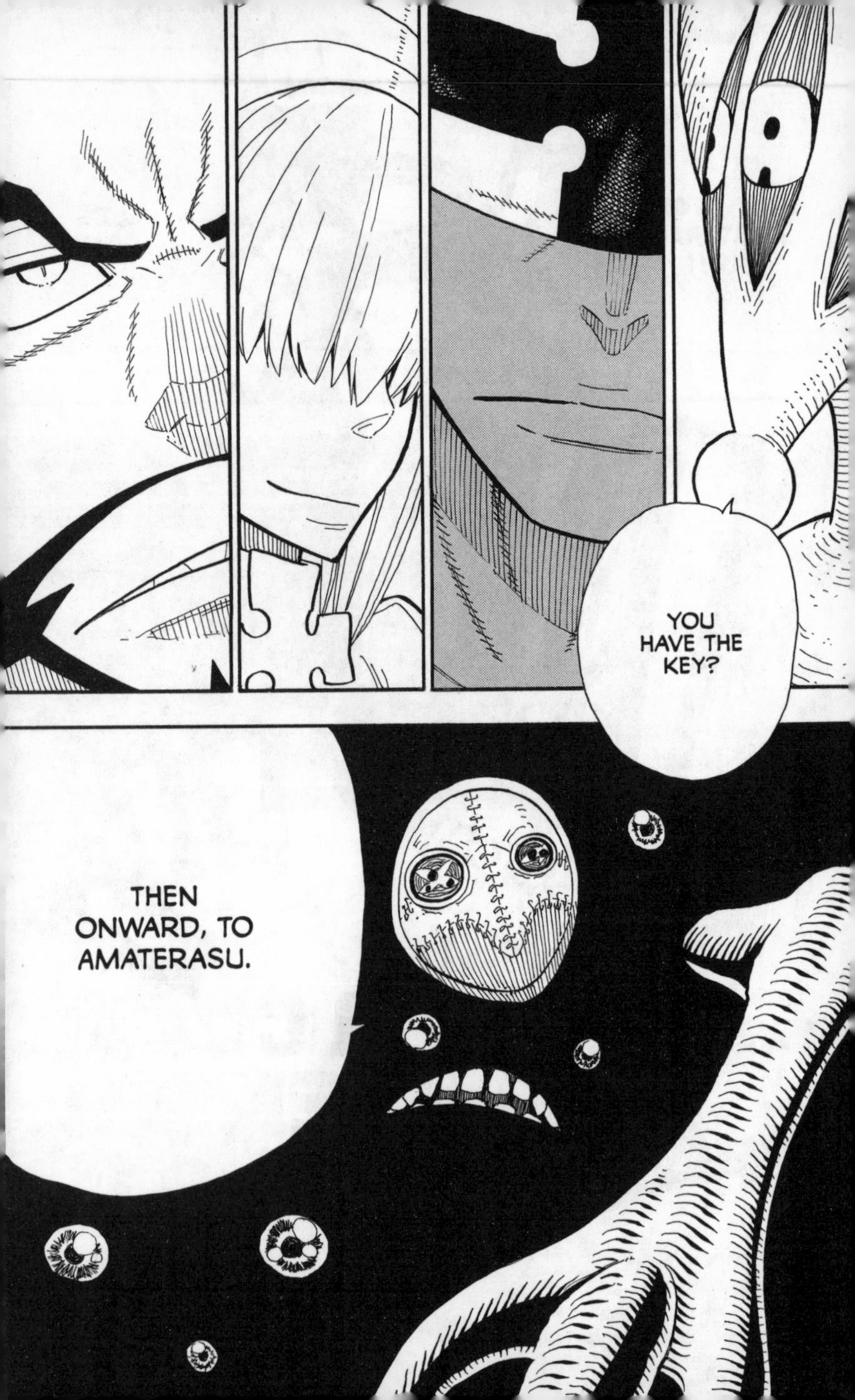
YOU HAVE THE KEY?
THEN ONWARD, TO AMATERASU.

CHAPTER CCXL:
AT THE CENTER
OF THE WORLD

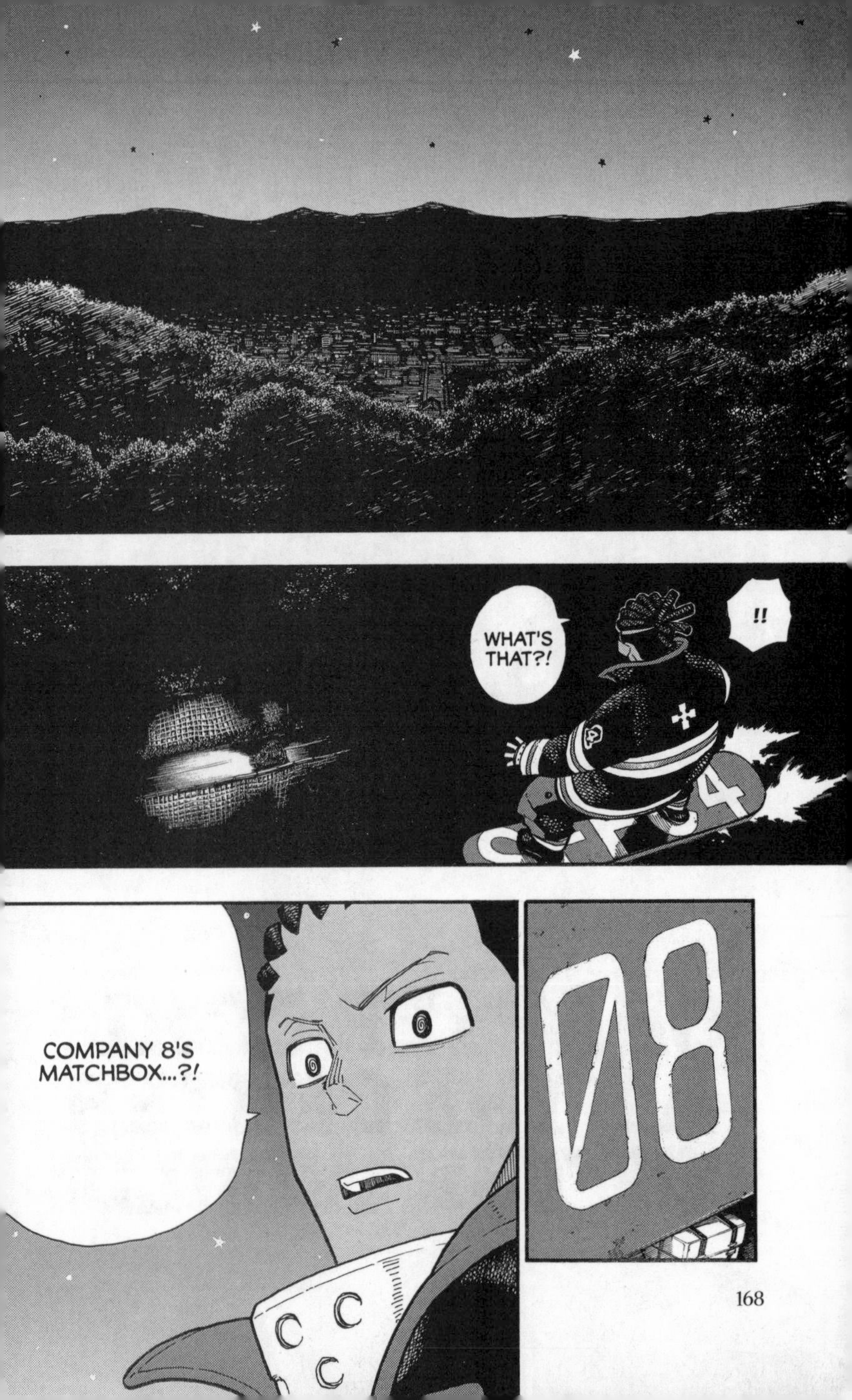
!!
WHAT'S THAT?!
08
COMPANY 8'S MATCHBOX...?!

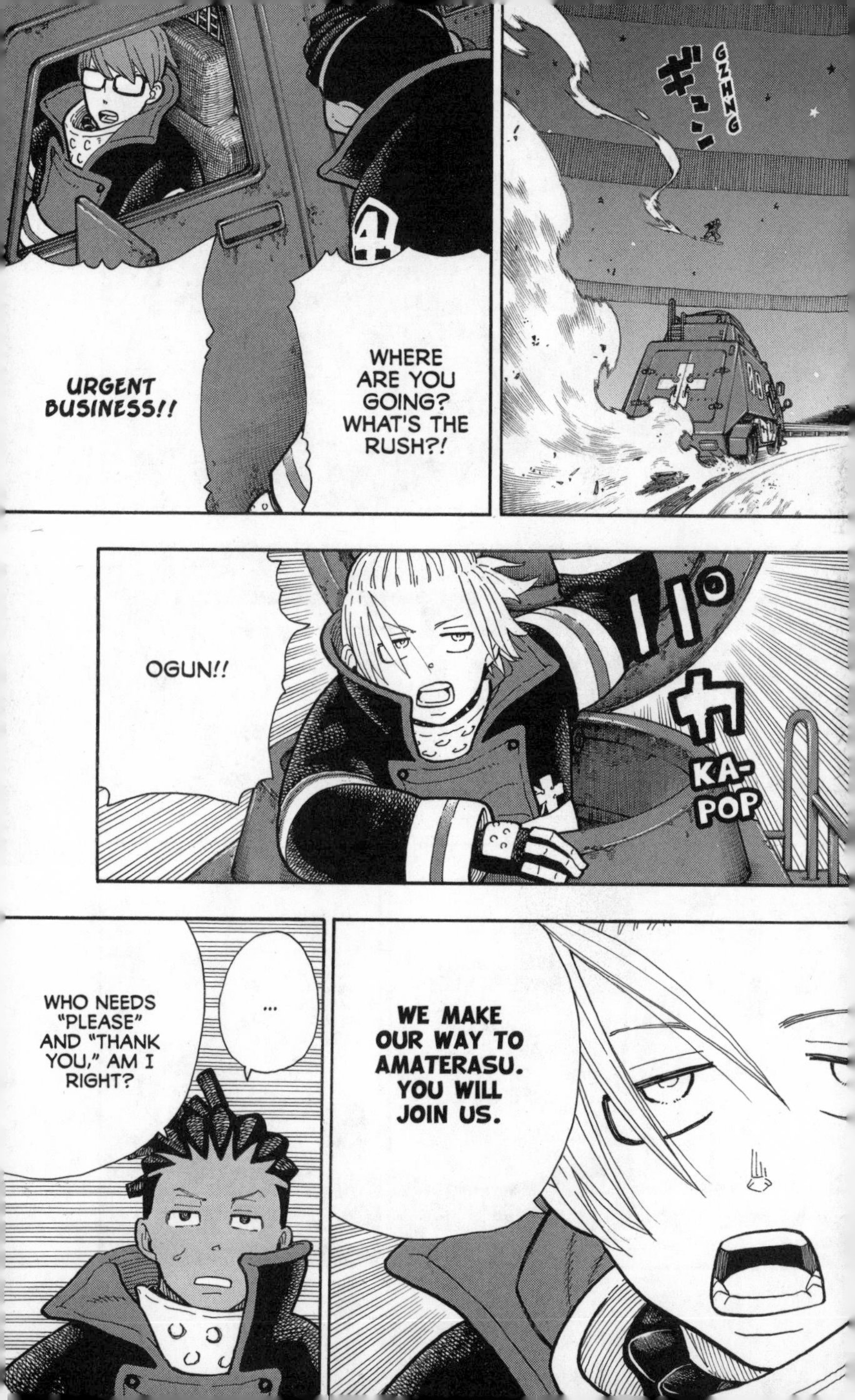
GZHNG
WHERE ARE YOU GOING? WHAT'S THE RUSH?!
URGENT BUSINESS!!
OGUN!!
KA-POP
WE MAKE OUR WAY TO AMATERASU. YOU WILL JOIN US.
...
WHO NEEDS "PLEASE" AND "THANK YOU," AM I RIGHT?

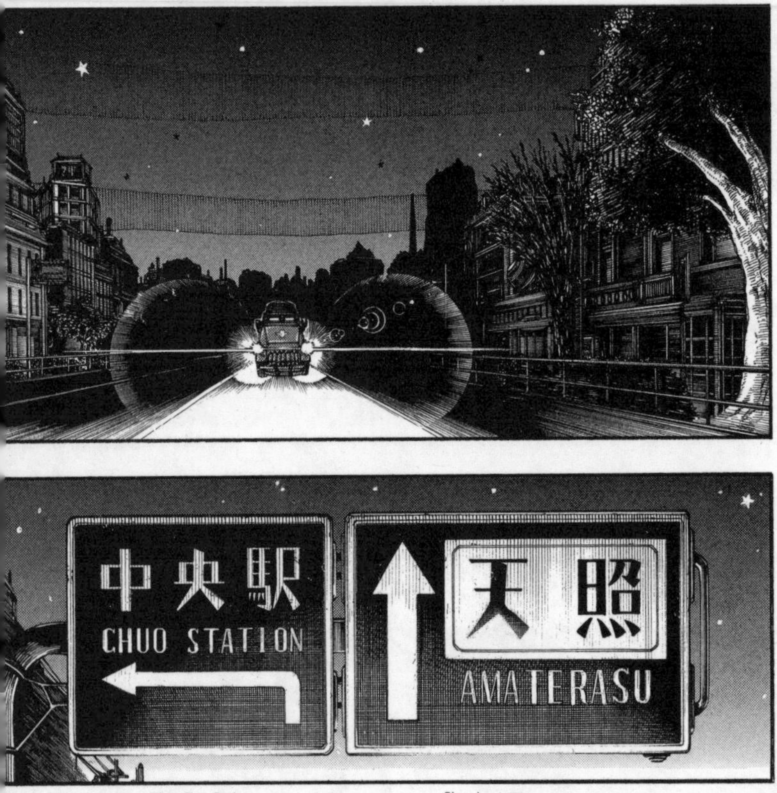
天照
AMATERASU
中央駅
CHUO STATION

Sign: Chuo Station Sign: Amaterasu

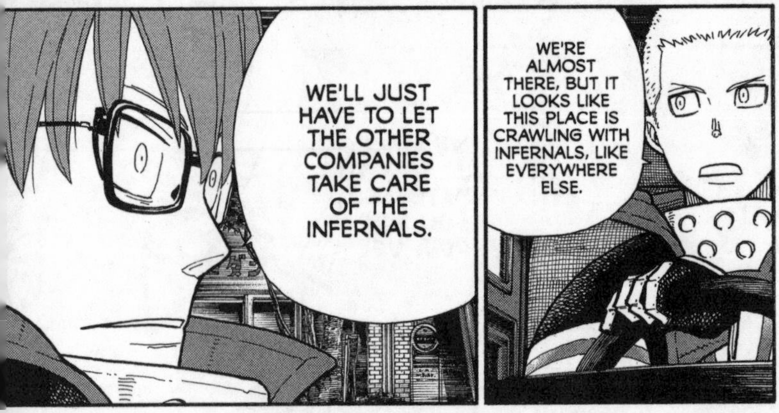
WE'RE ALMOST THERE, BUT IT LOOKS LIKE THIS PLACE IS CRAWLING WITH INFERNALS, LIKE EVERYWHERE ELSE.
WE'LL JUST HAVE TO LET THE OTHER COMPANIES TAKE CARE OF THE INFERNALS.

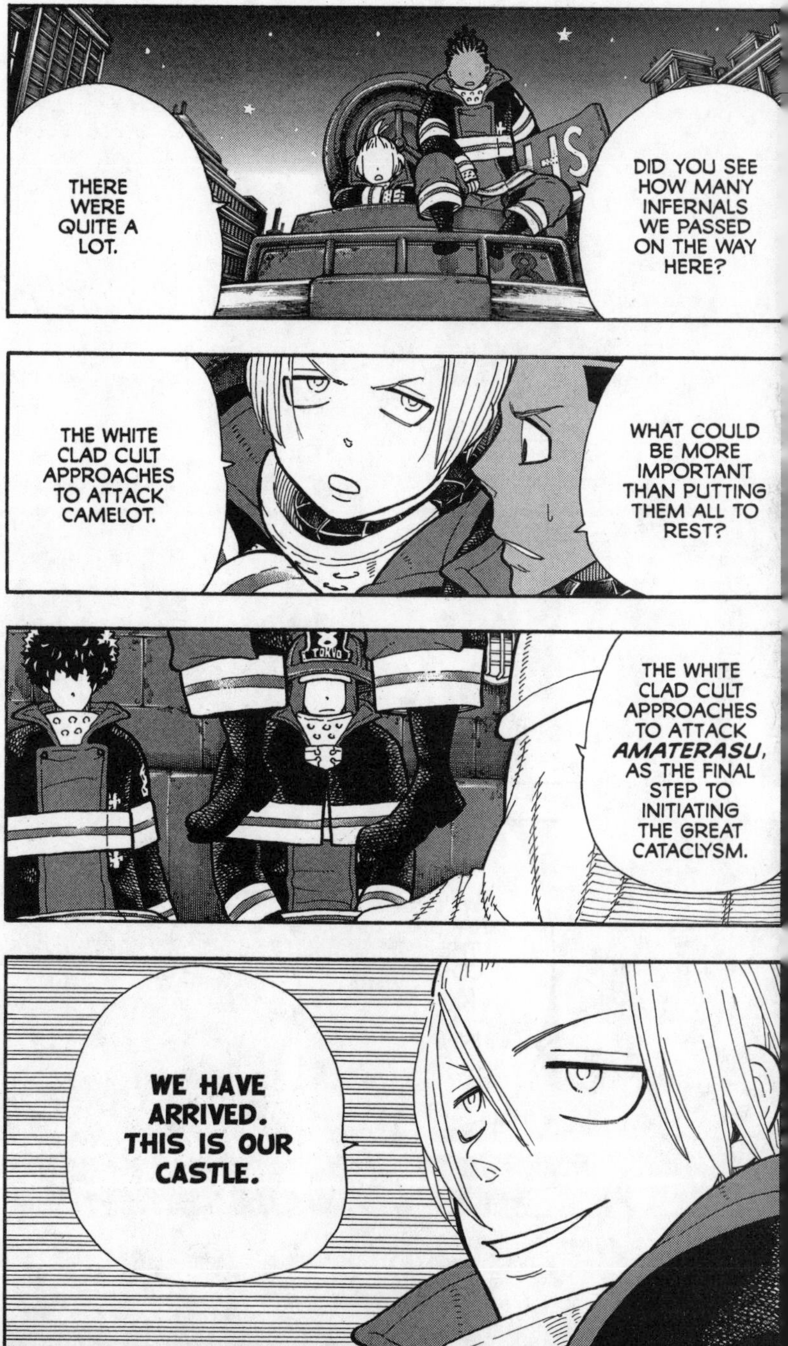
DID YOU SEE HOW MANY INFERNALS WE PASSED ON THE WAY HERE?
THERE WERE QUITE A LOT.
WHAT COULD BE MORE IMPORTANT THAN PUTTING THEM ALL TO REST?
THE WHITE CLAD CULT APPROACHES TO ATTACK CAMELOT.
THE WHITE CLAD CULT APPROACHES TO ATTACK *AMATERASU*, AS THE FINAL STEP TO INITIATING THE GREAT CATACLYSM.
WE HAVE ARRIVED. THIS IS OUR CASTLE.

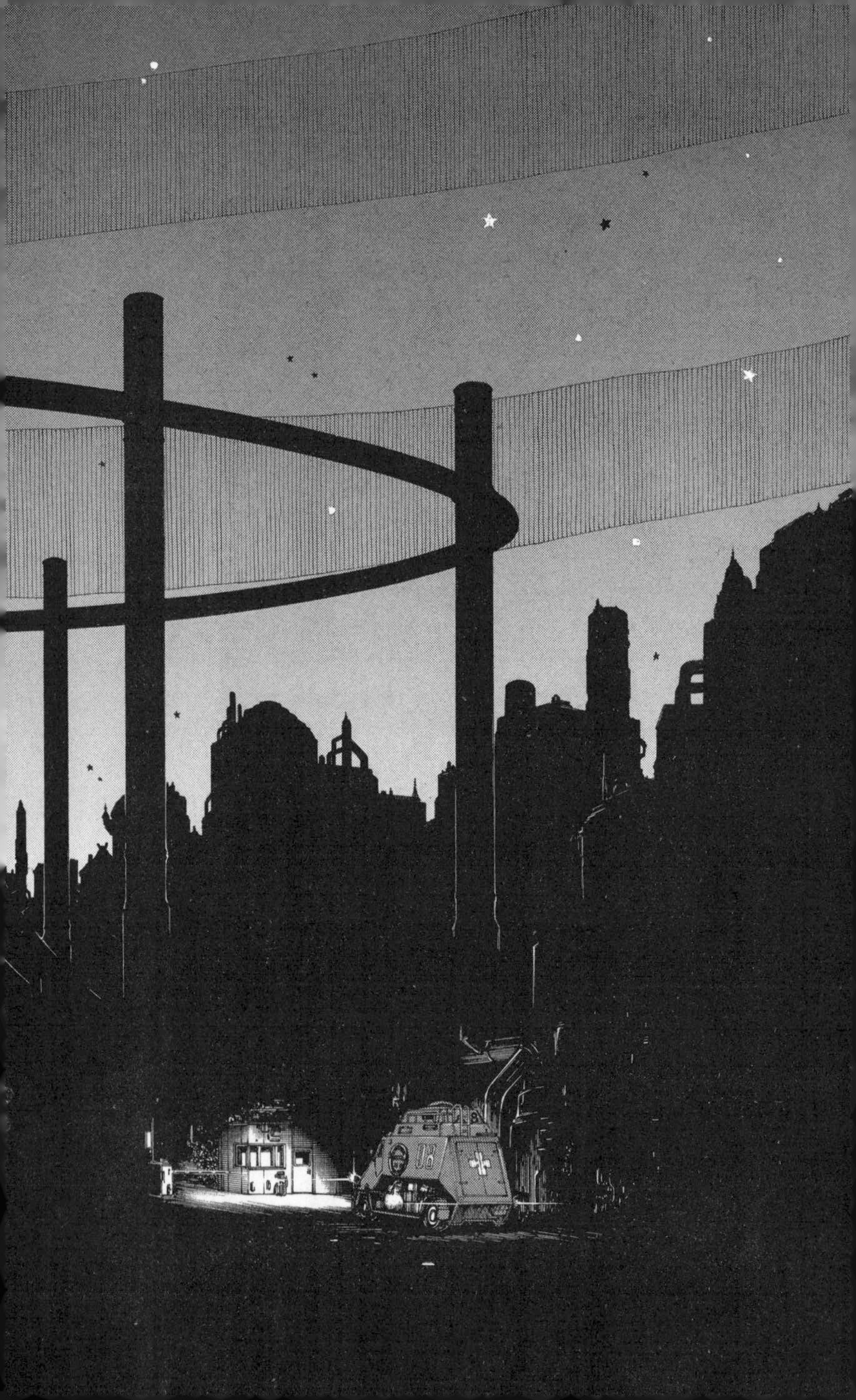
08

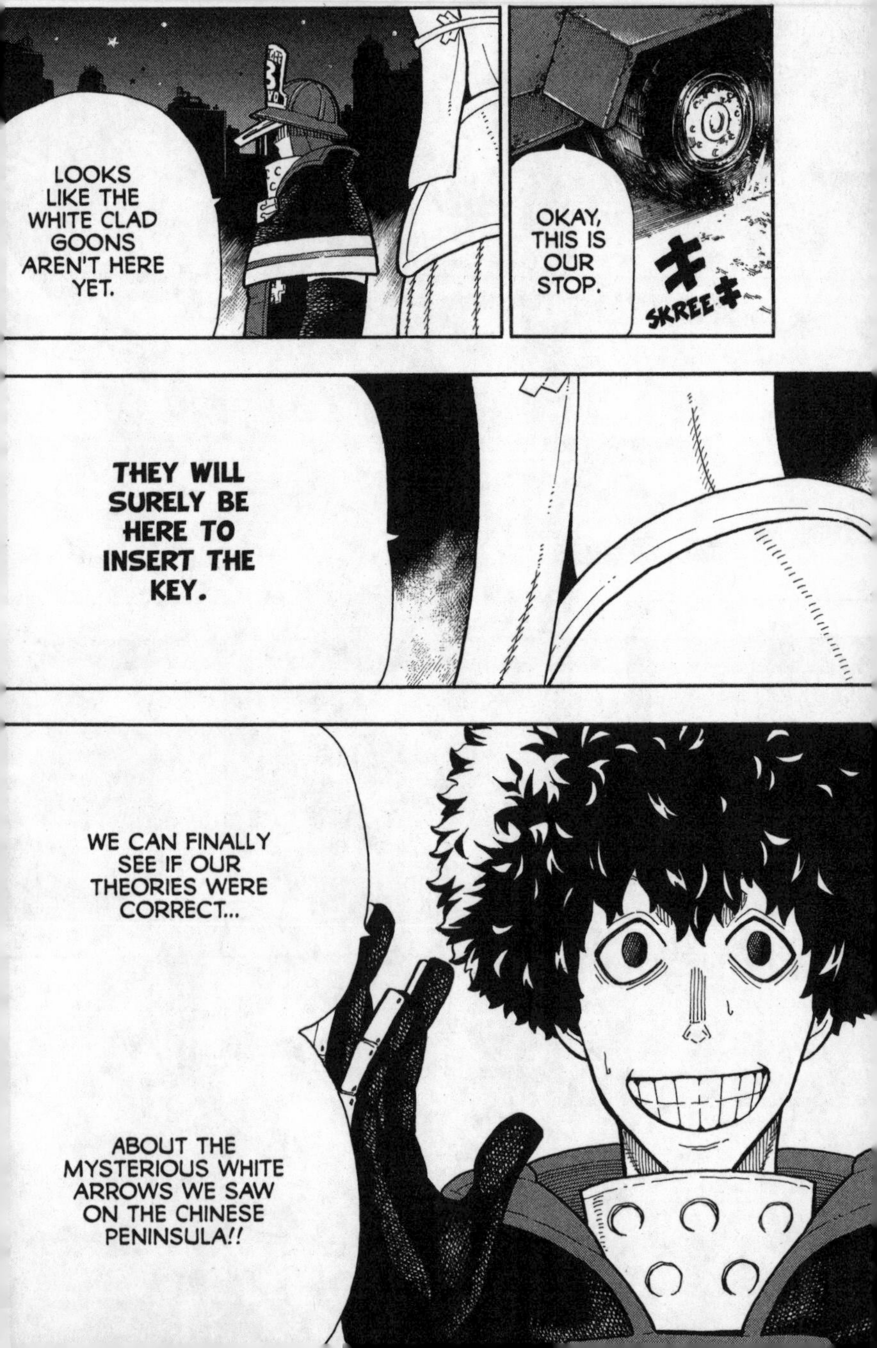
OKAY, THIS IS OUR STOP.
SKREE
LOOKS LIKE THE WHITE CLAD GOONS AREN'T HERE YET.
THEY WILL SURELY BE HERE TO INSERT THE KEY.
WE CAN FINALLY SEE IF OUR THEORIES WERE CORRECT...
ABOUT THE MYSTERIOUS WHITE ARROWS WE SAW ON THE CHINESE PENINSULA!!

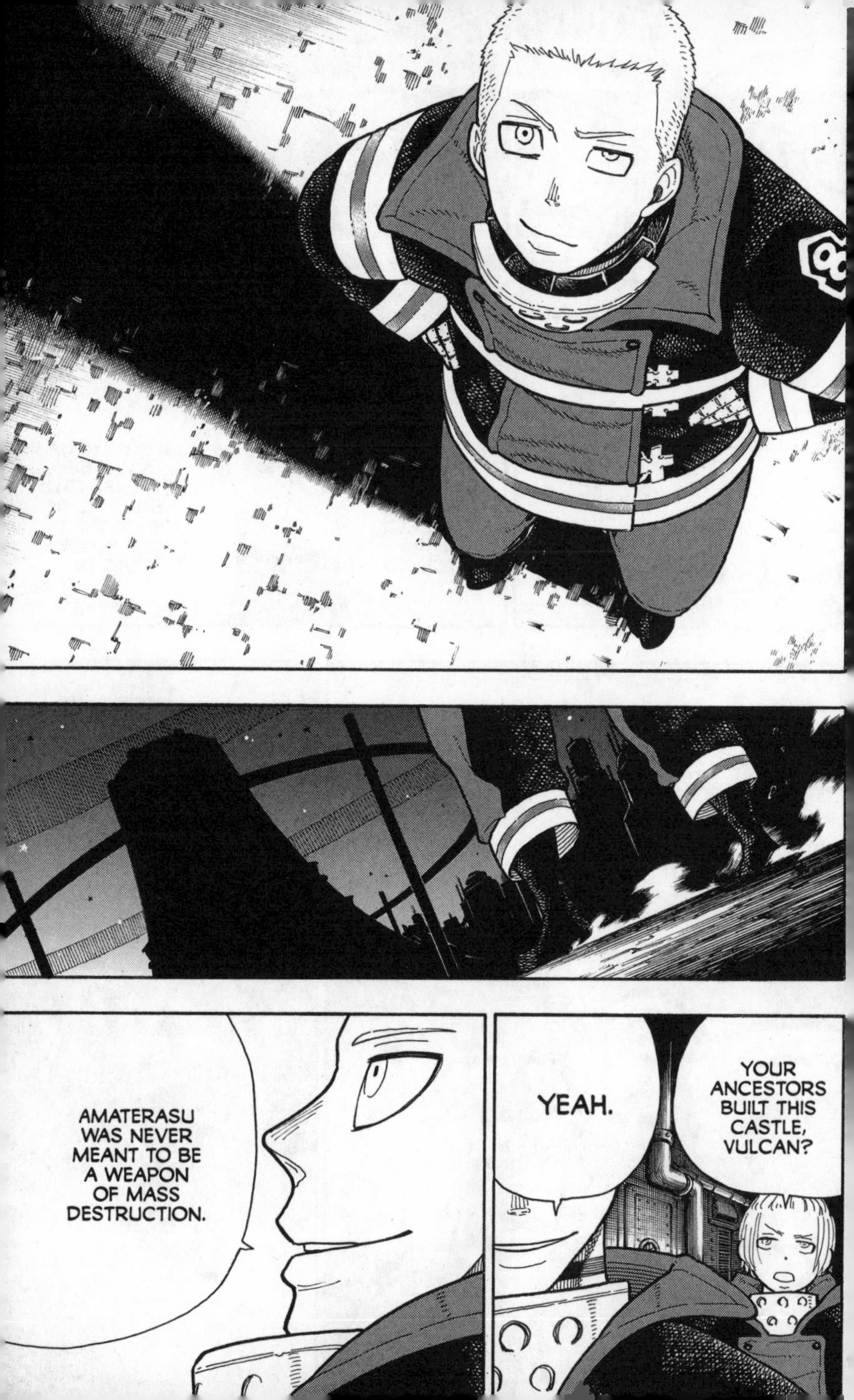
YOUR ANCESTORS BUILT THIS CASTLE, VULCAN?
YEAH.
AMATERASU WAS NEVER MEANT TO BE A WEAPON OF MASS DESTRUCTION.

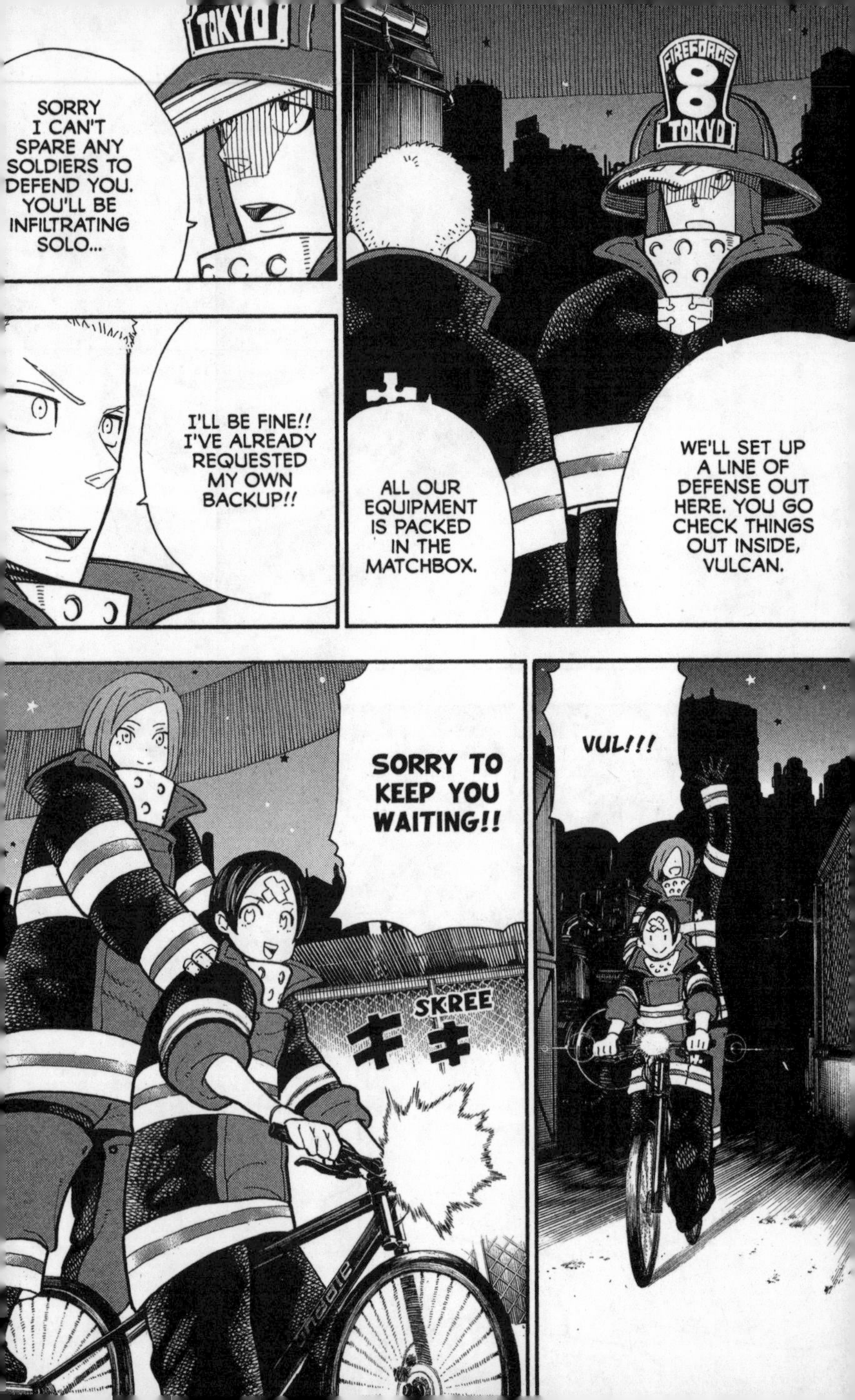
WE'LL SET UP A LINE OF DEFENSE OUT HERE. YOU GO CHECK THINGS OUT INSIDE, VULCAN.
ALL OUR EQUIPMENT IS PACKED IN THE MATCHBOX.
SORRY I CAN'T SPARE ANY SOLDIERS TO DEFEND YOU. YOU'LL BE INFILTRATING SOLO...
I'LL BE FINE!! I'VE ALREADY REQUESTED MY OWN BACKUP!!
VUL!!!
SORRY TO KEEP YOU WAITING!!
SKREE

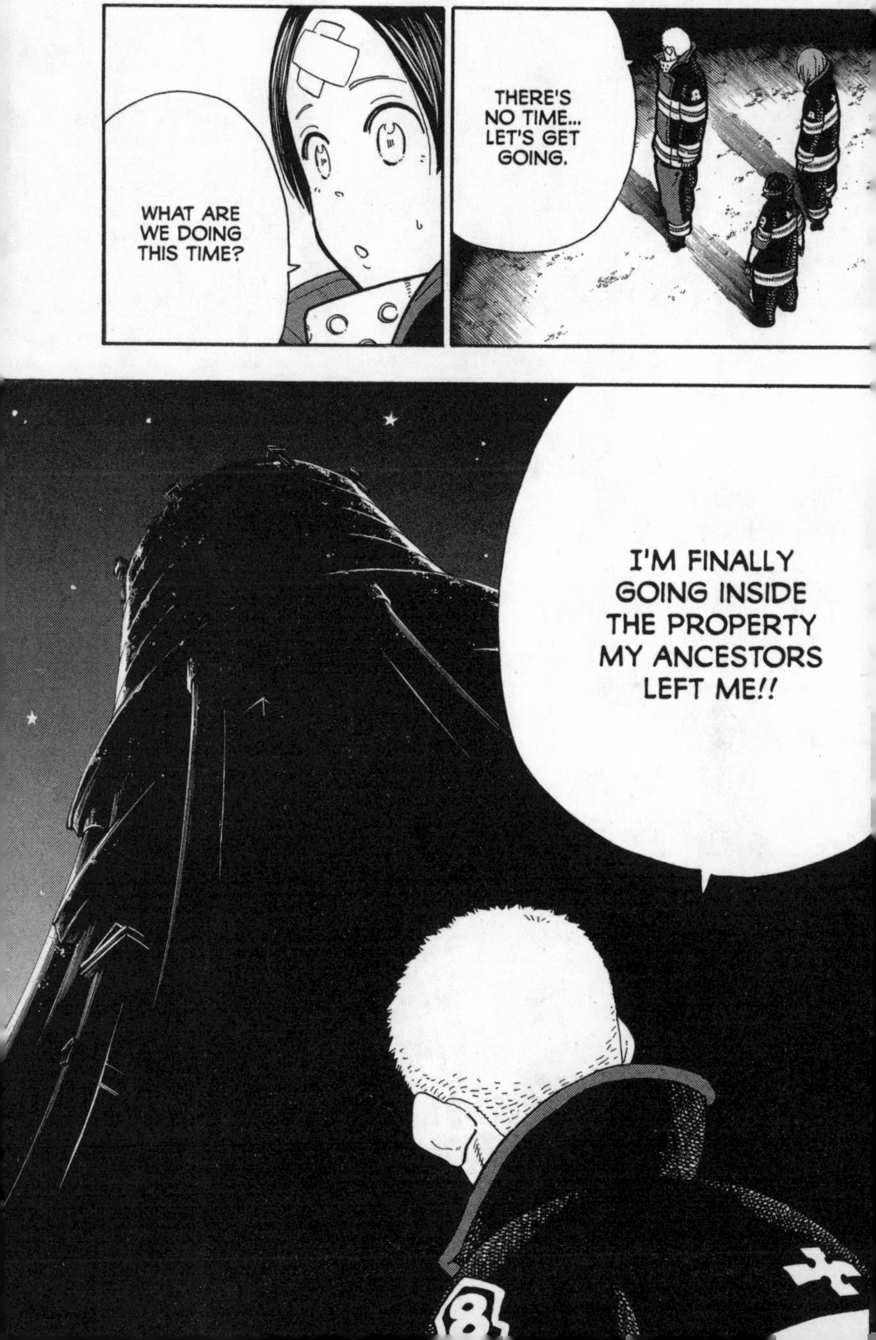
THERE'S NO TIME... LET'S GET GOING.
WHAT ARE WE DOING THIS TIME?
I'M FINALLY GOING INSIDE THE PROPERTY MY ANCESTORS LEFT ME!!

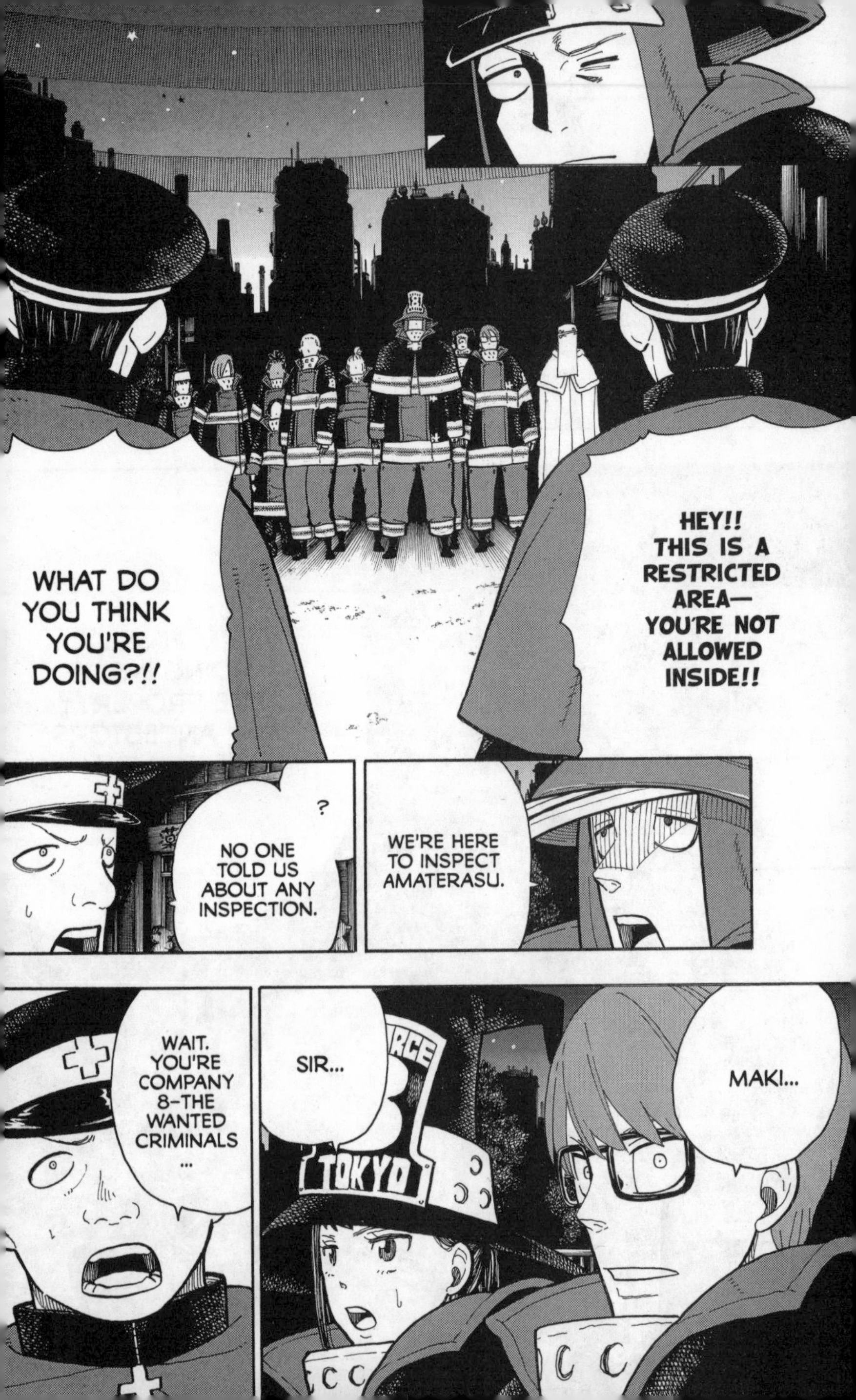
HEY!! THIS IS A RESTRICTED AREA— YOU'RE NOT ALLOWED INSIDE!!
WHAT DO YOU THINK YOU'RE DOING?!!
WE'RE HERE TO INSPECT AMATERASU.
?
NO ONE TOLD US ABOUT ANY INSPECTION.
MAKI...
TOKYO
SIR...
WAIT. YOU'RE COMPANY 8–THE WANTED CRIMINALS ...

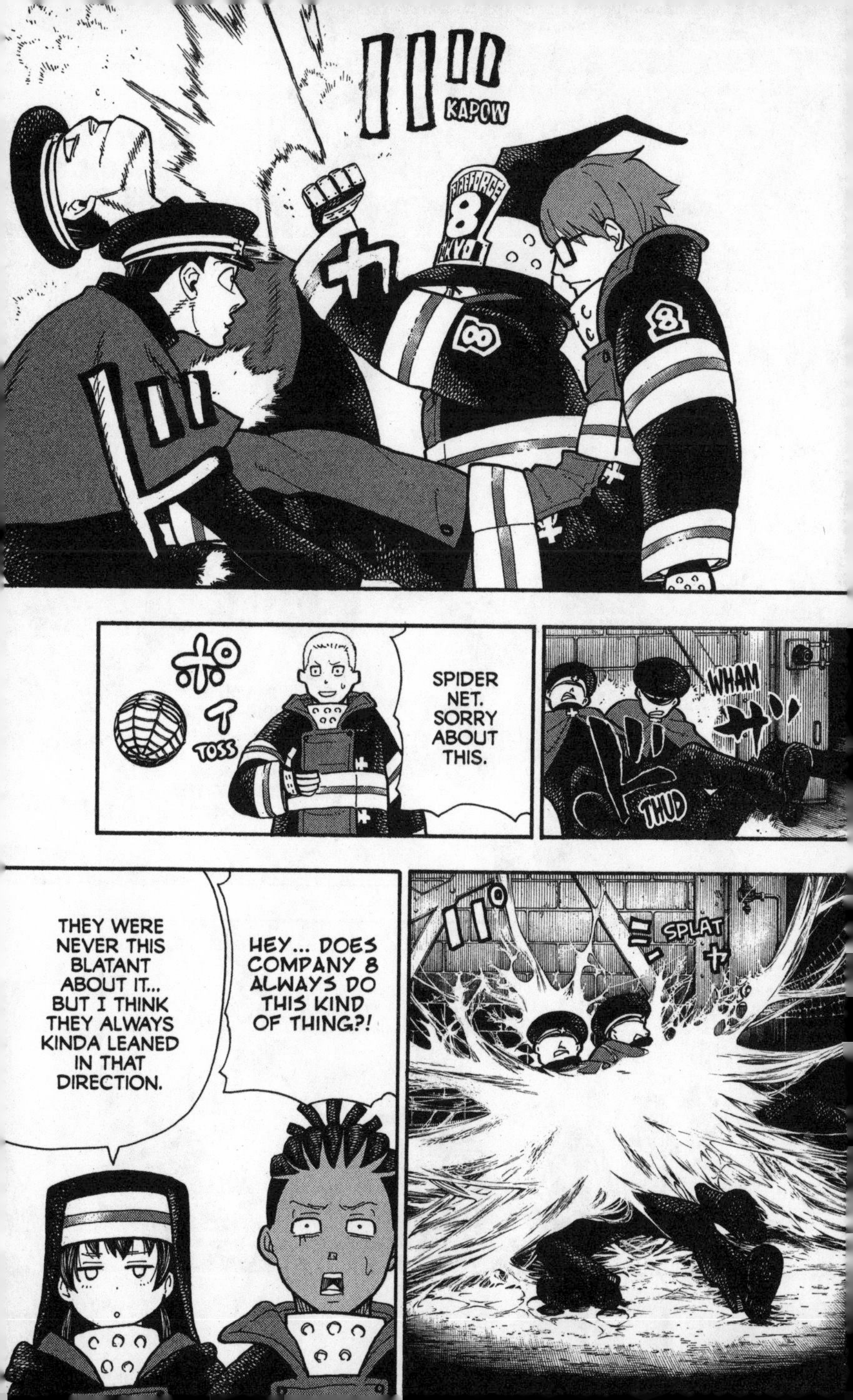
KAPOW
WHAM
THUD
TOSS
SPIDER NET. SORRY ABOUT THIS.
SPLAT
HEY... DOES COMPANY 8 ALWAYS DO THIS KIND OF THING?!
THEY WERE NEVER THIS BLATANT ABOUT IT... BUT I THINK THEY ALWAYS KINDA LEANED IN THAT DIRECTION.

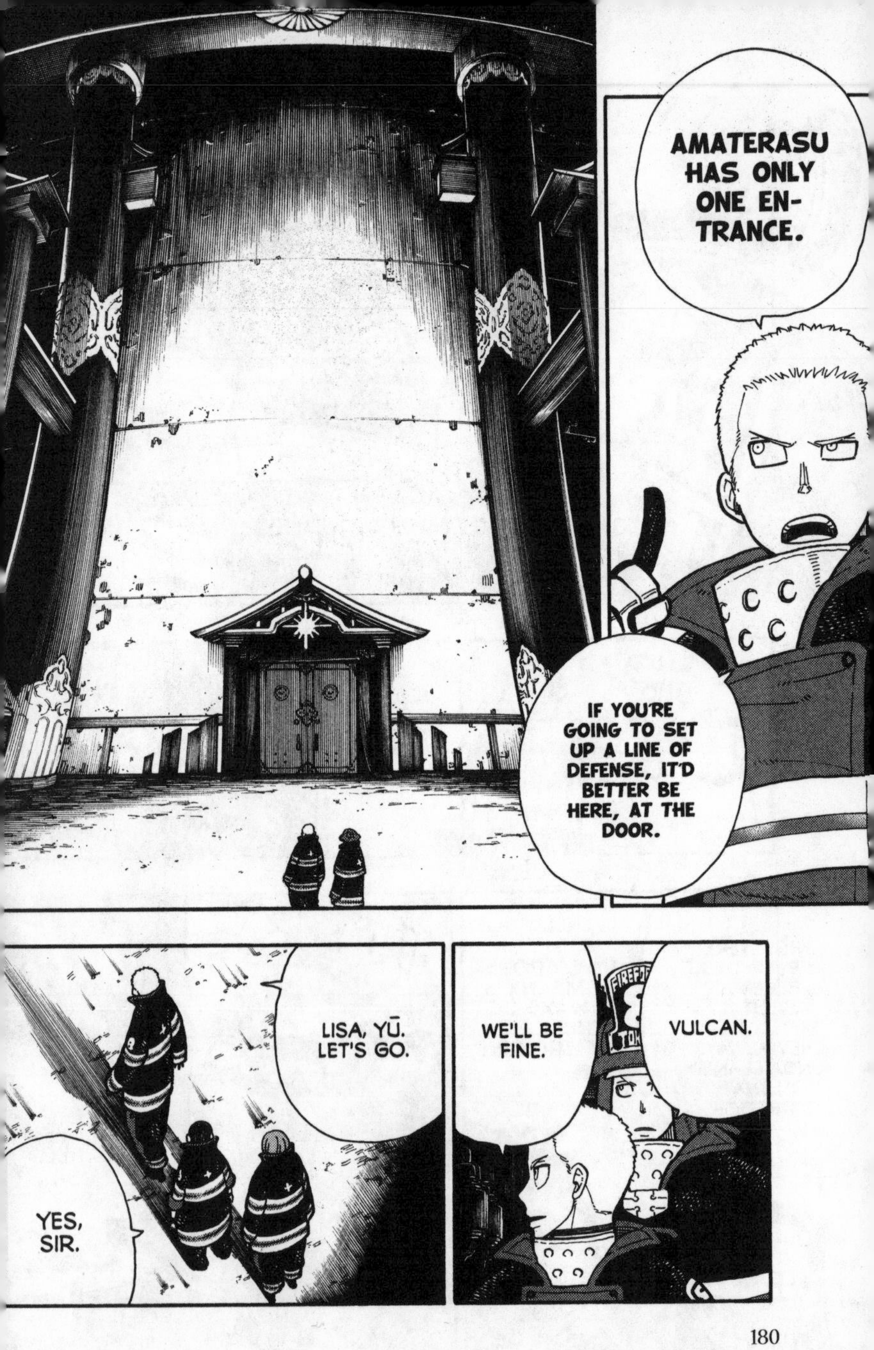
AMATERASU HAS ONLY ONE EN-TRANCE.
IF YOU'RE GOING TO SET UP A LINE OF DEFENSE, IT'D BETTER BE HERE, AT THE DOOR.
VULCAN.
WE'LL BE FINE.
LISA, YŪ. LET'S GO.
YES, SIR.

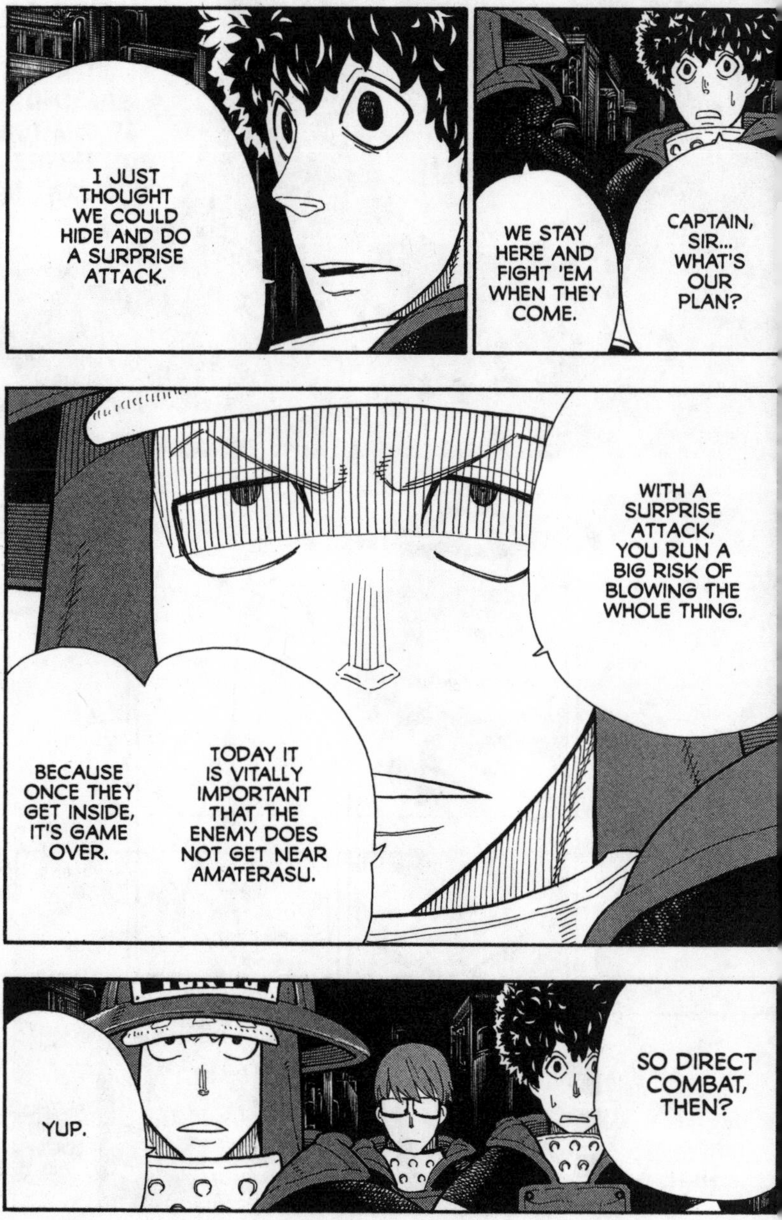
CAPTAIN, SIR... WHAT'S OUR PLAN?
WE STAY HERE AND FIGHT 'EM WHEN THEY COME.
I JUST THOUGHT WE COULD HIDE AND DO A SURPRISE ATTACK.
WITH A SURPRISE ATTACK, YOU RUN A BIG RISK OF BLOWING THE WHOLE THING.
TODAY IT IS VITALLY IMPORTANT THAT THE ENEMY DOES NOT GET NEAR AMATERASU.
BECAUSE ONCE THEY GET INSIDE, IT'S GAME OVER.
SO DIRECT COMBAT, THEN?
YUP.

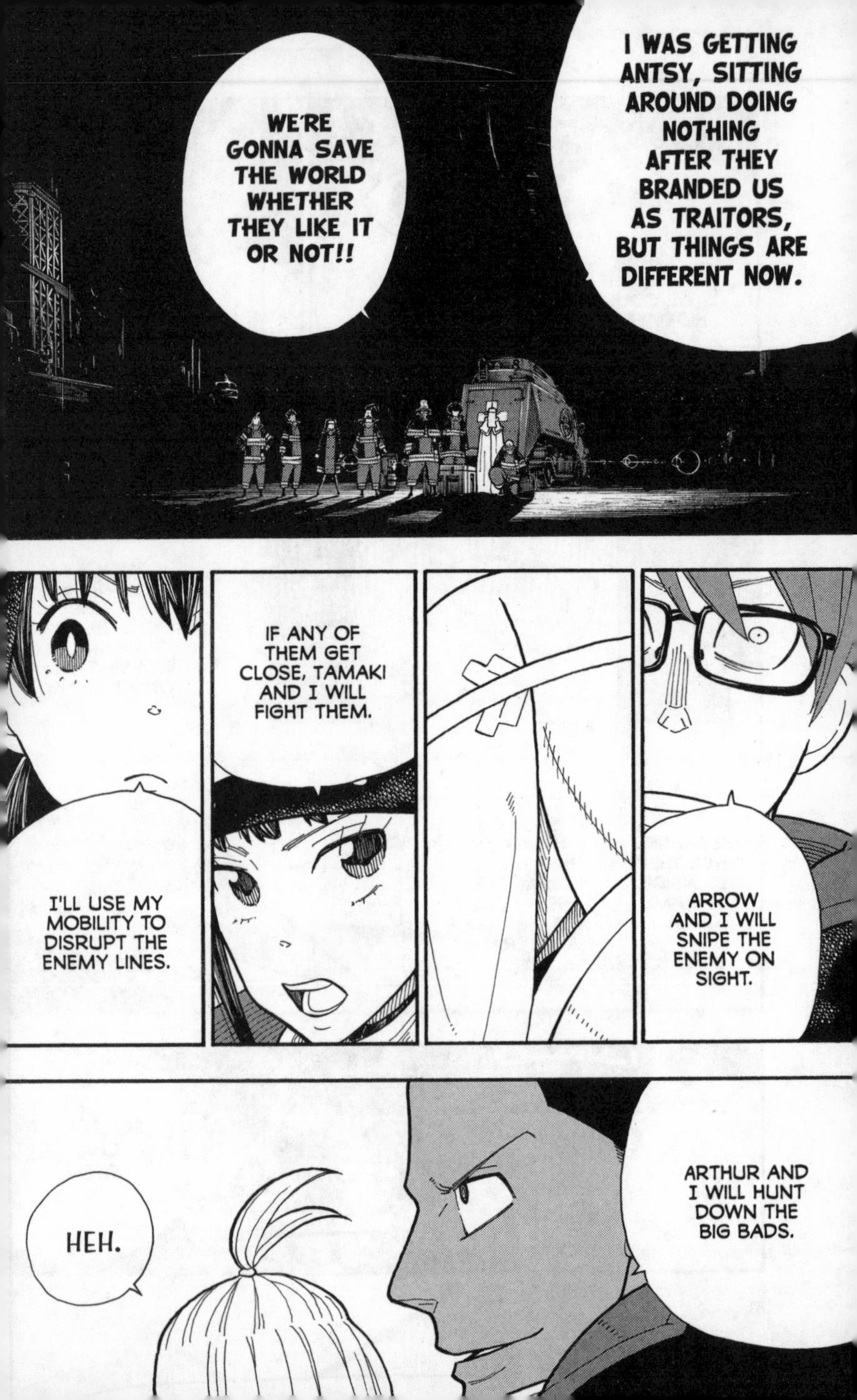
I WAS GETTING ANTSY, SITTING AROUND DOING NOTHING AFTER THEY BRANDED US AS TRAITORS, BUT THINGS ARE DIFFERENT NOW.
WE'RE GONNA SAVE THE WORLD WHETHER THEY LIKE IT OR NOT!!
ARROW AND I WILL SNIPE THE ENEMY ON SIGHT.
IF ANY OF THEM GET CLOSE, TAMAKI AND I WILL FIGHT THEM.
I'LL USE MY MOBILITY TO DISRUPT THE ENEMY LINES.
ARTHUR AND I WILL HUNT DOWN THE BIG BADS.
HEH.

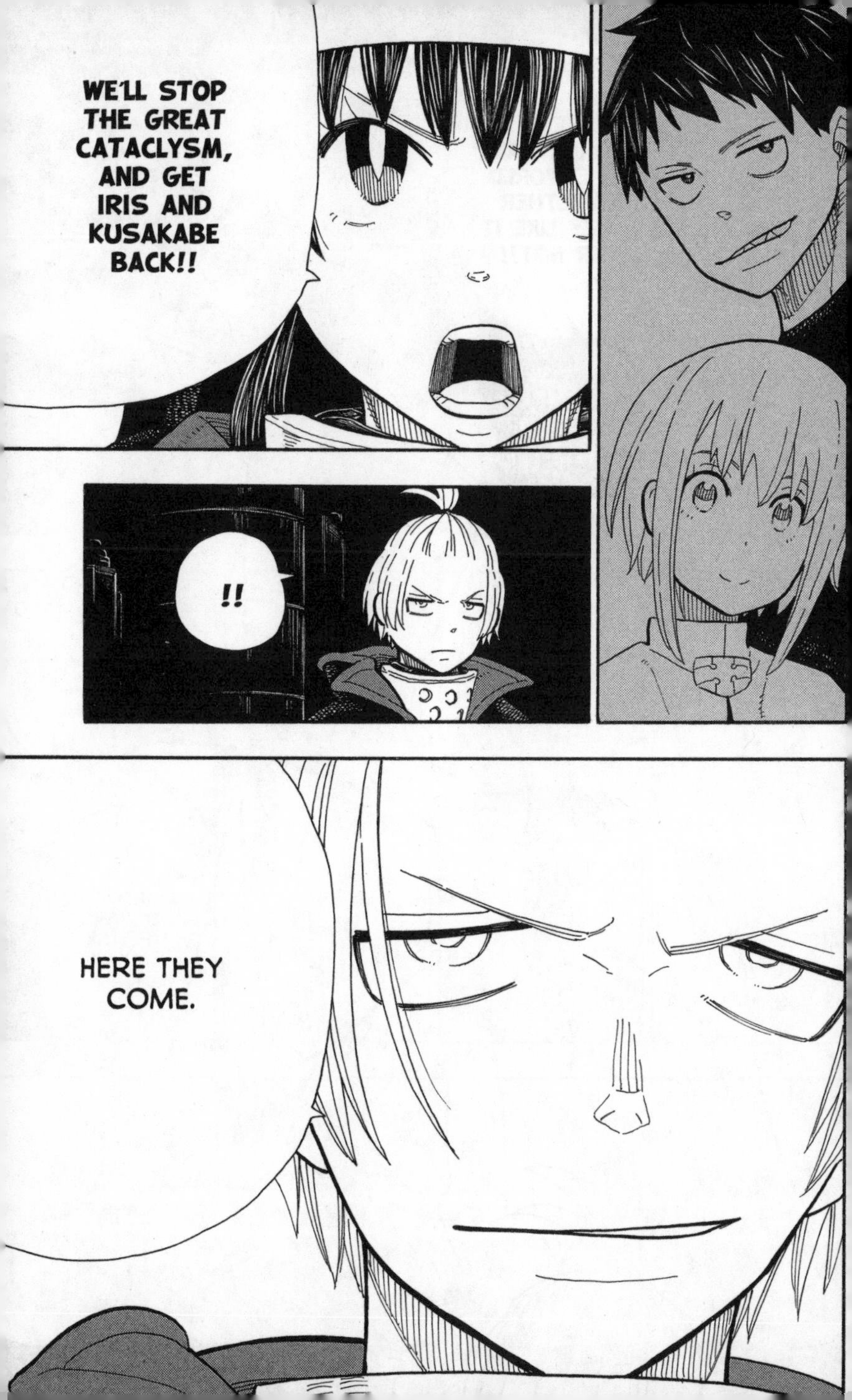
WE'LL STOP THE GREAT CATACLYSM, AND GET IRIS AND KUSAKABE BACK!!
!!
HERE THEY COME.

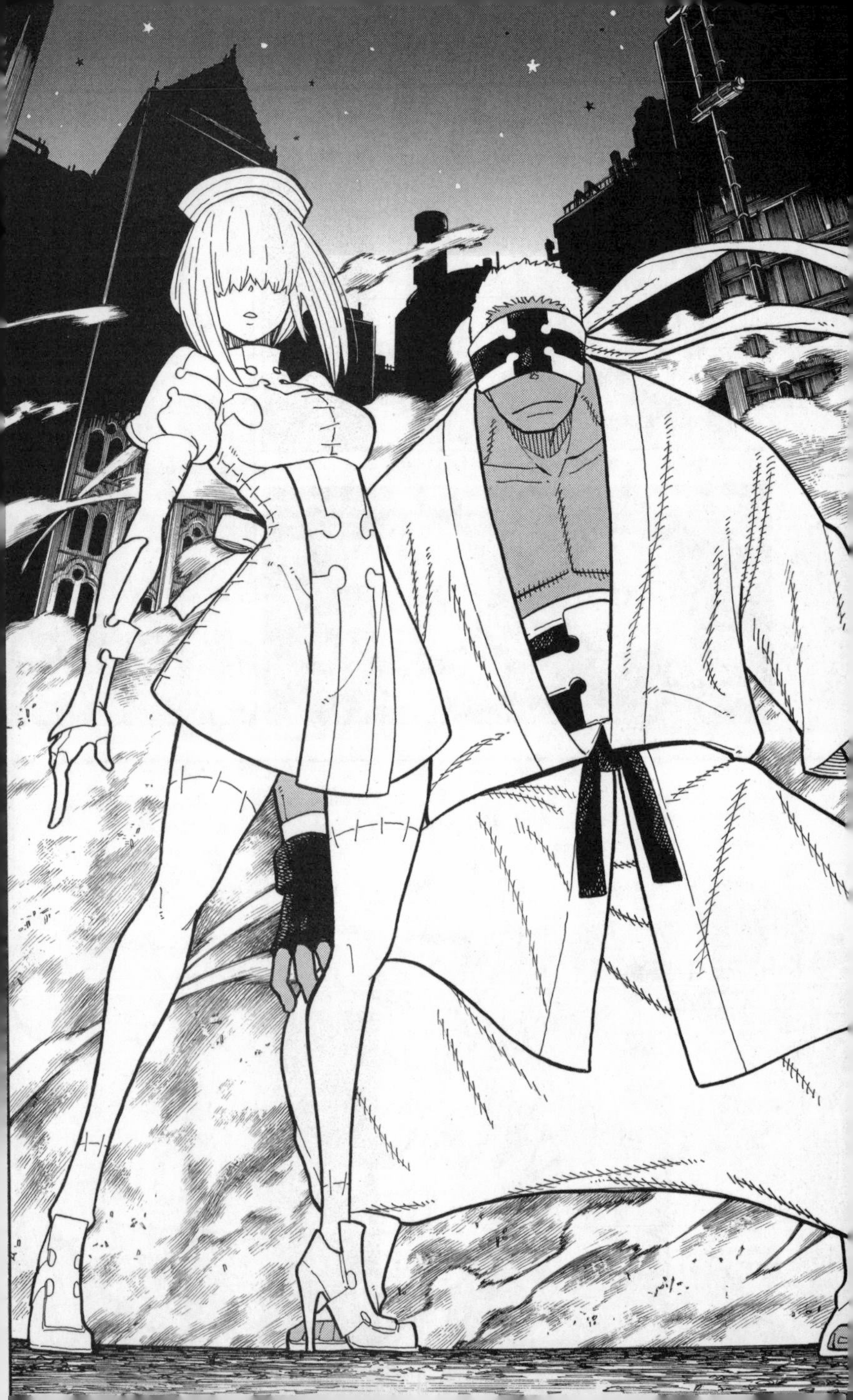

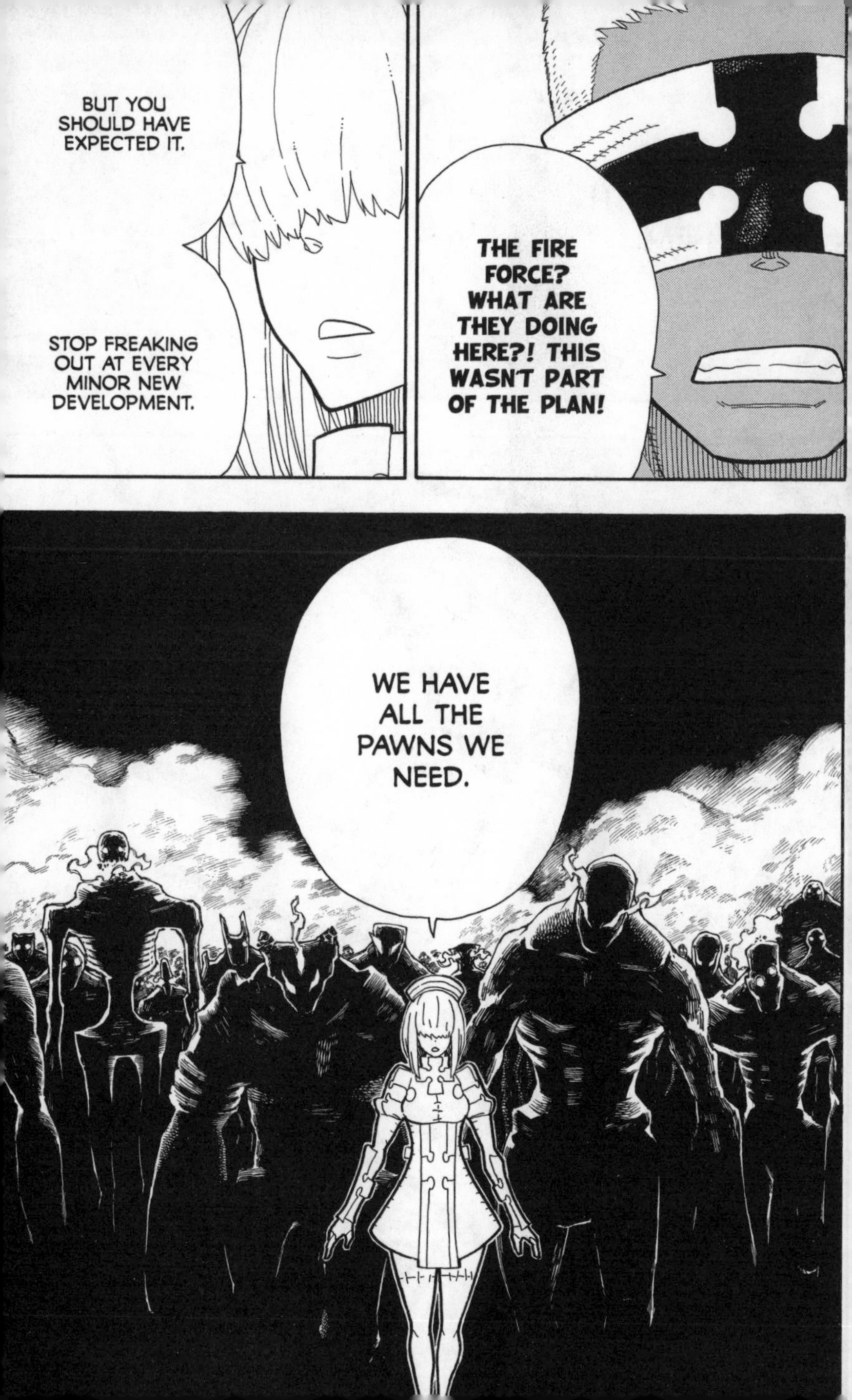
THE FIRE FORCE? WHAT ARE THEY DOING HERE?! THIS WASN'T PART OF THE PLAN!
BUT YOU SHOULD HAVE EXPECTED IT.
STOP FREAKING OUT AT EVERY MINOR NEW DEVELOPMENT.
WE HAVE ALL THE PAWNS WE NEED.

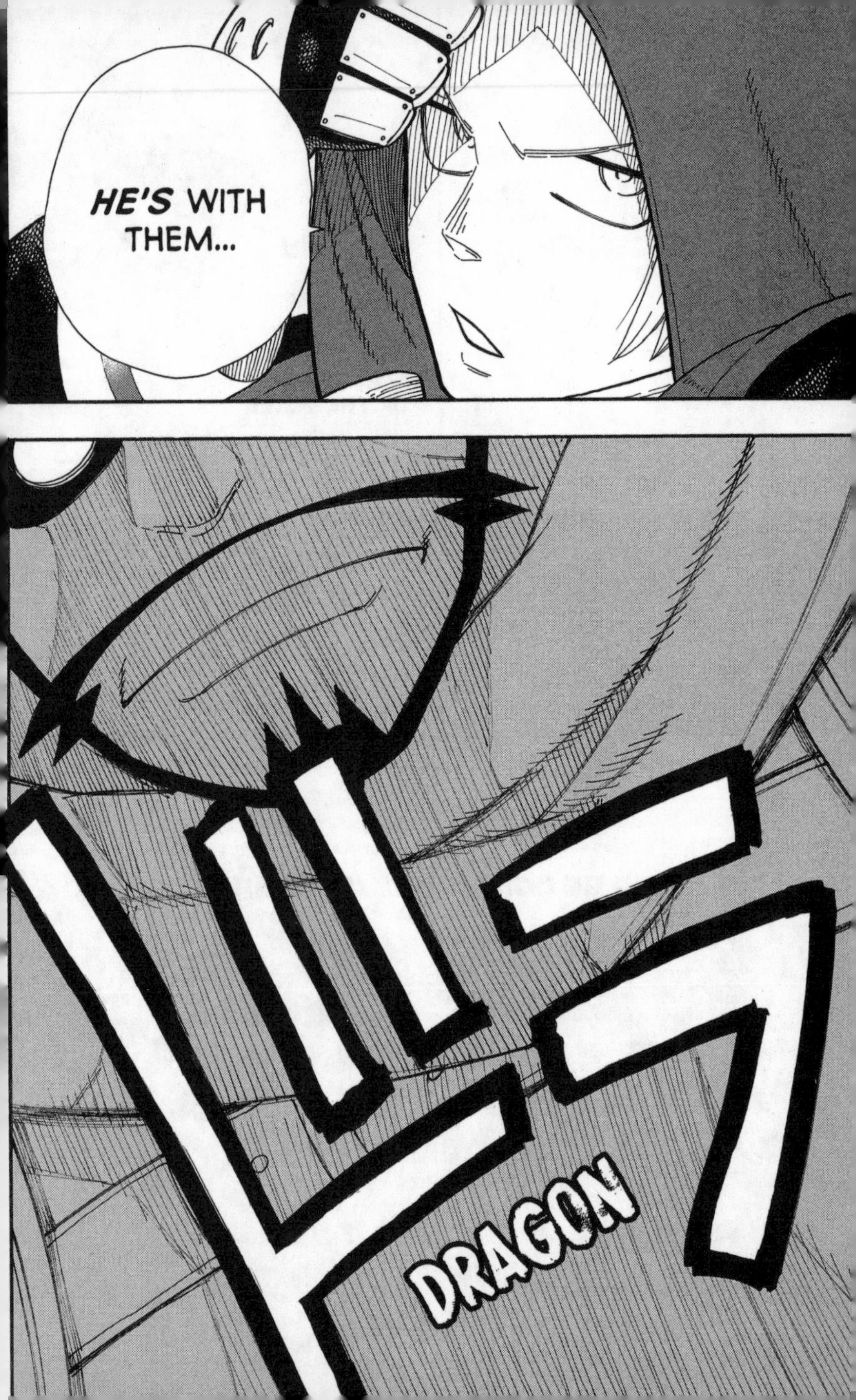
HE'S WITH THEM...
DRAGON

TO BE CONTINUED IN VOLUME 28!!

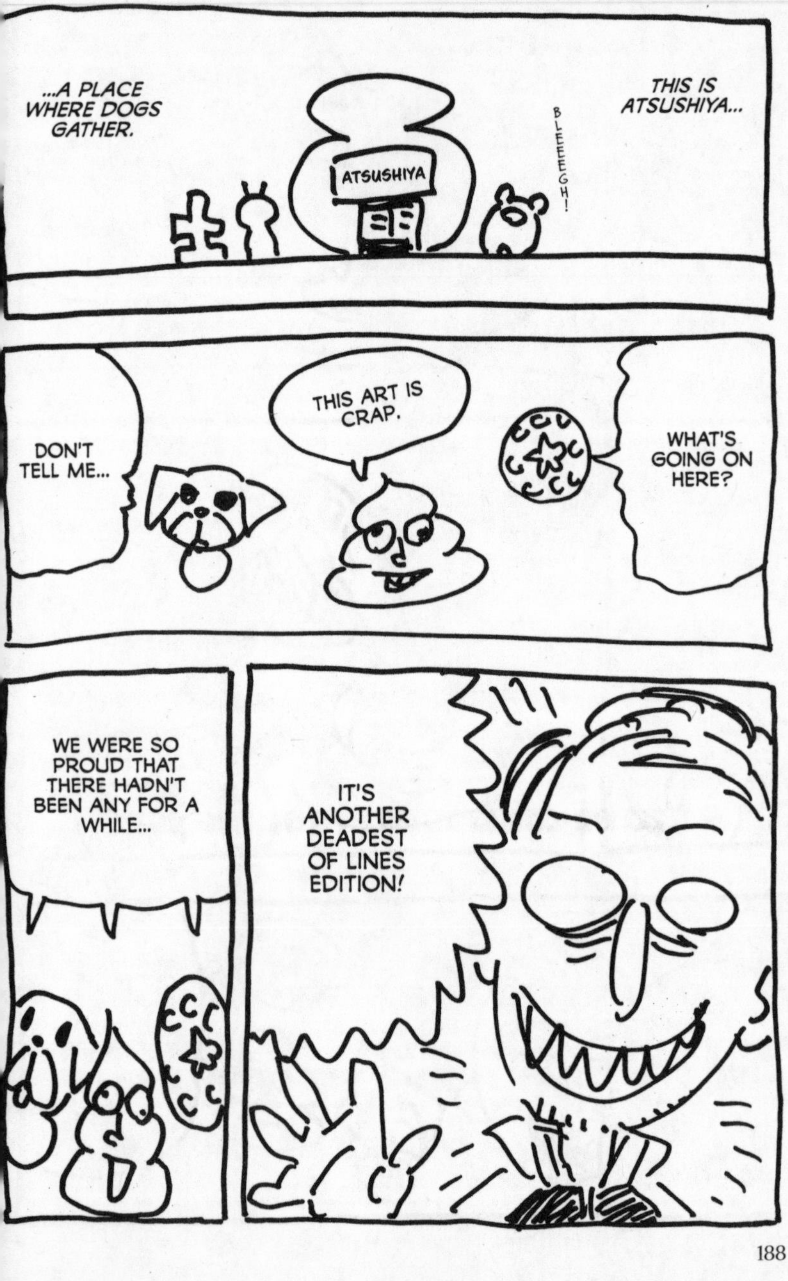
THIS IS ATSUSHIYA...
BLEEGH!
ATSUSHIYA
...A PLACE WHERE DOGS GATHER.
WHAT'S GOING ON HERE?
THIS ART IS CRAP.
DON'T TELL ME...
IT'S ANOTHER DEADEST OF LINES EDITION!
WE WERE SO PROUD THAT THERE HADN'T BEEN ANY FOR A WHILE...

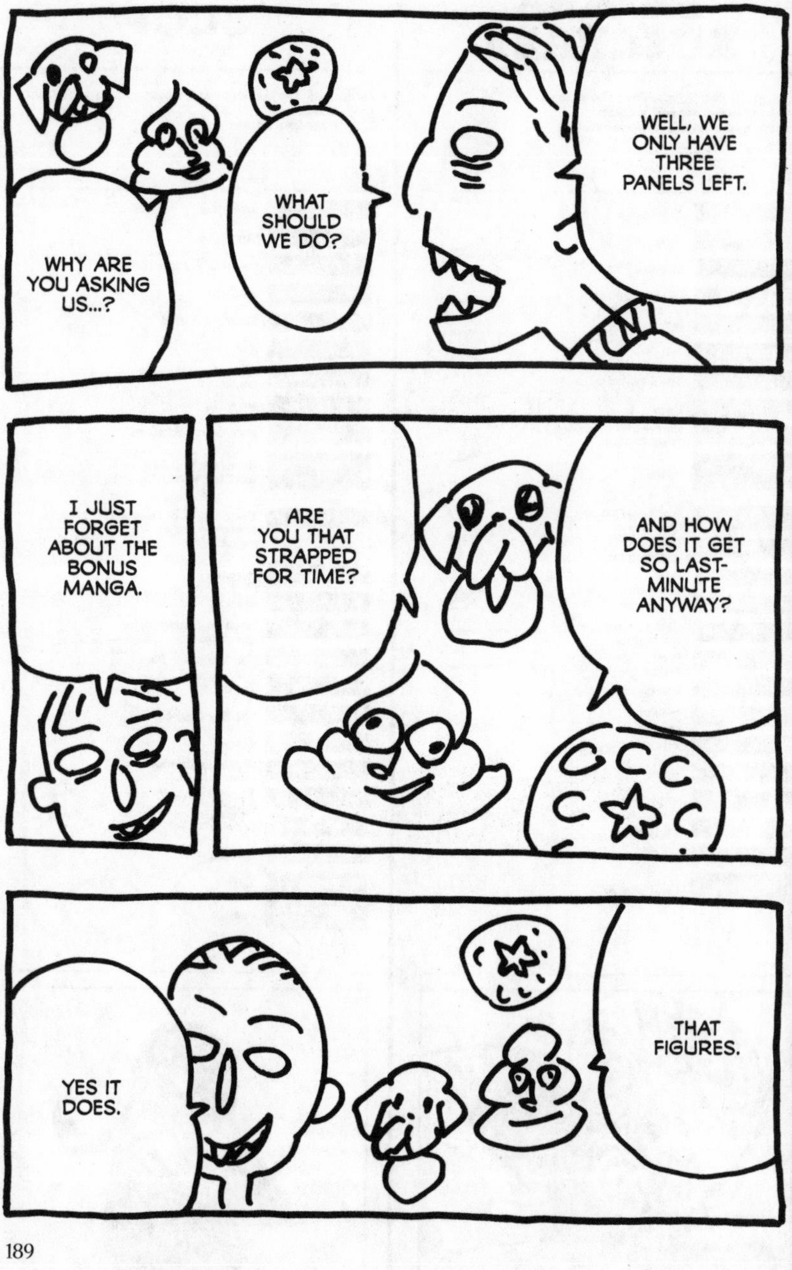
WELL, WE ONLY HAVE THREE PANELS LEFT.
WHAT SHOULD WE DO?
WHY ARE YOU ASKING US...?
AND HOW DOES IT GET SO LAST-MINUTE ANYWAY?
ARE YOU THAT STRAPPED FOR TIME?
I JUST FORGET ABOUT THE BONUS MANGA.
THAT FIGURES.
YES IT DOES.

SHINRA KUSAKABE

AFFILIATION: **SPECIAL FIRE FORCE COMPANY 8**
RANK: **SECOND CLASS FIRE SOLDIER**
ABILITY: **THIRD GENERATION PYROKINETIC**
Emits fire from his feet.

Height	173cm [5'8"]
Weight	67kg [148lbs.]
Age	17 years
Birthday	October 29
Sign	Scorpio
Bloodtype	AB
Nickname	The Devil's Footprints
Self-Proclaimed	Hero
Favorite Foods	Ramen, Hamburgers, Fried Chicken
Least Favorite Food	None
Favorite Music	Anything fast and awesome
Favorite Animal	Leopard Anything fast
Favorite Color	Red
Favorite Type of Girl	Pretty girls
Who He Respects	Commander Ōbi His mother
Who He Hates	Pretty girls Arthur
Who He's Afraid Of	The Lieutenant
Hobbies	Soccer Futsal
Daily Routine	Breakdancing
Dream	To become a hero
Shoe Size	27cm [10]
Eyesight	2.0 [20/10]
Favorite Subject	Math
Least Favorite Subject	Language Arts

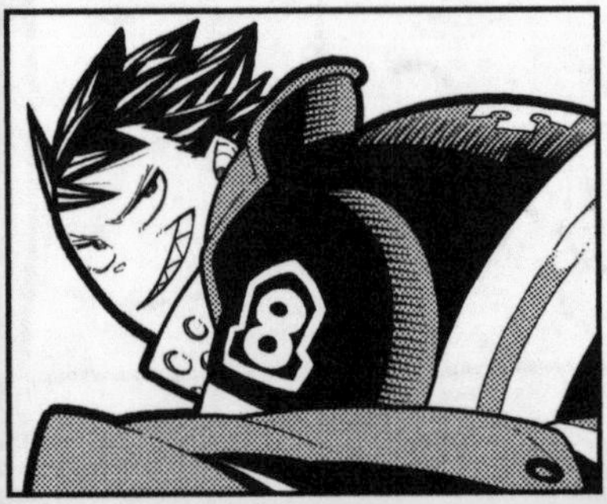

SCOP

AFFILIATION: **FANTASTICAL OASIS WORLD OF ANIMALS LAND**
RANK: **GENIUS!**
ABILITY: **DIGGING HOLES**

Height	23cm [9in.]
Weight	5kg [11lbs.]
Age	I want to live forever!
Birthday	Happy!
Sign	Stars are pretty!
Bloodtype	Red
Nickname	Gimme a really cool one!
Self-Proclaimed	Mr. Mole
Favorite Foods	Noto brand potatoes
Least Favorite Food	Here I am in Tokyo, so I want to try everything
Favorite Music	There's a lot of different sounds in Tokyo. It's exciting
Favorite Animal	Humans
Favorite Color	Black
Favorite Type of Girl	What an embarrassing question!
Who He Respects	The Woman in Black
Who He Hates	Tempe
Who He's Afraid Of	The Evangelist
Hobbies	Talking
Daily Routine	Digging a thousand holes
Dream	To build an underground empire
Shoe Size	I dunno
Eyesight	No idea
Favorite Subject	Talking
Least Favorite Subject	Fighting

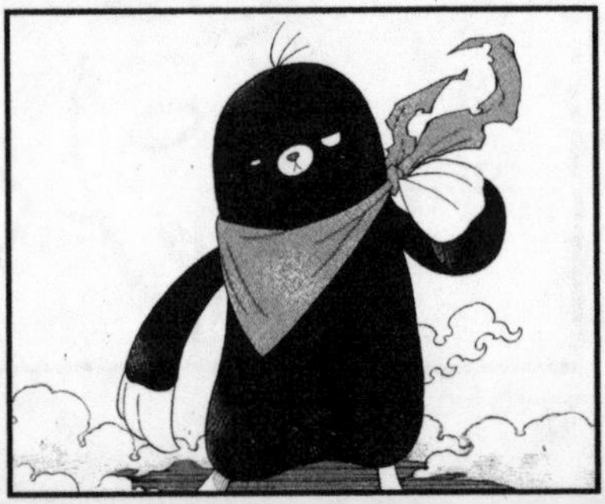

Translation Notes:

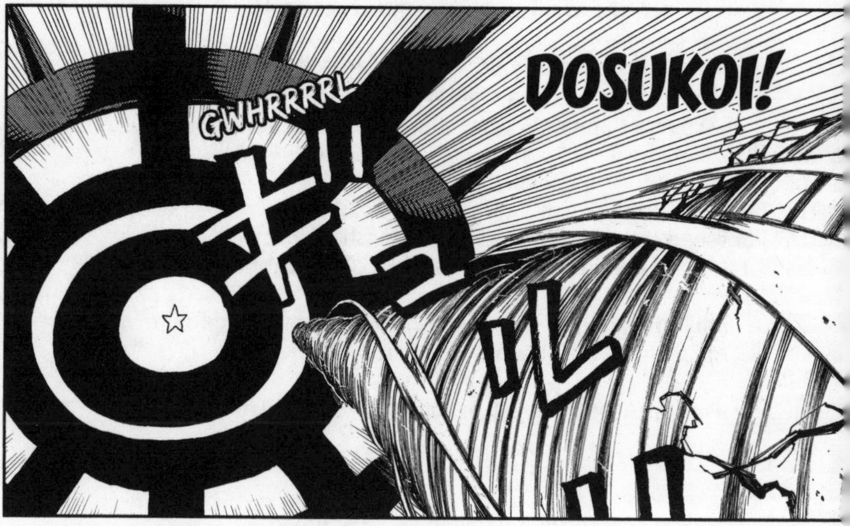
DOSUKOI!
GWHRRRRL
ギュル

Dosukoi, page 64

Dosukoi is an interjection used when doing manual labor and largely associated with sumo wrestling. Perhaps Captain Honda is channeling a Honda from another world—a sumo wrestler with the first initial E., who is a bit of a street fighter, and has a move called Oni-Muso, meaning roughly "the demon's muso," where *muso* is a sumo wrestling technique.

A Kodansha Comics Trade Paperback Original
Fire Force 27 copyright © 2021 Atsushi Ohkubo
English translation copyright © 2022 Atsushi Ohkubo

All rights reserved.

Published in the United States by Kodansha Comics, an imprint of Kodansha USA Publishing, LLC, New York.

Publication rights for this English edition arranged through Kodansha Ltd., Tokyo.

First published in Japan in 2021 by Kodansha Ltd., Tokyo.

ISBN 978-1-64651-420-5

Printed in the United States of America.

www.kodansha.us

9 8 7 6 5 4 3 2 1
Translation: Alethea Nibley & Athena Nibley
Lettering: AndWorld Design
Editing: Greg Moore
Kodansha Comics edition cover design by Phil Balsman

Publisher: Kiichiro Sugawara

Director of publishing services: Ben Applegate
Director of publishing operations: Dave Barrett
Associate director, publishing operations: Stephen Pakula
Publishing services managing editors: Madison Salters, Alanna Ruse
Production managers: Emi Lotto, Angela Zurlo